T0329861

THE CONSUMING TEMPLE

THE
CONSUMING TEMPLE

JEWS, DEPARTMENT STORES, AND THE
CONSUMER REVOLUTION IN GERMANY, 1880–1940

PAUL LERNER

Cornell University Press
ITHACA AND LONDON

Cornell University Press gratefully acknowledges receipt of a grant from the Dean's Office of Dornsife College of Letters, Arts and Sciences, University of Southern California, which aided in the publication of this book.

First published 2015 by Cornell University Press
Printed in the United States of America

Library of Congress Cataloging-in-Publication Data

Lerner, Paul Frederick, author.
    The consuming temple : Jews, department stores, and the consumer revolution in Germany, 1880–1940 / Paul Lerner.
        pages cm
    Includes bibliographical references and index.
    ISBN 978-0-8014-5286-4 (cloth : alk. paper)
    1. Consumption (Economics)—Germany—History.   2. Consumer behavior—Germany—History.   3. Department stores—Germany—History.   4. Jews—Germany—Social conditions—19th century.   5. Jews—Germany—Social conditions—20th century.   I. Title.
    HC285.L47   2015
    339.4'7094309034—dc23   2014033254

Cloth printing   10 9 8 7 6 5 4 3 2 1

The temptation was acute; mad desires were driving all the women crazy. The department store had been transformed into a white chapel.
—*Émile Zola, 1883*

Just as medieval society was balanced on God **and** the Devil, so ours is balanced on consumption **and** its denunciation.
—*Jean Baudrillard, 1970*

We need the department store. It belongs to us and we to it. . . . What is it that makes the department store so attractive? Its magic, its secret fluid. Therein lies the spirit of the department store which pulls us in whenever and wherever we find it.
—*Walter Schulz, 1929*

CONTENTS

ACKNOWLEDGMENTS   ix

Introduction   1

1 Jerusalem's Terrain: The Department Store and Its
Discontents in Imperial Germany   21

2 Dreamworlds in Motion: Circulation,
Cosmopolitanism, and the Jewish Question   56

3 Uncanny Encounters: The Thief, the Shopgirl, and the
Department Store King   94

4 Beyond the Consuming Temple: Jewish Dissimilation
and Consumer Modernity in Provincial Germany   139

5 The Consuming Fire: Fantasies of Destruction in
German Politics and Culture   179

Conclusion   212

NOTES   217

SELECTED BIBLIOGRAPHY   247

INDEX   257

ACKNOWLEDGMENTS

I am delighted at last to be able to acknowledge the support of the many individuals and institutions who made this book possible. A generous grant from the Alexander von Humboldt Foundation funded a year of intensive library and archival work in Germany, and a follow-up grant several years later allowed me to finish up my research there. Thanks to a fellowship from the American Council of Learned Societies, I was able to take another year away from teaching, allowing me to complete a draft of most of the manuscript. Additional funds were provided by the Dean's Office of USC's Dornsife College through the Advancing Scholarship in the Humanities and Social Sciences program.

I feel very fortunate to have been a guest scholar at several vibrant research institutes over the course of my work on this project. In Germany I was based first at the Moses-Mendelsohn-Center in Potsdam and later at the Simon-Dubnow Institute for Jewish History and Culture at the University of Leipzig. I thank Joachim Schloer in particular for bringing me to Potsdam and Karin Bürger for both her vital bibliographic assistance and her collegiality and warmth. In Leipzig Dan Diner, Nicolas Berg, Susanne Zepp, and Arndt Engelhardt welcomed me kindly, and I remain deeply indebted to Jörg Deventer for deftly helping me gain access to the Schocken materials in Chemnitz while the archive that housed them was closed for renovations. A semester at the Katz Center for Advanced Judaic Studies at the University of Pennsylvania, where I held the Charles W. and Sally Rothfield Fellowship, provided an ideal environment for conceptualizing parts of the book. I am grateful to David Ruderman for his hospitality and to my fellow fellows, above all David Sorkin, Derek Penslar, and Rebecca Kobrin, for challenging and inspiring me to think about Jewish history in new ways.

I am indebted to the many librarians and archivists in the United States, Germany, and Israel who made the research for this project possible, including Gisela Erler at the Landesarchiv Berlin and Dr. Tobias Crabus of the Saxon State Archive in Chemnitz. Above all let me acknowledge Michaela Ullmann, exile studies librarian at USC, for her invaluable assistance with many aspects of my research, particularly for digging up fascinating department store texts, unknown pieces by major authors, in the Feuchtwanger Collection. Racheli Edelman, granddaughter of Salman Schocken, graciously took an interest in my research and patiently answered my questions about her family. Several individuals generously shared material with me from their personal collections. I am especially grateful to Sarah Farmer and Bess Rothenberg for sending me family memoirs. Walter Arlen and Rudy Petersdorff kindly took the time to speak with me about their department store–owning families and to show me artifacts and photographs.

I have been moved by the generosity of a number of friends and colleagues who read parts of the manuscript, shared sources, or just helped me work through ideas. One bleak Berlin winter when I was despairing about the project, Julia Sneeringer advised me to "stick with the novels." She probably doesn't remember ever saying this, but her words stayed with me over the years, and anyone who reads this book will see their impact. Mila Ganeva shared pages and pages of notes with me, Joe Perry sent citations, sources, and even department store cartoons from his files, and Stefan Hofmann guided me to the Berlin Police Presidium's censorship records in Berlin's Landesarchiv for department store dramas and revues. I also thank the following friends and colleagues for their insights, support, and critique: Elinor Accampo, Leora Auslander, Ben Baader, Darcy Buerkle, Veronika Fuechtner, Sander Gilman, Jason Glenn, Joshua Goldstein, Atina Grossmann, Justinian Jampol, Karen Lang, Molly Loberg, Michael Miller, Leslie Morris, Boaz Neumann, Kirill Postoutenko, Ramzi Roughi, Gideon Reuveni, Miriam Rürup, Uwe Spiekermann, Michael Stanislawski, Scott Ury, Ben Veghte, Kerry Wallach, Liliane Weissberg, and Jonathan Wiesen. I have benefited from the opportunity to receive feedback on my work on many occasions in many locations and am especially grateful to Todd Presner for inviting me to deliver the Kahn Lecture in German Jewish Studies at UCLA's Center for Jewish Studies. Thanks also to the members of the Working Group on Jews and Popular Culture in Central Europe for reading a chapter in progress and helping me frame my project and to the Southern California German Studies Workshop where I also presented an early draft of a chapter. Finally, I am deeply grateful to Penelope Falk, Sharon Gillerman, Ann Goldberg, Wolf Gruner, Yaron Jean, Andreas Killen, Rachel Lerner, Lisa Silverman, and Pamela Swett for reading and commenting on chapters.

Working with Cornell University Press again has been a great pleasure. John Ackerman took interest in this project at an early stage and patiently waited for its completion. He read and reread the chapters with tremendous care, and the book is unquestionably better thanks to his keen editorial eye. I am honored that mine was the last manuscript he brought into production, capping off a long and distinguished career. Roger Haydon, taking the project over in midstream, immediately put me at ease with his efficiency, professionalism, and humor. Great thanks also to Karen Hwa for guiding the manuscript through the final stages before publication.

I owe a particular debt of gratitude to the two anonymous readers enlisted by Cornell University Press. Their reports were extraordinarily thorough and thoughtful, and as they will see, both had a significant impact on the book. A subvention from the USC Dornsife Dean's Office helped cover production costs; my thanks to Vice Dean Peter Mancall for making the funds available. Three fantastic research assistants helped out in various ways over the course of the project: Megan Mastroianni provided crucial research assistance in Los Angeles, Sarah Goodrum reliably tracked down sources on the ground in Berlin, and Sarah Rapaport has been a great help in finalizing the manuscript and chasing down permissions for illustrations.

Finally, I would like to thank my family, my parents, Jack and Carol Lerner, and my in-laws, Judy and Azriel Fellner, for their enthusiasm about my work and their endless willingness to help out with childcare. My boys, Etan and Noam, gamely put up with my absences for research and conference trips. I am thrilled that now that the book is finished I have time to join them on more "inventures." Michelle Fellner has lived with this project far longer and far more intensely than she could have ever imagined. Words cannot convey my gratitude for her incredible patience, and it is her encouragement, companionship, and love, not to mention her editing skills, that sustained me through this process. I dedicate this book to her.

THE CONSUMING TEMPLE

INTRODUCTION

In 1935, while he was on the run from the Nazis, the satirist and illustrator Thomas Theodor Heine wrote a fable called "The Devil in the Department Store."[1] Originally published in the Netherlands, the tale concerns one Siegfried Hagen, proprietor of a dry goods store in an unnamed town, who strikes a deal with Satan that rescues him from bankruptcy. The only stipulation is that he lower his prices continually. Customers flock immediately, lured by the amazing bargains, the "astonishing, remarkably cheap" prices.[2] Goods fly off the shelves. Customers queue up to wait for entry, while nearby stores remain empty, abandoned. Within two weeks, Hagen has sold out his entire stock. He places his new orders, incinerates the supply forms as instructed, and the new goods arrive without fail the next morning. Profits rise to astounding levels, and Hagen finds himself carrying his cash to the bank in barrels.

Hagen, soon with a gleaming new department store building, takes on hundreds of new employees. The richest man in the city, he now possesses a castle, luxury cars, even an airplane. He is named chairman of the chamber of commerce and basks in accolades and honors. Meanwhile, his prices are asymptotically approaching zero, and he is once again in the throes of anxiety attacks and insomnia. Finally, after consulting with his attorney, Hagen reverses course and suddenly raises his prices. Immediately the devil appears and ferociously demands his soul and the souls of his workers. Yet Hagen stands firm, asks Satan to leave, and threatens to call the police. He informs his otherworldly business partner that he has transferred ownership to his wife and put all assets in her name. Hagen assures him he would be welcome to discuss a new contract with her, but the devil quickly departs with a fearsome curse and a vaporous emanation. Hagen and his wife would have lived happily ever after in their palace, Heine adds wryly, except that they soon die and go to heaven.

Heine's tale contains many of the themes that run through this exploration of the department store and the consumer revolution in Germany. It narrates the department store's dramatic rise from humble beginnings to prominence and splendor, as it became a central urban destination, teeming with immense crowds, and a source of vast fortunes. It alludes to the discontent of traditional retailers who, unable to compete with the department store's stunningly low prices and magnetic draw, accuse the store owner of unethical, deceptive

I

I.1 The devil appears to Hagen. From T. T. Heine, "Der Teufel im Warenhaus."
© 2014 Artists Rights Society (ARS), New York / VG Bild-Kunst, Bonn.

I.2 Hagen's shop windows announcing astonishing sales. From T. T. Heine,
"Der Teufel im Warenhaus." © 2014 Artists Rights Society (ARS), New York / VG
Bild-Kunst, Bonn.

I.3 The devil returns to collect his due. From T. T. Heine, "Der Teufel im Warenhaus."
© 2014 Artists Rights Society (ARS), New York / VG Bild-Kunst, Bonn.

practices. The story nods facetiously to the principle of small profits / high volume—in this case the prices are minuscule and the profits enormous—a key commercial innovation at the heart of the department store's success. It also dramatizes the "special relationship" that developed between department stores and women. When neighboring retailers lodge complaints about Hagen's baffling sales tactics, no judge will rule in their favor, for none has the temerity to deny his wife the pleasure of such extraordinary bargains. Yet, above all, it is the fable's supernatural quality that makes it a fitting way to start this investigation of Jews, department stores, and consumer culture in modern Germany.

The emergence of department stores in Germany, like their predecessors in France, Britain, and the United States, generated great excitement. The enticing displays of their abundant products, their architectural innovations, and their prodigious scale inspired widespread fascination and even awe in Germany, as it had elsewhere, but at the same time Germans also greeted the department store phenomenon with considerable unease. With their mysterious powers, their amazing ability to entice and seduce customers and to grow seemingly without limit, department stores could be unnerving. Heine's tale satirizes the belief that preternatural forces were at work beneath the store's surface—what else but a pact with the devil could explain the magic of limitless price reductions, the remarkable magnetism of department stores, their profitability and constant expansion? And just as Heine's store functions as a smokescreen for a satanic plot, so does its Jewishness lie concealed behind "Siegfried Hagen," the most German of names.

This book recovers a set of unique German discourses about department stores, a widely shared sense that they were too powerful, that they brought hidden dangers to the individuals who frequented them and to the nation as a whole. While some of these ideas and themes appeared in other national contexts too, the German reception of department stores, and consumer culture more generally, was exceptionally conflicted, fraught, and intense. An extraordinary number of works from this period warned of the dangers of department store shopping. The morbid sensibility, the wild imaginings, and the sense of dread that pervaded many of these sources claimed to expose the dark side of the excitement and promise of the new consumer venues. Indeed, German responses to the department store were entangled with a broader unease about capitalism and modernity's revolutionary impact on commerce, culture, and daily life.

Max Weber famously characterized the modern era in terms of the disenchantment of the world, the banishment of myth through the rise of instrumental reason, rational explanation and calculability amid increasing bureaucratization and rationalization.[3] Walter Benjamin, nearly as famously, asserted that underneath modernity's rationalizing pull, myth and fantasy survived, even flourished in the traces left by the bric-a-brac of commodity culture in the unconscious. His *Arcades Project* posited, as Susan Buck-Morss writes, that "on an unconscious 'dream' level, the new urban-industrial world had become fully reenchanted."[4]

The department store embodied both modern tendencies. Thoroughly rationalized, centralized, and scientifically managed, the early twentieth-century department store was also a dreamworld, a site of fantasy, a magical place. It was an "enchanted forest" for two young lovers in a 1926 novel, as they strolled hand in hand from department to department after hours, as if in a fairy tale.[5] For some enthusiasts, the department store was a place of adventure, of seemingly endless possibilities, where customers could be transported in space and time, where they could fleetingly transcend the barriers of social class, where they could meet friends, or lovers, where they could fulfill basic needs and satisfy desires they did not even know they had. But it was also a place of mystery. The department store redrew the boundaries of intimacy. It made the private public. Beds were on display, undergarments could be purchased. The department store was nothing less than a "temple of love" and a "symbol of eros," according to one ardent observer.[6] Like the modern city itself, then, it offered unexpected encounters and transgressive possibilities.

Contemporary sources dramatized the stores' unnerving qualities, their impact on the psyche, and their power to unleash women's allegedly insatiable desire for goods. *Kauflust*—literally, the desire or drive to buy—became a leitmotif in department store representations of all kinds, an explanation for the stores' ability to enthrall customers and entice passersby. These consuming desires were said to be aroused through low prices, but were then intensified through manipulative techniques of display, presentation, and marketing. The stores' uncanny influence also preoccupied psychologists and psychiatrists, who diagnosed epidemics of kleptomania and "magasinitis" around the turn of the century and blamed many women's seemingly irrepressible drive to steal on both the temptations of the department store environment and the weaker female constitution. Kleptomania was considered so inevitable that in a 1933 Austrian play, *Zwischenfall im Warenhaus* (Incident in the department store), a wealthy man secretly purchased a major department store so that his wife could indulge her stealing habit without legal consequences—an inventive solution to be sure, which allowed for the safe and unthreatening expression of female desire.[7]

The department store was not only magical, it was also Jewish. The association between Jews and department stores ran so deep that for many Germans, from the late nineteenth century through the 1930s, the phrase "Jewish department store" would have sounded redundant. The Jewish ownership or "Jewishness" of the department store was obvious to contemporaries. It did not have to be uttered, forcing the historian at times to read between the lines. Take this passage from Alfred Döblin's 1929 novel *Berlin Alexanderplatz*, a work that makes repeated references to the giant Hermann Tietz emporium on the eponymous city square: "You can buy ties like this from Tietz or Wertheim, or if you don't like to buy from Jews [you can go] elsewhere."[8] Patronizing a department store meant buying from Jews. To be sure, Hermann Tietz and Wertheim, two of Berlin's major department store firms, were founded by Jewish entrepreneurs, as were the Leonhard Tietz and Schocken chains, and the Jandorfs, Knopfs, Baraschs, Alsbergs, Urys, Grunwalds, Wronkers, Adams, and many others. Only Karstadt, of Germany's five largest pre-1933 department store concerns, was not a Jewish firm; but it did have Jews in key management positions and was often assumed to be Jewish-owned by department store opponents.[9] Jews held, or at least started, the overwhelming majority of department stores and clothing and fashion houses throughout the country.[10] Yet, beyond these empirical realities, writers, cultural critics, political agitators, and shoppers associated department stores with Jews in a variety of ways.

Werner Sombart, one of the period's most prominent economic thinkers, argued that Jews demonstrated a unique, historically and racially determined aptitude for commercial capitalism and were thus the bearers of economic modernity. Sombart viewed the department store as a quintessentially modern development, the embodiment of the anonymous, objectifying forces of capitalism and marketing, which, he lamented, were displacing traditional retail practices based on personal connections and loyalty.[11] Operating with less nuance and on a less rarefied level, the pages of Germany's anti-Semitic press from the 1890s on rattled with debates about whether all department stores or only the Jewish-owned businesses deserved to be reviled and boycotted. The Nazis, in their 1920 party platform, famously called for department stores to be communalized, and Nazi activists urged boycotts and incited attacks against the stores in the late 1920s and 1930s.

Simultaneously, more neutral and even sympathetic voices, gentile and Jewish alike, simply assumed the "Jewishness" of the stores, a characterization that some businesses certainly embraced. Several firms closed their doors on major Jewish holidays—Berlin's Kaufhaus Israel was shuttered weekly for the Jewish sabbath—advertised with conspicuous Jewish symbols in the Jewish press, and made no secret of the fact that they carried kosher food and Jewish books, such as the abridged edition of the Babylonian Talmud that was available at the Kaufhaus des Westens (Department Store of the West, or KaDeWe).[12] The KaDeWe and Hermann Tietz stores also sold tickets to lectures and classes at Berlin's Jewish adult education center (Jüdische Volkshochschule), and a Hermann Tietz store was one of the few spots for obtaining entry passes to a 1931 pageant to crown the most beautiful Jewish woman in Berlin.[13] Store directors like Berthold Israel and Oscar Tietz were active, esteemed members of the Jewish community who understood both their commercial and philanthropic activities through a traditional Jewish framework, which obligated Jewish men to become financially self-sufficient, to support charitable causes generously, and to conduct their business fairly.[14]

GEGRÜNDET 1815

DAS
KAUFHAUS
IM ZENTRUM
DAS
ZENTRUM
DES EINKAUFS

N*JSRAEL

BERLIN C 2
SPANDAUER-KÖNIGSTRASSE

In popular culture, the world of retail became a kind of cultural code for Jewishness, reinforced by names, accents, and exaggerated physique and body language.[15] Supporters and foes alike represented department store owners with what contemporaries understood as typically Jewish features and characteristics. Despite his über-Germanic name, portly Siegfried Hagen, protagonist in the Heine story, cuts a recognizably Jewish figure. In Werner Türk's 1932 novel Konfektion (Ready-made clothing), store own-

I.4 Kaufhaus Israel ad, "The Department Store in the Center, the Center of Shopping," in Gemeindeblatt der jüdischen Gemeinde zu Berlin 18, no. 12 (December 1928).

ers Bohrmann and Mendel speak in a Yiddish-laden German—the author translates the Yiddish into High German in footnotes. They even argue about which of them looks more Jewish as they vie for the opportunity to represent the firm at a big sales event: "A goy could bump into your nose!" Bohrmann lashes out. "And what are you, a Teuton?" his partner fires back.[16]

Another way that authors denoted the department store's Jewishness was by inscribing Jewish features onto the stores themselves. For example, in *Das große Warenhaus* (The great department store), a 1926 novel by Siegfried Siwertz, the store's owner, Jeremias Goldmann, collects defamatory cartoons and caricatures, one of which depicts a prodigious nose and furrowed brow atop the store's portals.[17] This image strangely presaged a 1931 Nazi rally poster that used strikingly similar iconography in its depiction of the department store as a threat. Anti–department store material was indeed saturated with images of predatory store owners with exaggerated Jewish features. Exposing (or in fact fabricating) the ragged Jewish merchants behind the scenes of the modern, luxurious palaces of consumption, alarmists declared that the stores, like their owners, were trying to mask their rag-trade origins and the shoddy quality of their wares.

Both the German department store's "Jewishness" and its magical qualities intersected with a discourse that represented the department store as an ersatz church, a secular temple or indeed a cathedral of commerce. As Émile Zola observed in his notes for *The Ladies' Paradise* (*Au Bonheur des Dames*), "The department store tends to replace the church. It marches to the religion of the cash desk, of beauty, of coquetry, and fashion. [Women] go there to pass the hours as they used to go to church: an occupation, a place of enthusiasm where they struggle between their passion for clothes and the thrift of their husbands; in the end all the drama of life with the hereafter of beauty."[18] Zola's metaphor works on several levels. Most literally, department stores, like churches, were spaces outside the home where women could spend their leisure time without arousing suspicion. Zola's passage adds that money and commodities were replacing the divine as objects of worship, and that as a space the stores incited powerful feelings, staged dramatic conflicts, and gave access to the sublime, the province of the church in previous eras.

The cathedral metaphor appears throughout the novel. For example, Zola writes of Octave Mouret, the director of the fictional Ladies' Paradise department store: "His creation was producing a new religion; churches, which were being gradually deserted by those of wavering faith, were being replaced by his bazaar. . . . If he had closed his doors there would have been a rising in the street, a desperate outcry from the worshippers whose confessional and altar he would have abolished."[19] For Zola, then, commodity worship was filling a gap left by the waning of traditional religious devotion amid modernity's secularizing tug. And it was women who were the chief zealots of the new religion.

Zola's notion of the cathedral of consumption betrays a clear debt to Marx's concept of the commodity fetish. In volume 1 of *Capital*, Marx pointed out the gap between a commodity's value—expressed as a coefficient of the human labor that went into its production—and the value ascribed to it, which he illustrated through the fetish.[20] The separation of production and consumption under capitalism, the invisibility of the productive process—perhaps best embodied by the department store—prevents modern subjects from seeing their real value and allows us to mystify consumable objects. The fetish, after all, is a term Marx borrowed from the anthropology of religion, meaning an inanimate object that is endowed with supernatural power and theological significance.

The religious underpinnings of modern consumption, the comparison of the department store to a church or cathedral, runs throughout the European and American experience of early department stores and consumer culture. In the German case it was concretely embodied by the colossal building that the eminent architect Alfred Messel designed for the Wertheim firm on Berlin's Leipziger Strasse. When the store first opened in 1896, Berliners nicknamed it "the Cathedral" for its awe-inspiring vertical lines, its majesty, and its grandiose central atrium, which brought the eyes skyward and bathed the wares in rays of sunshine.[21] A journalist at the time controversially compared the edifice to the Gothic cathedrals of the Middle Ages, asserting that each structure embodied the spirit, aspirations, and greatest achievements of their respective times.[22]

In terms of their scale, department stores can also be compared to railway stations, museums, and exhibition halls. Each of these structures, new to later nineteenth-century cityscapes, could be seen as modern, iron-and-glass equivalents of the medieval church, but it was the department store, standing atop the transportation grids and circulatory networks of the modern metropolis and anchoring the new sites of middle-class leisure and entertainment, that inspired the comparison. Reflecting on Baudelaire's notion that the modern city caused a kind of "religious intoxication," Benjamin added that "the department stores are temples consecrated to this intoxication."[23]

Konsum-Tempel remains a common German vernacular term, an ironic, playful way of highlighting the secular condition of capitalist modernity, a tongue-in-cheek confession that we know we should not place too much value in material objects and consumer goods, but we do anyway. Jean Baudrillard described this dynamic of consuming and condemning consumption as two complementary parts, the discourse and anti-discourse, of the "myth of consumption." Ecstatic consumption and the act of morally critiquing consumer abundance together constitute a kind of game, a modern, secular replacement for the theological battles that captivated the conscience of prior eras.[24] The idea of the consuming temple bespeaks our condition of being too cynical to derive meaning from devotion to the divine, a state in which satisfying consuming desires shapes identities, provides meaning, and becomes ritual.

The term "consumption" has another meaning, of course, a usage that dates back to the nineteenth century and denotes destruction, specifically the eating away of the body from tuberculosis.[25] Consumption's destructive connotations have lingered. Indeed, destruction inheres in acts of consumption—eating, purchasing, using up—and it is no coincidence that so many of the period's imagined department store plots culminate in destruction, usually through fire. The department store then was perceived as a consuming temple in two senses, as both a temple of consumption and a temple that consumes—that is, a place of destruction, a Moloch, even, that greedily devours vulnerable customers and neighboring businesses.

These three intersecting themes—the department store's uncanny qualities, its Jewishness, and its religious connotations—shape the parameters of the book that follows. The operation of the supernatural in department store representations—the dreamworlds of Benjamin, and the Faustian pact dramatized by Thomas Theodor Heine—make more sense when seen in the context of the department store's status as ersatz cathedral. The department store's metaphysical qualities also intersect with its "Jewishness" and indeed with broader themes around German experiences of and encounters with the explosive onset of new forms of mass consumption. These themes come together in a 1935 psychiatric case history in which a kleptomaniac compared her condition to the protagonist of S. Ansky's classic Yiddish play The Dybbuk, identifying with the bride whose body is entered by a possessing spirit. Her dreams displaced the demons from the cemeteries of the Russian Pale to the emporiums of the German metropolis—that is, from one uncanny Jewish context to another. The demons came to her at night and compelled her "with an eerie force" to return to the store again and again against her better judgment.[26]

In a parallel discourse, political agitators used religious and supernatural imagery to characterize the stores as having seductive, even satanic powers and a parasitic effect on the German body politic. Oppositional literature depicted the department store as an angry god, a monster preying on traditional German businesses, and a vampire or "economic demon," as a 1928 work by a Nazi economist had it.[27] These responses were also related to the visible presence of Jewish businessmen, the elite commercial class whose fortunes flowed from the revolution in consumer goods. A great many of these entrepreneurs in fact had arrived in the massive migration of Jews from the Prussian province of Posen over the course of the nineteenth century, and thus the department store was represented by its enemies not only as Jewish but as foreign, un-German and "oriental."

From the 1880s, when German department stores first appeared, through the later 1930s, when they were "Aryanized," many Germans saw the department store not only as a modern secular temple, but specifically as a Jewish temple, a shrine for the worship of the commodity and for crass capitalism and profit mongering. The department store and the rapid onset of new forms of consumerism in Germany came to symbolize the Jewish presence in the economy, culture, and society, and Jews were often construed as the agents of modernity and secularization for better or worse. Erich Köhrer's 1909 novel *Warenhaus Berlin*, a story that dramatizes the uncomfortable position of the fictional Department Store Berlin adjacent to the Kaiser Wilhelm Memorial Church, provides a vivid illustration.[28] The juxtaposition of the Jewish temple of commerce and the traditional Christian cathedral, viewed as a provocation by city officials, works as an allegory for the conflicted culture of imperial Germany, a symbolic face-off between the old Prussia of throne and altar and the emerging new society, with its international entanglements, global commercial ties, social fluidity, and emancipated Jews.

The Consumer Revolution

The department store was hardly an isolated phenomenon. Along with the other elements that forged modern consumer culture—retail innovations such as vending machines, mail-order catalogs, and fashion houses; the daily illustrated press; the publication of low-cost, mass-marketed books; the proliferation of advertisements; phonograph recordings; and radio—the department store was perhaps the most conspicuous symbol of the broader transformation in European and North American life that occurred between the later nineteenth and the mid-twentieth centuries. Although it still accounted for a modest portion of the total retail volume in these places, the department store symbolized and stood at the center of what many historians call the "consumer revolution"—a set of dramatic economic, social, and cultural developments that altered the way people acquired and used goods, changed how they spent their time, transformed the face of the modern city, and challenged traditional social and gender roles and hierarchies.

While the onset of consumer culture brought controversy and conflict throughout Europe and North America, particularly in the years before World War I, the German experience was unique in many ways.[29] Like German industrialization, Germany's consumer revolution began later than in Western Europe and then developed with unparalleled intensity. Germany's path to a consumer society, furthermore, was marked by stops and starts throughout the modern period amid the devastation of wars, the resistance of threatened social groups, and the controlling grasp of dictatorships. The German twentieth century, as historians Michael Geyer and Konrad Jarausch have pointed out, oscillated between the heights of prosperity and consumer abundance and periods of abject deprivation and destitution. Together these two extremes make for a jarring picture that is difficult to square, yet this linkage of "hunger and affluence," Geyer and Jarausch write, "both as reality and as mentality . . . is imperative because one cannot be understood without the other. For the longest time, German dreams of consumption and consumer society were born from the nightmares of hunger and want."[30]

From its inception in the later nineteenth century through the Cold War era, German consumer culture has been laden with enormous political and cultural stakes. Consumer goods and access to them have fueled fierce debate over the integrity of culture, the nature of German society, the national welfare, the proper roles of women, and the survival of the "authentic" German middle classes. The department store, and the controversies and fantasies it inspired, were deeply intertwined with these broader processes and controversies.

Historians generally look to the early modern period, specifically the eighteenth-century Atlantic world, for the origins of modern consumer society. This was indeed a moment of increased international trade and heightened commercial activity and consumer spending in Britain and northwestern Europe, the era in which consumer demand first became a measurable entity and a demonstrable political force.[31] Over the course of the eighteenth century, more goods became available to broader segments of the population, and in France, for example, bourgeois alternatives to the courtly regime of consumption began to emerge and challenge the strict regulation of consumer practices encoded through archaic sumptuary laws.[32]

If these eighteenth-century developments revolutionized the distribution of dry goods, textiles, and some foods and expressed the new social power of the bourgeoisie, the changes that began in the mid- to later nineteenth century—often called a "second consumer revolution"—reached further down the social hierarchy and brought an array of new products and services to the middle and even working classes. Nineteenth-century innovations sped up the distribution and acquisition of goods and turned shopping into an activity that filled the increasing amount of leisure time enjoyed by members of the middle classes.

This late nineteenth-century "revolution" hastened the advent of what social scientists often call a consumer society, an amorphous state to be sure, usefully defined by the historian Jean-Christophe Agnew as "a whole way of life—[a] society-wide structure of meaning and feeling organized primarily around acts of purchase."[33] In such a condition, in a society beyond mere subsistence, a critical mass of citizens find themselves freed from concern about basic necessities and enjoy enough leftover income and leisure time to participate in the world of abundance around them. Henceforth, patterns of consumption begin to contribute more toward determining social position than one's place in the process of production, and consumable objects—or the "system of needs," to use Jean Baudrillard's terminology—play a disproportionate role in creating meaning and shaping individual and group experiences.[34] As the historian Ellen Furlough has written, "Objects are sold and exchanged as cultural bundles, wrapped in social, cultural and gender relations that signify a person's 'lifestyle' and personality."[35]

Social theorists from Thorstein Veblen to Pierre Bourdieu have studied the process of social distinction, how individuals in such a state distinguish themselves through their acts of consumption and display and how advertising and commercial capitalism can manipulate consumers and create "false needs." Jarausch and Geyer have described these various features and conditions aptly and with unparalleled exactitude: the concept of consumer society, they write, encompasses "the availability of an ample range of goods for a multiplicity of consumers, a system of mass media that allows for the collective attribution of meaning to objects, the differentiation of a world of objects into discrete spheres of taste, fashion, or style in which these objects and their meaning are appreciated and used as markers of distinction, and not the least a wholesale shift in the self-definition of society from production to consumption, from work to leisure, and, one might add, from producing destruction to creating waste."[36]

The department store was bound up with this transformation in crucial ways. It was a key site for the establishment of new forms of consumption and a powerful symbol of their social and cultural consequences. In his pathbreaking history of the Bon Marché, for example, the historian Michael B. Miller argues that the *grands magasins* shifted the terms of French bourgeois identity from participating in a particular style of living to purchasing the goods that enabled that life.[37] And in her important study of American department store workers and customers, Susan Porter Benson describes the department store as symbolizing "one of the most profound changes in recent history: the shift from a production-oriented society to one centered on consumption."[38] According to the sociologist Rudi Laermanns, the department store was the primary setting for the second consumer revolution. It was, he argues, the site for the aesthetization of the commodity, for turning processes of commercial exchange into cultural practice, associating the display and acquisition of certain commodities with cultural meaning.[39] Even if its share of German retail volume remained relatively limited in this period, the department store stood at the forefront of these developments. It was a privileged locus for the staging, performance, and contestation of the new consumer culture.

The Twisted Path to Consumer Society

France, Britain, the United States, and Germany each experienced these revolutionary upheavals in unique ways, but there were significant peculiarities in the German case that made its experience of nascent consumer culture uniquely fraught.[40] For one, department stores and the other trappings of modern consumerism came later; decades separated the opening of the pioneering French department stores (1840s) and the appearance of major urban department stores in Germany (ca. 1890). This lag can be explained by Germany's comparatively later industrialization, the later completion of its rail networks, the belated emergence of a middle class with buying power, and the persistence of cultural taboos against certain kinds of commercial activity, embodied by enduring craft and handworker traditions, and resistance to the leveling power of the market. Furthermore, while French, British, and American department stores originated in cities such as London, Paris, New York, Philadelphia, and Chicago, German *Warenhaus* firms began in places such as Gera, in east-central Germany, and Stralsund (on the Baltic Sea), and became full-fledged department stores only when they entered metropolises such as Munich and Berlin, in most cases not until the 1890s. Though German department stores came later, they expanded more rapidly—like German industry itself—than their counterparts in Britain and France. By the early 1900s, German department stores surpassed all but American stores in both number and sales volume. Finally, despite the significant Jewish presence in American, British, and French retail, nowhere outside of Germany did Jews own such a sizable percentage of department store firms, and nowhere else was the association between department stores and Jews as strong.

By the 1890s, the so-called consumer revolution was well under way. Germans suddenly experienced the new profusion of goods made possible by the country's rapid industrial growth that started in the 1850s and was spurred on by the economic boom of the early 1870s, the prosperous founding years of the unified imperial German state. Consumer cooperatives—in which individuals banded together to purchase items en masse to keep costs low—colonial shops, and special department stores for civil servants and military officers sprang up in the mid- to late nineteenth century and represented new alternatives to traditional retail, pioneering many of the practices associated with department stores.[41] German consumers could now make purchases through mail-order catalogs and could obtain certain products, such as sweets and cigarettes, from vending machines. Toward the turn of the century, wares began to carry brand names, and advertising, formerly limited to short, text-based newspaper notices, now featured eye-catching graphics and clever campaigns, directed by members of a growing and increasingly sophisticated profession.[42] Commodities and signs bearing their likeness became a conspicuous part of the urban landscape in Berlin and other major cities.

In Germany and elsewhere, these developments facilitated the emergence of department stores, whose success in turn accelerated the further expansion of consumer industries and the reach of consumer society. The construction of department store buildings catalyzed the growth of new urban districts for shopping and recreation. Shopping was then transformed from a set of neighborhood chores into a leisure activity that concentrated increasing numbers of consumers in distinct urban districts. As the historian

Erika Rappaport writes, referring to Edwardian London, the city itself was increasingly "a thing to be consumed."[43] Decades after London's West End and Chicago's State Street emerged as vibrant commercial and entertainment centers, the Zeil in Frankfurt and Leipziger Strasse in Berlin followed a similar trajectory.

While World War I put Germany's fledgling consumer economy on hold and stalled the spread of department stores, things picked up again in the Weimar years, especially in the period of relative economic stability between 1924 and 1929. This era witnessed not only the continued growth of consumerism, but a shift in its nature through the diffusion of radio, phonograph recordings, mass-produced books, and the cinema.[44] Encroaching commodification, the social impact of mass culture and the new culture industry (that is, its hold on fantasy life, and its power to manipulate) preoccupied many of the period's leading intellectuals, including Walter Benjamin, Max Horkheimer, and Siegfried Kracauer, whose encounters with modern consumer culture continue to shape today's theoretical horizons. Still, despite its vibrancy, Weimar consumer culture remained geographically and demographically circumscribed, limited, above all, to educated, middle-class urbanites.[45]

The Nazis, inveterate critics of the department store, promised to destroy this symbol of urban modernity, of the decadence of Weimar nightlife and the materialism of the Jewish- and American-influenced interwar culture. Although bitter opponents of the Weimar period's flourishing consumer industries, Nazi leaders nevertheless harnessed the power of these industries for the spread of their propaganda through the later Weimar period and introduced their own, racially exclusive forms of consumer culture in the 1930s and '40s.[46] Yet Nazi promises of material abundance for Aryan subjects went largely unfulfilled. Indeed, the Third Reich's more enduring legacy was one of wartime deprivation and scarcity, the memory of neckties made out of fish skins and potato peel threads, for example, and images of "rubble women" gathering scraps in the hollowed-out shells of Germany's war-devastated cities.[47]

It was only in the postwar period, and truly only in the West, when Germany became a full-fledged society of abundance, a time when department stores reached their peak share (12–13 percent) of national retail.[48] The West German citizen consumers of the 1960s and beyond did not have to worry about the scarcities that plagued their parents' and grandparents' generations.[49] Benefiting from the robust growth of the so-called economic miracle and the resulting plethora of commodity choices, the contented consumer came to be the face of a new peaceful and democratic Germany. Meanwhile, on the other side of the German-German border, the East German regime vacillated between trying to persuade its citizens to sacrifice consumer goods to the vaunted goal of building socialism, and issuing impracticable declarations that the East would surpass West German production levels and provide a better, more materially rewarding style of life.[50]

In these postwar years, indices of consumption and the availability of consumer goods lay at the root of key policy decisions and Cold War rivalries, and the GDR's failure to satisfy consumer demand or compete with the West's quality of life—visible to most citizens through West German television—certainly helped spell its doom in 1989.[51] In the West, on the other hand, consumer culture had largely lost its power to provoke. The debates that had preoccupied the anticapitalist Right and animated decades of department store critique had run out of steam. Consumer culture, as the historian Detlef Briesen observes, stopped being controversial in the Federal Republic of Germany.[52] To put it more accurately, anticonsumerism migrated from the Right to the Left, and became a pet cause of the Western European youth movements in the 1960s and 1970s. Drawing on the Frankfurt School's critique of the manipulative power of the culture industry, the New Left took over the anticonsumerism cause, aiming to shatter the complacency of (what they saw as) the self-satisfied, consumer subjects of the West German economic miracle who were simultaneously complicit in the crimes of the Third Reich and American imperialism in Southeast Asia.

The 1968 bombing of two Frankfurt department stores by left-wing activists provides a suitable end point for this short survey of German consumer culture and indeed for the broader exploration of the Jewish department store that follows. The event shows, as we will see, that the department store remained an "un-German" irritant—in this case, more American than Jewish—forty years after Aryanization put an end to actual Jewish ownership of these and all other commercial enterprises in Germany.

A Note on Sources, Method, and Organization

In this book I use a thematic approach in which I connect certain recurring motifs in the history and representation of department stores to themes in German and European Jewish history. The resulting work is both a cultural history and an investigation into social and business history. It is concerned both with discourses and representations and with social, political, and economic dimensions. The book attends therefore not only to the shaping of discourse by reality, but also to the shaping of reality by discourse. Jews and the figure of "the Jew," I argue, stood at the center of the raging controversies around consumer culture and the department store in Germany from the 1880s through the Nazi period and even into the postwar years.

As I began researching this topic, I was struck by the absence of works that engaged with the department store's Jewishness. Even with the groundswell of scholarship on European consumer culture and the department store that appeared in the 1980s and 1990s—and the somewhat belated emergence of historical literature on the German stores—scholars shied away from emphasizing Jewish ownership of the stores and Jews' economic power in pre-Nazi Germany, wary, perhaps, of recycling old anti-Semitic stereotypes and slander.[53] However, in recent years the taboos have fallen away, and scholars have been vigorously exploring the role of economic activities in a range of areas, including Jewish emancipation, Jewish-gentile relations, and Jewish cultural expressions.[54] I draw on this new historiographic wave in my treatment of the department store, striving to integrate the "new Jewish economic history" with modern European historiographic currents and insights from the history and theory of consumer culture.

Parallel to the reemergence of Jewish economic history, a new subfield of Jewish cultural history has recently arisen, consisting of works that assay the meaning and operation of "Jewishness" in particular cultural contexts and ask which institutions or practices can and should be treated as "Jewish" by today's historians.[55] Jewishness, to some, stands for the operation or performance of difference; its functioning can be fruitfully compared to the way feminist scholars have characterized the performance or operation of gender.[56] Just as Jewishness is a constructed category, always in flux, so, these authors remind us, the "non-Jewish" or "German" must also be understood as relational, as a product of social and cultural forces in specific contexts.[57] These analytical tools help locate and unpack the "Jewish" in the Jewish department store. They show how the Jewishness of an institution means much more than the ethnic identity or religious practices of its founders and facilitate a more nuanced approach than merely chronicling anti-Semitism for making sense of the bundle of associations that enveloped Jews and the new consumer culture in modern Germany.

The book operates by finding overlapping themes and following chains of associations through diverse material and media. Key sources include political writings and propaganda from newspapers, parliamentary debates, and agitational literature, such as the "Hammer-Schriften," a series of anti-Semitic booklets that devoted considerable attention to department stores; professional discourses, such as psychiatric writings on kleptomania and academic treatises on mass consumption and retail in the fields of economics and sociology; and business materials, including published reports, studies, and brochures, and unpublished archival material from department store firms. Although malicious and deceitful, the explicitly anti-Semitic materials did intersect at times with these more respectable sources—they drew on images of Jews that were familiar to contemporaries and fanned anxieties about economic and social change that were shared across the ideological spectrum.

Visual sources such as advertisements, photographs of store displays, architectural renderings, cartoons, and the occasional work of art and film play a role here too, sources whose production and dissemination, in many cases, were bound up with the same processes, the same engines of consumer culture, that gave rise to the department store. I also devote considerable attention to department store fiction—that is, novels, revues, plays, and stories where a good deal of the plot unfolds within and revolves around the functioning of a department store and where the store itself often becomes a kind of character. Fiction, going back at least to Gustav Freytag's 1855 novel *Soll und Haben* (Debit and credit), is a particularly valuable source for shedding light on images of Jews and the cluster of associations around Jews and capitalism in German popular culture. As the historian George Mosse argued in a classic essay, "When movements or classes used the appeal of anti-Semitism, they could rely upon a certain popular image whenever they used the word 'Jew,'" and such images, Mosse shows, were to a great extent developed and transmitted through literature, even by figures such as Freytag, a liberal opponent of anti-Semitism.[58]

Fiction and nonfictional writings intersected and cross-fertilized each other in astonishing ways—the same themes ran through very different kinds of source material, forming a coherent discursive field around the German department store. The evidence strongly suggests in some cases that these novelists read the same primary sources that I use. We will see passages from *Warenhaus Berlin* and *W.A.G.M.U.S.*, for example, that strikingly match descriptions in nonfictional department store texts by such writers as Leo Colze and Paul Göhre. The author of a planned department store novel called "Die Rolltreppe" (The escalator) corresponded with the directors of the Hermann Tietz, Leonhard Tietz, and Schocken firms and professed to base much of his narrative on four lectures sponsored by the German Department Store Association that were published in 1931, an important source for this book as well.[59]

I draw on several dozen examples of this strikingly abundant genre, ranging in prominence from best-selling author Vicki Baum's "Jape im Warenhaus" (Jape in the department store) and *Der Große Ausverkauf* (The great sale) to the abovementioned unpublished novel fragment "Die Rolltreppe" and plays that can be found in the Berlin Police Department's censorship files. My research clearly shows that some examples, such as Erich Köhrer's *Warenhaus Berlin* and Manfred Georg's *Aufruhr im Warenhaus*, were widely read and enjoyed, while others among the works I discuss languished in obscurity and were never even published or performed. Still, I would argue for the relevance of the unread, too, for they illustrate and work through the themes under discussion, attesting to the urgency of those themes and offering unique, historically valuable perspectives on the discursive field, on how department stores were seen, experienced, and represented.

The novelists read the psychiatrists, who in turn read the chroniclers, who often read the architects. And everyone read Zola. Zola's *The Ladies' Paradise* is a unique primary source. Zola himself researched his novel extensively in the archives of the Bon Marché. At times, I use his work to illustrate points about the department store under discussion; at other times, I show that it, along with the French experience in general, helped to shape the German perception and representation of department stores. Zola's work is the quintessential department store novel; slightly altered versions of its characters and plot elements appear throughout German fiction in the early twentieth century. *The Ladies' Paradise*, which was sold in translation in some German department stores and reviled as a bad influence by department store critics, thus has a special place in this exploration.

All the fictional works that I analyze were written in German in German-speaking Europe, with the exception of Heine's "Devil in the Department Store," Vicki Baum's novel *The Great Sale* and her novella *Dienst am Kunden* (Customer service), both of which were composed in American exile, but in German, and Siegfried Siwertz's 1926 novel *The Great Department Store*, which was originally written in Swedish and published in Sweden.[60] I have chosen to include it because it appeared in German, in Germany, in this period, which makes it a part of the cultural constellation that I am unpacking.

Each chapter in this book moves back and forth through different kinds of source material. Each treats the department store space as a microcosm for broader economic, social, and cultural change and conflict and shows how in each case these conflicts were intertwined with images of Jews and anxieties or fantasies about Jewish power—power over German women and ultimately over the German economy.[61] The book traces the most prominent of these themes in five chapters, which, organized in a loose chronological progression, cover the period from the 1880s, when the earliest department stores appeared in German cities and towns, through the late 1930s, when the Nazis took these businesses out of Jewish hands.

Chapter 1 focuses on the so-called department store boom of the 1890s, the explosive growth of this new retail form in German cities and towns. It surveys the central and conspicuous role of Jews in Germany's consumer revolution, in the development of department stores and in the other branches of Germany's nascent consumer culture, and charts a well-traveled trajectory in which such families as the Schockens, Tietzes, Urys, and Wronkers rose from itinerant peddlers to owners of giant emporiums in major cities. I analyze German department stores both in international context and in contrast to existing forms of retail and chart the emergence of the anti–department store movement, whose imagery and propaganda mobilized old anti-Semitic notions and constructed the department store as a Jewish encroachment on German territory, a parasite on the German middle classes, and an economic vampire.

In chapter 2 I approach the department store through the prism of mobility and circulation, motifs that run through European economic thought about the Jews and which inhered in department store representations and displays in multiple ways. A stationary spot, the department store was also a scene of perpetual motion. The hub of an international traffic in goods, capital, people, styles, and tastes, it survived by constantly changing, innovating, and expanding. Even as department store entrepreneurs embraced this condition and celebrated the stores' ability to imaginatively transport customers through time and space, their internationalism, and their stylistic cosmopolitanism, these very qualities became fodder for attacks on the stores as "un-German." The chapter thus connects cosmopolitanism and circulation to the position of Jews in European states and societies and to a tradition of thinking about the Jews—by anti-Semites, Zionists, and many in between—as ur-capitalist risk takers, and as restless, mobile, and circulating economic actors.

In chapter 3 I turn to the department store's sex-gender order. I focus on the representation (and actual conditions) of the iconic modern German shopgirl, the image of the store owner as a sexual predator, and the eroticization of the act of purchasing—or indeed stealing—department store goods. The store was cast as a safe, alternate domestic space for women on one hand and as a site of mystery, seduction, and danger on the other, a tension I frame in terms of Freud's notion of the uncanny. Behind these representations lurked the figure of the Jewish capitalist or department store king and anxieties about the special relationship between German women shoppers and Jewish store owners. Through a discussion of store mannequins and prostitutes, I stress the stores' uncanny qualities and their erotic dimensions, concluding by noting the tension between the new, Weimar-era shopgirl, who was in control of her own sexuality, and the exploitative department store director, as portrayed in a range of texts and sources.

The fourth chapter provides a case study of the S. Schocken concern—and devotes considerable attention to the Leonhard Tietz stores as well—chains that operated outside Berlin. These Jewish-owned firms brought modern business practices, modernism in architecture and design, and modern advertising to medium-size cities like Stuttgart and Chemnitz and even large towns like Crimmitschau and Waldenburg in Saxony and Oberhausen in the Ruhr area. I link Schocken's stunning modernist department stores—designed in three cases by architect Erich Mendelsohn—to developments in Jewish social and cultural history. Schocken and Mendelsohn's rejection of the "German"-style department store (best exemplified by Alfred Messel's 1896 Wertheim building) parallels the rejection of a German assimilationist course by Zionists and members of German Jewry's intellectual and cultural elite after World War I.

The fifth and final chapter turns to the problem of violence, both real and imagined, toward and within department stores, from early riots and opposition through the actions of Brownshirt thugs in the late 1920s and early '30s. It focuses above all on the department store fire, a preoccupation among turn-of-the-century agitators and a leitmotif in fictional representations. Voicing concern with fire safety was, on one level, simply one among many strategies by shopkeeper activists for curbing the growth of department stores in German cities. However, the ubiquity of the destructive fire as a motif signifies, I argue, the explosiveness of the German encounter with consumer culture and the wonders of modernity. The fire also brings to the fore the invisible violence veiled behind the process of mass production. The department store fire, finally, operates on a religious level, functioning as a symbolic purging of the Jewish temple of commerce from the modern cityscape. It thus resolves the contradictions and tensions around consumer society by doing away with the provocation of the Jewish department store, an alluring destination to be sure, but ultimately, in the eyes of its detractors, a false idol.

If the department store represented mass consumption at an unprecedented scale, scope, and tempo, the department store fire appears as its logical consequence, a spectacular, thrilling, and terrifying resolution of the tensions and ambivalences of modern mass consumption. This is the flip side of the spectacular consuming temple, and these tensions run throughout the five chapters of this exploration. From the department store boom of the early 1890s through Nazi-coordinated violence in the 1930s, the strong and conspicuous presence of Jews in Germany's modern commercial economy triggered a range of responses from simple pleasure through a collective unease that expressed itself in morbid, supernatural imagery and—both fantasized and real—acts of destruction.

1 JERUSALEM'S TERRAIN

*The Department Store and Its Discontents
in Imperial Germany*

The German department store had survived the childhood maladies of its
early years. It was no longer thought of as on par with rummage bazaars
and rip-off joints in the public mind; it had achieved prestige and the trust
of its customers. For big retail at this time the possibilities were nearly
endless. . . . Department store after department store has arisen in the past
few years, but much more damaging than this competition has been the
vilification and agitation by the owners of specialty shops. . . . All in all it
has been an intense time, a period of frenzied progress and simultaneously
of struggle, of self-defense and hard-fought success.

—*Margarete Böhme (1910)*

To talk about the department store question and not to emphasize that
Jews are the principal carriers of the department store idea would be just
as foolish as if someone were lecturing about cholera and did not wish to
mention the comma bacillus.

—*Emil Suchsland (1904)*

"Department store fever is raging in all cities," observed Leo Colze in a
1908 book on the Berlin department stores.[1] "If someone thinks he
has found a corner anywhere that seems suitable for a new department store building," Colze continued, "he immediately tries to drum up
interest in the project among investors." Colze was writing at the peak of
a veritable boom in German department store construction, the roughly
fifteen-year period from the end of the nineteenth century until the beginning of World War I. In these years new retail constructions were rising at
a frantic pace, rapidly creating new fortunes as well as the occasional bust.
Like many other commentators in this period, Colze marveled at the rapid
spread of new department stores and the enormous size and scale of new
store buildings, developments that he greeted with a great deal of excitement and some measure of concern.

Even a more dispassionate observer like Käthe Lux, the author of a scholarly study of the department store phenomenon in 1910, could not but note
how sensational department stores had become: "These vast enterprises," she
wrote, "arouse public interest in the big cities on a daily basis. This is especially the case for women who follow their announcements in the morning

papers with the most excited attention."[2] This sensationalism was captured in a 1912 musical revue called *Chauffeur ins Metropol!* (Chauffeur into the metropolis), one of dozens of theatrical, literary, and cinematic representations of the department store from this period. The revue, which was performed at Berlin's Metropol Theater, began its second act with the following refrain:

Where does Berlin go in and out today?	Wo geht Berlin heut ein und aus?
In the department store	Im Warenhaus! (Im Warenhaus)
Where is there endless luxury?	Wo ist ewiger Saus und Braus?
In the department store	Im Warenhaus! Das Warenhaus!
Where do you see the people going up and down the stairs,	Wo sieht die Leut' man Treppab— und Treppauf geh'n,
Where do you see the money so quickly disappear?	Wo sieht die Gelder am schnellsten daraufgeh'n?
What for the small shopkeeper causes so much fear?	Was ist dem kleinen Geschäftsmann ein Graus?
The department store!	Das Warenhaus!
The department store!	Das Warenhaus!

A tongue-in-cheek, satirical show to be sure, *Chauffeur ins Metropol!* nonetheless reflected the excitement modern Germans experienced around department stores, and with one well-placed line about small shopkeepers, it simultaneously signaled awareness of the other side of the picture, the vocal opposition by proprietors of smaller specialty shops, many of whom saw the department store as a grave threat to their livelihoods and to traditional German economic and social values.

Not simply a department store booster, Colze saw both sides of the issue. He credited department stores with helping to turn Berlin into a metropolis, a widespread source of satisfaction in Germany, as the recently unified state flexed its muscles in world affairs, embarked on a course of imperial expansion, and wracked up accolades in science, medicine, and increasingly the applied arts.[3] He also praised the new stores for helping to modernize the German economy and to display and broadly distribute tasteful objects, necessary for the aesthetic education of the German people. Colze pronounced: "If today commercial palace after commercial palace is lining up along the major traffic arteries of the imperial capital; if illuminated display windows showing the most superb products of the collective industry of the civilized peoples are luring people in, not only for acts of purchase, but also for purely aesthetic reasons; if today even the little man is in a position to obtain luxury articles which are otherwise scarcely of any practical utility, then this is solely and singularly the achievement of the modern department store organism."[4]

Colze was clearly impressed, even awed by the department stores for their architectural beauty, their feats of engineering and design, their modern commercial methods, and perhaps most of all their tremendous power and scale. Yet his text registers a certain ambivalence and subtly attends to the more ambiguous consequences of the "department store organism." He expresses genuine consternation about the destruction of apartment buildings that was required for building the Kaufhaus des Westens (Department Store of the West, or KaDeWe) in Berlin's still mostly residential and verdant west. He rues the increasing influence of big banks and foreign capital over the new department store businesses. (Several of the major firms in fact became publicly financed ventures early in the twentieth century, and new construction typically required enormous bank loans, such as the 2 million mark capital infusion from Deutsche Bank behind the KaDeWe.) Colze also muses about the fate of smaller merchants and specialty retailers suddenly forced to compete with these mighty department store firms. Finally, he predicts that the stores' tremendous profits will soon wane; now that the department store phenomenon has passed through its childhood and entered maturity, he concludes, the era of rapidly acquired fortunes and new retail empires has nearly run its course.

Colze's perspicacity, his ability to see both the department store's contributions and its drawbacks, was rather unusual in the highly polarized department store debate that took place amid Wilhelmine Germany's divisive political culture. German society in this period was riven by the demographic and social consequences of rapid industrialization and urbanization. To many, particularly spokesmen for the shop-owning middle classes, the department store was the very symbol of the threatening future, a seemingly untamable economic juggernaut, a conduit for American ways, and a potential leveler of the distinctions that had made social standing and gender roles legible, segmented, and stable in the old order. New store openings became flashpoints in the confrontation between a political system that was still in many ways premodern and the forces of economic modernity.[5]

Not merely grist for the mill of German cultural pessimists, the department store issue quickly took on political dimensions. To many critics, the new stores represented a conspicuous embodiment of the international—and specifically the Jewish—presence in Germany. At the very moment in which a handful of Jewish businessmen were creating vast, attention-getting edifices in major German cities and helping transform daily life and culture, there was a revival of anti-Jewish rhetoric throughout German-speaking Europe, carried by new political groupings and organs that decried the Jews in the shrill tones of a new era of mass political mobilization. The department store became a convenient target just as a new generation of demagogues was seeing the political utility in harnessing economic resentment and whipping up anti-Semitic rage in Germany and Austria-Hungary.

The department store, then, almost as soon as it appeared on German soil, became a lightning rod for social and political conflict, and its dynamic growth incited several waves of controversy in Germany, and elsewhere, in these years. Starting already in the late 1880s, street protests greeted new department store openings in several German cities. The issue was also debated fiercely in the public sphere, taken up in state parliaments across the country, and even addressed in the Reichstag. "Hardly a state parliamentary session goes by," observed Lux, "without some new petition being brought forward [against] the department stores, these social-politically 'undesired enterprises.' "[6]

In June 1899, for example, the Reichstag held a debate about department stores and how to regulate them, one of dozens of clashes between economic liberals and Social Democrats on the one side and defenders of the interests of the *Mittelstand*—the shopkeeping and artisanal middle classes—on the other. During this particular session, Hermann Roeren, a Center Party delegate—later known for exposing scandals in the German colonial administration of Togo—denounced the rapid spread of these "colossal businesses," which, he lamented, were expanding and spreading at a terrifying rate, or "sprouting up like fungi," as he put it.[7] This great expansion, Roeren added, could be attributed not to the skill or cleverness of their proprietors but to the influence of the big banks and big capital. As a result, he claimed, "these businesses are engulfing the whole country; they are beginning to reach their tentacles even into the countryside and into the little towns."[8]

What Colze and Roeren had in common, despite the significant differences in their temperament and tone, was a sense of astonishment at the tremendous growth and the seemingly boundless expansion of the department store phenomenon. They shared a belief in the department store's revolutionary potential, its tremendous power over individual Germans and over the national economy, even if they assessed that power differently. Colze, for example, continually refers to department store businesses as dynasties and their directors as "kings," who exercised sovereignty over large groups of subordinate, fawning subjects, their eager customers. He writes, for example, that "in thick packs and ceaselessly they stream in: the ruler calls, they follow gladly."[9] Such evocations of the department store's power course through the abundant contemporary literature on the phenomenon by the stores' boosters and critics alike.

A great many of those accounts, to be sure, trafficked in anti-Semitic imagery, and their authors portrayed the department stores as a manifestation of Jewish capitalism, as the latest example of pervasive and nefarious, but often hidden, Jewish economic power. "Once a Jew always a Jew [Jud' bleibt Jud']," mused Theodor Ribbeck, an artisanal shopkeeper in Margarete Böhme's 1911 novel *W.A.G.M.U.S.*, as he pondered the ambitious expansion plans of the (baptized) department store owner Josua Müllenmeister (né Manasse). "A Christian wouldn't be able to pull all of this off. Whether

Müllenmeister or Manasse, Israel holds all the cards. Step by step Jerusalem increases its worldly terrain."[10]

Other than a minority of non-Jewish businessmen, who did in fact "pull it off," Germany's leading retail entrepreneurs at this time, Nathan Israel, Adolf Jandorf, Oscar and Leonhard Tietz, and Abraham Wertheim, were of Jewish origin. Jews founded the great majority of department stores throughout Germany, and Jewish businesses accounted for around 80 percent of total department store sales volume in the Weimar period, according to one frequently cited but not wholly reliable estimate.[11] The number was most likely higher before World War I, before many small, Jewish-owned firms were absorbed by the Karstadt company. Most of Colze's readers would have certainly been aware of the department store's entanglement with Jews and Jewishness: the affluent Jewish department store owner had become a stock character in novels like *W.A.G.M.U.S.*, and was emerging as a political scapegoat and even a cultural cliché. Indeed, the department store itself was widely seen as a Jewish phenomenon, by opponents, supporters, indifferent passersby, and eager customers.

Colze's text, however, differs from the standard anti-Semitic critiques and caricatures. A reference to Rabbi Akiva in the middle of the book is the first hint of the author's Jewish background. In his subsequent discussion of his maternal grandfather, whom he calls the Marshall Field of the 1860s, the "department store king" of his shtetl, the author subtly but unmistakably reveals his Jewish identity. Colze, it turns out, was actually one of several pen names used by the writer, publisher, and corporate attorney Leo Cohn.

Notwithstanding the idiosyncrasies of Colze's position, the department store debate was generally conducted in shrill and hyperbolic tones, with little room for nuance. Anti–department store writings were suffused with dire warnings of Germany's demise and filled with morbid, even supernatural images meant to lay bare the parasitical effects on the German middle classes of Jews, commercial capitalism, or both. Similar debates occurred elsewhere, chiefly in France, and also in the United States and Britain, but the German debate was marked with a particular venom against department stores and what they were believed to represent. It also started later and lasted much longer, marked by several distinct phases: first from the 1890s through the early 1900s, briefly, again, after World War I when the Nazis joined the fray, and then again in the later 1920s. It reached a crescendo with the economic crash of 1929, the subsequent unemployment crisis, and the Nazi rise to power.

A Revolution in Retail? Department Store versus. Specialty Shop

The nine years between Roeren's Reichstag speech and Colze's volume bookend the first of two peaks of German department store expansion.

A second department store boom occurred in the 1920s, during the brief but dynamic years of economic stability in the Weimar Republic. A decade before Roeren's 1899 address, there were scarcely any department stores in the German Empire. Large specialty stores and ready-made clothing shops certainly existed, along with other innovative retail establishments such as consumer cooperatives and shops for colonial wares, but department stores in the strict sense of the term, defined as highly capitalized retailers who carried multiple types of products that bore no inherent relationship to one another, in one, single-owned establishment, had only begun to appear.[12] Yet, in the 1880s and '90s, the retail landscape began to undergo a drastic and profound transformation. Two years before Roeren's speech, amid much fanfare, Berliners witnessed the opening of Warenhaus Wertheim on Leipziger Strasse, an enormous commercial palace on a key thoroughfare in the heart of the capital. The Wertheim store became the iconic department store in the Wilhelmine era, the fullest, and most influential architectural expression of the German department store idea. It was also a site of continued controversy and critique.

In a 1903 article, architecture critic Marie Netter described the revolutionary changes that had transformed commercial life over the past twenty years. It was now taken for granted, she noted, that even the most trivial consumer items appeared in tastefully arranged window displays. Modern department stores had replaced venerable old specialty shops, and glitzy commercial structures stood where there were once dank, cobweb-covered shacks. Netter speculated about the possible sources of what she labeled a revolution in retail: a more relaxed attitude about life among members of the consuming public; growth in industry, which was now able to supply cheaper, mass-produced goods; changing fashions, news of which now circulated the globe instantaneously; or some combination of all three.[13]

The department store's essential departure from traditional retail lay in its extremely wide selection of products. This distinguished it from so-called specialty shops (*Spezialgeschäfte*), which traded in one particular type or category of article. As they grew and expanded their offerings, department stores strove for comprehensiveness, so that all of a customer's consuming needs and desires could be satisfied in one location. The common motto "everything under one roof" (*alles unter einem Dach*) expressed the early twentieth-century department store's aspirations. Werner Sombart wrote that the department store "strives to bring more and more goods together in one business to be able to satisfy the wishes of the buying public as much as possible," thus becoming, "a store for every need" (*All-Bedarfsartikelgeschäft*).[14]

The department store's all-inclusiveness was the subject of a song-and-dance number, part of the musical revue *Es Liegt in der Luft* (It's in the air), performed on the Berlin stage in 1928. While flashing lights illuminate the store's many departments, the elevator operator invites passersby into the department store, his song humorously listing the store's various wares:

Women's clothes, stationery,	Damenkonfektion, Schreibwaren,
Storage units, cravats, tchotchkes,	Wirtschaftslager, Schlipse, Nippes,
Leather, books, sporting goods, paper,	Leder, Bücher, Sport, Papier,
Bridal department, funeral attire,	Brautabteilung, Trauerwäsche,
Rubbish, tripe, baby clothes,	Tinneff, Schmonzes, Babywäsche,
Passport photos, a chamber and a fuss,	Paßfotos, ein Gemach und ein Getu,
Art department, powder room,	Kunstabteilung, Erfrischungsraum,
gentleman's clothing.[15]	Herrenkonfektion,

The list continues with such items as herring, whipped cream, and cheese, and so on, until, in a nod to contemporaneous political events, it veers into absurdity as he begins to sing about democracy, government, and ministers of state. The point, in any case, is made: everything from the most trivial bauble on up can be found in the department store.

Exactly three decades earlier a cartoon had captured the stores' comprehensiveness in a way that evoked the heated context of the debates of the 1890s. Appearing in the humor newspaper *Simplicissimus*, the cartoon bitingly satirized both the department store's claim to all-inclusiveness and the pessimism

1.1 " 'I've come to tell you that you've brought me to complete ruin with your dastardly pricing policies. There is nothing left for me but put a bullet in my head.' 'May I kindly direct you. The weapons department may be found on the first floor.' " *Simplicissimus* 3, no. 14 (1898).

of many shopkeepers in the face of the great stores' rapid expansion. The scene takes place in a department store with ladies and several gentlemen picking through dresses and shoes in the background. On the left, a shopkeeper (tall, wan, clearly suggestive of a non-Jewish German of modest means beaten down by economic struggle) has entered the department store to inform the owner (drawn with stereotypically Jewish features: short, stout, with a bulbous nose and spectacles) that he has given up the fight, that the department store's low prices have run him out of business. He reports, "There is nothing left for me to do but put a bullet in my head."

The Jewish department store owner, betraying not a hint of emotion, addresses him as he would a customer and casually directs him to the weapons department on the first floor. The message is clear: competing with the department store is hopeless. Independent of its economic veracity, the cartoon provides a glimpse into popular attitudes and gives a sense of the department store's perceived inevitability and all-inclusiveness.

Significantly, the department store, like its cousins, the ready-made clothing store and the consumer cooperative, separated the acts of consumption and production. Disconnected from their origins in the process of mass production and exhibited in increasingly palatial and grandiose settings, goods were easily incorporated into the kinds of fantasies that the fully formed department store cultivated in its displays, promotions, and spectacles. In the department stores the banal and discrete act of purchasing was transformed into the activity of shopping, soon to become a major leisure activity and source of (at least some measure of) independence for bourgeois women. The new stores encouraged casual browsing (*freier Eintritt*, or *entré libre*). Shoppers were invited, even urged, to enter without any obligation to purchase (*ohne Kaufzwang*), a practice unheard of in specialty shops, where a store's proprietors welcomed only serious inquiries.

Department store directors calculated that more traffic inside their premises would lead to more purchases, and they counted on the stores' tempting displays, their suggestive powers, to arouse consuming desires and hence entice even stubborn customers into becoming impulsive buyers. As entrepreneur Josua Müllenmeister, the protagonist of *W.A.G.M.U.S.*, explained to a skeptical potential investor: "Believe you me: of every ten people who enter a department store with the intention of not buying anything, at least eight leave with a package, even if it's only a matter of a pound of grapes or a couple meters of ribbon or a scrap of calico . . . buying will happen under any circumstances."[16] "Thus," Müllenmeister continued, "the best and most effective advertising consists of attractions that have no apparent connection to the business, but which bring a great stream of people in and through the building." This approach, the attempt to create a fantastical experience that in turn was meant to arouse the desire to consume (*Kauflust*), accounted for much of the excitement and the controversy surrounding early department stores.

In a 1912 book about department stores and retail business architecture, Alfred Wiener contrasted the specialty shop, which waited for customers to enter, with the department store, which endeavored to pull people in by "displaying the goods from the best angle and making a visit to the store and the shopping experience as pleasant as possible." Wiener continued: "Everything that the department store has and is must contribute to attracting the public. . . . The fact that [visitors] can stroll freely through the department store's beautiful spaces, that they can observe everything without having to buy something . . . draws many people into the department store who had no intention at all of buying anything."[17] Consider also this passage from an 1898 newspaper article about department stores:

> It rustles and sizzles, gleams and glitters. Parisian bronzes and Meitzen linens. Cigarette boxes and bridal blouses woven with breath and fragrance, wheels and suitcases for journeys, dolls and umbrellas—what is there that these department stores do not have! . . . The more you look, the more you covet. You buy and buy. So that on the next day when the delivery wagon comes with the package, you can say that you got the better of the frugality that reigns in all virtuous households.[18]

But what turned curious onlookers, drawn in by the store's beauty and eye-catching lighting and window displays, into buyers? What led them to overcome the virtue of frugality? For Wiener it had to do with both women's nature and department store planning: "But when they see the goods on display, they are easily induced to buy this or that. This is why most of the spaces for resting and relaxing are located in a place where you first have to traverse the greater part of the department store, usually multiple levels, before you reach them. The department store thus is counting on, above all, the psychological characteristics of the world of women, who just by seeing things are induced to buy them."[19] The department store therefore operated on its customers—the women especially—psychologically, as Arthur Wilke claimed in a 1905 essay.[20] It functioned by awakening *Kauflust*.

Large crowds of shoppers and browsers made the department store seem like the place to be, an exciting and modish destination, which in turn attracted even more attention and consequently larger crowds. A visit to the store was thus transformed into an experience, a new mode of activity and spectatorship structured around commodities, as European and American department stores became safe, respectable places for bourgeois women to spend their time—for many, a more compelling alternative to the church. This in turn generated new concerns about women's independence, their use of money, and the consequences and power of their desires.

By the eve of World War I, department stores were attracting more attention to themselves with special events like fashion shows, performances, and art exhibitions.[21] Such attractions, along with the ancillary services the stores began to provide, enticed more potential customers, further distinguishing the department stores from specialty shops and turning them into leisure destinations and tourist attractions in their own right—theaters, so to speak, for the staging of acts of consumption.[22] In the words of Rosalind Williams, "As environments of mass consumption, department stores were, and still are, places where consumers are an audience to be entertained by commodities, where selling is mingled with amusement, where arousal of free-floating desire is as important as immediate purchase of particular items."[23] Exhibitions, concerts, and shows drew in curious spectators, while restaurants, banks, theater ticket offices, travel agencies, hair salons, newspaper reading rooms, letter-writing areas, and public telephones, among other services, enabled shoppers to manage their affairs, conduct personal and household business, rendezvous with friends and associates, and while away the day within the major department store's portals. One Berlin department store even created a supervised play area for children, so that mothers could shop freely while their little ones were entertained.[24] Saying "we're going to Wertheim," wrote Gustav Stresemann, in 1900, did not mean going shopping to fill a household need, but rather signaled an outing like a day trip. The future foreign minister and chancellor described the experience:

> You choose an afternoon on which you have as much time as possible, and whenever possible, you make a plan with acquaintances. Having arrived at Leipziger Strasse, you first spend a good deal of time admiring the display windows and then you perambulate the ground floor, look at the most varied displays, perhaps buy a thing or two, let yourself be conducted by the elevator to the first upper floor and enjoy if possible a cup of chocolate with the obligatory slice of torte or apple cake. If you've found or brought along acquaintances, you may stay here for a long time sitting and chatting, showing each other your various purchases and spurring each other on to new selections.[25]

The swarms of department store shoppers and the enormous sales staffs created a more impersonal or anonymous consuming experience, a striking contrast to the specialty shops, where customers usually knew the owner and his family and often had patronized them for years, even generations. Sombart described a visit to the specialty shop this way: "You were known and would be greeted as an acquaintance when you entered. . . . You would chat about this and that and also about the item that you were interested in."[26] Not so in the department store, where, as Rosalind Williams puts it, "Active verbal interchange between customer and retailer was replaced by the passive, mute response of consumer to things."[27] In the specialty shop customers and storekeepers customarily engaged in a dialogue about a product's qualities, notes the historian Wolfgang Schivelbusch, but in the age of department stores, posted price tags squelched that conversation, turning value primarily into a function of price and goods into bearers of exchange value.[28]

Entering the department store meant stepping into a world of things. The customer or casual browser had an unmediated, even intimate relationship with the goods. Most products could be touched and held, at least until glass cases, increasingly implemented in the early twentieth century to prevent theft, became more prevalent; but even then consumers could see all the merchandise and were free to run their hands through fabrics, sundries, and other assorted items stocked on tables, in racks, and on floor displays.[29] They could sit on furniture, try on neckties or scarves, and fiddle with the knobs and dials on household appliances like kitchen gadgets or radios.

In specialty shops, on the other hand, the counter served as a barrier that separated the customer from the products. Before purchase, commodities were hidden, as though shrouded in shame, a stark contrast indeed to the department store's often ostentatious showcasing of its products.[30] Goods sold by specialty shops, furthermore, were frequently ordered through intermediary brokers, meaning that customers often had to wait for weeks before they were available. Department store patrons, on the other hand, left the store with their purchases in hand or waited at most a day or two for the delivery truck to bring larger and bulkier items. The department store brought immediate gratification.

Another significant difference between the two retail settings is that department store prices were fixed and prominently displayed, whereas in specialty shops they were typically negotiated and often adjusted in accordance with the customer's ability to pay. It would have been unthinkable to charge a rich customer and a poor customer the same price for an item, Werner Sombart recalled.[31] Sales and special promotions, another department store feature that contradicted traditional German retail practices, simultaneously drew in more customers through enticing spectacles and decorating schemes—like the so-called white weeks, when often elaborate, themed displays took over the central atriums—and helped clear out inventory.

At department stores, furthermore, goods were usually returnable and exchangeable soon after they were bought, turning purchasing decisions into far more whimsical, inconsequential acts. In the words of fictional department store proprietor Friedrich Nielandt in Erich Köhrer's novel *Warenhaus Berlin*: "One of the most attractive things about the department stores is that we treat you with the utmost politeness if you come in to exchange an item. . . . The public and especially the female public buys away with such crazy reckless abandon because, as people say, 'Ah, if we don't like it, or if it turns out we don't need it after all, we can always just bring it back.'"[32]

Finally, department stores generally accepted only cash, whereas specialty shops typically worked on credit, both for buying and selling merchandise. Consequently, the specialty shops' accounts were often settled slowly and inefficiently—"the more elegant the lady, the more nonchalant they are about paying [their bills]," mused a struggling but resigned shoemaker in *W.A.G.M.U.S.* "If you express your warnings a little more bluntly, they get extremely insulted and you run the risk of losing their business."[33]

Because of their size and their considerable expenses, department stores faced great pressure to turn over goods rapidly and to keep their shelves clear for new merchandise. The key to their success was their high volume: "high volume, small margin/profit" (*Grosser Umsatz, kleiner Nutzen*) was the business motto of the Hermann Tietz firm and a principle adopted by most of its competitors too, whereas specialty retailers generally tried to charge as much as they could for their wares.[34] Goods were thus marketed at lucrative prices, often barely above cost, or occasionally even below, for quick clearance to make room for new stock. In such a way, department stores could sell goods at prices 25–30 percent lower than their competition.[35]

Department store companies, often composed of several, even dozens of affiliated stores, were able to buy in extremely high volume and pay manufactures in cash and up front, in contrast to specialty shops, so that the producers in turn gave them better prices. Most department store firms also produced some of their own textiles. These stores' favorable prices, as we will see, baffled and infuriated critics and fueled the opposition, which constantly accused the store owners of improper sales practices and deceptive advertising. With its low prices, high sales volume, and rapid turnover, the department store was characterized by constant motion and instant satisfaction—all in stark contrast to the image, if not always the reality, of the traditional, unchanging German specialty shop.

Since the mid-1890s, department stores had devoted increasing resources to print advertisements and soon developed more elaborate and eye-catching advertising techniques, superseding the sober announcements in the daily press that had constituted early advertising efforts by department stores and specialty shops alike. Aggressive self-promotion, in the eyes of traditional retailers, amounted to *Kundenfang*, the attempt to capture another business's customers, and was thus looked at with disapproval.[36] By the first years of the twentieth century, department store ads could be found across major cityscapes, on autobuses, on bridges, and in large letters on store buildings. Even smaller shops' resistance to the practice had waned, and their proprietors now joined the advertising frenzy.[37] Window displays became increasingly attractive, bright, and skillfully designed, in contrast to the cluttered, dank, and chaotic shop windows of the earlier nineteenth century.

To be sure, many specialty shops grew rapidly in these years, too, and adopted more modern business practices, and not all department stores, especially outside the metropolis, reached this enormous scale, featured such a diverse array of goods and services, and attracted so much attention. Nevertheless, in general, early twentieth-century department stores were distinguishable by their size, their broad selection of products, their often ornate designs, and their spectacles, services, and entertainment. Their low prices made certain kinds of products that were once available only to elites accessible to broader sectors of the middle class, and even the working class. Advertising and mail-order business furthered the early department stores' reach into the countryside and sped the onset of imperial Germany's nascent mass consumer culture.

The Department Store and Its Discontents: Modern Retail in France, the United States, and Britain

The department store and the trappings of consumer culture incited controversy in all national contexts, but nowhere were these controversies as biting and enduring as in Germany. The opposition to department stores, however, began in France, with the appearance of the first *grands magasins*. Educated German readers, if they followed French developments, were generally aware of the department store debate long before they ever set foot in such an establishment. Because department stores originated in France and then spread through Britain and the United States before they reached Germany, nationalist German critics continually associated them with non-German cultures and contexts. In fact, department stores were often represented as a French phenomenon internationally—hence the proliferation of (unaffiliated) stores called Bon Marché in Great Britain and the United States—until around World War I, when America replaced France as the seat and symbol of international consumer culture.

Historical consensus generally views the Bon Marché in Paris, immortalized as the model for Émile Zola's *Au Bonheur des Dames*, as the most influential early department store and its new 1869 building as the first purpose-built department store edifice, marking a crucial turning point in the history of retail and commercial architecture.[38] The Bon Marché originated as a drapery shop. Taken over by Aristide Boucicaut in 1852, the store grew rapidly over the succeeding decades, and Boucicaut continually added new departments, increased staff, and expanded its premises.[39] By 1887, the store took up an entire city block and had some eighteen hundred employees. By 1906 the staff had expanded to almost seven thousand.[40]

The 1869 building, codesigned by Gustave Eiffel, pioneered the style that became emblematic of department store architecture worldwide. An iron-and-glass construction featuring an enormous inner courtyard topped with a glass skylight, a wide central staircase below, and upper selling departments oriented around the courtyard, the building remained the model for department store construction until the modernist designs of the 1920s. Its ornate flourishes, dramatic lighting, and massive scale inspired Zola to compare the department store to a cathedral, a church for the worship of the commodity.

Other *grands magasins* followed in the years to come. Like the Bon Marché, many quickly outgrew their original quarters and constructed new, purpose-built, palatial edifices. In 1877 Les Grands Magasins du Louvre opened its impressive new facilities, and in 1883 Printemps rebuilt its quarters on a comparable scale. Like the Bon Marché, these stores originated as smaller operations that specialized in a particular kind of merchandise, usually draperies.[41] The entrepreneurs who created them, like Boucicaut, were mostly men of modest means and generally of provincial origin, and while several were Jewish—the owners of the Galeries Lafayette prominent among them—Jews represented a fairly small minority of department store directors in France. Strategic marriages, the historian Philip Nord points out, supplied the necessary capital for the rapid growth of several of these stores. In other cases, the ability to sway potential investors (and customers) was of crucial importance.[42]

In their development from specialty shops into department stores, most of these businesses passed through an intermediate phase as *magasins de nouveautés* (drapery and fancy goods stores), establishments that featured such products as silks, woolens, cloths, shawls, lingerie, hosiery, gloves, ready-to-wear clothing, and sometimes furs, umbrellas, and sewing goods, at the time an unprecedented combination of wares.[43] These precursors hastened the so-called second consumer or retail revolution, presaging many of the department store's innovations, including stocking a diverse array of wares, free entry, returnable goods, and conspicuous advertising.[44]

The rapid growth and spectacular trappings of early French department stores do not mean, of course, that they were universally welcomed. Critical voices ill at ease with the stores' seductive qualities and their apparent influence over eager women shoppers portrayed them as dens of iniquity, corrosive to the moral fiber of the French bourgeoisie. Journalist Pierre Giffard, for example, condemned the department store in 1882, highlighting the alleged proliferation of transgressions like kleptomania and prostitution and recounting salacious tales of debauchery among female sales workers and customers.[45] These scandalous reports, doubtlessly highly exaggerated, reflected above all an anxiety around the degree of independence and agency bourgeois women enjoyed in the department stores and also a kind of titillation about the increasingly youthful and female workforce who dwelled and worked within the store building.[46]

Simultaneously there emerged a political and economic critique of the stores and their apparent impact. Perceiving that the new stores were endangering their livelihood, small shopkeepers banded together in 1888 and formed the Ligue syndicale du travail, de l'industrie et du commerce (the Syndical League of Labor, Industry, and Commerce), a group that came to include over 140,000 members in the 1890s.[47] The league, together with other petit-bourgeois groups, pressed the state to levy taxes on these massive stores and sought other means of leveling the commercial playing field, even though, as Philip Nord has demonstrated, specialty shops and department stores were usually not in direct competition, and the latter did not hamper the fortunes of the former in any appreciable way.[48] In many cases, department stores actually improved the fortunes of neighboring small businesses by bringing in more pedestrian traffic and thus increased exposure beyond circles of loyal local clientele.[49] Department stores, furthermore, despite the lip service they paid to "everything under one roof," were slow to enter into certain retail sectors and did not compete with specialty stores for such items as bicycles, lamps, and photographic equipment until into the twentieth century.[50]

Although shop owners greatly exaggerated the threat posed by department stores, their political allies denounced the stores vociferously in the public sphere, criticizing working conditions and accusing the stores of engaging in deceptive sales practices that threatened the integrity of the French nation. Ultimately, they achieved only minor legislative gains in the form of extra taxes on the *grands magasins*, but their condemnations reverberated not only in the political life of the French Third Republic but also wherever new department stores appeared, including the United States, the next site of major department store construction.

The growth of American department stores occurred slightly later than in France. Most of what would become the leading department store firms were established between 1870 and 1890 and gradually evolved, continually adding more departments and services, culminating in what the historian Susan Porter Benson called a "new world of retailing."[51] In her now classic study of American department store workers and customers, Benson shows that the early department store entrepreneurs did not operate with a vision of the fully formed store; rather, they experimented and improvised constantly in the hopes of maximizing revenue and earning returns on their enormous capital expenditures. Thus many of the department store's key attributes came as expedient tactics for increasing profitability and surviving amid fierce competition.

The "palaces" that Scottish Irish immigrant A. T. Stewart built in New York between the 1840s and the 1860s represented an American equivalent to the *magasins de nouveautés* and pioneered many sales techniques and business approaches that we associate with department stores. Yet most of Stewart's business was wholesale, and he carried only fancy dry goods.[52] By the 1890s American department stores began to take shape in recognizable form, first with the Siegel-Cooper stores and then Wanamaker (originally in Philadelphia), Marshall Field's and Carson, Pirie, Scott in Chicago, Macy's in New York, Filene's in Boston, and a bit later Famous-Barr in St. Louis. In the 1880s, most American stores had only fifteen departments. By 1910, many exceeded 125.[53]

The expansion of American department stores, like that of their counterparts in France, was met with opposition, chiefly by representatives of small shopkeepers, who agitated for the state to intervene to curb their growth.

As William Leach recounts, "Laws were introduced in state capitals from California to New York to tax 'the octopus which has stretched out its tentacles in every direction, grasping in its slimy folds the specialist or one-line man'—the florist, the shoeman, the grocer, the jeweler, the furniture dealer, and the like. Butchers and liquor dealers often led the fight."[54] In one incident activists threatened John Wanamaker's life and attacked his stores with bombs.[55]

Nevertheless, the resistance, intense at first, proved short-lived. Efforts to impose special department store taxes failed in the United States, and the issue had faded away by the beginning of the twentieth century. American culture was certainly less ambivalent about commercial capitalism than the French, and the anxieties about the new consumer culture, so salient in the French and German contexts, with their strong handworker and shopkeeper traditions, yielded to an American embrace of entrepreneurship, modernity, and convenience.

Developments in Britain paralleled those in the United States in many ways. Department stores and the new consumer culture made themselves felt in London first in the 1860s and '70s with the arrival of Whiteley's Universal Provider, a kind of department store precursor akin to the *magasins de nouveautés* or A. T. Stewart's marble palace. British department stores, such as Marks & Spencer, Selfridges, and Harrods, were founded at the same time as their American counterparts, but it took them longer to rival the American firms in size. British stores were not only smaller than American and French department stores in the later nineteenth century, but they also had fewer departments and catered to a narrower demographic group.

Despite the long history of consumerism in Britain, the department store and newer forms of retail were often treated as foreign, that is, French or American imports. Thus, not only did the stores incite the same moral panic and political opposition that we saw in France and the United States, but they also were construed as an unwanted international presence, best embodied in the figure of the flamboyant American Henry Selfridge—erstwhile second-in-command at Marshall Field's in Chicago—who strove to introduce Londoners, men and women alike, to the joys of shopping.[56] Selfridge's early ads proclaimed that shopping was "an important part of the day's PLEASURE, a time of PROFIT, RECREATION, and ENJOYMENT."[57]

Family Matters: Jews and the Rise of the Department Store in Germany

Developments in German retail had much in common with these French, American, and British trajectories, but there were also significant differences that help explain the depth and duration of oppositional movements there. For one, as we have seen, department stores as such appeared later in the German Empire and also in Austria-Hungary than in Britain and the United States and significantly later than in France.[58] Most of the major German department store families, including the Wertheims, the two Tietz branches, the Karstadts, Wronkers, Urys, Knopfs, and Jandorfs, were founding their first, modest establishments—dry goods or textile stores—in the German provinces in the 1870s, precisely during the great wave of Parisian department store openings. Most of these families, although notably not the Wertheims or the Karstadts, migrated from Posen (Poznań), and a great many, including the Tietzes, Schockens, Urys, and Wronkers, hailed from the same general area, the district of Birnbaum (today Międzychód), toward the west of the erstwhile Prussian province. These families were part of the wave that brought some fifty thousand Jews from Posen into central and western Germany between 1824 and 1871, and a great many of these migrants had a background in retail and were able to launch new commercial enterprises in German cities and towns.[59]

Why were Jews so heavily represented in the department store sector in Germany? Only the American case offers another example of such major Jewish representation; but with the exception of the Strauss family (Macy's), the Filenes of Boston, and the Kaufmanns of Pittsburgh, most of the pioneering American entrepreneurs were not Jewish.[60] Historians have seldom addressed this topic directly. Jewish presence in the department store business might in fact have more to do with the experience of migrant groups than with any Jewish specificities. Newcomers, searching for economic opportunities, tend to enter into newer, less prestigious commercial niches and are generally more open to innovation and less inhibited by the taboos that may influence more established populations. Long excluded from the German guild system, Jews were prohibited from practicing many traditional branches of manufacture and commerce and had to improvise in ways that proved beneficial in the long term. Those commercial spheres that were open to Jews, already less prestigious, became doubly tabooed, marked as all the more undesirable because of the pronounced Jewish presence.[61] Nevertheless, some Jews benefited from positions in economic and commercial sectors that proved to be useful gateways into more diversified retail. In the early nineteenth century, Jewish manufacturers entered the textile trades, and through technical innovations and lucrative contracts—supplying uniforms for the Prussian army, for example—they came to dominant the trade in ready-made clothing. Several Jewish entrepreneurs, such as Hermann Gerson, went on to found most of Germany's major fashion houses.[62]

In some cases Jewish entrepreneurs benefited from international connections—the Tietzes, for example, had close relatives in the United States and Belgium—and were more informed about foreign commercial innovations than other German businesspeople. Family connections helped. The Wronker brothers married two Tietz daughters, for example, and Julius Bamberger worked for the Ury department stores in Saxony before starting his own store in Bremen in 1907.[63] Young Jewish men typically apprenticed at the firms of family friends or relatives.[64] To make a place for themselves in the competitive world of German retail and manufacture, Jews relied on the solidarity of family and took advantage of their religious and communal bonds.[65]

Many department store families had started out in peddling, and the experience of bringing together goods of diverse origin and selling them to different populations may have proved useful, as they transplanted their family businesses westward. Moreover, peddling and junk dealing, typical Jewish occupations in Europe, had one crucial element in common with the department stores: they sold a diverse collection of goods and as such differed from mainstream retail traditions. Nevertheless, the exceptions, most notably the highly successful Karstadt firm, the Althoff concern, which flourished before World War I, and the Rudolph Hertzog store in Berlin, a major, proto-department store, preclude sweeping explanations for the preponderance of Jews.

Unlike the French, British, and American department stores, which catered mostly to bourgeois shoppers at this time (the low-cost basements that became common in American stores were an exception), early German department stores were essentially discounters providing quality goods at reasonable prices for predominately working-class and lower-middle-class customers. Only in the mid- to late 1890s, beginning most notably with the Wertheim store on Leipziger Strasse, did the German department store begin to reach higher up the social hierarchy and become a site for acquiring more elegant goods. Being able to sell luxury articles at reasonable prices, argued Salman Schocken, required an enormous store facility, one with a selling area large enough that fine goods could be vended in high quantities.[66] This increasingly characterized the stores that were built after 1896; and even after they attained the heights of luxury and elegance, German department stores could not entirely free themselves of the criticism, leveled repeatedly by their opponents, that they were no more than spruced-up junk dealers or shabby discounters passing as elegant purveyors. Kaufhaus Israel's directors were clearly responding to this label when they published a tourist's account of her "three days in Berlin" in the 1902 edition of their annual album. "The catalog had given us ladies a rough sense of what we would be able to find in the store," the author recounted, "but I was nonetheless surprised at what a cornucopia of goods lay before me. And everything was displayed so elegantly. There was no ballyhoo, no pushing and shoving!"[67]

Also distinguishing the German case is that its firms generally developed into regional, but not national, retail chains. Most got their start in smaller cities and even large towns in the 1870s and 1880s before entering the bigger markets of Hamburg, Munich, or Berlin toward century's end, and most retained their regional focus. The Wertheims, for example, started out in Stralsund. Brothers Hugo and Georg Wertheim entered their family business in 1876 and persuaded their father Abraham to begin innovating and expanding their cramped facility, soon pioneering such practices as accepting returns and exchanges and taking only cash.[68]

Georg Wertheim opened a second branch in the Hanseatic city of Rostock in 1884. The next year came the first Berlin shop, and they added a second in 1890 and a third two years later; only at that point did they begin diversifying their stock to the point where they could be classified as department stores. The Leipziger Strasse store, however, represented a dramatic shift for the company and for the German department store as a whole. Its prodigious size dwarfed its predecessors, and Alfred Messel's design—implemented in several stages over the 1890s and 1900s—inspired widespread admiration and imitation.[69] The store's elegance captivated the Berlin bourgeoisie. Its exquisite tastefulness and subtlety were meant definitively to distance it from its humble origins, to silence the critics who slandered the stores as glorified rummage bazaars or junk dealers or who complained of their crass commercialism. The Leipziger Strasse store became not only a famous department store, notable for its fusion of German historical styles and its cathedral-like splendor, but also the most influential piece of commercial architecture in Wilhelmine Germany.

Not long after Wertheim's grand opening on Leipziger Strasse, the Hermann Tietz concern—a rival firm that had started out in the Thuringian town of Gera with 1,000 marks in capital in 1882 and then expanded into Munich in 1892—purchased a neighboring property and constructed its own flagship emporium, an attention-getting glass-and-steel colossus that opened up with tremendous fanfare and a major advertising blitz.[70] It was soon followed by another major construction at Alexanderplatz, a more conservative and less controversial affair architecturally. In 1892, the Hamburg-based entrepreneur Adolf (Abraham) Jandorf was sent to Berlin by his employer, H. J. Emden Sons, to open the first of what ultimately became seven major department stores in the capital under the direction of the four Jandorf brothers.[71] Jandorf's typical customer, in contrast to the patrons of Wertheim and Tietz, came from Berlin's sizable working class, except at his KaDeWe, which, completed in 1907, rivaled Wertheim as the capital's most elegant and exclusive shopping destination. The KaDeWe, the massive "retail palace" that inspired Colze's book and Köhrer's novel *Warenhaus Berlin*, helped shift the capital's center of gravity and catalyzed the commercial development of Berlin's residential west.

Thus, most department stores, at least in their initial form, began outside the capital, and it was in the towns and medium-size cities in the industrializing pockets of provincial Germany that they experienced some of their fastest growth. Leonhard Tietz, Oscar's brother, began in Stralsund, just down the street from the original Wertheim store. In 1890 he moved his base of operations to Elberfeld (adjacent to and later incorporated into Wuppertal in North-Rhine Westphalia) and then in 1895 to Cologne, from where he directed a growing chain of department stores centered in the Rhineland and scattered throughout Germany's west, and including affiliated stores in Belgium.

Rudolf Karstadt started out with a large retail store in the town of Wismar, on Germany's northern coast, in 1891. In 1912 he moved his headquarters to Hamburg, from where he directed a similarly large chain of stores concentrated in Germany's north. Karstadt's first Berlin store was opened only in 1929. By that time, the firm employed over twenty-four thousand workers in 112 stores and factory sites.[72] The two Tietz brothers and Rudolf Karstadt had agreed not to go into direct competition with each other, hence their complementary regional emphases; and this arrangement, first only an oral pact, and written down after Leonhard Tietz's death in 1914, lasted until 1923 when the H. Tietz firm attempted a hostile takeover of L. Tietz.[73]

Theodor Althoff, who had inherited his widowed mother's woolens business, quickly expanded his scope of operations and began opening up new affiliates in 1886, above all in the heavily industrialized and densely populated Ruhr area. Althoff became one of Germany's largest firms, but after falling into financial distress, it was taken over by the Karstadt company after World War I. The picture begins to fill in with the addition of the Wronkers in Hessen, the Alsbergs around North Rhine–Westphalia, the Urys and Schockens in Saxony, the Barasch brothers in Breslau, the Knopfs in southwestern Germany, and dozens of local enterprises throughout the country.[74]

Reliable numbers are difficult to find, particularly owing to the fluidity of the department store concept and the slippage between true department stores (*Warenhäuser*) and large retail shops (*Kaufhäuser*). In his 1907 book on Wertheim, Paul Göhre estimated that there were between forty and fifty department stores in Berlin and some two hundred in Germany as a whole, and these figures do stand up to scrutiny.[75] By 1914 the country had approximately four hundred department stores, according to a contemporary estimate by the leader of the German department store association.[76] Looking at taxation records, Käthe Lux counted about ninety department stores in the state of Prussia in 1906 and some forty-one in Bavaria.[77] Roughly 71 percent of these firms were founded after 1890, and those whose origins predated that year had started out as specialty stores and slowly evolved into full-blown department stores in the 1880s and '90s.[78] Erich von Wussow reached similar conclusions in a 1906 study. Circulating questionnaires among department store founders, he found that the majority of German department stores had emerged within the preceding decade and that even the oldest businesses had existed for less than twenty years.[79] Despite their later beginning, department stores in Germany were proliferating faster than anywhere else, with the possible exception of the United States.

Netter captured this frenetic growth in a 1903 newspaper article about department store architecture:

> Twenty years ago in all the notable city centers there still stood a grand row of respectable old retail shops in the old buildings in which they had been founded, which had been passed down from generation to generation with the nondescript selling areas and the worn-out furniture, without the slightest changes in business practice. The bare selling areas fit with the exterior, a clean coat of paint, a sign over the entry, the goods arranged artlessly in little display windows. The personnel in these solid old businesses were polite but taciturn, and the boss looked on with condescending scorn on all the efforts that the new competition was putting into getting the customers to pay attention to it.[80]

Since then, Netter declared, everything had changed. Retail had been revolutionized faster and more thoroughly than any other branch of business. The two preceding decades had given birth to the commercial building, she wrote, and the new consuming palaces (*Kaufpaläste*) in Berlin, Vienna, Munich, and Frankfurt had supplied "architecture [with] a gratifying new challenge, had inspired technology and creativity in equal measure, and had stamped the image of the city with the mark of modernity."[81]

This period had also created vast fortunes. At the beginning of the twentieth century, only Berthold Israel, director of the eponymous department store in Berlin, ranked in the upper echelons of the Jewish economic elite, somewhat below the bankers and big industrialists, whose economic prominence traced back to the early modern period. Israel's fortune was estimated at the time to be between 10 and 20 million marks.[82] The two Tietzes and the Wertheims ranked slightly lower, although their businesses had already become larger and more profitable than Israel's.

The stores' sales volume and profitability are difficult to recover. One of the few useful sources for this kind of information is a 1910 study by Julius Hirsch. Hirsch estimated that the Wertheim Leipziger Strasse store was worth 33 million marks, a figure that included the cost of the valuable central Berlin property.[83] He put the value of all the Leonhard Tietz stores at 14.25 million marks. Wertheim's sales, according to Hirsch, totaled some 60 million marks for the year 1905, which was more than twice the sales of the L. Tietz stores; annual profits for L. Tietz amounted to between 3 and 4 percent of those sales figures—that is, around 1 million marks each year between 1905 and 1910.

It bears emphasizing that despite the precipitous and arresting growth of department stores in Germany, at their pre–World War I peak they constituted only around 2.5 percent of German retail volume, and their highest interwar levels scarcely exceeded 4 percent.[84] (In 1957 they reached around 12.4 percent of total retail volume, their high-water mark for the twentieth century.)[85] On the other hand, it is also important to note that the numbers alone do not tell the whole story. In Wilhelmine and Weimar Germany, the department store generated attention far beyond what these numbers would suggest. It was a highly fraught and hotly contested part of modern life, a flash point for dramatic changes, a source of cultural conflict and political controversy about, as we will see, class, gender, urban space, German cultural heritage, and the place of the Jews in European cultural and economic life.

The Department Store under Attack: The *Warenhaus-Debatte* in Germany

The political fault lines of the department store question varied regionally and depended on party alliances and constellations in the various German states. Above all, the debate expressed the anxiety of the traditional middle classes in an era of rapid industrialization, squeezed, as they increasingly found themselves, between big capital on the one side and the expanding ranks of the working class on the other. Attempts to curb department store expansion, as the historian Uwe Spiekermann argues, had more success where shopkeeper activists—who positioned themselves as the defenders of throne and altar and guardians of traditional German values—were able to win members of the bourgeoisie over to their cause by depicting department stores as beholden to foreign interests, friendly to socialism, and threatening to traditional German mores.[86]

Liberals, at least in principle, thought department stores made good business sense and admired the efficiency of their models for supplying and distributing goods and materials, while the social democratic Left typically welcomed the material benefits the stores brought to the working class. The Marxist Wilhelm Liebknecht, for one, celebrated the department store in an 1898 essay. He admired the way such stores modernized and simplified the economy by centralizing capital, and cast them as a harbinger of socialist economic conditions. Writing about department stores in general—he listed the Louvre in Paris, Stewart in New York, and Wertheim in Berlin—and London's Spiers & Pond in particular, Liebknecht remarked:

> Should I wish to have my laundry washed, a flat furnished, a meal hosted, one word to Spiers & Pond and my wishes are fulfilled as promptly as the genies of *A Thousand and One Nights* and with quite the same ability of traversing through time and space. Should I require a piano, a lobster or a leg of mutton . . . one word to Spiers & Pond, and if it is at all humanly possible, I receive what I requested. In short, there is nothing—in any case I have not yet found anything—that can't be had at Spiers & Pond for money. If it weren't for the money, it would be the true state of the future.[87]

Liebknecht of course conceded that the department store was a capitalist, profit-driven enterprise, yet he argued that by centralizing mass production and distribution it facilitated the transition into a socialist economy, representing a "growing into socialism" (*Hineinwachsen in den Sozialismus*).[88] Since economic power had been transferred into fewer hands, it would be easier for the state to take over the reins.

The support of the Social Democratic Party (SDP) for the stores became a major theme in what became the anti–department store movement. From the perspective of the embattled *Mittelstand*, the SPD's defense of department stores represented a kind of nightmare scenario, an alliance of their two major class foes, the capitalist upper middle classes and the socialist workers. Nevertheless, Social Democratic support of department stores was rock solid, at least during the Wilhelmine and early Weimar periods. The more radical Left, however, soured on department stores decades later, seeing them as exploitative of the working class and responsible for arousing false needs in financially strapped workers as the economic crisis of the late Weimar years took its toll.[89] At the same time, department store employees rejected social democracy and tended to affiliate with white-collar interest groups that defended their status as members of the middle class.[90] These groups, amid Weimar economic uncertainty, tacked strongly to the right, embracing anti-Semitism and largely sympathizing with the Nazi cause in the later 1920s.

Even before department stores had become an important fixture in German commercial life, the new emporiums found themselves under attack by coalitions of small shop owners and anti-Semites. The organized shopkeeper movement, the Zentralverband Deutscher Kaufleute und Gewerbetreibender (ZDK, or Central Association of German Shopkeepers and Artisans), like its French counterpart was founded in 1888 when a series of local organizations came together and established common leadership. The association's membership, which hovered around four thousand in 1889/90, reached about ten thousand in 1894/95 and around fifteen thousand in 1897/98.[91] Its rapid growth thus occurred just as department stores were spreading and expanding so conspicuously.[92] In other words, the ZDK emerged not as a response to the damaging effects of department stores, but rather in anticipation of their potential consequences. In fact, the league originally targeted consumer cooperatives, and only around 1896 did it begin to shift its attacks from the Social Democratic co-ops to the department stores.[93]

One of the ZDK's primary goals was to enact national legislation against dishonest or unfair sales practices (*unlauterer Wettbewerb*), which they associated chiefly with the department stores. Their efforts reached fruition in 1896 when the Reichstag passed a law for the "combatting of dishonest sales practices." The law, which went into effect in July of that year, covered four areas: excessive advertising, obfuscation of the quantity of goods, defamation, and disclosure of trade secrets. Violations were to be punished with fines of up to 1,500 marks. The shopkeeper movement succeeded in having the legislation sharpened in 1909. Among its new provisions was the tighter regulation of clearance sales.[94]

ZDK activists also condemned advertising (for both ethical and aesthetic reasons) and joined cause with early environmental groups who claimed that billboards and conspicuous signage marred the natural beauty of surrounding landscapes.[95] They pushed, furthermore, for state and federal intervention against department stores through building regulations aimed at limiting the size of commercial buildings and the number of customers stores could accommodate. They also invoked the fear of fire to scare away potential department store consumers and to justify their appeals to building authorities. Most notably, the ZDK agitated for department store taxation, efforts that bore some fruit as special department store taxes were adopted by the state governments in such places as Saxony (1897), Bavaria (1899), Prussia (1900), Brunswick and Baden (1904), and Hessen (1911).[96]

The new tax laws first had to define their targets, since there was no consensus either about what constituted a department store or how a department store differed from a large shop. Further complicating the issue is the existence of two German terms, *Warenhaus* and *Kaufhaus*, which though often used interchangeably had different meanings and different connotations. The Prussian legislation established a formal distinction by defining department stores—*Warenhäuser* or *Waarenhäuser*—as commercial enterprises whose sales volume exceeded 500,000 marks annually and which carried goods from each of four different categories: (1) colonial goods (spices, tea, coffee), food and beverages, tobacco, pharmaceuticals, etc.; (2) textiles: yarn, threads, knit goods, ready-to-wear clothing, curtains, rugs, etc.; (3) household, kitchen, and garden wares; and (4) gold, silver, jewelry, paper goods, books, music, weapons, bicycles, toys, etc.[97] *Kaufhäuser*, on the other hand, were simply large retail enterprises that did not meet the criteria for taxation. For many people, however, the word *Kaufhaus* had a more refined ring to it, as in the Kaufhaus des Westens, a store that was technically a *Warenhaus* but aspired to great elegance. Further muddling the issue are examples like Kaufhaus N. Israel, which although it began as a *Kaufhaus* had developed into a *Warenhaus* by the late nineteenth century, yet continued to bear its original name.

The department store tax amounted to about 1.5 to 2 percent of profits, with a ceiling of 1 million marks. The laws also stipulated that proceeds were to be earmarked for the protection of smaller enterprises. As the historian Uwe Spiekermann has argued, the influence of the ZDK on retail taxation was somewhat indirect, and the legislation probably resulted more from regional political alliances than from the ZDK's propaganda campaigns. The taxes, furthermore, were ultimately more of a nuisance than a hindrance and did little to inhibit the growth and spread of the new stores. In fact, they probably aided the larger enterprises—the principal targets of the ZDK—who were able to absorb the added costs and renegotiate with suppliers to the detriment of smaller and newly founded firms.[98] The taxes were revoked after World War I by the SPD-led government, only to be reinstated on the local level with Nazi electoral gains in the early 1930s.[99]

Probably the ZDK's major achievement in these years was to dramatize the condition of small shopkeepers and bring the department store issue to state and national attention. The direct influence of anti–department store propaganda is difficult to assess—in 1906 one observer claimed that it back-fired completely, arguing that all the attention to the department store issue inspired curious onlookers to come investigate these controversial entities, with the result that many were impressed and became loyal customers.[100] What is clear, however, is that in the years around the turn of the century the movement assailed the stores in the harshest possible terms. These relentless attacks forged popular associations between department stores, Jews, and the specter of national decline, associations that would be resurrected and find greater resonance in times of economic crisis.

Some participants in the anti–department store campaigns were mo-tivated by sincere, if misplaced, economic anxiety. At a time of increas-ingly sharp anti-Semitic political rhetoric, they may have found it useful to ally themselves with outspoken anti-Semites or to stress the stores' Jewish origins and bang the anti-Semitic drum to attract attention and generate support. Others came to the issue precisely because of anti-Semitism. The department store represented an ideal target for anti-Semites. Its rapid ex-pansion in these years could be exploited to stoke fears about the increasing influence of Jews over German economic and cultural life. The two types of critiques overlapped and cross-fertilized to the point that they were es-sentially indistinguishable and constituted a common discursive formation about Jews, department stores, and German national well-being. This dis-course mobilized age-old images of Jews as hucksters and speculators, as greedy, exploitative capitalists who enriched themselves on the toil of others and to the detriment of the public good.[101]

Department store directors did not sit idly by as the shopkeeper move-ment condemned their businesses in the political sphere and pushed for additional taxation and other regulations. They created their own interest group in 1903, the Association of German Department Stores (Verband Deutscher Waren-und Kaufhäuser), founded at an assembly in Berlin and spearheaded by Oscar Tietz and Johannes Wernicke with a board of twelve officials. The association's stated goals were "above all to defend modern business developments against the onslaught of reactionary elements, to enlighten the government and the public about the advantages and necessity of this modern development, and to combat the degradation of department stores and large retail shops in the public mind."[102] The association fought against the constant attempts to raise department store taxes, to impose stronger laws against "unfair competition," and, along with the Associa-tion to Combat Anti-Semitism, they countered the calumny and exposed the false accusations made by department store foes and worked to improve the image of large retailers in the public eye.

Economic Vampires: Shopkeeper Propaganda and Fantasies about the Jews

Even as the anti–department store movement adjusted its political aims, championing different issues at different times, its critique of the emporiums was remarkably consistent from its beginnings through to the revival of anti–department store activism in the late years of the Weimar Republic. Critics repeated several themes with little variation: the chaotic nature of the stores, their fraudulent and unethical business practices, their moral turpitude, and the hazards they posed to upstanding German tradesman, the German family, and the whole German nation. Each of these themes intersected with anti-Semitic notions; whether or not they explicitly invoked anti-Semitism, anti–department store writings and propaganda frequently deployed images of Jews and capitalized on stereotypes about Jews' role in the German and European economy.

Perhaps the department store's most crucial departure from traditional retail was the way it grouped together goods that had no logical connection to one another. Well-run department stores, with their hundreds of employees, enormous capital flow, and abundance of goods and services, had to be tightly organized and efficient. Paul Göhre likened the stores to ocean liners for their compartmentalization and scale, and many other contemporaries described department store sales staffs as army-like, in their level of discipline, regulation, and regimentation. Nevertheless, despite the enormous attention department store managers paid to the organization of goods and workers, critics derided the stores as scenes of chaos, claiming that goods were crammed together haphazardly and that navigation through the aisles was confusing, disorienting, and potentially dangerous.

Turn-of-the-century department store opponents made use of a rich vocabulary, denouncing the stores as *Ramschbasare* (rummage bazaars), *Schleuderbasare* (discount bazaars), or *Großbasare* (large bazaars), terms that implicitly challenged the quality of their goods and the legitimacy of their business practices.[103] The word "bazaar," furthermore, a label some French and German department stores adopted to sound exotic and enticing, was deployed here to make the stores seem foreign and Near Eastern—coding for chaotic and fraudulent. In a similar vein, critics equated the so-called rummage or junk bazaars with peddling and other traditional Jewish economic activities. In an 1899 text, Paul Dehn posited a "psychological connection" between "grand bazaars" and the hawking of goods. Both department stores and peddlers' carts, he wrote, "deal predominately with knickknacks. Both also use teasers [*Lockartikel*], which they price cheaply or under cost so that they can charge all the more for other goods. They operate similar kinds of deception. They're only decorated differently."[104]

A 1910 article set out to shed light on the "dark business" of the department store, which, according to its anonymous author, sold whatever goods its managers could acquire cheaply—another reference to peddling. The author charged that the department store sold not what people needed, but what it could unload profitably, and that it then sought to convince people that they wanted or needed these shoddy, out-of-date, or defective goods.[105] The department store's most valued customers, the writer concluded, were those who would happily receive a 1906 calendar for a Christmas present in 1909.

Critics like Dehn insisted that department stores were fundamentally a scam, simply a glossy, spruced-up version of the rummage shops and dry goods stores that preceded them. Unable or unwilling to understand the commercial principles that enabled their low prices, such opponents assumed that the department stores' pricing was based on chicanery, that the merchandise was of poor quality, that cheap goods simply functioned to lure in naïve customers who could be easily tricked into making more purchases at higher prices, or that prices would skyrocket as soon as a department store had eliminated its competition.[106] Department store goods were simply "cheap and bad" (*billig und schlecht*), railed the anonymous author of an 1898 tirade in the anti-Semitic press.[107] The stores sold "inferior" wares, according to an 1899 article in the same newspaper, "knickknacks and rubbish."[108] The fact that German department stores grew out of dry goods stores and discounters gave such attacks a patina of veracity and prevented the department store owners and their self-defense association from ever completely discrediting these exaggerated, even fully fabricated rumors.

The idea that the stores used *Lockartikel* or teasers echoed throughout these attacks, since the department store's success required attracting eager browsers and curious onlookers and turning them into buyers. Critics (and more sympathetic observers, too) focused on the two stages of this process: that is, how the stores brought people in from the street and then how they conjured up *Kauflust* to turn passive browsers into active buyers. In both areas critics alleged that the stores acted fraudulently and disingenuously. They spilled a great deal of ink complaining about these teasers or lures, attractively priced goods that were displayed in shop windows or in advertisements. Good prices, special bargains, exciting merchandise—no matter what the department store was touting, there was always a catch. As one 1894 commentator put it: "The assumption that if someone sells one item for 30 percent less than his competitors, then he is cheaper across the board is certainly made by the great majority of women, but in reality most of the goods in these stores are not less expensive."[109]

J. W. Hausschildt devoted attention to teasers in his 1899 screed, claiming that the stores provided the illusion of good bargains with a few strategically placed items, while most goods were sold at high prices and profit.[110] The accusation appeared in nearly identical form in an anonymous book that was published more than three decades later. This author (one H.M.) set out to reveal the department store's hidden deceptions and counteract its power over and appeal to gullible customers—taking a swipe, along the way, at the failure of the (Jewish-owned, bourgeois) press to report on these violations. Window display lures, he cautioned, employed various means of chicanery such as vague, deceptive pricing or subterfuge, as in the old "sock trick." In the window display a sign reads "socks: 25 pfennig." Catching sight of the tantalizing bargain, a man enters the store, asks for the socks, and hands over his money. The salesclerk then presents him with a single sock. Like any rational consumer, he had assumed that the socks came in pairs.[111]

A 1913 article in the viciously anti-Semitic *Hammer* newspaper set out to catalog and expose common department store tricks.[112] The *Hammer*'s founding editor, Theodor Fritsch, writing under the pseudonym F. Roderich Stoltheim, listed the following tactics: deceiving the customer by selling trinkets at very cheap prices and giving the impression that all prices were reasonable, when in reality prices on larger items were quite high; displaying "show pieces" in the shop windows, that is, goods that were actually not available but functioned to lure interested parties inside; mixing goods up in large piles that contained an assortment of both high-quality and defective articles, usually with the better ones nearer the top; and listing deceptively precise prices such as 98 pfennig, or 2 mark, 98 pfennig, to give the impression that exact calculations were used to set prices, when in truth fairly arbitrary figures were employed. Department store foes seized upon these kinds of anecdotes and used them to claim that the stores were engaging in practices that made it extremely difficult for the honest competition to survive. They railed against city officials for failing to take action just as they vilified the liberal press for its alleged failure to report these abuses.

Indeed, intending to spur outrage among readers and propel legislative action, the pages of the *völkisch* press overflowed with tales of alleged department store abuses. A common accusation against large retailers in the 1890s was that they concealed their names, that is, they either failed to hang an identifying sign or listed a deceptive name, presumably in an effort to hide their Jewish or foreign identity.[113] Anti-Semitic authors persisted in referring to Adolf Jandorf by his original name, Abraham, to call attention to his Jewishness, and continued to treat members of the Wertheim family as Jewish or "Mosaic," even though they had converted to Christianity.[114] The anti-Semitic press delighted in exposing, or in fact inventing, department store accounting errors or cases of extortion or in pointing out, for example, the Jewish ownership of an elegantly named shop.[115] According to Hausschildt, the department store's vagueness about its name and its other duplicitous strategies—such as displaying goods with cheap prices on Sundays when the stores are closed and then charging a higher price when the store reopened on Monday—were "reprehensible methods to be sure, but highly effective weapons in bringing down the respectable competition."[116]

In addition to their frequent complaints about petty schemes to increase floor traffic and prey upon naïve consumers, critics condemned the stores' "extremely baleful influence on the moral posture of their employees and customers."[117] One detractor claimed that the stores sold salacious reading materials in their book departments—directly adjacent to the children's section, no less—including "trashy," lowbrow novels like Zola's *The Ladies' Paradise*, all the more incendiary because of its department store setting.[118] Some critics focused on sexuality, circulating rumors about the sexual proclivities of department store directors and the corruption of young saleswomen either through employer molestation or the need to supplement their insufficient incomes by engaging in prostitution.[119]

Here, as in the French case, the idea of a largely female sales force was clearly provocative and a bit scandalous to many observers.[120] Other opponents depicted department stores as hotbeds of crime, blaming them for creating the kleptomania epidemic—turning upstanding *bürgerlich* women into compulsive shoplifters—and harboring rings of thieves and swindlers. The stores' morally corrosive environment not only affected customers, wrote Fritsch, but also took its toll on employees who "stand under the constant influence of the lax department store morality and must help deceive and hoodwink the public."[121] These concerns reflected a profound unease with the power Jewish businessmen were thought to be gaining over German women—both department store employees and customers—and the perception, common in the anti-Semitic imagination, of Jewish men's sexuality as distorted and rapacious.

Oppositional imagery portrayed the department store as a kind of trap, a monster even, or a creature with tentacles that reached out onto the street and pulled in unsuspecting passersby. Lured in by cheap prices, the illusion of convenience, or a stunning window display, there innocent pedestrians were held

1.2 *The Department Store Plague.* G. Gerber, 1932. © Herzog August Bibliothek Wolfenbüttel <http://diglib.hab.de/inkunabeln/14-astron/start.htm>.

captive, seduced into making additional purchases, or corrupted by the store's debased moral order, as in the case of the naïve young woman who entered Wertheim simply to purchase a hairnet and ended up ensnared in the tea salon, a known cauldron of illicit behavior.[122] Ominous descriptors like *Fangarme* (tentacles), *Bauernfänger* (peasant catchers), *Gimpelfang* (sucker traps), *Mausefälle des Todes* (deadly mousetraps), or *Fallstricke* (snares) fill the pages of anti–department store rants, calling attention to the stores' insidious powers and admonishing readers that deadly traps lurked behind the glitzy, inviting surfaces.[123] This kind of imagery can be seen starkly in a Nazi Party sheet that depicts the department store as a many-armed creature attacking and engulfing the surrounding small businesses: a butcher, a leather worker, and a small grocer. There is nothing subtle about such representations; the department

1.3 Flyer for an anti–department store demonstration sponsored by the Munich branch of the Nazi Party, June 23, 1931. Bundesarchiv Berlin.

store, with crowds of eager shoppers surrounding it, has a figure with stereo-typical Jewish traits standing above its front portal, and the monster atop the store also has Jewish facial characteristics and an evil, rapacious grin. Here then the store is not only coded as Jewish, but is personified as a Jew as it grabs and pulls in eager onlookers and consumes the surrounding small businesses.

A 1931 rally poster by the Kampfgemeinschaft gegen Warenhaus und Konsumverein (Combat League against Department Stores and Consumer Cooperatives), with its calls for Germans to buy only from "Germans" and to avoid department stores and consumer cooperatives, shows a dragon-like beast coming out of the department store and preparing to devour a line of specialty shops. Unlike the previous image, however, this one suggests that there is hope, namely in the chivalric figure, poised to rescue small German businesses and slaughter the monster with a swing of his sword.

Other voices articulated a more general, moral critique of the department store, accusing it of enshrining greed and the worship of false idols and el-evating the pursuit of profit over serving the public good.[124] Critics attacked department store owners for their indifference to the social consequences of their business schemes and charged that the stores were detrimental to German social and cultural life, ignoring of course the major philan-thropic activities of some of these men. "The fact is that with the arrival of the department stores, morality in all circles has seemed to plummet," opined the anonymous author of a 1912 *Hammer* article on "morality in the department store."[125] And as Fritsch put it in 1915, "The department store principle is immoral, and a spirit rages from these dazzling suns that threatens to poison nearly all social classes; the spirit of the base pursuit of profit and the hunt for material gain, the spirit of vain ostentation and the

1.4 Newsletter of the Combat League against Department Stores and Consumer Cooperatives, August 10, 1931. Bundesarchiv Berlin.

addiction to luxury, a spirit of flippancy and wastefulness, even delusions of grandeur."[126]

This alleged disregard for the common good again drew on stereotypes about Jewish avarice. To quote a 1903 polemic from the anti-Semitic *Staatsbürger-Zeitung*: "Just how little right to existence these department stores have, which endanger the public in the most serious way, is shown by the fact that nearly all of these economic vampires lie in the hands of international Jewish families, whose goal it is to plunder the toiling classes, to grab Germany's national wealth for itself, and to take hold of the state of the future."[127] The stores then were represented as snarling monsters on the one hand, but also as vampires, parasites that existed by feeding off the labor of the nation and sapping its productive energies. This image is well captured by Ribbeck the gentile cobbler in *W.A.G.M.U.S.*, who rebuffs the Jewish department store proprietor who wants to buy him out and use his space: "Big department stores like yours are bloodsuckers, a kind of organized thievery that attacks and suffocates us little business operators."[128] Decrying department stores as vampires or bloodsuckers had a strong anti-Semitic resonance. Contemporaries would have certainly made the association with blood libel, and these charges would have gained additional rhetorical power from newer, racial notions of Jewishness, which, portraying Jews as pollutants to the healthy German bloodstream, were gaining traction in the 1890s.[129]

Above all, anti–department store agitators warned that the new stores represented a grievous threat to the whole German middle class, contrasting the clever, opportunistic Jew with the honorable, hardworking German. Activists depicted this threat in stark and morbid terms, treating the stores like a pestilence and making constant reference to the stores' deadly consequences. On the occasion of the Kaiser's highly publicized visit to Wertheim's Leipziger Strasse store in 1910, one writer, even as he confessed begrudging admiration for Wertheim's business skills, asked "how many corpses, how many thousands and thousands of existences has he trampled" in constructing this department store empire? "Not only in Berlin," the author continued, "but in other cities as well, the danger of Wertheim [*Wertheimgefahr*] is extraordinary."[130] He continued by calling the department store the "gravedigger" of the "honorable middle classes who, standing in loyalty to the Kaiser and the empire, are being driven out of their businesses and their livelihoods in great numbers."[131] On the same occasion, Paul Dehn estimated that with the opening of the Leipziger Strasse store, some five thousand lives would inevitably be destroyed.[132] Another critic, writing in the *Hammer* in 1912, depicted the department stores as economic parasites that could thrive only by destroying other businesses. He pointed to the "18,000 boarded-up businesses in Berlin" as evidence of the department store's destructive consequences.[133] And in the same year, the *Staatsbürger-Zeitung* charged that the "Jewish department store" Wertheim had on its conscience the destruction of the German middle class.[134]

As they drove small business to bankruptcy, the department stores were, so it was claimed, leading to the proletarianization of the shop-owner class. This was all the more tragic, Dehn asserted, because these proprietors were too honorable to declare bankruptcy or seek the aid of the state.[135] Others alleged that this was the very reason the Social Democrats defended department stores—that is, that the stores, by liquidating the entire petite bourgeoisie, were swelling the ranks of the proletariat and creating more potential SPD constituents.[136] The alleged hypocrisy of the Left, its unflagging support for department stores, a symbol of commercial capitalism, was a thorn in the side of the shopkeeper movement, and their attacks on the SPD were frequent and venomous and replete with anti-Semitic imagery.

H.M. chimed in on this issue too, attacking the SPD for hypocritically supporting an institution that did harm to the working class. "Thus the worker who has been lured into the department store by the ads in the Social Democratic press will have the last pennies which he desperately needed for himself and his family drained out of his pockets."[137] Neither the leftist nor the liberal press dared criticize department stores, he claimed, lest they lose the advertising revenue the stores brought.[138] But he saved his most cutting comments for the Marxists, who "are of course unmoved when a department store Jew threatens his poor saleswomen with dismissal right before Christmastime."[139]

Christmas, in fact, and specifically the concern over its commodification at the hands of the department store, represented yet another key theme in the anti–department store program. Christmas was indeed a significant source of revenue for department stores, and the idea of Jewish businessmen profiting from the Christian holiday rankled anti-Semites and members of the shopkeeper movement. Jews, they charged, viewed Christmas merely as a business opportunity to exploit, an occasion for pressing cheap wares on gentile celebrants, as a Nazi newspaper put it in 1929.[140] Agitation against department stores generally picked up in intensity around the holiday, observed Johannes Wernicke, head of the Association of German Department Stores, with the appearance of newspaper ads, brochures full of spurious accusations, and calls for boycott.[141]

Articles in the *Staatsbürger-Zeitung*, for example, admonished readers to stay away from the "big bazaars, whose owners for the most part hardly understand the Christian meaning of Christmas."[142] In the years around the turn of the century, members of the *völkisch* German National Party handed out flyers at Christmastime in front of Jewish-owned department stores urging potential customers to avoid the stores and warning, for example, that Jewish fraudulence toward Christians was rooted in Talmudic dictates. The historian Joe Perry notes that anti-Semites and anti–department store activists even established an "anti-Semitic Christmas market" in Berlin in 1891, where Berliners could shop without fear of supporting Jewish-owned enterprises, although it seems that the market was not terribly successful and thus short-lived.[143] In his 1897 polemic *Behind the Scenes in the Modern Store*, Dehn claimed that a department store could earn as much as 60,000 marks a day during the Christmas season and condemned even well-meaning charities that purchased Christmas presents for orphans and impoverished children at department stores. "Is that good for the community?" he railed. "Is it Christian?"[144]

Anti–department store propaganda was stuck in the 1880s. Its writers, losing influence over the increasingly pro–department store middle classes, failed to notice or deliberately ignored the dramatic changes of the mid '90s, the architectural innovations and stylistic upgrades of the modern department store, the clearly marked prices, publicized return and exchange policies, and emphasis on customer service. To call Wertheim's Leipziger Strasse branch, the KaDeWe, or the Leonhard Tietz store in Düsseldorf junk bazaars was to miss everything that was innovative and appealing about them: the remarkable efficiency, tight organization, and reliability at the root of the department store's success. Yet anti–department store writings operated with the assumption that these changes were superficial at most, that the shiny, elegant facades of the modern stores concealed scenes of depravity, exploitation, and moral turpitude, representing the sophisticated trickery of the Jewish economic interloper.

Not all opponents of the department stores, of course, resorted to such extreme language or used anti-Semitic notions. Some critics were themselves Jews, and concern over the fate of the "Jewish shop-owning middle classes" at the hands of the department stores—a topic that has received scant historical attention—appeared in the German-Jewish press in the 1920s. The aspiration of every young Jewish man, according to a 1929 article, was, after several years of apprenticeship and employment at a firm, to become self-sufficient and open his own shop. The age of the department store, with its concentration of capital and consolidation of retail, had eliminated this possibility.[145]

Finally, we should note that the years of intense criticism seem to have had little or no effect on the department stores' appeal to broad sectors of the German population and did not appear to threaten these stores' economic viability. Despite Colze's admonition that the great age of the department store was drawing to a close, department stores remained vibrant, profitable, and dynamic establishments through 1914 and again after the stabilization of the Weimar economy. However, Colze was indeed correct in noting that by 1909 the field was too crowded for newcomers, and, especially after the war, smaller, independent stores began to fail at an increasing rate, only to be swallowed up by Karstadt, Hermann Tietz, Leonhard Tietz, or Schocken, the four most successful and durable chains. Independent of the intense department store debates of the Wilhelmine period and the later Weimar years, the great emporiums, and the retail revolution that accompanied their spread, remained popular across the social spectrum.

"What would the present age be without the department store?" asked Walter E. Schulz in a 1929 volume on the Hermann Tietz concern. "We need the department store. It belongs to us and we to it. . . . What is it that makes the department store so attractive? Its magic, its secret fluid. Therein lies the spirit of the department store, which pulls us in whenever and wherever we find it."[146] Judging by sales figures and rates of expansion, the secret fluid worked its magic. Jerusalem, as the fictional shoemaker Ribbeck put it, continued to increase its worldly terrain.

2 DREAMWORLDS IN MOTION
Circulation, Cosmopolitanism, and the Jewish Question

> The old retail trade was static; the department store is dynamic.
> There everything was fixed, here everything is fluid; before small,
> now big; before dark, now bright; before spirit, now intellect.
> — *Werner Sombart (1928)*

> The customer was kept in motion; he traveled through the department
> store as a train passenger traveled through the landscape.
> — *Wolfgang Schivelbusch (1986)*

Department stores often had deep local roots, and many evolved over decades from neighborhood dry goods shops or *Konfektionshäuser* into full-fledged retail emporiums. The wave of new department store construction of the late 1890s and 1900s and the massive expansion of existing stores made the turn-of-the-century consuming palace a conspicuous urban landmark that in turn changed the dynamics of the city, affected the flow of traffic, and redrew the boundaries of commercial and residential life. As firms such as Hermann Tietz, Leonhard Tietz, Wronker, Althoff, Karstadt, and later Schocken, began to evolve into major regional and supra-regional franchises, they became points of contact between local residents and international currents, products, and styles, conduits of regional and global circulatory networks, and purveyors not only of products, but of identities and experiences. German department stores then started to aspire to a kind of worldliness or—to use a term that resonates more profoundly in Jewish history—cosmopolitanism.[1] This development occurred at precisely the moment when the German Empire was starting to play an increasingly active role in global affairs, becoming simultaneously more internationally engaged and more prone to nationalist fervor.[2] This chapter investigates the department store's unique position in time and space, exploring its multiple and overlapping identities as local, national, and international, and German, Jewish, and cosmopolitan.

Over the last several decades of intense scholarly interest in modern mass consumption, commodity culture has often been depicted in historical, sociological, and anthropological studies as a kind of world: several seminal works thematize, for example, consumers' encounter with the "world of goods" (Douglas and Isherwood) and their entry into "dream worlds" of mass consumption (Williams).[3] In his structuralist period, Jean Baudrillard influentially characterized the consumer society as "a sign world," a universe of meaning that we produce, and through which we see ourselves reflected, but which ultimately stages our own alienation.[4] Whichever particular direction the metaphor is taken, these and other works portray commodities as elements that constitute a world or as having a world of their own, as existing in a kind of parallel universe, an enchanted mirror world that stimulates our imaginations, triggers our fantasies, and, in some formulations, molds and even creates our identities.

Baudrillard's theorization of consumer society draws on Marx's treatment of the commodity fetish in volume 1 of *Capital*, whereby the commodity appears to take on a life of its own, becoming animated, so to speak, as the labor that goes into its production is concealed from consumers by the conditions of bourgeois economic relations.[5] Our haunting by the commodity world, and the eeriness of department store encounters, are themes that reverberate throughout this book, but for the purposes of this analysis the key point is that Baudrillard, among others, portrays commodities as a symbolic field, a sign system that, in a sense, fills the world with meaning, and that the consumer encounters commodities not as individual objects, but as a parallel world, which captivates and entertains but also troubles and even haunts us.

The department store, "a world of beautiful things,"[6] offers an ideal context for exploring the connections between consumption and worldliness, that is, not only that commodities exist in a world of their own, but that modern consumption represents a dynamic meeting between local consumers and goods that have traveled far. Marx, adopting the labor theory of value, defines a commodity's value as a function of the accumulated or "crystallized" labor within it, the cumulative human labor power required for its production. In the *Grundrisse*, he also considers the *movement* of commodities, maintaining that it is the process of transporting a product, taking it to the market, that transforms it into a commodity.[7] The mobility of goods is a key component of modern mass consumption, which is characterized by the ability to consume goods from afar—new types of products newly available from other points in a shrinking globe—with the aid of mechanized systems of distribution and circulation. The department store appears then as a kind of station, a depot of sorts where people, goods, and capital are brought together from disparate points of origin. It also functioned as a primary site for the display and consumption of commodities, exchangeable goods stripped of their local context, their "spatial-temporal presence" or "aura," to use Benjamin's term.[8]

In its golden age, from the end of the nineteenth century through the early 1930s, the German department store embodied what I am calling cosmopolitan consumption. Akin to a permanent, enclosed international exposition, the department store exhibited and marketed a world of goods, and the motifs of cosmopolitanism, exoticism, distance, and mobility appeared throughout its self-representations.[9] These themes characterized department store advertisements, goods, and displays and underlined the department store's position as a hub of concentric circulatory networks. The emphasis on mobility, this sense of relentless motion and circulation, intersected with a tradition of characterizing Jews as circulating, mobile economic actors. The overlap between the department store's cosmopolitanism and political economists' assertions about "the Jew" amplified the construction of the department store as a Jewish phenomenon and further attests to the intertwining of Jews with the German experience of commercial capitalism and modern mass consumption.

The World of the Department Store

"The department store, we can say without sounding supercilious, is a world in miniature, a microcosm," declared the urban chronicler Max Osborn in a 1932 celebratory volume about the Tietz stores.[10] "The Hermann Tietz concern today," wrote Doris Wittner in the same volume, "which now encompasses seventeen department stores, including nine palatial buildings in the capital city alone, comprises a world in itself in which national economic problems are effortlessly solved, a world that has put the discipline of economics on a whole new footing, a world that possesses its own rhythm and exerts a suggestive magnetic pull on the public."[11] We will come back later in this chapter to the notion of the department store's rhythm. First I want to emphasize the idea that a store—or in this case, a series of stores—constitutes a world, and relatedly, reaches out and covers the world.

Like an exposition, the department store touted the far-flung origins of its products, a motif that appears repeatedly in contemporary accounts. Lion Feuchtwanger's "Warenhaus-Revue" (Department store revue), for example, an imagined cabaret act about a Berlin store, echoes the theme that all the world's treasures could be found in the store:

> Inside are piled up
> All the treasures of the world from Greenland to India
> Great and small.
> Crude and fine,
> Loose and tight, mild and spicy,
> Ultimate luxury, bare necessity.[12]

In Vicki Baum's 1937 novel *The Great Sale*, decorator Erik Bengtson gazes at the department store at night and delights in its fullness, pronouncing it

the "abundance of the world."[13] The historian Christiane Lamberty writes
of this sense of abundance and the appearance of cornucopia in department store advertising. "The unlimited availability of wares," she observes,
"was meant to cradle the consumer, to soothe his concerns and take his
mind away from the limitations of his wallet. Progress presented itself as an
endless stream of goods; participation in consumption appeared to be the
epitome of modern life."[14]

Department store publicity and sumptuous window displays sustained
the illusion of abundance even in times of economic crisis and consumer
deprivation. One way that the department stores maintained the fantasy of
consumer abundance was through repetition. Typical displays featured a
particular kind of item, usually something banal like umbrellas, shoes, or
tinned food, for example, stacked or piled up in neat patterns, in staggering,
awe-inspiring amounts. In his "Warenhaus-Revue," Feuchtwanger satirizes
this practice, the grouping of piles of trivial consumer goods into elaborate
patterns and shapes, describing a pyramid of artfully stacked toothbrushes
in the store's display window.[15]

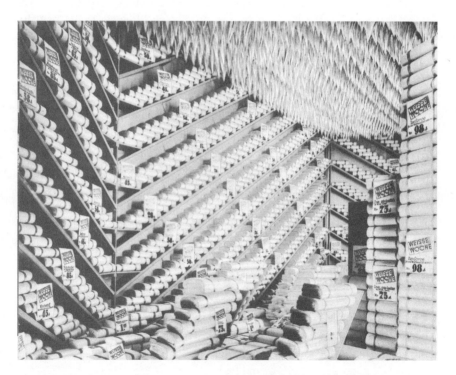

2.1 "Modern Window Display Art," from *Das Kaufhaus des Westens: Festschrift
zum 25 jährigen Bestehen 1907–1932* (Berlin, 1932). Bpk, Berlin/Art Resource, NY.

Rosalind Williams observes that the effect of repetition was to numb the viewer. With reference to Zola's *The Ladies' Paradise*, she writes:

> When rugs are placed on the ceiling, walls, and floor of the vestibule, when the same item is repeated over and over with minor variations . . . the sheer accumulation becomes awesome in a way that no single item could be. The same effect is achieved when Mouret fills an entire hall with an ocean of umbrellas, top to bottom, along columns and balustrades and staircases; the umbrellas shed their banality and instead become "large Venetian lanterns, illuminated for some colossal festival," an achievement that makes one shopper exclaim, "It's a fairyland!"[16]

In addition to repetition and abundance, advertisements commonly boasted that the stores offered a comprehensive shopping experience, with "everything under one roof" (*Alles unter einem Dach*), as a common slogan put it. Newspaper advertisements and publicity (which in the 1920s were increasingly text-based and sober in contrast to the fantastical imagery of the window displays) frequently featured A to Z lists—"everything from *Anzugsstoff* [material for suits] to *Zimmereinrichtungen* [room furnishings]" was a common formulation—to illustrate the stores' extensive lines of products, and they frequently emphasized the diverse origins of their styles and wares.[17]

Kaufhaus Israel's colorful and panoramic annual promotional albums, issued between 1901 and 1914, took their readers on ethnographic journeys through time and space with such themes as "Woman and her world," "The world of the German colonies," "Above and below the earth," and "A world journey: Battle sites, world exhibition."[18] These lavishly illustrated volumes reflected and furthered the association between the pleasures of commodity culture and the edifying experience of (reading about) global travel, so crucial to both the culture of Wilhelmine-era exhibitions and the department store.[19] Clearly geared for bourgeois women readers, the albums aimed to inform and educate the sensible female consumer while feeding the fantasy of global mobility.

Feuchtwanger's "Warenhaus-Revue," finally, emphasizes the distance the goods have traveled and the work that went into their production, in a poetic evocation of the commodity fetish and the harmony of worldwide laborers:

> It was not easy, shopper, to make it this way
> That the things lie so conveniently at your disposal.
> Many had to slave away in heat and frost
> To put your goods together for you. . . .

In the Canadian forest quiet men fell trees,
float them to the valley over still waters and rapid currents.
In another part of the world they make machines,
To saw up the trees. . . .
Yellow, black, white hands worked together
So that, shoppers, table and chair are pleasing to you.[20]

Notably, the globe became a symbol for many Wilhelmine department stores. It signaled the stores' global reach and cosmopolitanism, their ability to collect and display goods from all over the world and also their power and majesty. Many Hermann Tietz buildings, including the arresting Berlin Leipziger Strasse structure (1899), featured a globe adorning the store's portals in a triumphant, muscular way, an emblem that made the store highly visible and established Tietz as a conspicuous presence in the cityscape. Kaufhaus Israel designated itself a *Welthaus* (global concern) in 1906, and Wertheim, Hermann Tietz's biggest competitor in Berlin, represented its business as a "world city department store for the world" and also used an image of the globe as its insignia (above a large *W* that suggested Wertheim and also *Welt*) on advertisements, catalogs, and stationery.[21] Indeed, Georg Wertheim designed the symbol himself and even initiated legal action to prevent Tietz from using the globe too, but lost the case in the Berlin courts.[22] Enormous globes also crowned several of H. Tietz's other Berlin stores, the firm's branches in Stuttgart and Dresden, and the Roman Emperor Department Store, a Tietz affiliate in Erfurt.[23] Globes similar to Tietz's appeared on many other stores between 1900 and World War I, including the Barasch Brothers in Breslau (1904), the Karstadt branch in Braunschweig (1903), and the Julius Bormaß Department Store in Wiesbaden (1905).[24]

Department store firms then were competing with each other over their claims to worldliness, both in the sense of domination—the tallest, most commanding presence in the cityscape (and rooftop terraces were popular spots for employees and customers to relax)—and in the comprehensiveness, abundance, and diversity of their wares. The department store's expansion and its cosmopolitan aspirations coincided with Germany's increasing involvement in global affairs. Overcoming his initial opposition to imperialism, Chancellor Otto von Bismarck oversaw the formation of a colonial empire, beginning with Germany's acquisition of colonies in West and South-West Africa in 1884. German imperialism, although shorter-lived and never as extensive as French, British, or Dutch empire building, nonetheless furthered the deep imbrication of the German economy in international systems of trade, labor migration, and resource extraction and internationalized the focus of German culture and the activities of the German military. German commercial culture and the advertising industry, as the historian David Ciarlo points out, developed in tandem with these processes, and they deeply influenced the visual vernacular of German ads, especially after Germany's brutal suppression

2.2 Tietz department store, Berlin Leipziger Strasse. Reprinted from Antonia Meiners, *100 Jahre KaDeWe* (Berlin, 2007).

of the Herero uprising in what is now Namibia. The German "advertising empire," Ciarlo asserts, "was built, in part, on the advertising *of* empire," and his fascinating book presents skillful analyses of a sizable archive of racially fraught advertising imagery.[25]

2.3 Kaufhaus Israel annual album, 1908.
"Below and Above the Earth."
Landesarchiv Berlin.

Notwithstanding Ciarlo's compelling analysis of German advertising culture, imperial scenes and explicit racial imagery seem to have made little mark on the department stores. Contemporary department store observers seldom commented on or documented imperial scenes, and they rarely occur in the extant visual sources. One example can be found in Kaufhaus N. Israel's album of 1901, its first annual album, which was devoted to "the German colonies" and included tales of adventure from Togo, East Africa, and China and colonial battles on land and

2.4 KaDeWe rooftop terrace with Kaiser Wilhelm Memorial Church in the background. Reprinted from *Das Kaufhaus des Westens: Festschrift zum 25 jährigen Bestehen 1907–1932* (Berlin, 1932). Bpk, Berlin/Art Resource, NY.

at sea.[26] As vivid and fraught as these images were, they were not associated with particular goods; nor did the album use racial imagery directly in its product promotion.[27] The paucity of this kind of imagery suggests that the department stores may have ceded this role to colonial stores, and it was coffee, chocolate, and other imported, "exotic" goods that often bore labels with racialist and imperialist content. Among German department store entrepreneurs, only Rudolf Hertzog seems to have involved himself actively in colonial affairs, having established a branch of his store in Swakopmund in German South-West Africa (Namibia today).[28]

When they marketed goods from their empires, French and British department stores reinforced and glorified their dominant place in the world. German stores, in contrast, served up a panoply of styles from around the world. Unlike the French, they did not further nationalism through aesthetics—at least not before 1933—but instead offered up a kind of cosmopolitan vision.[29] Their displays, decorations, and promotions celebrated (and marketed) their openness to the world, their ability to provide access to goods from afar and to uplift the bourgeois consumer into a sphere of elegance and fantasy. This quality ultimately made them vulnerable to accusations of being un-German, a critique aimed at the stores' cosmopolitan ambitions, which dovetailed with discussions of their Jewishness.

The metaphor of the department store as world was closely tied to another frequently appearing image, which portrayed the department store as a metropolis. Both metaphors expressed the store's aspiration to comprehensiveness both in the range of goods it sold and in the kinds of experiences it offered. The major urban department store represented a kind of microcosm of the city itself, an alternative reality where one could take care of all of one's needs. Feuchtwanger writes that the department store satisfies needs from "cradle to grave," selling articles for birth, wedding, and burial.[30] A satirical commentator joked about a time "when department stores will have all of the living and dying needs of the man of the future: hotel rooms, a justice of the peace and a marriage chapel for the recognized religious communities, and all of the other human needs between marriage and burial."[31] This notion is dramatized in the Sigfrid Siwertz novel *The Great Department Store*, in which a child is conceived after hours in the store's bedding department and raised in the store by store owner Jeremias Goldmann and his staff.[32] The boy becomes the "child of the department store," for whom the store really was his lifeworld.

Larger stores aspired to comprehensiveness not only in the kinds of goods they sold, but also in the services they began to provide. From their inception, major department stores featured rooms for reading periodicals and writing correspondence, and cafés and restaurants. By the 1920s many boasted of additional features, including hair salons, banking services, and theater ticket offices, photography studios, occasional art exhibitions and fashion shows, and even supervised play areas for children.

The store became a kind of fantasy city, where women could stroll and spend as much time as they desired, insulated from the dangers of the greater urban environment and the disapproving glances of men. Traversing the department store's aisles became a version of walking in the city.[33] Gerhard Tietz, Leonhard's son and successor, noted in 1928 that customers identify with their department stores as they do with their home cities, and they "see it as self-evident that they can move about in a department store every bit as freely as they can move on the street or at home."[34] Friedrich Nielandt, the department store proprietor in Erich Köhrer's novel *Warenhaus Berlin*, a melodramatic story that takes place in a fictionalized version of the KaDeWe, decides that "Warenhaus Berlin" is the only appropriate name for his giant new emporium because the department store itself was a symbol of Berlin. As he explains:

> The department store, as I see it, is a microcosm in which all aspects of life reverberate most strikingly . . . and life in Berlin seems to me more and more like a great department store. Cold and foreign, everyone stands cheek by jowl, [and] everywhere you look, the most varied things are on offer. . . . In our Berlin you can no longer spend your life tranquilly as in the old days, when you could pleasantly satisfy all of your needs in the peaceful specialty shops. Rather multiple currents and streams crash into each other wildly and surge by each other like the hustle and bustle of a department store.[35]

Simultaneously, then, the German city itself was becoming more like a department store—a bustling site of commerce and consumption, a scene of unprecedented mixing and intermingling of social groups and styles, and part of widening, global circles of transport and circulation, as newly united Germany asserted its influence in world affairs, gained overseas colonies, and began hosting international exhibitions. The department store, meanwhile—through its rapid expansion and diversification and through its comprehensiveness—was becoming more like a city, a place to wander around, explore, meet people, and encounter the unexpected. Kaufhaus Israel devoted its 1904 album to "Greater Berlin," and its 1902 album featured a lengthy exposition of how the evolution of the store went hand in hand with Berlin's development into a metropolis.[36] The 1912 revue *Chauffeur ins Metropol!*, which was performed at Berlin's Metropol Theater, illustrates this equation between the department store and the big city. It takes place in a department store called "Warenhaus Gross-Berlin" (Greater Berlin Department Store). The set, like a department store, featured a staircase leading to the upper floors on the right and left of the stage, with the actors standing in the central atrium. In the first scene, the emcee "Madame Sensation" sings:

Berlin itself is a department store	Berlin ist selber ein Warenhaus
All the departments are represented—	Alle Branchen sind vertreten—

It swarms with customers	Von Kunden wimmelt's
day and night!	tagein—tagaus!
Every hour brings new sensations!	Jede Stunde bringt Novitäten![37]

Like the metropolis itself, then, the department store is portrayed as "having it all" and swarming with people. "Where does today's Berlin go in and out?" the narrator asks. "The department store."

Department stores, furthermore, represented themselves and were depicted as meeting points for both planned rendezvous and unplanned encounters. Different worlds existed side by side in the department store, which often made for unexpected, sometimes awkward encounters. As they traversed the store's aisles, displays, and exhibitions, shoppers and strollers embarked on imaginary journeys to different parts of the world. Writing on the psychology of the department store, sexologist Josef Bernhard Schneider portrayed the shopping floors as a meeting point of East and West: "Here people buy everything, and they also live everything [*man lebt hier auch alles*]. Indeed, they really live here, as in the fable *A Thousand and One Nights*, since here the Orient is united with the Occident, and while you sit in a palm grove amid the rushing of a fountain there rises the aroma of all the goodies of the world right in front of you."[38]

Different social worlds also collided on the shopping floors. Here is how Köhrer describes the teeming throng of shoppers outside Warenhaus Berlin's fashion salon: "A thick crowd of women of all classes surged, their faces pressed excitedly against the glass display cases . . . ladies of the elegant world in pricy fur coats and working-class women in plaid woolens, dressed crudely and ostentatiously, gussied up Jewesses from Berlin's West alongside tall blond, officers' wives of simple, cultivated elegance."[39]

Paul Göhre, in his 1907 work *Das Warenhaus*, a treatise devoted chiefly to Wertheim's flagship store on Berlin's Leipziger Strasse, noted that the department store led to a kind of social leveling, since women from different social groups encountered one another in front of the display tables and in the elevators. After spending a morning observing people on the shopping floors, he reported that he saw "Protestant deaconesses and Catholic nuns, women from the demimonde, honorable bourgeois women, elegant society ladies, mourners, children, young wives and little old mothers, hideous women, beautiful women, the fresh, the vibrant, the slow, and occasionally even a man."[40] Similarly, in his department store commentary from 1900, Gustav Stresemann noted, "Indeed women of the most varied social classes all feel the attraction or pull that Wertheim exerts. The most elegant wives of officials from western Berlin or Charlottenburg give themselves over to the madness just as willingly as the petit-bourgeois or working-class wives from the east and north of Berlin, who put on their 'good dress' otherwise reserved for Sundays and holidays, when they go to Wertheim."[41]

To be sure some department stores catered to particular social groups and reinforced hierarchies of wealth and status; the Jandorf stores in Berlin, with the exception of the KaDeWe, were aimed at working-class customers and promoted themselves primarily as discounters, while most of the Wertheim and Tietz locations targeted consumers from the *Mittelstand*, and the KaDeWe and the Wertheim store on Leipziger Strasse attracted a markedly wealthier clientele.[42] Yet, despite the reality of social stratification, huge stores like Tietz and Wertheim enticed mixed crowds. Oscar Tietz reported that educated, well-to-do women were drawn to his stores but ashamed to be seen in them, thus often justified their presence as "on behalf of the servants" and asked that their goods be packaged in plain brown bags to conceal their origins.[43]

Significantly, the major department stores represented themselves as sites for the mixing of worlds, the juxtaposition of commodities of disparate origins and an escape from the social segregation of real life into unregulated, often uncontrollable encounters between people from different regions and social sectors. Many fictional plots turned on the meeting of a poor shopgirl and a rich and powerful department store "king." Other stories probed the social tensions and resentment between smart, savvy salesgirls and the wealthy women of leisure they served. As we have seen in the rhetoric of oppositional groups, department store consumption brought with it concern about the so-called democratization of luxury, which represented the threat of social leveling and the abolition of the exterior and easily legible signs or markers of social status.

The department store also served as a gateway to the wider world, and shopping exposed consumers to distant reaches, accessible through the fantasy of mobility that they promoted. The stores—above all, the renowned Berlin emporiums such as the KaDeWe and the flagship Tietz, Wertheim, and ultimately Karstadt stores—offered the possibility of imagined escape, of travel to distant parts of the world, by virtue of their displays and spectacles. Persian rugs, Chinese silks, and French *mode* gave the shopping floors a distinctly international feel; simultaneously, the addition of travel agencies and window and product displays promoting luggage and other travel accoutrements further emphasized the way in which the stores positioned themselves as a point of entry to the wider world that could be experienced, either through actual travel, or through simple acts of spectatorship and consumption within the store's walls. In *The Great Department Store*, Siwertz writes:

If someone buys a fur coat or even a packet of needles just once at Goldmann's, it is already clear to them what a fantastic thing a large department store is. Wander the halls for just five minutes, and you will see silks from China, Japan, and Lombardy, woven woolens from Australia and Argentina, furs from Siberia, Alaska, Australia, whalebone from the Arctic, paradise feathers from New Guinea and Borneo, rice from Malacca, ivory tusks from the Sudan, diamonds from South Africa, tobacco from Cuba and Sumatra, not to mention the fruit and colonial goods from Sicily, Asia Minor, Tasmania, California, India, the Moluccas, Java, and the West Indies.[44]

The department store thus offered more than mere access to consumer goods. Like the international expositions that began in the later nineteenth century, department stores offered browsers the chance to experience and traverse the world through exposure to commodities.

Shopping and Mobility: The Department Store on Rails

In many ways the department store resembled a railway station. Both gateways, the two kinds of structures were of comparable size and scale, and both helped transform nineteenth-century urban topography. In this passage from *Das Warenhaus*, Göhre describes the main *Lichthof* (light court or atrium) of the famous Wertheim department store in central Berlin:

> Think of the largest and most magnificent assembly hall in Germany, of the mightiest arrival terminal of the most modern central rail station, of the most magnificent coronation hall in our princely palaces, of the crepuscular vessel of the Cologne Cathedral. This space has something of all of those in it . . . . It seems essentially compatible to all of them, but yet it is a thing all its own, having been developed to meet completely unique needs for completely new purposes, as the foyer of a world department store, as the central point and the festival space [*Festraum*] of a completely new organism, which represents the peak of the world economic traffic in goods.[45]

Göhre's depiction thus puts the department store's religious grandeur side by side with its position as a hub of global commodity circulation. He stresses economic circulation, worldliness, and the stores' impressive architecture, and like Zola in *The Ladies' Paradise*, he brings trains and train stations into the picture.

Zola's novel begins with his protagonist Denise Baudu and her two brothers arriving in Paris by train, having left their provincial home in search of a livelihood with their shopkeeper uncle. Its opening sentence mentions that the siblings arrived in Paris at the Gare Saint-Lazare, and in the second sentence the reader learns that they had taken the train from Cherbourg and slept in an uncomfortable third-class carriage. When they arrive at her uncle's shop, the department store across the street, the Ladies' Paradise, whose ceaseless expansion threatens to destroy Baudu and all the neighboring shops, fascinates and enthralls Denise, who gazes longingly at it for much of the first part of the novel. The Ladies' Paradise, furthermore, is described as emitting a "steam engine sound," and Zola repeatedly refers to its "gnashing wheels" and machine-like movements. Throughout the narrative, Zola emphasizes the store's restless energy, its rapid turnover, constant motion, and position within the expanding trade and transportation networks, the broad new arteries of Haussmann's Paris.[46]

Department stores, notes the Zionist spokesman David Littwak in Theodor Herzl's *Old New Land*, "were inevitable in an era of steam engines and railways."[47] Indeed, the similarities and connections between department stores and railway stations were not lost on contemporary observers, and the history of the department store is deeply intertwined with the history of the railroad both materially and in the realm of representation.[48] Todd Presner compares railways and arcades, the department store's nineteenth-century predecessors, as two dream spaces of modernity, both of which were bound up with notions of mobility, progress, and capitalization.[49] And in his classic book *The Railway Journey*, Wolfgang Schivelbusch likens the late nineteenth-century department store consumer to the railway traveler. Both activities created a new kind of spectatorship, which he terms "panoramic perception." Schivelbusch writes: "We call the appearance of the goods in a department store 'panoramic'—to distinguish them from their appearance in shops of the old type—because those goods participated in the same acceleration of traffic which generated the new mode of perception on the railways and boulevards."[50]

In architectural terms, as Göhre observes in the passage quoted above, the only structures that rivaled early department stores for their size and scale, their high ceilings, vaulted roofs, and vast open spaces, were train stations and cathedrals. In terms of economic relations and business history, the completion of rail lines made the comprehensive department store possible, by enabling the rapid and high-volume transportation of products from afar. Trains also made customers mobile and thus enabled stores to be stationary, a reversal of older economic arrangements whereby the peddler circulated and the stationary customer awaited his arrival, or the newer practice of provincial customers purchasing goods from mail-order catalogs. As Salman Schocken pointed out, new train connections facilitated travel from the countryside and provincial settings into the big cities with the result that wealthy provincial women undertook regular shopping trips to the metropolis with increasing frequency.[51]

Consumer mobility was a precondition for the concurrent development of the tourism industry and the emergence of travel as a bourgeois leisure-time activity. Whiling away the hours in department stores and embarking on packaged tours and vacations were both new bourgeois pursuits, and department stores reinforced (and commodified) emergent travel cultures and simultaneously offered an alternative to actual travel.[52] Schivelbusch quite succinctly illustrates the interdependence of modern rail travel and department store consumption: "From that time on, the places visited by the traveler became increasingly similar to the commodities that were part of the same circulation system. For the twentieth-century tourist, the world has become one huge department store of countrysides and cities."[53]

By the late twentieth century, urban reformers in the United States began turning defunct railway stations into malls to revitalize desolate urban landscapes, and functioning stations, like major airports, began to feature extensive retail offerings, further sealing the association between shopping and travel. These connections with railroads were palpable in the early twentieth-century department store; they made themselves felt in its organization and were expressed in its advertising and through its exhibits. One year, for example, the Tietz store on Berlin's Dönhoffplatz was decorated to look like a giant train station as part of its summer travel promotions.[54]

Like a central railway station, the department store served as a depot for arriving goods and people, a hub that lay at the center of a grid or transit network within the city and also throughout the European continent and even beyond. The theme of the stores' centrality and their place in urban and regional circulatory networks appears again and again in contemporary sources and formed a conspicuous part of the department store's identity. In *Berliner Warenhäuser*, Leo Colze describes the way the department stores, or "retail palaces," lined up along the great traffic spokes (*Verkehrsrädern*) of imperial Berlin. He characterized the KaDeWe as lying on the nodal point of Berlin traffic, right at an urban fault line at the center of the metropolis's vast, pulsating public transportation system:

> Here, where the bustling, industrious and commercial Berlin comes into contact with the elegant, primarily residential West, where numerous electric tram lines ceaselessly connect all parts of Berlin and points farther west, Charlottenburg, Schöneberg, and Wilmersdorf, and guide thousands upon thousands of people, and where the subways constantly release new streams of people into the light of day, several minutes away from the Berlin Zoo Station for commuter and long-distance rail, this is exactly the spot where a great department store could be certain to develop effectively.[55]

It seems likely, especially given the similar titles, that Erich Köhrer read the Göhre book as part of his research for *Warenhaus Berlin*; the Köhrer novel features a strikingly similar description of the fictional department store's location, likewise emphasizing its connection to tram lines linking it to the entire city.[56] "Der Treffpunkt Berlins" (Berlin's meeting place) was one of the KaDeWe's advertising slogans, again emphasizing its centrality in the city and in the lives of its inhabitants. To be sure, Wittenbergplatz, site of the KaDeWe, was served by the new *U-Bahn* line, completed in 1902, that linked eastern and western Berlin. Another line, finished in 1906, connected it to Berlin's wealthy western suburbs.

A speech given on the ceremonial reopening of the newly remodeled Kaufhaus Israel in Berlin in 1928 evokes the same imagery, namely the centrality of the store to the urban environment and even to customers' lives. The company's slogan was "Das Kaufhaus im Zentrum"—the department store in the center. In advertisements in the late 1920s the motto was accompanied by an additional tagline: "Das Zentrum des Einkaufs"—the center of shopping. The speaker at the 1928 event began by affirming that the store's slogan rings true because Kaufhaus Israel stands not only in the center of Berlin, but also in the middle between producers and consumers. Das Kaufhaus im Zentrum actually became Kaufhaus Israel's official name after Aryanization in 1939.[57] Finally, the name of the store in Vicki Baum's *The Great Sale* was "Das Warenhaus-Zentral," or the Central Department Store, and the novel's English title in its 1940 translation was "Central Store."[58]

The speaker at the Kaufhaus Israel opening noted further that the internal organization of the store also follows the principle of concentric circles, with particular departments radiating out from a central nucleus. He concludes: "This notion of the centralized large retail firm must take effect more and more internally and also toward the outside, and as we wish, hope, and believe, it must work in the service of our customers, in the service of the whole consuming class, in the service of and simultaneously for the advancement of our father city Berlin."[59]

The internal organization of the stores is discussed below, but it is worth noting here that Salman Schocken's business plan for his department stores, based on his application of Taylorism and economic rationalization, incorporated similar notions of centralization and circulation. Schocken centralized all business operations, that is, all buying, price setting, and decision making (and even window display design) and treated the Kingdom of Saxony as his field of operations, with stores radiating outward from his central offices in Zwickau, which in 1931 employed some five hundred workers.[60] According to Georg Manasse, managing director of the Schocken concern, "The same goods that are bought for Zwickau also go to Nuremberg or Stuttgart or Waldenburg. The selling prices, which are established in the center, apply to all locations where we have branches. This then determines that our customers receive the same quality in all our establishments and that they can conduct their shopping in our houses with blind trust."[61] Centralization and rationalization were key concepts for many department store firms and helped guarantee both quality and profitability.

An advertisement for the Karstadt department store in Berlin likewise emphasized the store's topographical centrality in the metropolis and reinforced the equation of the stores with railway stations. In the early 1930s, Karstadt circulated pamphlets that positioned its imposing new Hermannplatz store—actually a bit removed from both the city's old textile center (Konfektionsviertel) near Hausvogteiplatz and the new commercial center in the west—on the metropolitan transportation grid, literally by superimposing it on the transit map. The construction of the enormous store in fact went hand in hand with the expansion of the Berlin public transportation system.[62] Another image in the same pamphlet shows the store building in front of Berlin's major rail stations and linked to them with a kind of red carpet. The accompanying text urges visitors to Berlin not to pass by this attraction, which a later page identifies as a sightseeing destination and a shoppers' paradise. The brochure also shows the roof terrace as a beach-style vacation spot. These Karstadt folios, which stressed the store's centrality, its position on the rail network, and its accessibility by public

2.5 Advertisement for Karstadt department store (probably 1935). "Whoever visits Berlin may not pass this house by." Bundesarchiv Berlin.

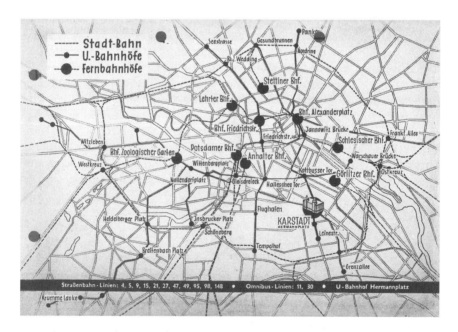

2.6 Advertisement for Karstadt department store (probably 1935). Bundesarchiv Berlin.

transportation, were placed in trains, behind the seats on Berlin-bound lines, in an attempt to drum up business from tourists and other visitors to the city.

To complete the circle, this Karstadt store was actually located directly above an underground rail station, and passengers could enter the store straight from the *U-Bahn* without going outside, a sensational phenomenon when the store first opened in 1929. "Direct from the train platform into our shopping floors" stated a newspaper ad, and this further testifies to the connections, even the sealed system between department stores, rail networks, and urban and commercial circulatory networks.[63] Karstadt ads referred to the Hermannplatz station as Bahnhof Karstadt—Karstadt Station.[64] (Similarly, years earlier, when horse-drawn trams stopped at Leipziger Platz, conductors typically called out simply "Wertheim" instead of the name of the stop, a practice that enraged anti–department store activists.)[65] Customers could purchase tobacco, newspapers, flowers, or snacks in a corridor right at the platform, which was linked to the store's shopping floors by stairways, escalators, and an elevator with room for three passengers.[66]

Another elaborate Karstadt advertisement featured, in addition to the elements noted above, trams, buses, and even airplanes, again stressing the accessibility of the store and its integration into local and even more distant

2.7 Karstadt, Berlin, 1929, direct entrance from Hermannplatz *U-Bahn* station. Landesarchiv Berlin.

transit networks.[67] "From East, North, West, South," it read, also noting that Berlin's Tempelhof Airport was not far from the store for potential customers arriving by air. The Karstadt company could not pretend that its store lay in Berlin's center, as noted above, but it made the most of the situation. "In the center of the South," the ad optimistically declares. This advertisement also refers to the passage leading directly from the underground into the department store, which it places alongside a list of Berlin's most noteworthy tourist attractions.

The idea of a passageway from the subway station into the store, emphasized so pointedly in Karstadt's ad campaigns, had aroused great controversy decades earlier with the expansion of the Wertheim store on Leipziger Strasse. Rumors abounded in the early 1900s, especially in the anti-Semitic press, that the Wertheims had commissioned the construction of an entrance directly from the *U-Bahn* station at Leipziger Platz, an idea supposedly inspired by their visit to New York. This prospect triggered a series of polemics about the enormous power allegedly wielded by Jewish entrepreneurs, enabling them to shape the urban landscape and to expose innocent passersby to the seductive reach of the department store.[68] The underground passageways provided fertile ground for the imaginations of anti–department store agitators, who depicted them as sites of the kinds of immoral and lurid activities that the department stores promoted.[69] These

2.8 Store guide, Karstadt department store, Hermannplatz, Berlin. Stiftung Deutsches Technikmuseum Berlin, Hist. Archiv.

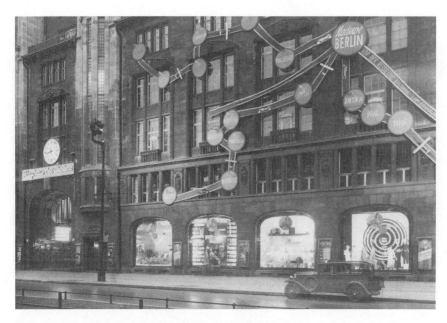

2.9 "Before the trip, go shopping at the KaDeWe." KaDeWe facade, 1935. Reprinted from Antonia Meiners, *100 Jahre KaDeWe* (Berlin, 2007).

condemnations assumed that Berliners would be powerless in the face of the department store's magnetic pull, which would divert innocent pedestrians straight into the Moloch's ravenous maw. Significantly, these objections overlooked the fact that Georg Wertheim, like the Karstadt firm in 1929, was actually cooperating with municipal authorities who had asked for permission to run underground tracks below his store.[70]

A KaDeWe promotional campaign from 1935 affixed to the storefront mock tracks linking the emporium to various German and Central European cities, again putting the department store on the transit grid—and in this case the transit grid directly on the store. At first glance the spurs appear to be railroad tracks, but closer inspection reveals not trains but small airplanes and automobiles. Like Karstadt in its ads, here the KaDeWe appears as both a destination and a point of departure. Indeed, the KaDeWe lies at the center of the rail system, and all the tracks and spurs lead to it. Significantly, the large hub in the center is labeled "Kadewe Berlin," serving to equate the store and the city and placing the KaDeWe, rather than the surrounding metropolis, at the center of the rail grid. The department store is the ultimate destination, but it also serves as a point of departure, the place to go to buy all of one's travel needs before embarking. As the text states: "Before the trip, go shopping at the Kadewe." To illustrate that the KaDeWe was an ideal place to purchase luggage, clothes, and other travel accessories, a display window showed four comfortable, sophisticated, and smartly outfitted mannequins relaxing in a train compartment.[71]

2.10 KaDeWe window display. Reprinted from *Das Kaufhaus des Westens: Festschrift zum 25 jährigen Bestehen 1907–1932*, ed. Franz Arnholz and Max Osborn (Berlin, 1932). Bpk, Berlin/Art Resource, NY.

In other ways too the department store functioned as the point of departure for journeys real and imaginary. The maritime and harbor scenes painted on the atrium walls in Wertheim's Leipziger Strasse store further underlined the notion of the store as a port, as a hub for the global transport of goods and a jumping-off point for distant journeys. The KaDeWe was replete with nautical themes, notably in the sail-like curves in its entryway, and the store's seal included a ship motif through the end of the twentieth century.[72] Paul Göhre, as we have seen, compared the Wertheim store to an ocean liner.[73] He also reported the existence of "swimming department stores" in Japan, built out of remodeled Russian merchant ships that the Japanese had seized in the Russo-Japanese War—a dubious claim to be sure, but one that helps illuminate contemporary German mentalities, if not Japanese realities.[74] Department store architecture and other commercial constructions in the 1920s often featured explicit nautical references; the steamship effect in Erich Mendelsohn's buildings accentuated their dynamism and made them appear ready to embark on a journey through the city streets.[75]

The stores gestured at air travel too, a source of tremendous excitement in the German 1920s. Karstadt and the KaDeWe, as we have seen, incorporated airplanes and airports into their ad campaigns. In a 1929 promotion, tied to the national week of celebrating flight (*Luftfahrt-Werbewoche*), Wertheim displayed an entire airplane in its central atrium. The exhibition also included a parachute, gliders, and other objects that celebrated humanity's conquest of the skies.[76]

2.11 Wertheim department store, Berlin 1929. Stiftung Deutsches Technikmuseum Berlin, Hist. Archiv.

2.12 Tietz department store, Berlin, 1924. Reprinted from Antonia Meiners, *100 Jahre KaDeWe* (Berlin, 2007).

Major department stores sold travel gear, of course, and their in-house travel agencies booked vacations. Karstadt's advertisements juxtaposed pictures of their store travel agency with their imported-rug section, implying, perhaps, that a trip to the store meant a possible journey to distant, exotic places. That is certainly the case with the paintings that adorned the KaDeWe's "silver terrace" by noted Berlin Secession artist César Klein. The text accompanying its 1932 reproduction—in a volume celebrating the KaDeWe's twenty-fifth anniversary—proclaims it a "dream image from distant southerly worlds."[77]

The widespread use of Asian and Near Eastern motifs and imagery emphasized the notion that a department store visit could transport the customer to faraway, exotic places. In a 1924 product display, for example, the Hermann Tietz store on Leipziger Strasse constructed a Sphinx out of kerchiefs and hand towels to promote the store's annual linen sales event, the so-called *Weisse Wochen*, or white weeks.[78] Like the dioramas and panoramas that became an urban craze in Berlin and other European cities in the nineteenth century, the department store offered the experience of dream encounters with distant worlds past and present that promoted and accompanied mundane consumer transactions.[79] A stationary spot of iron, glass, and concrete, it also embodied mobility and dynamism, serving as a portal to distant worlds of discovery.

The Human Stream

Business writers and department store entrepreneurs were also concerned with the circulation of people within the stores, indeed with managing the flow of customers and goods through the enormous and complex structures with their many dozens of departments. As we have seen, the department store embodied a rationalized and highly organized commercial operation, one where nothing was left to chance and where even the smallest details were planned out and scientifically managed. On the other hand, the store created a dreamworld, a fantastical experience, and a business's success depended on inherently unpredictable variables such as customer desire and the ability to provoke *Kauflust*. We see this tension vividly in the problem of managing human circulation.

This concern reflected the preoccupation with traffic and the problem of movement through urban spaces that held the attention of city planners, architects, and social theorists, especially in the Weimar period. Helmut Plessner, distinguishing between community (*Gemeinschaft*) and society (*Gesellschaft*), characterized society as an "open system of traffic among unconnected individuals," in contrast to the stultifying air of the traditional community.[80] The historian Wolfgang Schivelbusch writes that "whatever was part of circulation was regarded as healthy, progressive, constructive; all that was detached from circulation, on the other hand, appeared diseased, medieval, subversive, threatening."[81] Traffic, argues Helmut Lethen, was coded as movement and dynamism, and peacetime urban circulation—as opposed to the mobilization of wartime—formed a central theme in the culture of New Objectivity of the mid 1920s.[82] We see this same preoccupation with movement in the work of Georg Simmel, specifically in his writings on the circulation and flow of money through the capitalist economy.[83] Finally, the architect Erich Mendelsohn conceived of the department store as part of a dynamic, ceaselessly moving urban fabric. "The building is not a passive spectator of the racing autos, of the traffic flowing this way and that," he wrote; "rather it has become an integral, contributing part of this movement."[84]

The department store's position on the urban grid and indeed its relationship to the streets that surrounded it preoccupied many early twentieth-century and interwar observers. Contemporary depictions of the stores' success tended to emphasize efficiency, rationalization, and the movement of people from the streets through the department store's portals and the smooth circulation of people, goods, and money.[85] Eager shoppers within and the crowds on the street and outside the display windows, in all kinds of representations, are depicted as a *Menschenstrom*, a stream of humanity, which needed to be guided and routed through the store's various departments, as if department store design and good retail practices were matters of hydraulic engineering.

The human stream as metaphor also underlines the sense of dynamism, haste, speed, and motion, and even the dangers that appear in so many kinds of representations of the department store and also of urban modernity as a whole. Speed, after all, was crucial to the department store's profitability. Rapid turnover and enormous sales volume allowed the stores to turn prodigious profits while keeping prices low. It was thus crucial that the stores be kept crowded, that "masses" of customers be constantly brought in, guided around, and kept in motion. "The customer is usually in a hurry," noted Gerhard Tietz of the Leonhard Tietz concern, in a 1928 essay; "in fact he comes to the department store so that he can take care of all of his shopping, if possible, at a single location. But even if he is not in a hurry, all of the department store bustle brings about a certain nervousness that makes him buy faster, or may make him unstable and indecisive."[86]

The department store's dynamism reflected what Werner Sombart identified as the acceleration of modern life ushered in by the newly emerging consumer society, in which goods needed to be replaced with increasing frequency, and consumers began to expect instant gratification. These changes in turn forced the acceleration of the processes of production and distribution, which then further intensified the consumer's experience.[87]

Describing the street scene outside the KaDeWe, Leo Colze observed: "A spruced-up human stream flows along the street, laughing and flirting, full of life, taking their time."[88] The Köhrer novel depicts the mass of humanity (*Menschenmasse*) that streams through Warenhaus Berlin and leads the "stream of gold" (*Goldstrom*) right into Nielandt's hands.[89] In the "Warenhaus-Revue," Feuchtwanger portrays the scene outside the store with the same metaphor: "People like water flow back and forth, ebb," and then, in the department store, "the porter guides the human masses in."[90] Walter E. Schulz, writing in a promotional volume on the Hermann Tietz stores, observed the "nearly limitless streams of buyers and lookers who writhe through the gates and halls, unceasingly, indefatigably."[91] Siegfried Kracauer compares the crowds at Berlin's Karstadt store, the "popular stream," to blood running through the circulatory system, but he notes that in light of the high unemployment—this was 1929—the stream had thinned out a bit and no longer completely covered the floors.[92] In *Arbeit: Ein Warenhausroman* (Work: A department store novel), author Oscar Schweriner opts for a different set of metaphors, comparing the crowds of female shoppers to a huge swarm of bees competing for the same flower and likening women following signs for a sale to soldiers marching in lockstep behind a banner.[93]

Department store crowds could get unruly. Journalists and novelists described department store sales as "battles" and scenes of "warfare," noting the danger of being caught in the consuming current. One contemporary recalled a turbulent visit to Wertheim: "The crowd [*Menschenmenge*] pushed me back and forth. I wanted to go to the perfume counter and ended up in the notions section; suddenly I was standing in front of a lady who showed me handkerchiefs, and half an hour later I had landed in the middle of the enamel kitchenware."[94] Here yet again the crowd is compared to a river whose current violently pushes customers through the store and whose flow was strongest during sales or at the unveiling of new product lines, times when the individual consumer could most easily find herself submerged.

Whereas some depictions characterized the crowd as military-like in its seriousness of purpose, intensity, and forcefulness, other accounts emphasized its wild, spontaneous, and even dangerous qualities. Drawing on Gustave LeBon's notions of crowd psychology and his assertion that crowds acted like an irrational, debased, and pathological entity, writers treated the shopping crowd as feminine and hysterical. Just as LeBon's crowd endangered the polity with its irrational, shortsighted behavior, the consuming crowd represented the antithesis of the rational shopper or the sophisticated Weimar housewife, two icons of savvy consumption from the 1920s.[95]

The hysterical consumer, in contrast to the competent household manager, embodied loss of control and rational subjectivity, becoming a collective mass of women driven mad by the forces of *Kauflust*. In *W.A.G.M.U.S.*, Margarete Böhme describes the scene at the beginning of the December shopping season as a gushing river of people impatient to trade in their money for wares: "An uneasy restlessness accompanied the crowd that streamed in the various entrances, as though every person was simultaneously gripped by the feverish longing to sacrifice part of his weekly earnings, which he had just now received, at the altar of the temple of goods."[96]

The crowds that gathered in front of exciting new window decorations or at displays mounted during the Christmas shopping season or other promotional events alarmed Berlin city officials. Department stores began opening on Sundays in the weeks leading up to Christmas, having been given special dispensation by the authorities to violate the prohibition of Sunday trade, and the preceding Advent Sundays were termed "Silver Sunday" and "Golden Sunday." A Copper Sunday was introduced some time after 1900.[97] The holiday shopping crowds in Berlin were so enormous in December 1901 that one newspaper account reported a "colossal stampede" into the department stores, which even the day's terrible weather did not deter.[98] The police responded by posting dozens of officers in all major department stores. To curb the unruly crowds that gathered to admire window displays, police ordinances prevented shop window displays that were deemed too exciting or stimulating, particularly anything with moving figures.[99]

By the Weimar period, moving store-window installations had become standard in major cities. Increasingly elaborate displays began to feature projected images and animatronic characters and started to resemble theatrical, even cinematic productions. The historian Janet Ward writes that "actual movement in the window that mirrored the circulating movement in the city street outside was understood to be a key factor in arousing pedestrians' buying desire."[100]

The goal was of course to maximize the flow of traffic from the streets into the department store's doors. Store designers contemplated the problem of transportation and flow, of channeling streams of consumers through the stores' multiple departments to maximize profitability and retain a sense of excitement. Like Kracauer, the writer Kurt Pinthus, son of a department store executive, compared the sensation of customers circulating through the store to the pumping of blood through the body: "Since childhood I experienced it semiconsciously but yet I felt it physically like the circulation of my blood, the numbing effect of this endless, always forward-driving flowing of the human masses [*Umströmens der Menschenmassen*] which were sucked in through the department store's doors, forced into ceaseless motion through the corridors, stairways, and elevators, and finally, after this zigzag, pushed back out the doors and poured back into the linear flow of the street."[101]

Paul Göhre, also using the metaphor of flowing and rushing water, added that the department store's magnetic pull was so mighty that it seemed as though its customers, the stream of humanity, would not only flood the store itself and the surrounding streets but would spray out the roof and through the floors down to the earth's core.[102] The stores indeed often had a significant vertical dimension, consisting of three, four, or even more floors—or a sixty-story skyscraper in one fantastical literary account.[103] The writer Joseph Roth dubbed the enormous Karstadt store on Hermannplatz, whose towers evoked American skyscrapers and eclipsed surrounding businesses, the "very large department store," in contrast to the other, merely "large department stores."[104]

Customers also had to be directed up and down the store's many floors. Elevators were first used at the beginning of the twentieth century, and the first escalator in Germany appeared at a Leonhard Tietz department store in Cologne in 1925. Memoirs from the period often note that the author's first elevator or escalator ride occurred in a department store. Customers' first experiences of escalators could be frightening or exhilarating, as recorded, for example, by staff members after the installation of Zwickau's first escalator in the town's Schocken store. "Customer behavior on the escalator varies widely: Many run and scream 'keep going! keep going!' Many want to fully savor the experience of being on the escalator and stand still. Some have a deadly serious expression. Others laugh and titter with pleasure. Several applaud at the end, their first escalator ride in the books."[105]

The sociologist and journalist Wilhelm Carlé titled his planned serial department store novel "Die Rolltreppe" (The escalator), maintaining that the escalator symbolized "the perpetual motion in the department store by the consumers as well as the capital."[106] Roth joked in his musings on the "very large department store" that the stores waxed their steps to make them slippery and dangerous so that customers would avoid these old, outdated relics and opt for the more modern conveyances like escalators and elevators.[107] Escalators, Roth pointed out, were good for business. They took shoppers to the upper floors, where they saw merchandise that they might not have bothered to look at if forced to exert themselves by climbing steps. He noted that taking mechanized conveyances renders people so passive that they begin to resemble the store's merchandise. Ultimately, Roth concluded, "it does not matter at all if the goods are brought to the waiting customer on a downward moving stairway or if the customer is brought upward to the waiting goods."[108]

Apparently Roth's observations were not far off the mark. In taking on the problem of leading the "stream of people" through the department store, one business writer, an H. Wagner, noted that extra efforts had to be made to ensure that shoppers went to the upper stories, since the natural tendency would be to stay close to the ground floor.[109] Wagner proposed placing the enticing food section at the top, so that (female) customers would go there first, generally riding an escalator or elevator all the way up and then working their way down, the very idea that Roth had put forth in a humorous vein, without the waxed steps.[110] This mode of circulation would increase the chances that consumers would be lured into making extra purchases by attractive displays and appealing product choices as they made their way down the stairs, having already accomplished their food shopping.

It was not just customers whose movements were studied and channeled by the directors of these highly rationalized businesses. Wagner also drew up a series of charts that schematized the movement of goods through department stores. Several illustrated the circulation of goods and slips for purchases conducted with credit. Others diagrammed the paths of returned goods back to the shelves, or the ways in which wares entered and left the stores for delivery or for the important mail-order business. The KaDeWe featured a centralized cash register on the ground floor, and all purchases were routed through this system. Sales slips, placed in small cases, were shot thorough a comprehensive network of pneumatic tubes that propelled them through the store's departments. Eleven miles of tubing stretched through the building, with 154 stations, and cash could be carried at a speed of one kilometer per minute, at least until the cumbersome system could no longer be maintained and had to be replaced with more conventional registers.[111]

The department store thus had to manage the movement of goods from its loading docks through its retail departments and the flow of people from its entrances through its shopping floors and attractions. Its location facilitated the efficient management of goods and provided the easiest access for potential consumers whatever their means of transportation. The department store was also a hub from which goods emerged and were rapidly delivered. Stores like the KaDeWe and Wertheim boasted of their fleets of trucks, which enabled delivery teams to take large items to customers' houses on the day of purchase. In 1932 the H. Tietz concern publicized its two-hundred-vehicle fleet enabling rapid delivery to customers' homes.[112] Kaufhaus Israel advertised as early as 1906 that it shipped abroad. Goods that cost more than twenty marks could be ordered by catalog and received in Austria-Hungary, Denmark, Luxembourg, France, Belgium, Switzerland, and the Netherlands.[113]

The stores, then, served as the base of operations for the mail-order business, another way in which they were embedded in regional circulatory networks. Mail order, an increasingly important source of revenue for department stores and other large retailers, depended on the completion of an efficient railway system and two key innovations of the 1870s: COD and a fixed, fifty-pfennig tariff on packages weighing five kilograms.[114] These developments allowed stores to recruit new customers in the surrounding countryside through catalogs and newspaper advertisements. Traveling salesmen also fanned out from the stores to reach customers in more remote settings whom they exposed to the most current products and styles.

Efforts to manage the circulation of goods and the flow of people show how the stores cultivated a kind of programmed chaos. A rationalized layout and thoroughly planned store organization were, on the one hand, necessary for efficiency and safety; on the other hand, stores sought to stimulate consumer desire and let the shopper lose herself in the frenzy of the crowd, which was necessary for profitability. Together these two dimensions show both sides of commercial modernity: rationalization and scientific planning here worked to set the stage for the mysterious magic of commodity culture, which turned the stationary store edifice into a site of dynamic encounters, ecstatic consumption, and constant motion.

Cosmopolitan Consumption and the Jewish Question

In his 1844 text "On the Jewish Question," Karl Marx somewhat infamously identified the Jews with self-interested economic behavior and demanded society's emancipation from Judaism. Theodor Herzl, coming from a radically different position over half a century later, sought to emancipate the Jews through economic change. Herzl's Zionist vision, at least the eclectic utopia of Jewish modernity presented in his 1902 book, *Altneuland* (*Old New Land*), describes the Jewish state as filled with department stores that rival Paris's Bon Marché in their splendor—modern grand emporiums and bazaars that have all but replaced small-scale shops. Through the department store, we are told, the Jews have been emancipated from their economically degrading position as small shopkeepers and especially peddlers, the most Jewish and least modern of all economic pursuits.[115]

Significantly, for Herzl, there was nothing Jewish about the department store. The department store actually represented the negation of (economic) Jewishness, defined as petty merchandizing and peddling. Some department stores in his imagined Jewish state were owned by Jews, but others were in the hands of Armenians, Greeks, Persians, and others. It also bears pointing out that in Herzl's fantasy, Jerusalem was linked by good rail connections, which bridged the Bosporus, to major European capitals from Amsterdam through St. Petersburg, and it lay "at the exact geographical center of traffic between Europe, Asia and Africa."[116] Central, in other words, like a department store at the hub of a transit grid. For Herzl, the department store represented deracinated cosmopolitan modernity, and the proliferation of the department store in the new Jewish state bespoke its modernity and symbolized the economic emancipation of the Jews. In some ways Herzl's vision resembled what was realized by the S. Schocken concern two decades later; but before turning to Schocken, we first need to flesh out cosmopolitan consumption and its multiple valences in nineteenth- and twentieth-century Germany.

The department store's cosmopolitanism was both a source of pride for entrepreneurs (both Jewish and presumably non-Jewish) and grounds for disapproval by department store opponents, for whom the stores seemed suspiciously and threateningly un-German. Here then we see the negative side of cosmopolitanism. Going back to the middle of the nineteenth century, cosmopolitanism was construed as a threat to the project of German national and cultural unification and associated with the Jews, the perennial outsiders. Todd Presner has traced this discursive formation to the 1830s and '40s, the same period that saw the initial establishment of rail networks in parts of Germany, a development that was greeted as the key to increasing unity among German polities and populations. German state governments, Presner shows, limited the ability of Jews to invest in railroads out of concern that German unity be achieved at the hands of stateless, cosmopolitan agents. Whereas the generation of Goethe had hailed cosmopolitanism and viewed it as fully compatible with the project of building a common national literature and culture, by the middle of the century, cosmopolitanism, mobility, and the technological assault on borders and boundaries were reconfigured as threats to German nationhood, and the Jew, in turn, on the verge of emancipation, was constructed as the cosmopolitan negation of Germanness.[117] Yet, long after cosmopolitanism fell out of favor among German nationalists, some Jews in Germany embraced it as a model for their own emergent nationalism through the Zionist movement. Cosmopolitanism for German-speaking Zionists meant the establishment of the Jews as a people of world-historical significance by demonstrating Jews' mobility and modernity, a vision clearly indebted to early nineteenth-century German philosophy.[118] For non-Zionist intellectuals like Hannah Arendt, on the other hand, cosmopolitanism denoted the reality of Jewish life in interwar Europe, describing the condition of being at home everywhere and yet nowhere, being a transnational people in an increasingly national world.[119]

Critics of the Jewish department store revived the mid-nineteenth-century notion of cosmopolitanism as subversive to German nationhood and used the stores' own claims to cosmopolitanism to denounce them as un-German. Writers like anti–department store crusader Paul Dehn, and Theodor Fritzsch, editor of the *Hammer*, characterized department stores as a Jewish economic plot, an unwanted import, or a foreign invasion from "the East," which threatened to bury the upright German *Mittelstand*.[120] The East could denote the Polish East or indeed the Near East. As Dehn wrote in 1897, amid heightened Jewish movement into Germany from the Russian Empire, "Dubious elements have immigrated here from the Orient, where different notions of business morals obtain."[121] In this text Dehn never explicitly identifies these "dubious elements" as Jews, but there can be no doubt about his meaning. He chastises them for lacking a national identity, accusing them of having no homeland but of making themselves at home in other lands—cosmopolitans, in other words: "The bearers of this fraudulent industry are in fact neither Germans nor Austrians. They're not even Poles, rather new arrivals from the East."[122]

Like Sombart, Dehn implicitly equated the desert, the alleged source of Jews' economic peculiarities, to the modern city. Fritsch, writing as F. Roderich Stoltheim, furthered the association between the Jews' Near Eastern origins and their approach to commerce, declaring, "The prototype of the department store is the oriental 'bazaar.'"[123] Both authors argued that the department store was essentially a sham. Its glamorous facade concealed the shady business practices that Jews had imported from the East, the hucksterism and chicanery of the open-air market. Hence, the title of one of Dehn's works was *Hinter den Kulissen des modernen Geschäfts* (Behind the scenes of the modern store), which formed part of the genre of exposing the supposedly nefarious hidden workings beneath the glitzy surfaces.

The attempt to orientalize department stores and their owners probably explains the peculiar and wholly unsubstantiated accusation that major department store entrepreneurs Wertheim and Jandorf had personal harems. The anti-Semitic press accused these men of seducing female employees and customers and depicted them as sexually voracious predators who took advantage of innocent German women.[124] Such smears not only characterized Jewish businessmen as a morally corrupting force, but through repetitious use of the word "harem" they implied that these men were of Near Eastern origin and mores, again conflating the actual East-Central European origins of many department store families with the "oriental" East.

Hans Buchner, a Nazi economist, was another vociferous critic of department stores and modern mass consumption. Writing several decades later, when the National Socialists revived the department store critiques of the earlier part of the century, Buchner crusaded against the perceived threat of big retail in the name of Germany's embattled middle classes and attempted to articulate a Nazi vision of consumption, an alternative to the Americanizing (and "Judaizing") influence of the department store.[125] In both his 1928 screed *Dämonen der Wirtschaft* (Economic demons) and its 1929 sequel, *Warenhauspolitik und Nationalsozialismus* (Department store politics and National Socialism), Buchner treated the department store as a fundamentally Jewish phenomenon and as part of a Jewish plot to undermine Germany's economy and society.

Commenting on a brochure that the German Association of Department Stores had published in celebration of department stores' successes, Buchner heaped particular scorn on a portrait gallery, a page of photographs of Germany's leading department store entrepreneurs—or "department store kings," as they were frequently called. "There you see them all together," he wrote, "as if to facilitate the work of the race scientists. The (in part) racially pure types of Schocken, Grünbaum, Knopf, Hirsch. And the half 'hucksters' [*Talmiköpfe*] Tietz, Wronker, Joske, Ury, and whatever all of their names are, those who came from Birnbaum and points farther east, from those places where the caftan and the earlock are to this day the requisite signs of ethnic/national belonging [*Volkszugehörigkeit*]."[126]

Buchner's provocative anti-Semitism and his vicious depictions were intended to shock. He hoped to sound a wake-up call to German consumers who may have enjoyed shopping and passing the time in department stores. Buchner and other critics, motivated by a combination of anti-Semitism and concern for the economic livelihood of the German middle classes, characterized the growth of department stores as a severe threat. Buchner sought to warn complacent German consumers of the pernicious forces at work behind these appealing, even exciting locales, claiming that they resulted from a conspiracy hatched in the shtetl to conquer the German retail market. Recycling the propaganda of an earlier generation of anti–department store activists, he sought to expose the stores' splendid luxury goods as merely repackaged junk and rummage and the stores as parasites sucking the blood out of the German *Mittelstand*. The department store Moloch devouring the world represents the antithesis of cosmopolitan consumption, as in the incongruously provocative cover art for a rather anodyne and mind-numbingly detailed 1908 treatise on comparative department store retail.

As we have seen, department stores frequently used Middle Eastern design motifs to further their claims to worldliness and promote products such as rugs; they sometimes referred to themselves as bazaars, and several French and German department stores even used *Basar* in their names. As Walter Benjamin observed, "The first department stores appear to be modeled on oriental bazaars."[127] Critics like Buchner seized on these motifs in their efforts to castigate the stores as "oriental" and threatening to German ways.

In his department store texts Buchner claimed to be revealing a pattern, a trajectory from the small-time trade in secondhand clothes and dry goods of Birnbaum and other small towns around Posen through Berlin, Munich, and other German cities. Jews, for Buchner, and for other contemporary economic thinkers too, were reduced essentially to an economic category, a commercial class, which was characterized by amorality and greed, and the trajectory from Birnbaum to Berlin of men like Salman Schocken and Adolf Grünbaum represented an invasion from the East, an assault on traditional German economic and social forms by "wandering Jews with their rummage carts."[128] Buchner here used language reminiscent of Heinrich von Treitschke's infamous 1879 condemnation of "pants-peddling Jews" streaming into Berlin from the "inexhaustible cradle of Poland," the touchstone of the Berlin anti-Semitism debate of the 1880s.[129] Like his recycled, recirculated wares, the Jew in these portrayals is himself forever cycling and circulating to exploit economic niches: from the peddler who does the circulating himself to the stores that then become the fixed destination for the circulation and further distribution of goods.

These motifs appeared in a number of tracts from the turn of the twentieth century through the 1930s, in which Buchner, Dehn, Fritsch, and others used cosmopolitanism as a code for the threat of Jewish economic power, for the circulation of Jews—who in turn lived from the circulation and recirculation of goods and capital—and for the associated danger to existing German businesses, rooted in worthy but threatened German craft traditions. This dichotomy drew on images popularized by Gustav Freytag's 1855 *Soll und Haben* (*Debit and credit*), which chronicles the rivalry between an honorable, upright German merchant house and its hateful Jewish competition.[130] German businesses, so the logic goes, were fixed and embedded in long historical traditions, with close ties to communities and customers. The upstanding German *Mittelständler* worked with their hands and made an honest living through steady, careful production. The merchant stood behind his counter, wrote Werner Sombart in a 1908 article on advertising, and waited for his customers to come to him, "just as self-evidently as they went to his father

2.13 Anonymous, *From the Department Stores of Both Worlds: The Organization
of the Great Berlin, Parisian, and American Department Stores* (Berlin, 1908).
Bpk/Staatsbibliothek zu Berlin.

and grandfather."[131] The notion of "German work," the historian Sebastian Conrad writes, became increasingly bound up with anti-Semitic stereotypes in the late nineteenth century, which contrasted Germans' productive occupations with the haggling and profiteering of the Jews.[132]

The Jews, then, in contrast to German fixity, represented fluidity, flux, and circulation. Sombart characterizes this age of high capitalism as one of "nervous, feverish activity," a constant struggle to attract customers and outdo the competition.[133] He was one of many observers to point out commercial capitalism's acceleration of time, the lightning-fast decisions, rapidly changing fashions, and quick turnover of goods that marked department store consumption. "In the specialty shops the owner or the salesman often waits for the customer," wrote A. Waldmann in a 1932 article on the H. Tietz stores, "but in the department store the floor burns under your feet. There's no time to be tired."[134] Similarly, Kurt Pinthus contrasted the old-fashioned store in which customers rang a bell to alert a salesman, with the modern department store with its "whirring elevators" and the "guidance of the managers and porters that sets the public masses in motion, in ceaseless circulation through the labyrinth of sales counters, which itself is a component of this perpetual mobility [*Perpetuum mobile*] which we call the rhythm of the metropolis."[135] The department store, then, like the Jew, was restless and pulsating, just like the modern metropolis whose rhythms and tempos it reflected and helped constitute.

For Sombart, the department store emphasized the profit principle above all else, and thus its directors were constantly trying to expand, to add new departments and to increase earnings, hence the notion of its frenetic dynamism and ceaseless growth. Old retail looked backward, and was firmly rooted in tradition; new retail, the department store above all, looked forward. Old retail had soul; new retail, intellect.[136] (Simmel, too, wrote of the intellectualism and calculability that capitalism requires of modern urban subjects at the expense of our "vital impulses" and "instinctive human traits."[137]) The juxtaposition of soul and tradition with intellect and modernity is vividly expressed in Margarete Böhme's *W.A.G.M.U.S.*, in which the department store run by Israel Manasse and later his son Josua Müllenmeister—who converts to Christianity and takes his non-Jewish wife's surname, lest anti-Semitism interfere with his business plans—expands and innovates breathlessly, taking risks, overwhelming smaller businesses and annexing their buildings. "The house," Böhme writes, "grew and grew, grew monstrously [*ins Ungeheuer*], grew still more, without coming to rest, without stopping."[138]

Meanwhile, the gentile shoemaker, Manasse's erstwhile friend Ribbeck, stubbornly clings to his old ways, emphasizing craft over business and tradition over growth, even as his business slowly dries up in the face of new commercial realities. Josua Müllenmeister, much like Mouret in *The Ladies' Paradise*, operates his business through ceaseless expansion and innovation, culminating in the construction of the W.A.G.M.U.S.—Warenhaus Aktien-Gesellschaft

Müllenmeister und Söhne (Müllenmeister and Sons Department Store Inc.)—an enormous and bold new emporium that required extraordinary amounts of capital and represented a tremendous risk. As Josua's son Friedrich points out, "Wagmus" could be broken down into the words *Wagen* (to risk/dare/bet) and *Müssen* (must), a succinct expression of the Jewish businessman's credo.

In a 1906 book about the clothing industry in Berlin, Moritz Loeb described the fashion business as inherently speculative and risky and subject to sudden, unpredictable changes. It was thus a stressful, nerve-taxing industry that took its toll on those involved in it. Consequently, the fashion trade, a sector dominated by Jews, was known as a "nervous" field, and the directors of Berlin's major houses were twitchy, anxious men, gamblers and players, furthering the association between Jews, nervousness, and risk in turn-of-the-century Europe.[139] Even Max Weber wrote about Jewish "adventurer capitalism," which he contrasted to Puritan notions of work.[140] Zola also echoes these associations about Jews, capitalism, and risk. Mouret, his non-Jewish protagonist, calls himself "more Jewish than all the Jews of the world" when he undertakes an enormously ambitious and risky expansion of his store.[141]

In Sigfrid Siwertz's novel *The Great Department Store*, Jeremias Goldmann, one of the richest men in Sweden and the proprietor of Stockholm's most magnificent department store, is plagued by (apparently baseless) financial insecurity, a fear that his business could fail at any moment and that his riches are simply speculative and lacking any actual value. This was a typical Jewish anxiety, according to Goldmann's associate, a collective unease that resulted from generations of persecution and catastrophe, and of the need to keep moving and fleeing hostile lands. In other words, it is part of the Eastern Jewish experience. But it is not a bad thing. Indeed, it is this insecurity that leads the Jewish store owner to expand, innovate, and risk. "Here this same anxiety," Goldmann's colleague muses, "has built up a retail palace."[142] Goldmann's associate is rehearsing a point made by Sombart and others, namely Jewish conditions—in this case, Jewish insecurity and restlessness—bred a remarkable affinity with modern commercial capitalism.

Werner Sombart characterized Jews as restless, mobile merchants, as circulating economic actors, whose nomadic roots prepared them for the restive commercial activity of the modern city. Furthermore, the Jews' intellectualism and ability to calculate—stemming from centuries of desert life and the need to keep track of flocks of sheep—endowed them with a cold commercial acumen that found expression in modern business techniques.[143] Sombart's ruminations about the Jews falls into an interpretive tradition that traces back to Marx and all the way forward to the historian Yuri Slezkine, who labels this cluster of characteristics "Mercurian" in his 2004 book *The Jewish Century*.[144] (Not coincidentally, the Schocken stores were renamed "Merkur"—Mercury—after the swift-footed god of commerce when they were Aryanized in 1939, and the Wertheim store on Leipziger Strasse featured a Mercury gargoyle on a side facade.) Sombart wrote extensively on the Jews' affinities for capitalism and their role in modernizing European economies.[145] Despite—or perhaps because of—Sombart's unflattering depiction of the Jewish influence on European economic life, his writings were well received by Zionists who sought to expose Jews to work that was physically and spiritually healthier than commercial capitalism and speculation.[146] Arthur Ruppin, an important Zionist official and pioneer of the field of Jewish sociology, wrote in 1930 that "the Jews are more mobile, more nervous, more excitable than their neighbors, especially the Northern Europeans," qualities that predisposed them to "business, to the highs and lows of the daily business cycle."[147]

Lacking Sombart's sophisticated theoretical and historical framework and his dispassionate approach, Buchner also portrayed Jews as economic modernizers, as the bearers of the anonymous, objectifying tendencies of the market economy. He excoriated the Jew as no more than a mediator between producers and consumers, an agent of the circulation of goods and capital and therefore an economic parasite. One of the many flaws in this specious argumentation, it bears pointing out, is that major department stores such as Karstadt, Schocken, and Hermann Tietz built up their own manufacturing sites and produced a significant portion of the goods they sold. Karstadt alone operated over one hundred factories by 1927.[148]

Though the critical assessments of German department stores we have canvassed in this and the preceding chapter were saturated with vicious anti-Semitic stereotypes and had at best dubious basis in fact, they nevertheless merit closer scrutiny. I suggest that the department store in effect gave institutional form to certain Jewish economic roles—Jewish not in any essentialist way, and certainly not as a function of their origins or racial composition, but Jewish in the sense that Jews often filled distinct economic niches in premodern Europe and through the eighteenth and nineteenth centuries. Prohibited from tightly regulated guilds, Jews were prevented from becoming landowners or laborers in most European contexts and had little choice but to innovate and take risks to achieve economic stability and social mobility. Jews in Prussia's Polish provinces, furthermore, where many department store families originated, were seasoned at bridging cultural worlds. Their livelihood depended on mediating between producers and consumers, on the ability to transport goods across borders and communicate and do business with Polish villagers, Ukrainian peasants, German burghers, and others. The department store in a sense institutionalized the circulation of the itinerant peddler, bringing diverse goods and populations together under one roof, but in a setting where the consumers, modern mobile spectators, circulated around stationary displays of commodities that had come to rest after their long journeys.

As we have seen, Köhrer, in *Warenhaus Berlin*, compared living in the modern metropolis to being in a department store. Both settings are characterized by speed, fleeting stimuli, crushes of people, and the need to act quickly without time for reflection. Kurt Pinthus recalled that the department store has a rhythm like a world unto itself, one formed by the unity of its various departments and the speed and constant motion of customers and salespeople. When the poetic narration in Feuchtwanger's "Warenhaus-Revue" enters the department store, the stage notes tell us that the music switches to jazz, for what other form of music could capture a department store's pulsating rhythms, its modernity, its international dimensions, and its relentless motion? Jazz, like the modern German department store—oscillating between tight organization and explosive desire—harnessed an energy that was at once highly regimented and wildly unpredictable.

3 UNCANNY ENCOUNTERS

The Thief, the Shopgirl, and the
Department Store King

In my opinion, one cannot overestimate the influence of the department store on women.

—*Hans-Bernd Thiekötter (1933)*

Purpus—for women that is not a department store. . . . Purpus is the name of a man who adorns them and dresses them, who adorns them tenderly and dresses them lovingly, and to whom it matters not if they are customers or employees.

—*Wilhelm Stücklen (1918)*

Emil Kläger's 1933 play *Incident in the Department Store*, like so many other plays, novels, stories, and films that take place in a department store, includes among its characters a shoplifter and a store detective. In this case, Herr Kaliwoda, an employee at the Kreis department store in a city that closely resembles Vienna, observes Grace, a bourgeois woman, engaged in suspicious behavior. He escorts her to a special room for questioning and examination. Grace cooperates, digs into her handbag, and gamely hands over a swath of silk, some stockings, a pair of gloves, and a nickel-plated watch. She knows the drill; evidently this is not the first time that she has been apprehended. The salesman accuses her of also having stolen the fine outfit she is wearing, but she denies that adamantly. At this point a police inspector appears. He tells Kaliwoda that he has been on the woman's trail for some time, and that she habitually grabs cheap wares and hides them under her shawl. Grace wearily informs the inspector that it would be pointless to arrest her, for reasons that will soon become clear.

To this point nothing distinguishes this case from the numerous others that appeared in the mainstream press, medical and psychiatric literature, department store and retail trade journals, and contemporary fiction, beginning in the 1890s with the emergence of the major urban department store in Germany and waning by the 1930s. All of the outlines of the event conform neatly to the basic profile of the kleptomaniac, who was, according to general psychiatric consensus, usually, although not always, a woman, and typically a woman of some means who stole for psychological reasons as opposed to economic necessity.[1] The value of the items she pocketed was generally negligible, but she was driven by some kind of irrepressible compulsion and in some cases accumulated enormous collections of stolen wares, once taken, no longer desired, and often heaped up in piles, even occupying entire rooms at her (often spacious) residence.

Kläger's version, however, deviates from the typical profile when we learn that Grace is married to a Monsieur Malinet, a mysterious French scientist who happens to be a co-owner of the department store. In fact, Malinet invested in the store for this very reason—that is, so that his wife could have a safe venue for practicing her habit. When Kreis, his partner and the store's majority owner, learns all of this, he is impressed by Malinet's ingenuity. "So that your bride may have a regular spot [*Stammlokal*] for her passions . . . stealing in her own department store. A brilliant solution!"[2]

Frau Malinet's case, absurd as it is, reveals a great deal about the kleptomania phenomenon and contemporary perceptions of department stores and theft. It suggests that a kleptomaniac's drive to steal was seen as a powerful urge, one that could not be suppressed, and could, at best, be channeled into a safe environment without legal consequence or embarrassment. In his 1907 work on department store theft, the psychiatrist Leopold Laquer reported that when a major department store opened in a central German city, a high-ranking municipal official asked its owner proleptically to bill him for any items that his wife might steal.[3] Apparently the man knew his wife's tendencies, correctly anticipated her behavior, and created acceptable conditions for its pursuit.

Incident in the Department Store, although certainly somewhat satirical, is also consistent with psychiatric and psychoanalytic writings from the 1920s and early 1930s, which emphasized the sexual dimensions of the shoplifting act. Filled with frank dialogue about sexuality and modern gender roles, the play signals an awareness of psychoanalysis and also raises broader issues around gender, sexuality, and commodification. Kläger's stage notes, for example, describe Grace Malinet as appearing elegant, but nervous, sexually pathological and prone to hysteria, suggesting that she may be erotically unfulfilled and implying that her shoplifting tendencies worked as a kind of compensation for her frustrated erotic urges. The end result, in any case, is a brilliant solution for Grace (as for the city official's wife in Laquer's account). The department store then has been transformed into a woman's fantasyland, a zone for the free expression of her otherwise frustrated desires.

A German play from fifteen years earlier, *Purpus*, by Wilhelm Stücklen, deals with many of the same themes. It also features a store investigator very busy with shoplifters; he announces in the opening scene that he had caught twenty-seven female thieves the preceding day. In this play, department store owner T. T. Purpus, a professed lover of all women, pines away for a young lady whom he has observed but whose name and whereabouts are unknown to him. Obsessively smitten, he waits, confident that she, like all women, will inevitably return to his store. When she fails to appear he concludes that the store lacks the necessary magnetic pull. Hence Purpus decides to expand and enhance his department store, to make it so enticing that no woman could resist it. "And eventually," he continues, "I practiced the dodgiest schemes for luring women in. Only women!"[4]

Purpus finally does meet the young woman again, but under quite unexpected circumstances. The object of his longing, the twenty-four-year-old Hulle, is apprehended by the store inspector for stealing. Once seen, she throws the stolen objects at the inspector's face and makes for the window with the intention of jumping out. Purpus intervenes in the proceedings. Recovering from the shock of recognizing her, he treats her graciously and sympathetically. Learning that she is engaged to an unemployed salesman, Purpus hires her fiancé in order to keep her close to the store. As Purpus relentlessly pursues Hulle's affections, Orge, the fiancé, is caught embezzling, hoping to become rich for Hulle's sake. (Purpus had put him in a situation where he could easily be tempted.) Hulle, who had been flirting rather brazenly with Purpus, does not return the director's affections, the plan fails miserably, and Hulle, enraged, accuses Purpus of "tempting away young men [so that] you may steal their brides."

In both *Incident in the Department Store* and *Purpus*, women are portrayed as constitutionally unable to resist the department store and the lure of its wares. The two dramas present the department store as a place created for women, a safe setting for the fulfillment of their needs and the satisfaction of their desires. At once a woman's space, an "Adamless Eden" in the words of American entrepreneur Edward Filene, the department store was simultaneously a space created and managed by men who profited enormously from women's presence and purchasing power.[5] At first glance a safe and respectable place for women, it was also a dangerous space, where women could be preyed upon by lecherous store owners, where hidden threats and dangers lurked, and where the frightening power of women's dormant desires was aroused and unleashed.

In this chapter I treat the department store as a woman's space, foregrounding the tension between female safety and danger and between women's emancipation and their exploitation both in concrete social terms and in the realm of visual and literary representations. It is a place that shifts the boundaries between public and private and puts private, intimate acts on public display, encouraging highly charged, erotic, and even eerie encounters of various kinds, between (women) shoppers and goods and between men and female employees and even mannequins. I characterize these encounters as "uncanny," or eerie in the sense of Freud's term *unheimlich*, to evoke the dark and supernatural forces believed to be at work in and behind the department store, a notion that appears again and again in contemporary fiction, in anti–department store materials, and even in medical and psychiatric writings. The uncanny, which for Freud was closely connected to the compulsion to repeat and the death drive, also ties into the behavior of many women consumers, their alleged inability to stay away from the department store and their purported urge to visit it and revisit it daily or even multiple times a day.[6] The uncanny or *unheimlich*, Freud argues, also connects to its ostensible antonyms, *heimlich* (and *heimelich* or *heimelig*), words denoting home or familiarity. In this sense the department store becomes a woman's home, an alternative domestic space and simultaneously a place for uncomfortable, dangerous, and even violent occurrences and encounters.[7]

The discussion that follows concentrates on three interrelated topics: the kleptomania panic, the shopgirl or *Verkäuferin*, and finally, the prostitute and the mannequin, two liminal figures that embodied women's dual position as consumers and as objects to be consumed. Linking these topics is the perception of the department store as a morally (and indeed physically) corrosive environment that had the power to corrupt formerly upstanding employees and customers. Concerns about Jews, Jewish power, and Jewish masculinity run through and inhere in discourses on the gendering and eroticization of the department store space. And at the center of any discussion of these subjects stands the (Jewish) department store king, a stock character in department store fiction and theater, and an object of fascination, admiration, and fear in a wide range of contemporary accounts.

Many of these themes had already found expression in the original department store novel, Émile Zola's *The Ladies' Paradise*; they reverberate throughout the book's rich descriptive passages, as in the following example: "And if, in the shops, Woman was queen, adulated and humored in her weaknesses, surrounded with attentions, she reigned there as an amorous queen, whose subjects traded on her, and who pays for every whim with a drop of her own blood." Like T. T. Purpus, Zola's store owner Mouret devoted enormous energies to luring women into his ever-expanding store, simultaneously adoring and destroying them: "Beneath the very charm of his gallantry, Mouret thus allowed the brutality of a Jew selling Woman by the pound to show through; he was building a temple to Woman, making a legion of shop assistants burn incense before her, creating the rites of a new cult . . . and behind her back, when he had emptied her purse and wrecked her nerves, he was full of the secret scorn of a man to whom a mistress had just been stupid enough to yield."[8] Not himself a Jew, Mouret is depicted as seeming Jewish as he at once worships women and exploits them for his own profit. In the words of a German commentator, "Colossal creations like the huge department store are [made] from the flesh and blood of woman. There lies the secret of their success."[9]

The Thieves' Paradise: Shoplifting, Kleptomania, and Magasinitis

Kleptomania, as a psychiatric diagnosis, predates the appearance of department stores by decades. It was christened in the early nineteenth century by André Matthey, a French psychiatrist, who belonged to the circle of doctors around Jean-Étienne Dominique Esquirol at the center of French mental medicine. Esquirol and his students innovatively called attention to the role of the mind and "the passions" in triggering mental illnesses and created new syndromes and disease entities, primarily the manias, around pathological behaviors, ideas, or delusions. This was the context for the emergence of "klopemania," as Matthey labeled the phenomenon, until his colleague C.-C. Marc modified it to kleptomania.[10]

Among Matthey's lasting contributions were the stipulations that kleptomaniacs tended to come from the upper classes—Victor Amadeus, king of Sardinia, and the sister of the lord mayor of Edinburgh were particularly noteworthy cases—and that the objects they stole were usually valueless and inconsequential, hence distinguishing acts of kleptomania from the desperate, economically motivated crimes of the underclass.[11] The explanation of a store detective in a 1926 novel succinctly illustrates the distinction: "A kleptomaniac is a rich person who steals something he could get without stealing. It's called theft when someone takes something that they wouldn't have been able to get any other way." The detective recounts an incident in which he had observed a refined lady letting "black silk stockings of the nicest sort disappear into her bag."[12] He followed her home only to discover that she was the wife of one of the country's most important judges.

Shoplifting and what was later construed as kleptomania certainly occurred in a variety of retail settings before the emergence of department stores, but the department store occupies a special position in the history of kleptomania. The abundance of wares, unrestricted entry, and direct access to goods—especially before the widespread use of glass display cases in the early twentieth century—the vast, bustling crowds, and the anonymity of the shopping floors all must have contributed to making the department store the "paradise of kleptomaniacs and thieves."[13]

While men were also known to steal, the shopping floors of the department store were seen as women's spaces. As numerous contemporaries observed, male shoppers tended to enter, make planned purchases, and depart, while female shoppers often lingered for hours, taking advantage of the stores' many attractions and services. In the words of the fictional Purpus, "The gentlemen are such uninteresting buyers. They always know what they want before they enter, and you can't mislead them. They only buy with their heads [Verstand], while women buy with all five senses."[14] Store attractions were in fact usually designed for women and intended to cater to their senses. Department store cafés welcomed even unaccompanied women on a break from shopping, in contrast to typical urban cafés, and many stores also featured powder rooms and other services intended to pamper women and make them relaxed, comfortable, and carefree.[15] Since a loitering man would have aroused suspicion, department stores typically hired female detectives who could roam the shopping floors inconspicuously. Men were often associated with directing organized crime rings that used women or store employees to do the actual stealing, but they were seldom implicated in the impulsive acts associated with kleptomania or pathological shoplifting. Male crime, like men's purchasing, was typically portrayed as rational, premeditated, and purposeful, in contrast to the irrational action of the female consumer and shoplifter.

Contemporaries often pointed out that women's accessories facilitated department store theft. Handbags, shawls, and loose frocks provided easy cover for stolen trinkets, pieces of fabric, watches, or knickknacks, and women were even caught hiding stolen goods in their hair or wrapping them up in blankets with their babies.[16] "When you see a sleeve or skirt noticeably sagging in one spot," wrote Leo Colze, "you can be sure that 'there's a secret hidden inside.' "[17] Another common trick, one that required a bit more premeditation, involved carrying empty packages or hatboxes into an establishment and surreptitiously filling them or switching their contents with goods from the store. A 1910 article reported on such creative techniques as the use of suitcases with false bottoms and a rather outlandish scheme that made use of a gloved, artificial hand that enabled the thief's actual hand, secretly ensconced in her overcoat, to emerge far enough to pull objects into the pockets.[18]

Hard-core shoplifters and thieves might attempt to steal in any number of environments, but there was a whole class of women who, according to psychiatric observation, only stole in the department stores.[19] Department stores generally kept quiet about theft to avoid bad publicity and apparently also to prevent gaining the reputation that they were easy to steal from. Suspected shoplifters were typically brought into a private room where they were searched and questioned in a polite, businesslike manner. If the suspicion was confirmed, the thief was asked not to return to the store.[20] At that point, in most cases, the matter was laid to rest. Since store authorities generally reported only repeat offenders and habitual criminals to the police, it is impossible to provide a statistical account or to know just how great a problem department store theft actually presented. Furthermore, police records did not separate department store theft from general larceny, so they provide little insight into the actual extent of the problem.[21]

Leo Colze simply concluded that each store had to accept a certain percentage loss through theft in its yearly budget calculations. Other anecdotal evidence includes the report from a major Cologne department store that on busy days typically dozens of pairs of stockings and about twelve silk garments for men were taken.[22] Several authors pointed out that department store theft was more rampant in Berlin than in other parts of Germany, rehearsing the well-worn theme that the metropolis posed particular dangers or perhaps simply alluding to the observation that the greater anonymity of the big city and the massive size of its department stores made it more conducive to the shoplifting act. Colze, for example, noted that ninety-six thieves were apprehended in Berlin's department stores just in the days leading up to

Entlarvte Ladendiebinnen.

In demselben Maße, in dem das Warenhaus die Kauflust der Damen im allgemeinen weckt, üben die offen zur Schau gestellten Kostbarkeiten ihre suggestive Anziehungskraft auch auf jene Elemente aus, die es verstehen, sich in den Besitz eines gewünschten Gegenstandes zu setzen, ohne den üblichen Weg der Zahlung zu wählen: auf das große Heer der Ladendiebinnen. Die Warenhausdiebin ist erfinderisch, schlau und verwegen; mit Leichtigkeit gelingt es ihr zumeist, die Wachsamkeit der jungen, unerfahrenen Verkäuferin zu täuschen, und selbst dem geübten Auge des Berufsdetektivs entzieht sich oft mit Hilfe genial

Der Trick mit dem Koffer ohne Boden.
Dieser Koffer wird über andere kleinere Koffer oder Gegenstände gestülpt, die dann durch eine Vorrichtung darin festgehalten werden.

Entlarvte Ladendiebinnen: Die künstliche Hand,
ein Hilfsmittel der Gaunerinnen.

ausgedachter „Tricks". Einige von diesen seien hier erklärt und hoffentlich unwirksam gemacht. Einer der beliebtesten und verbreitetsten ist der sogenannte „Muff-Trick": In dem Futter eines Muffes ist unauffällig eine Diebstasche angebracht, in die kleinere Gegenstände, gewöhnlich Bijouterien und Juwelen, vom Ladentisch versenkt werden können, ohne daß die Verkäuferin, mit der die Diebin harmlos plaudert, mehr merkt als eine leichte Bewegung des ruhig auf dem Tisch liegenden Armes der Kundin. — Sehr beliebt ist auch der „Trick der dritten Hand". Er besteht, wie die hier reproduzierten Photographien zeigen, darin, daß in dem Aermel einer Damen-

Die künstliche, mit einem Handschuh bekleidete Hand
bleibt zur Täuschung des Verkäufers unbeweglich und sichtbar, während die rechte Hand der Diebin, unter dem Jackett versteckt, die Beute packt.

gut tun, allzu ruhigen Händen mit dem gleichen Mißtrauen zu begegnen, wie auffallend geschäftigen. — Wenn es sich darum handelt, größere Gegenstände zu stehlen, wird oft ein offener Koffer oder Karton ohne Boden angewandt, den die Diebin über das zu stehlende Gut, oft auch über ein von einer anderen Dame im Erfrischungsraum sorglos neben ihn hingelegtes Paket stülpt. Natürlich ist die Warenhausdiebin stets elegant gekleidet; je vornehmer sie aussieht, desto unbeobachteter kann sie ihre Diebstähle ausführen, und desto weniger wird man es wagen, sie zu verdächtigen.

Die Diebstasche im Jackett.

jacke oder eines Capes eine künstliche Hand befestigt wird, während die natürliche Hand und der Arm der Diebin unter dem Kleidungsstück verborgen bleiben. Die künstliche Hand ist mit demselben Handschuh bekleidet, den auch die sichtbare echte Hand trägt, und ruht bewegungslos auf einem Stück Stoff oder auf einer kostbaren Spitze auf dem Verkaufspult, indes die Diebin unter ihrer Jacke die verborgene „dritte Hand" eifrigst dazu benützt, den Gegenstand, der ihr Gefallen erregt hat, in der Diebestasche des Jackenfutters zu verbergen. Die Verkäuferin wird von diesem Vorgang nur in den seltensten Fällen etwas bemerken, sie kann auch wohl kaum Verdacht schöpfen, denn sie hatte ja beide Hände der Kundin unausgesetzt beobachten können! Auch für einen etwa aufgestellten Aufseher im Rücken der diebischen Kundin bleibt das Manöver völlig unsichtbar. Die Verkäuferinnen werden also

Der Muff als Deckung für die diebische Hand.

3.1 "Store thieves exposed," from *Die praktische Berlinerin* 34 (1910), 11.

Christmas. Another study estimated that Tietz's Berlin stores had to reckon with several hundred cases per year; and the dramatic claim circulated that so much was stolen from Wertheim's flagship store on Leipziger Strasse that it would be enough to stock a whole store.[23] In Oscar Schweriner's 1912 novel *Arbeit: Ein Warenhausroman* (Work: A department store novel), Herr Heimberg reckoned that his store (the fictional Warenhaus Heimberg) lost a thousand marks a day to theft.[24] The ten plainclothes officers supplied by the police department and his own staff of twenty female detectives were a mere "drop in the ocean." This was a work of fiction to be sure, but like several other department store novels the text clearly indicates that Schweriner had carefully researched his topic. While the sum itself has little credibility, it does indicate the extent of contemporary concern. Finally, the historian Uwe Spiekermann has estimated that around two thousand women stole from department stores in Germany each year in the later 1890s, a useful figure but, as he concedes, an extremely rough estimate at best.[25]

The ubiquitous references to shoplifting and kleptomania in contemporary writings suggest that these topics were very much on the minds of department store owners and the stores' critics, and as Elaine Abelson shows for the United States, the kleptomaniac became a widespread motif in the period's popular culture.[26] Kleptomania was even the subject of one of the earliest American films, Edwin S. Porter's *The Kleptomaniac* (1905), which contrasted the fate of a wealthy lady who is exonerated after stealing from a department store (Macy's at New York's Herald Square) with a poor woman who takes a loaf of bread out of desperation and suffers the consequences.[27] In *The Ladies' Paradise*, Zola's department store owner expresses exasperation at the vast sums he loses to shoplifters. Zola apparently had read contemporary psychiatrists as part of his painstaking research, and his protagonist describes kleptomania as a "new kind of neurosis which had been scientifically classified by a mental specialist who saw it as a symptom of the acute temptation exercised by the big shops."[28]

Kleptomania, like the department stores themselves, came to Germany a little later than it appeared in France and the United States, but was attracting attention by the first decade of the twentieth century, the time when the major French medical treatises were being translated into German. *Kleptomanie: Schwank in einem Aufzug* (Kleptomania: An elevator story), by Max Hartung, a 1900 play that might be the first work of fiction or drama in German to deal with the phenomenon, begins with a young woman reading about a case of shoplifting in the newspaper. In this case, an elegantly clad lady had grabbed a child's jacket on her way out of a linen and fabric store.[29] The humor magazine *Lustige Blätter* (Funny pages) devoted a special issue to the topic in 1906 with short stories, puns, vignettes, and cartoons, suggesting that kleptomania was very much on the minds of the magazine's bourgeois readers by then.[30]

Kleptomania reached German medicine just as psychiatry was undergoing rapid professional expansion and effectively asserting its authority on legal questions and in political affairs. This was also a moment of major diagnostic upheaval. German mental medicine, chiefly under the influence of the Munich psychiatrist Emil Kraepelin, had begun to simplify and rationalize its diagnostic approach and broke down mental illnesses into several major categories based on their patterns, course, and prognosis. In this context, kleptomania lost its status as a malady unto itself and came to be seen as a tendency or drive, a behavior exhibited by patients with pathological personality types.[31] Hence, in psychiatric terms a person did not suffer from kleptomania per se, but rather succumbed to certain impulses due to a weak or compromised mental and nervous constitution.

In the discourse of German psychiatry, then, kleptomania depended on two factors: the subject's disposition on the one hand, and, on the other, the environment or the influences that might trigger the behavior. Mental constitution and disposition were, of course, vague concepts that resisted clear definition and could never be empirically established. This diagnostic position also left open several key questions: Could kleptomaniacs be held accountable for their actions? The department store's livelihood depended on its ability to pull customers in and stimulate their desire for goods, so could the store be blamed for turning shoppers into shoplifters? What caused healthy consumer desire to lead to pathological acts, and where did the boundary between them lie?

Psychiatric experts weighed in on this question in various ways, and their descriptions dovetailed with other contemporary discourses on the department store's powers, on its magnetic pull, and indeed on the dangers of female desire. Several doctors characterized the female shopper's state as akin to a hypnotic trance: she was easily mesmerized by the goods for sale, the fantastic displays, and the distractions and stimuli of the store environment. The stores exerted "an intoxicating and dizzying effect" on customers, wrote psychiatrist Gerhard Schmidt.[32] "The temperature, the sounds, smells, colors, and lights bring about a clouding of the consciousness. . . . They even call forth a hypnotic-like state, in which the impulse theft is conceived."[33] Similarly, in his description of the department store's effect on the psyche, Emil Raimann noted, "One can only think of hypnosis: the tiring of the eyes and the ears are old, well-known methods, the fixation on a glittering object can bring forth a state of autohypnosis. . . . In women with such a disposition, and here one must include a great many psychopaths, the department store easily creates a state of consciousness that is comparable, at least, to the early stage of hypnosis."[34]

Such perspectives reflected the contemporary fascination with hypnosis in medicine and popular culture. Fears of hypnosis-induced crime overtook the French and German imagination in the early twentieth century, as traveling hypnotists dazzled audiences, and doctors experimented with scientific applications of the technique.[35] Like the hypnotized killers of film and scandal sheets of the time, department-store consumers were allegedly plunged into a dream-like state in which they lost control of themselves and had at best a partial awareness of what they were doing. In more recent popular culture, reflecting the influence of Frankfurt-school-style mass-culture critiques, shoppers in department stores and malls are often equated with zombies, represented as brainless or semiconscious beings manipulated by the predatory forces of commodity culture and advertising.[36] The kleptomaniac, then, embodies the extreme case of the culture industry's victimization, where the impulse to consume has overridden all normal boundaries and checks. Manipulated by the power of advertising and the department store's allure, the consumer loses herself in the irrational human stream, the frenzied, hysterical masses who crowded around shop windows and pressed at the store's gates.

For psychoanalyst Wilhelm Stekel, "all kleptomaniacs are daydreamers."[37] Those caught shoplifting frequently testified that they "lost their heads, what with the crush of people and the glittering lights, and didn't even know what they were doing," that "their vision got cloudy as they looked at the object," or that a strange feeling came over them and intensified with each additional step.[38] The term often used to describe this state, again borrowed from the French, was "magasinitis," or department store / market affliction.[39] Magasinitis denoted this feeling of numbness or intoxication that apparently came over women in the department store and compelled them to transgress. In his 1907 treatise, the most authoritative German text on kleptomania and department stores, Leopold Laquer described magasinitis as a kind of poisoning or contamination.[40] Writing the same year in a women's periodical, Dr. Caius Nordmann characterized magasinitis as the dark side of the department store's excitement and wonder. Normal, healthy people could handle the intense covetousness that the department store aroused, but for weaker women, he warned, the store milieu obliterated their resistance and plunged them into an acquisitive frenzy.[41]

Such accounts placed a good deal of the blame for shoplifting on the department stores themselves and the environment that their owners and managers intentionally created. In the words of a French psychiatric commentator: "It is impossible to spend time in one of these enormous establishments without feeling . . . a very particular sense of nervous depletion, of physical exhaustion and stupefaction. The sights, the atmosphere, the aroma, our delicate senses quickly become exhausted in this swarming, raucous, aromatic mass; you become fatigued very quickly, whether you stay calmly in place or circulate even a little."[42] For Hans-Bernd Thiekötter, author of a 1933 law dissertation, "The Psychological Roots and Penal Status of Department Store Theft," the whole point of a department store was to lure women in and arouse their desires. Department store owners, he claimed, knew that women were less in control of their desires than men and that fancy displays and attractive products created cravings in women who tended to leave the department store weighted down with much more than they originally intended to buy.[43]

Most women who entered the department store, of course, did not steal, but the idea that they were buying too much and the leitmotif of women bankrupting their husbands through their excessive spending appear throughout department store writing, again going back to Zola. Near the beginning of *Purpus*, to cite a German example, store owner T. T. Purpus hires a new worker for the establishment. Purpus explains to his assistant that the new employee had been brought to financial ruin by his wife's uncontrolled shopping at Purpus's store, and thus he had come to plead for a job. He argued that the only just thing to do would be for Purpus to help him get back on his feet by hiring him. Purpus concedes that the man's logic is "irrefutable."[44] A character in the Siwertz novel, a department store executive whose own wife had cost him a fortune with her uncontrolled spending, gamely accepted the irrational behavior of his "precious doll" (*teuere Puppe*), noting that the department store relied on female folly. It was, he maintained, something they counted on, a necessary part of the store's business plan.[45]

Shoplifting, then, represented the extreme end of a spectrum and was seen as the natural, if excessive, expression of women's powerful desire for goods, having been incited and unleashed by the department store. Uncontrolled, excessive buying, another recurring theme in discourses around the department store, lay on the same spectrum, a parallel response to the store's temptations and a similarly transgressive expression of these desires. When Purpus declares that stealing is ubiquitous, his detective, Kalender, shifts the blame back onto the store. Stealing may be ubiquitous, he responds, but "we use every means possible to get people all worked up."[46]

Kalender even doubts his own ability to withstand this intense seduction. In a similar vein, a 1900 newspaper article on the Tietz and Wertheim stores in Berlin claimed that the department store owner "has the woman caught in the trap. Now he can trust in the allure of a thousand ringed fingers tempting her to buy something, and he can be certain that even the most thrifty of housewives, who has come because of an unprecedented bargain, will go home weighed down with items she does not need."[47] A similar perspective can be found in Gustav Stresemann's description of a visit to Wertheim's Leipziger Strasse store in 1900:

> The time flies by as you look at the most diverse fabrics, at the outfits of the shopping ladies, the entertainment and everything else, and then when you suddenly look at the clock and realize that it's time to head home, you notice that instead of the necktie that you originally intended to buy, you are weighted down with a bundle of the most diverse items. For a while you feel remorse and vow not to be so frivolous again, but then as soon as you enter a department store for a small purchase the whole thing begins again anew.[48]

The itinerant preacher and lecturer Prentice Mulford, an American who traveled around Germany, wrote emphatically of his efforts to combat the "mysterious and dangerous influence that emerges from department stores, [the power] to make useless things seem desirable." Stresemann and Mulford indicate that men, too, were vulnerable to the department store's powers. Desperately trying to avoid buying something, Mulford recounted that he was only able to navigate through its "ocean of rubbish" by hoisting his "willpower sail" so that he did not succumb to the tremendous force of the store and its relentless salespeople.[49]

The notion that the department store was a trap that lured in and preyed upon innocent women drew on the same assumptions that animated the shopkeeper movement's anti–department store campaigns. Though anti-Semitic caricatures from those campaigns never made their way into the medical and psychological literature in an explicit way, anti–department store activists (anti-Semitic and not) used the perceived epidemic of kleptomania to further their cause, emphasizing the store's deleterious effects on women's behavior. For example, in his 1899 polemic against "grand bazaars" and "mass retail stores," Paul Dehn claimed that the stores turned women, especially vain and fashion-addicted women, into thieves.[50] With outrage he reported that department stores had to constitute their own security forces to deal with this raging problem of their own creation. Thus the implicit medical and psychiatric critique of department stores furthered belief in the mysterious and corrosive powers of these retail establishments and their owners. Dehn in particular made an explicit connection between Jewish store owners and shoplifting and warned about the power of Jewish men over German women.

Once inside the department store, some women were apparently unable to resist the operation of these powerful forces; but beyond that, psychiatrists suggested that certain women suffered from a kind of compulsion to return to the stores again and again. Laquer, for example, wrote of possession by a department store demon that compelled women to make multiple department store visits each day.[51] In a 1935 article, psychoanalyst Leo Deutsch presented two patients who suffered from this form of demonic possession, one of whom compared her affliction to possession by a Dybbuk, an evil spirit from Yiddish lore. And Caius Nordmann, in his 1907 article on kleptomania, referred to the "department store demon" as a "very dangerous seducer."[52] Significantly, these medical representations, with their references to the stores' supernatural forces and power to possess, shared a vocabulary with the propaganda pamphlets of the anti–department store movement, which also referred to the stores' uncanny atmosphere and their use of mystical, demonic forces to seduce and swindle.

Given the influence of the department store environment, the disorientation and hypnotic effect and the intense desire for goods provoked by displays and product promotion, why did some shoppers, especially women, give in to the temptation to steal while most were able to resist? Prevailing psychiatric opinion pointed to the influence of female anatomy and biology. The Italian psychiatrist and criminologist Cesare Lombroso, for example, noted "women's organic inability to resist stealing."[53] Acts of kleptomania, according to several studies, correlated directly with menstruation, pregnancy, and menopause. "Above all," wrote the anthropologist and physician Georg Buschan in his 1908 study of gender and crime, "department store theft is the typical crime of the menstruating woman."[54] Buschan cited a French investigation that found that 63 percent of apprehended shoplifters were menstruating.[55] For Leopold Laquer, menstruation, pregnancy, and even orgasm could cause women of relatively sound mental health to fall into a kind of stupor in which they steal.[56] And according to Thiekötter, "female department store thieves fight a continual battle with their desires, which appear with particular intensity during times of pregnancy, menstruation, or climax."[57]

Menstruating or menopausal women, then, along with pregnant, hysterical, and neurasthenic women were often seen as most suggestible and therefore most likely to succumb to the shoplifting temptation.[58] Or as the psychiatrist Arthur Leppmann put it in a 1901 lecture, neurasthenics, and especially women weakened by pregnancy or complications in childbirth, were the most vulnerable population.[59] It is no coincidence that kleptomaniacs were often discussed in the same context as prostitutes, another group that, as we will see, epitomized women's inability to control themselves and the perils of women mixing into the male economic sphere.[60]

These assumptions about the somatic basis of women's lack of self-control, based on long-standing medical tendencies to portray women as constitutionally inferior and even pathological, were reflected in popular culture as well.[61] Zola writes that Jouve, the venerable store detective in *The Ladies' Paradise*, always on the lookout for thieves, would "follow pregnant women, when the feverish look in their eyes made him suspicious."[62] The detective in Sigfried Siwertz's *The Great Department Store* similarly notes that women stole in far greater numbers than men and that the temptation of so many splendid wares grouped together, of glimpses of luxury in a time of deprivation—much of the story takes place during World War I—proved too great for women, and especially pregnant women, to resist.[63]

The crude stereotypes about women that dominated the discourse of kleptomania in Wilhelmine Germany began to change after the war. They had been based on archaic assumptions about women's constitutional inferiority and pathology, perspectives whose influence had begun to wane in the later nineteenth century. Not that medical misogyny had disappeared; rather belief in the somatic underpinnings of female inferiority had lost adherents as neurology and psychiatry took a more psychological turn in the first decades of the new century. References to the hysterical or neurasthenic nature of female shoplifters lingered well into the Weimar era, but the discourse was now more psychologically nuanced on the one hand and more sexualized on the other.[64]

Indeed, studies of kleptomania became a point where psychoanalysis and discourses around consumer culture converged. This convergence should not come as a surprise. Modern psychology and psychoanalysis, like advertising and consumer culture, were products of the late nineteenth century, and their developments were intertwined in the early twentieth. Psychoanalysis studies the way the mind handles desires; consumer culture arouses and channels desires, projecting affective attachments onto commodities. As Rachel Bowlby has written, "The marketing concern to discover what might persuade people to make purchases was intimately bound up, both institutionally and intellectually, with the contemporary psychoanalytical focus on the conscious and unconscious determinants of choices in life and love."[65]

Wilhelm Stekel, a rather unorthodox and "wayward" follower of Freud, framed psychiatric and psychoanalytic perspectives on the temptations of consumer goods for the interwar period. In his 1922 work on the psychology of impulsive acts, Stekel shifted the focus from the effects of the department store environment on the individual to the subject's internal state during the commission of the theft.[66] The term *Rausch* or *Berauschung*, which had been used to denote the intoxicating or numbing impact of the store, came to describe the mental state of the shoplifter as she committed her crime.

The 1915 novel *Der große Rachen* (The great gap), by Olga Wohlbrück, uniquely captures the voice of the shoplifter herself and tries to elucidate her perspective and mental state.[67] On the novel's first page Susanne Graebner, the bored and neglected wife of a music professor, is caught stealing by two female store detectives. Susanne had been more or less in a daze when it happened, and after the ordeal she asks herself how she could have done this and then thinks back to the first time that she stole. "There was no covetousness bound up with it and also no ghastly, shameful intentions. Just a peculiar feeling, a tingly sensation, an irresistible temptation to hold the glistening objects lying there and run them through my fingers."[68] The detective in Siwertz's *The Great Department Store* describes the would-be shoplifter's state in a similar way. "They get an itchy feeling in their fingers and then they can't stop themselves. That is the thief's nature."[69]

Stekel's psychoanalytic observations parallel these literary descriptions. The kleptomaniac, he claimed, steals for the act of stealing, for the transgressive thrill of crossing the line into forbidden behavior.[70] In contrast to earlier commentators, Stekel focused on the sensation of grasping goods, that is, the way they felt in the hand of a potential thief, which seems to be the motivating factor for Wohlbrück's and Siwertz's fictional characters. He also called attention to the choice of object and the symbolic meanings objects evidently carried, issues mostly ignored by his prewar predecessors. The theft of pencils and cigars and other phallic objects had an obvious symbolic meaning, Stekel noted. Hans-Bernd Thiekötter reviewed this list over a decade later and added that umbrellas, another commonly stolen item, unfolded in a manner that evoked the erect penis.

Stekel might have approved of a 1928 musical revue, *Es Liegt in der Luft* (It's in the air), a witty satirical comedy that takes place in a department store, with text by Marcellus Schiffer and music by Mischa Spoliansky.

The show, which featured Marlene Dietrich in its original cast, included a kleptomania song-and-dance number that begins with the "she" character recounting the universal joy of department store theft:

All women	Alle Frauen
who look at wares	welche Waren sich beschauen
love the feeling of stealing.	lieben das Gefühl zu klauen!

The song's chorus humorously reinforces the notion that kleptomania compensated for a lack of erotic fulfillment:

Such a thing lures us in hypnotically	Sowas zieht uns an hypnotisch
and satisfies us erotically!	und befriedigt fast erotish!
We have a little itch	Wir haben einen kleinen Stich
We steal like ravens!	wir stehlen wie die Raben!
In spite of the fact that	Trotzdem wir es ja eigentlich
None of us really need to!	gar nicht nötig haben!
We are driven not by financial need	Uns treibt nicht finanzielle Not
No, by an entirely different reason!	Nein, ein ganz anderer Grund!
We do it for sexual need!	Wir tun's aus sexueller Not!
But we're otherwise healthy. . . .	aber sonst fühln wir uns gesund
Such a thing lures us in hypnotically	Sowas zieht uns an hypnotisch
And satisfies us erotically!	und befriedigt fast erotisch![71]

Wilhelm Carlé's 1932 work, an unfinished novel called "The Escalator," provides another clear illustration of the psychological and sexual turn in the Weimar period's kleptomania discourse. The narrative begins with a store detective apprehending a kleptomaniac. As she starts to explain her irrepressible compulsion, the detective interrupts: "Examining the sexual-pathological dimensions behind your motivations would be a matter for a doctor," he intones, "and if that were our task, we'd have to open our own sanatorium."[72] Carlé gives his characters an awareness of and even a wariness toward these more sophisticated, nuanced, and sexualized perspectives.

A final literary example can be found in "Dienst am Kunden" (Customer service), an unpublished novella by Vicki Baum most likely from the 1930s or early 1940s that takes place in a New York department store. The protagonist, Mike Ingram, is a psychology graduate student doing field research in department store "Kietz," a pun on the name Tietz. The choice of name suggests that although the story is based in New York, the Vienna-born writer was thinking about Central European department stores, and it might signal that her perspective on department stores was shaped by her experiences in Germany in the late 1920s. For his fieldwork Ingram has invented for himself a job as the store's official sacrificial lamb. Whenever a shopper complains about poor service, Ingram is called in to the director's office and ceremoniously dressed down and dismissed, to the great satisfaction of the complaining customer.

The novella is full of psychological and psychoanalytic language; Ingram's doctoral thesis, for example, is called "Report on the Psychological Causes and Consequences of the Typical Neurotic Symptoms in the Female Consuming Public and Their Relationship to the Economic Structure of the U.S."[73] (With this Baum may have been gently mocking some of her fellow German-speaking émigrés who worked at the intersection of psychoanalysis and social theory.) Ingram hypothesizes that watching him being fired would satisfy most female consumers by giving them a sense of their own power and would validate their latent sadism. He claimed to observe this in action in well over a hundred cases. His provisional conclusion, which is alas finally undermined by a virtuous shopper who becomes his love interest, is that shopping in the department store gives women the illusion of power and allows them to express their sadistic tendencies. Although the novella does not deal with shoplifting, it nevertheless helps link our discussion of stealing and kleptomania to broader perspectives on women, sexuality, and power in the department store.

Similar terms appeared in German legal and psychiatric accounts during the interwar period. Drawing on the work of sexologist Otto Gross, both Stekel and Thiekötter equated the transgressive thrill of the kleptomaniac's act with the fulfillment of a repressed sexual wish. In an early case study, Stekel analyzed a seamstress who confessed to experiencing sexual arousal during the shoplifting act.[74] And in cases that bring to mind Frau Malinet from *Incident in the Department Store*, Stekel noted that department store theft could act as compensation for unfulfilled sexual urges. He pointed out that the cycle of expectation, tension, and release that accompanied a theft paralleled the experience of sex. Certain frequently stolen objects, furthermore, such as toys, along with shiny jewelry and other kinds of glittery knick-knacks, could be explained in terms of infantile regression, which again, in Freudian terms, is associated with the release of sexual energies.[75] Stekel, uniquely at the time, wrote of curing kleptomaniacs—in this case, through psychoanalysis—and also read the kleptomaniac's repetitive behavior in the context of Freud's repetition compulsion, that is, in terms of the economy of emotional energy served by the repetitious cycle of stealing and confessing.

Underlying both the more somatic prewar explanations and the psychological and psychoanalytic turn in the interwar period was the assumption that department stores caused, or at least catalyzed, unhealthy, untoward, and transgressive behaviors. The department store was conceived of as a woman's space, to be sure, but it was simultaneously seen as a potentially dangerous place that mesmerized and seduced its denizens, an artificial world that gave them a temporary and false sense of their own power for the enrichment of male businessmen. We have seen some of the ways that the stores were believed to be harmful to female shoppers and browsers, and this same tension—between the department store as a site of women's emancipation and independence and as a place for their corruption—inheres in the representation of female department store workers and, indeed, the iconic German shopgirl.

Shopgirls

In characterizing the department store as a women's space, we have thus far focused on the shoppers and the flâneurs, those customers and onlookers who frequented the department store, crowding around its display windows and filling its shopping floors. Women also constituted the great majority of department store workers by the early twentieth century. In the 1850s and '60s, when dry goods, linen, and clothing stores were still small-scale enterprises, employees were almost exclusively male. Generally the only women who worked in the stores were members of the owner's family. Employees lived in the stores, took their meals alongside family members, and often married into the family. However, as the stores expanded dramatically in the later nineteenth century, the older patriarchal model gave way to more modern business arrangements, and as women streamed into the growing white-collar sector in the later part of the century, sales jobs became increasingly female occupations. By the early twentieth century, saleswomen typically outnumbered men many times over, and while stores employed men to manage the selling of "masculine" goods like cigars, furniture, appliances, and of course men's suits, saleswomen filled most of the remaining departments.[76]

The modern department store thus presented a new phenomenon, a massive female workforce. By the early twentieth century, major urban department stores generally employed several thousand workers, and the majority, often more than two-thirds of the total, were women. Paul Göhre estimated, for example, that far more than 2,000 of the 3,200 employees at Wertheim's Leipziger Strasse store were women.[77] Julius Hirsch reported that in the Leonhard Tietz department stores, scattered around western Germany, more than 2,400 of the 3,000 total employees were women; and a 1908 study by the Association of German Department Store Owners found that a full 80 percent of department store employees throughout Germany were women.[78] Werner Sombart reported a similar, although slightly lower figure for the year 1925.[79] Finally, an article from 1931 estimated that there were more than 80,000 full-time female department store workers in the country.[80] A 1932 essay on the H. Tietz concern noted that the female workforce had grown from one single helper at the family's first store, in Gera, in 1882, to some 20,000 five decades later.[81]

Women worked in department stores in many capacities. Significant numbers of female employees performed clerical work in the stores' administrative offices, worked as store detectives, designed shop windows and in-store displays, and operated cash registers. Others answered the telephones, packed goods for delivery, ironed clothes, cooked for employees, and did custodial work. The highest rank that women employees could achieve in the major German department stores was that of *Aufsichtsdame*, or (female) supervisor, a job that carried significant power over the fates of the regular sales personnel and consequently was a role depicted in nearly all department store novels and stories from the period, and often portrayed as an intimidating and vindictive character.

Sales positions accounted for by far the single largest share of women workers. They made up some 43 percent, not including the large number of apprentices, of women employed at the L. Tietz stores in the early 1900s, and in the sales force women outnumbered men by a factor of eight to one in 1910.[82] "Young girls and women have a natural disposition for the sales profession," according to Kaufhaus Schocken's fifteen guidelines for sales personnel, a document written around 1926. "What task could be more natural for young females than . . . making carefully selected and tested wares available to the general public in an appropriate manner."[83] To be sure this occupation required knowledge, and Schocken, along with other companies, trained and educated their sales workers rigorously. However, the Schocken passage here seems to imply that women had a natural affinity for consumer goods and that there was a scientific basis for the strict division of department store labor. Salman Schocken rebuffed the concern that women workers were taking retail jobs away from men by avowing that women sales staff added to the "youth, beauty, and joy" of the department store environment. "I am convinced," Schocken wrote, "that if you took away the youth and freshness—which owes mostly to the women—you would diminish one of the chief advantages that department stores have over older forms of retail."[84]

Indeed, the saleswoman, or shopgirl, was also a figure that provoked elaborate fantasies across the spectrum of department store observers and resonated powerfully in popular culture. Karl Hubbuch's 1921 engraving *Der Traum des Tietzmädchens* (The dream of the Tietz girl) evokes the dark and disturbing currents in early Weimar culture. Hubbuch's work is a troubling, cluttered image, in which bodies and goods are thrown together in a crowded department store scene. The bodies, voluptuous shopgirls, some with modern *bubikopf* haircuts, are naked. The dummies are clothed. A naked male figure stands at the top of the steps and peers down blankly on the scene, perhaps supervising the proceedings. A bed in the lower left foreground might be where the dreaming Tietz girl is sleeping—and from its canopy she observes the room—and also seems to gesture at the connections between commercial culture, domesticity, and sexuality. In the words of the art historian Dorothy Rowe, who notes that Hubbuch's other subjects

3.2 Karl Hubbuch, *Der Traum des Tietzmädchens*, 1921. By permission of the Karl Hubbuch Foundation, Freiburg.

included prostitutes and shopgirls, "Headless mannequins are interspersed with the naked figures to evoke a surreal image of consumer desire in which female breasts and buttocks—interspersed among luxury fabrics, porcelain, shoes and other home-furnishing items—are foregrounded and displayed for the viewer's gaze and consumption."[85] The shopgirls' dream, then, a threatening vision of exploitation, is nonetheless served up for the consuming pleasure of a presumed male spectator.

Literary representations of the shopgirl trafficked in these themes, too, but generally stressed her youth and beauty, and sometimes also her humble, possibly provincial origins, her wholesome disposition, and her sensible, resourceful ways. Beyond this level of stereotype, department store fiction offered a variety of trajectories and outcomes. For every plot involving the ruin of an innocent salesgirl by the store's corrupting powers or a predatory boss, one can find a rags-to-riches story in which a good-hearted, innocent girl is rescued by the department store, which brings her happiness, security, and love. Her savior, often the store director, generally bears implicit or explicit Jewish characteristics and typically owns a villa in Berlin's affluent western surroundings. In the Weimar period, however, the department store novel is marked by a shift parallel and related to changing views of shoplifting. The innocent but naïve protagonists of the Wilhelmine-era works—though still very much alive in the melodramatic 1923 series *Süße Geschäftsmädels* (Sweet shopgirls)—gradually gave way to more sophisticated heroines who displayed an awareness of their own commodification and were able to use it to their advantage.

W.A.G.M.U.S., Margarete Böhme's 1911 novel, captures both sides of the shopgirl's experience and trajectory. Similar to *The Ladies' Paradise* in multiple ways and probably influenced by it, *W.A.G.M.U.S.* also expresses contemporary ambivalence about the department store. Böhme puts the case against department stores in the mouths of characters, and her narrative, like Zola's, shows these new retail establishments outcompeting long-standing specialty shops and thus threatening the livelihoods of worthy, traditional businessmen, a widely held, if inaccurate perspective. On the other hand, both novels revel in the department store's spectacular splendor and treat it as a sign of modernity, an irreversible development that, despite its lamentable consequences, ultimately had to be accepted and embraced.

W.A.G.M.U.S. portrays the plight of the department store shopgirl in particularly vivid terms. At a meeting of store employees, Frau Henriette Iversen, a longtime employee described as an old maid, works up the courage to address the crowd. Böhme writes, "She sketched with extraordinary eloquence the trajectory of the female department store employee. How they come into the establishment at sixteen or seventeen, with the color of youth in their unblemished faces, the brightness of life's joys in their eyes, a thousand hopes in their hearts . . . after two years the girl is a withered bud."[86] Frau Iversen goes on to describe the way in which the store dehumanizes its employees and robs them of their youth and their spirit. "The department store's hot, stimulating air has sucked the life out of her movements, the brightness out of her eyes. . . . She remains a shade plant her whole life, a tapped-out, spiritless being, a thing, an object, a depersonalized, mechanically functioning, wares-selling automaton, who says nothing and wants nothing, just does."[87]

In contrast to other occupations where employees establish increasing security and deeper roots if they remain in the same job for a long time, the department store, charged Frau Iversen, brought deepening insecurity with each passing year. By the time an employee is thirty-five, "she is withered, limp, a ruin. Perhaps one in ten find their way to a supervisory position, but the other nine are spit out, tossed out like cadavers into the street; the machine demands fresh fodder, young labor power. . . . The department store, which they serve, takes their best qualities away from them: their character, their will, that which distinguishes man from beast."[88]

Significantly, Frau Iversen does not argue that department store workers are exploited, that they are overworked and underpaid. Rather, she points to the dangers of the store environment and the enduring physical and psychological consequences of prolonged exposure. She describes the "enervating, effeminizing [*verweichlichende*] atmosphere that saps the physical strength from their [salesgirls'] bloodstream, devours their youth and beauty like a wild animal, strangles their entire personality, suffocates their soul, murders their self confidence."[89] Once young beauties, widely admired by men, these women elected to remain at the department store rather than marrying, a decision that, Iversen avers, leads to their gradual mental, physical, and spiritual destruction until they become too aged and unattractive for sales positions and are eventually discarded by their employer.

Given Iversen's scathing condemnation of the department store, her reconciliation with it a few scenes later comes as quite an unexpected plot turn. Josua Müllenmeister, now director of his father's store and the guiding force behind the new W.A.G.M.U.S.—in other words, the man ultimately responsible for her miserable situation—saves her. Having eavesdropped on her desperate peroration, and impressed by her savvy and intensity, Müllenmeister offers her a job as an undercover store detective to help deal with the increasing incidence of shoplifting, which, he correctly suspects, involves some of his own employees. Frau Iversen accepts the job and thrives in her new position, eventually catching the culprit and breaking up the ring. Yet the happy ending is unsatisfying, at least to today's reader. Frau Iversen's words hang in the air; that she is now an exception to the trajectory she identified scarcely nullifies the critique.

What Iversen's case does show is the power of the department store director or "king," as he is so often called, to destroy and to save (women's) lives. Elsewhere in the novel we read that "all of Berlin is subordinated to Müllenmeister . . . he is like a king who dictates the laws, to whom Berlin pays its taxes, who reigns over his people."[90] One finds this equation throughout the popular culture of the period, the department store director as king, as a Jewish king of Berlin, with awesome powers over the capital city's women. In Hans Fallada's best-selling 1932 Kleiner Mann—Was Nun? (What now, little man?), for example, Herr Lehmann, the imposing boss at Warenhaus Mandel, fires a shopgirl for having an affair with a male staff member (whom he also lets go), brandishing the power of the store (and its directors) over employees: "Mandel's department store feeds and clothes you, Mandel's department store makes your existence possible. It goes without saying that you need to think about Mandel's department store first in all of your doings."[91]

Just a few years before Böhme's W.A.G.M.U.S. was published, Leo Colze wrote in his little book on the KaDeWe: "There are four rulers in Berlin, uncrowned kaisers, whose iron dominion is heeded as widely as [Wilhelm II's]. . . . These uncrowned kaisers are the department stores: Jandorf, Tietz, Wertheim, and since roughly the beginning of the year, the Kaufhaus des Westens."[92] Near the end of W.A.G.M.U.S., the reader is told that since she was instated as house detective, Frau Iversen "revered the young boss like a demigod."[93] And in Erich Köhrer's Warenhaus Berlin, the owner Friedrich Nielandt relished standing alone on the store's balcony and peering over the space. It gave him a feeling of power, "like a ruler who had succeeded in subjugating a huge city with its millions."[94] The author describes Nielandt as a "dictator over the masses" who stream to him "like flies into a spider's web."[95]

Frau Iversen's dramatic indictment of the department store stresses the way it exploits young women, how it chews up its female employees who toil "from morning till evening for pennies while the colossal profits flow into Jewish wallets."[96] A related discourse charges that department stores were a physically unhealthy environment and that prolonged exposure to the store environment could cause physical and mental disability. In *W.A.G.M.U.S.*, Josua Müllenmeister is pressured by the police to create better ventilation, to expand the sales rooms and the narrow corridors and doorways to relieve the pressure from overcrowding. According to newspaper coverage (in the world of the novel), saleswomen fainted with regularity in the oppressive heat of summer days, and shoppers, upon completing their purchases, raced out the exits for a much-needed breath of fresh air.[97] Unable to redress these problems in the old department store, Müllenmeister hatches his plan to create an enormous new retail palace, the eponymous W.A.G.M.U.S.

Agnes, a pale blond beauty from the lower middle class, resembles the archetypal *Verkäuferin* of popular culture. A pastor's daughter no less, she is the lust object of Josua Müllenmeister's son Friedrich and becomes his fiancée early in the novel. Agnes suffers from nervousness and declining health (and morality) throughout the story—her beauty is magnified as her condition worsens. With a family history of nervous and mental disorder, she is portrayed as a decadent, frail beauty. "Our poor little sister," explains Hans Matrei, Agnes's brother, an anti–department store crusader, "suffers from the malady of our time. . . . I believe that one finds this sort of nervous anxiety and distractedness [*Zerfahrenheit*] among all department store girls. The department store in its present form is a cauldron of all possible dangers and infirmities for its employees."[98] With each successive appearance in the novel, the salesgirl sinks further and further into weakness, paleness, and fatigue, a condition that although amplifying the character's tragic beauty illustrates the department store's alleged effects.

In Matrei's indictment of the department store, as in Frau Iversen's critique, Böhme's characters were articulating widespread, contemporary concerns. The notion that department store salesgirls faced exploitation in addition to a range of physical and moral dangers—from overwork, inadequate conditions, and the crowds of demanding, even abusive customers—resonated widely in German culture. The plight of the salesgirl is depicted in equally dire terms in a 1922 novel, *Warenhausmädchen: Roman aus Berlin der Gegenwart* (Department store girls: A novel of present-day Berlin), by Josef Wiener-Braunsberg, where we read: "Most of the young girls who day in and day out had to endure patiently the demands of often moody and ruthless customers were meager and badly nourished creatures in whom you can see [the effects of] overexertion and only modest pay."[99] Prentice Mulford also concerned himself with the psychological effects of the stores, which he compared to insane asylums: "It is a wonder," he mused, "that salesmen and saleswomen do not go mad, when you consider the brain-addled, fidgety, restless herd, which they have to deal with from morning till night."[100] Like residents in an asylum, he continued, workers in a department store risk insanity from prolonged exposure to the insane behavior of others.

Beyond such obviously trumped-up claims about the insane-making and physically debilitating nature of the work, it is clear that department store jobs were difficult and demanding. Hours were long, and standards and expectations consistently high. Even a study published by the Association of German Department Store Owners had to concede that the work was difficult because of the "pushing and pulling" of the customers, especially on days with special promotions, and because of the quick rhythm and tempo of the job.[101] However, an early twentieth-century study showed that illness rates for department store employees were no higher than those for sales workers in smaller shops; in fact in 1907 and 1908, department store workers took about half as many sick days as their specialty store counterparts.[102] And despite the difficult work, department store jobs continued to pull experienced saleswomen away from specialty shops. The stores' size and seemingly constant growth gave the (often justified) impression that they provided opportunities for advancement.

As the stores grew from small enterprises into enormous retail palaces, the relationship between employees and bosses changed in significant ways. The extended-family model was replaced with a new model, that of the giant machine or the huge organism, in which each individual had a distinct part to play. The haste and urgency of modern life, according to Colze and other observers, left no place for the sentimentality and sociability of the old days. Division of labor and specialization characterized the modern retail workplace with its inevitably more distant and anonymous worker-employee relations. For Colze, "The individual is a number, which is put in its place to work, a little cog in a great, giant mechanism, which, when it becomes useless, is replaced with a new part so as not to obstruct the operation of the whole. The employees themselves . . . view this situation as the most desirable and most comfortable."[103]

Colze's words again were echoed in *Warenhaus Berlin*: "The employees in Warenhaus Berlin, as in any great department store, were at the forefront of the new development in our commercial life, as they sunk from [the status of] people to numbers. Nothing remained of the earlier personal relationship between boss and employee."[104] In fact, Colze recounts an incident in which the owner of a major department store on Berlin's Leipziger Strasse pretended to be a customer and went unrecognized by the saleswomen, one of whom chastised him for his impatience.[105] A similar, albeit more fraught event occurs in Siwertz's *The Great Department Store*. In this case the saleswoman tries to direct the rumpled and unkempt store owner Jeremias Goldmann to the soap department so that he can clean himself up.

Werner Sombart decried the depersonalization of the seller-customer relationship, claiming that department stores had rendered saleswomen interchangeable.[106] There were some twenty thousand department store employees in Berlin at the beginning of the twentieth century and several thousand in each of the major houses, making individual workers, like the objects for sale, seem more and more like exchangeable parts.[107] Berliners joked that a tiger had escaped from Tietz's (fictional) in-house zoo and devoured fourteen saleswomen without anyone noticing the loss.[108]

One novelist described the women in the sales force as uncannily identical in appearance, a representation that evokes the Tiller Girls, who with their rhythmic, synchronized steps, seemed to embody the pace and regimentation of modern, rationalized culture.[109] This connection appears in even stronger form in Maria Gleit's novel *Abteilung Herrenmode* (Men's fashion department) of 1932, where the shopgirls are described as

> all the same size and all equally long legged and narrow hipped, all painted with the same rouge, brunette and black, all with the same lock of hair fastened to the right side of the face, all with the same cap tilted over the pretty head, all with the same sailor pants, narrow, long, and burnt red, all with the smart, tightly fitted Eton collars, the same soft, white, low-slung shoes, with the artificially exaggerated heels, all hands placed equally seductively on the slender arms, all nails lacquered the same pink on the long white fingers.[110]

Paul Göhre also called attention to the loss of individual identity among large cohorts of saleswomen, describing store employees as nothing more than "cogs and chains in a giant working machine" and characterizing the organization of the department store workforce as "military and bureaucratic."[111]

The military metaphor echoes throughout descriptions of department store employees. Store workforces were often represented as "armies of employees," which emphasized the size of the workforce, the harmony between the different parts, the eclipsing of individuality, and the demand for strict discipline. Major sales events were frequently portrayed as battles or wars, an image that goes back to Zola and runs through the later German literature as well.[112] Describing H. Tietz's twenty thousand employees, A. Waldmann writes, "It is an army that marches anew every morning to conquer the customers, on whose favor every member of the enterprise depends."[113]

Like the store's wares, the workers were divided into different departments and situated within a rigid hierarchy with clear delineation of responsibilities. Performing one's job well therefore meant not standing out. The stores emphasized punctuality, neatness of appearance, and proper comportment toward fellow employees and customers. Wertheim prohibited workers from addressing each other with the informal *Du* during business hours, even in conversations between employees who were related to each other.[114] Lapses such as allowing customers to overhear private discussions between sales workers, using telephone or mail privileges for personal affairs, and smoking or drinking alcohol in the sales areas were strictly forbidden, and infractions against these rules led to fines or even immediate dismissal.[115] Some stores prohibited employees from meeting other employees in front of the store gates or near the store's entrance, in an effort, it seems, to underline the separation between work and leisure and to prevent customers from seeing saleswomen as anything but professionals.

A typical workday at a store like Wertheim, Tietz, or the KaDeWe lasted between eleven and a half and thirteen hours, although the days were punctuated with breaks. Notably, more-modest department stores and stores in smaller cities and towns generally had shorter workdays.[116] A two-hour lunch break, a short breakfast, and a late afternoon pause broke up the day, and as in all major department stores, subsidized meals and coffee along with comfortable chairs and staff lounges gave workers opportunities to rest their weary feet, breathe fresh air, and, where possible, enjoy the view from the rooftop terrace.[117] Some stores boasted that they provided lending libraries for employee enrichment; Hermann Tietz stores offered exercise classes for workers' relaxation and physical hygiene on Sundays, and Schocken instituted classes in rhythmic gymnastics in 1926 and offered subsidies so that workers could swim or take gymnastics courses at nearby facilities.[118] To boost morale, the Leonhard Tietz concern hosted employee festivals featuring singing and dancing by store workers, and each of its stores featured an intramural sports league, the Eltag (short for L. Tietz AG), in which employees competed in soccer, swimming, and track-and-field events. Each year the firm organized competitions between the workers in its different branches for the L. Tietz championship.[119]

Sales workers earned relatively high wages, especially in the Berlin stores, and contrary to the claims of the stores' opponents, department store workers were paid at significantly better rates and had more opportunities for advancement than sales personnel in specialty shops.[120] Major stores like H. Tietz and Wertheim also provided their own health insurance and pension schemes, which in many cases included benefits that exceeded legal minimums. They also offered banking services to their employees, allowing them to accrue interest if they set aside part of their regular earnings.[121]

Store workers were also eligible for vacation days—the annual number, at Wertheim, ranging from four to twenty in most cases, depending on position and seniority. At Schocken in the early 1930s even apprentices received two-week vacations, and regular employees' vacation time was extended to three weeks.[122] Several retailers created special inns in scenic spots for department store workers to spend their holidays; the Schocken concern and its sister store, Kaufhaus Manasse, for example, offered workers free stays at their employee vacation home in Rautenkranz in the Erz Mountains.[123] Many firms offered supplementary financial assistance during vacation time.

3.3 Courses in "rhythmic gymnastics" for store workers, Kaufhaus-Schocken, 1926. Sächsisches Staatsarchiv, Staatsarchiv Chemnitz, 31451 Schocken AG, Zwikau und Nachfolger, No. 307.

Schocken and others provided financial incentives for their workers to leave home and take their holidays in a more salubrious environment.[124] The Oscar and Betty Tietz Foundation paid out up to 40,000 marks a year for needy employees and provided travel subsidies for workers considered in need of a sanatorium or spa visit. Colze characterizes the heightened sense of social responsibility that store directors had for their employees as a holdover from the older, patriarchal days, when employees lived in the store and the boss's wife provided their meals and took care of their laundry.[125] Directors like the Tietzes and Salman Schocken, who gave generously to charities, also understood these programs in the context of Jewish philanthropic imperatives.[126]

Department store shopgirls may have done better than other women in the retail workforce, but there were clear limits. Saleswomen generally received less than half of what their male counterparts earned.[127] The heroines of department store novels, the shopgirls of modest background, for whom the store represented salvation or ruination, did reflect actual social conditions in at least one way. Saleswomen did in fact tend to come from the lower middle classes. Daughters of artisans made up the largest share, at least according to one study, and the descendants of functionaries and minor state officials (lower *Beamten*) also represented a sizable fraction.[128] Shopgirls occupied a somewhat ambiguous class position, toward the lower rungs of the middle classes—that is, below the level of their (mostly) bourgeois customers, but clearly distinct from the working class and often with opportunities for social ascent. Through their work with luxury goods, many acquired a sophisticated habitus that placed them beyond their actual class status. As Zola writes of shopgirls in *The Ladies' Paradise*, "The worst thing of all was their neutral, ill-defined position, somewhere between shopkeepers and ladies. Plunged into the midst of luxury, often without any previous education, they formed an anonymous class apart. All of their troubles and vices sprang from that."[129] Of course this too was a matter of perspective. A pro-Tietz article celebrated the stores for giving opportunities to working-class women who otherwise would have been forced to live in cramped, dark conditions and associate with uneducated acquaintances: "In the department store, on the other hand, the worker finds herself in cheerful, light surroundings. Contact with refined and educated customers is always stimulating . . . and facilitates their rise into higher social orders."[130]

In light of the apparent shortage of skilled saleswomen in Germany, Hermann Tietz was one of several department store firms that opened up its own school for salesgirls, a practice it pioneered in 1906. The school, whose enrollment started at fifty, increased to five hundred in its first decade of existence, and reached around twenty-one hundred in 1928, gave young women a basic education along with training in sales methods, home economics, bookkeeping, and advertising calligraphy.[131] Starting in 1913, apprentices and salesgirls enrolled in the Tietz school were released from their obligation to attend municipal schools. Tietz absorbed all the costs.[132]

3.4 Schocken store workers on holiday at Bad Rautenkranz, Erz Mountains, 1930.
Author's private collection.

The Leonhard Tietz firm opened up its "education department" in 1924, a supplement to its in-house vocational school, which stressed, among other topics, "consumer psychotechnics"—how to handle certain types of customers and respond to challenging situations on the shopping floor.[133]

All in all, a department store sales job appears to have been solid, steady, and fairly well-compensated work for a young woman of modest background. Although the work was exhausting and standards were high, the benefits, the opportunities for advancement, and the stability—certainly superior to what smaller shops could offer—would seem to balance out the difficulty of the work in most cases. Yet the salesgirl was often seen as a pitiable figure, a vulnerable and exploited young woman, trapped in a dreary, airless prison. To be sure, some department store novels had happy endings and depicted a salesgirl's rise through the system, or more often, her redemption through marriage to a handsome and wealthy man.[134] Yet other novels and other contemporary writings emphasized the abjectness of her position, her alleged poverty, desperation, and indeed vulnerability to the predatory advances of the boss. "It's a shame that the little doll has to spend her life behind the stone walls of the department store," says Werner Jahn in Wilhelm Rubiner's *Warenhausgräfin* (Department store countess)—part of the "Sweet Shopgirls" series—about the shopgirl who becomes his love interest. "It's a veritable prison compound for a blossoming young life."[135]

These images, common throughout department store discourses, were particularly freighted in the anti-Semitic press. Starting before 1900, radical right-wing newspapers made explicit connections between the plight of the *Verkäuferin* and the Jewish management of the department store, attributing the salesgirl's "dehumanization" to Jewish business practices. If modern retail, and above all the department store, were created by Jews, the argument went, then Jews were to blame for the salesgirl's exploitation and her status as a replaceable, consumable object. This logic also opened the door for a rich tableau of fantasies about Jewish sexuality, greed, and depravity, in which Jewish department store owners were viewed as ruthless and sexually rapacious.

A 1907 article in the populist anti-Semitic newspaper *Die Wahrheit*, for example, titled "Terrorism in the Ready-Made Clothing Shop" (Terrorismus in der Konfektion), noted (accurately) that strict rules prevented department store workers from having romantic relationships with customers. However, the article charged, these women were expected to be at their bosses' disposal. "If this forced familiarity is not welcomed, the women are let go or bullied until they give up their positions voluntarily."[136] Other interventions blasted department store owners such as Wertheim and Jandorf for having store mistresses, even harems of saleswomen, and for causing the moral corruption of young female employees. Not long after he opened the KaDeWe, accusations circulated that Adolf Jandorf, a married man, kept mistresses at several of his Berlin department stores—surely, his accusers claimed, a bad example for the morally impressionable staff.[137] The sexologist Josef Bernhard Schneider alludes to a scandal in which a man in a position of authority at a major department store faced trial for extorting sexual favors from his female employees.[138] Department store critics alleged further that young girls, often attracted by the lure of a career in sales, were forced to work in the store salons and restaurants, allegedly sites of illicit behavior and solicitation.[139]

Independent of the overblown accusations against department store owners, the sex lives of shopgirls was the subject of intense prurient interest and speculation. Department store fiction from Zola through his German imitators reflected this fascination, portraying shopgirls as in the market for husbands and depicting rituals like the regular Sunday outings or forays into the decadent nightlife of the metropolis. In his book on the Bon Marché in Paris, the historian Michael B. Miller attributes this voyeuristic fascination to the fact that the saleswomen were living away from home and in the stores, concentrated in great numbers and working in close contact with men.[140] These conditions were accompanied by a loosening of moral standards; liaisons, even prostitution, were considered normal occurrences.

A 1926 *Simplicissimus* cartoon captures contemporary perceptions of the shopgirl and her relationship to her superiors. The cartoon depicts several young women passing an acquaintance, another shopgirl, on the street. One says to another, "Look, Elli is going with the boss. Quite a feat. She's well on her way. She's been promoted after three years of department head!"[141] Like the perception of Agnes in *W.A.G.M.U.S.*, this woman is "working" her way up the department store hierarchy with her body.

Gender relations in Weimar culture, not unlike those in early twentieth-century Paris, could be described in terms of the slippery slope between courtship and prostitution, especially during the Republic's crisis-laden last years. Nowhere is this gray area more tellingly portrayed than in Irmgard Keun's 1932 novel *Das Kunstseidene Mädchen* (*The Artificial Silk Girl*), which lays bare the brutal economic realities under the

3.5 "Look, Elli is going out with the boss. Quite a feat. She's well on her way. She's been promoted after three years with a department head!" *Simplicissimus* 31, no. 5 (May 3, 1926).

surface of romance and love amid depression and desperation.[142] Although it does not speak to the theme of department stores per se, *The Artificial Silk Girl* draws explicit connections between Weimar's nascent consumer culture and the commodification of women, themes that we examine below through the figures of the prostitute and the department store mannequin.

As we have seen, the initial wave of anti-Semitic, anti–department store activism waned shortly before the First World War, but a new wave appeared at the end of the 1920s amid the period's economic hardships and inflamed by the increasing power and visibility of the Nazis. The scarcity of jobs, and the keen competition for them, increased the power of the department store king, rendering the workers even more expendable. Again the shopgirl played a highly visible role in these representations. Anti–department store and anti-Semitic writings targeted the stores anew for the way they treated female employees, framing their attacks in broader and more ominous terms than had their more gossipy Wilhelmine predecessors, who contented themselves with exposing (or often inventing) scandals.

A 1929 article in the Nazi organ *Illustrierter Beobachter*, for example, depicted the plight of female department store workers in dire terms, comparing them to prisoners and cogs in a machine ground down by their dehumanizing service to a Jewish industry.[143] "The human being is shut down, [as] thinking in numbers, sizes, and prices begins. . . . What's missing is the connection between the shopper and the goods, as it exists in all of the still small specialty shops. . . . 'Customer service' is replaced with service to the department store Jews."[144] The article emphasizes the way in which the department environment—the crowds, the scale, the hectic pace—allegedly affected the shopgirls' mood and mental health, using terms similar to what we saw in the kleptomania literature. Now, however, the connection between these working conditions and the greed of Jewish department store owners is made explicit.

Employees, the article charged, were required to remain in the store from sunup through sundown, leaving little time to shop for their own needs. This claim was partly accurate. As we have seen, the typical workday for many big city department store employees lasted twelve hours or more, and went even longer during holidays, when the crowds, the working hours, the pressure, and the financial stakes rose substantially. However, employees were in fact generally given time to do their own shopping.[145] Wertheim, among others, allowed its women workers to shop in the store for thirty minutes twice a week; they received a small discount on store goods and could also purchase damaged items and groceries that could not be sold at reduced prices.[146]

Nazi writings even decried the stores' organized leisure activities, like the Sunday gymnastics classes, characterizing them as coercive and suffocating. The salesgirl, one anonymous author maintained, is paid too little to take advantage of the city's booming leisure sphere and is so overworked that numbers, prices, and regulations come to her in her dreams. Finally, he describes shopgirls as having indifferent or blasé faces and lying around during their afternoon breaks like "patients in a sanatorium," returning us, once again, to the notion of the department store as a breeding ground for madness and psychopathology.[147]

Women for Sale: Shopgirls, Mannequins, and Prostitutes

The tension between the department store as a site of female emancipation and exploitation is vividly embodied in the figure of the mannequin. Wax dummies were used to display clothing as early as the seventeenth century. By the nineteenth century they had started to look a lot more realistic, only to be gradually replaced in the 1920s by highly stylized creations. The term *Mannequin* in German denoted both inanimate dummy and living store model for much of the century, and live women appeared in window displays starting in the 1890s, and lasting through the 1920s.[148] The mannequin functions in many department store representations to evoke the difference between people and things and the power of consumer culture to bridge this divide, to objectify consumers, and indeed to bring things to life through our fantasies. The idea of a dummy or doll coming to life in fact resonates with Freud's notion of the uncanny, and he introduces the concept in his discussion of the living doll in E. T. A. Hoffmann's "Sandman" story.[149]

In *The Ladies' Paradise*, upon noticing the mannequins in the store window, Denise Baudu observes that "the dummies' round bosoms swelled out the material, their wide hips exaggerated the narrow waists, and their missing heads were replaced by large price tags with pins stuck through them . . . while mirrors on either side of the windows had been skilfully arranged to reflect the dummies, multiplying them endlessly, seeming to fill the street with these beautiful women for sale with huge price tags where their heads should have been."[150] These lines, near the beginning of the novel, powerfully presage many of the themes that run through *The Ladies' Paradise* and this chapter. The image of decapitated mannequins with price tags above their necks acutely symbolizes the ways in which the department store commodified women and female beauty and indeed did violence to women. Zola describes the dummies as "women for sale," suggesting a slippage between inanimate mannequins and actual women. This slippage is reinforced by the fact that women worked as "mannequins" or store models who exhibited and tried on dresses and gowns before the development of the modern fitting room for customers.

Vicki Baum's *The Great Sale*, from 1937, also uses the figure of the mannequin to address women's commodification in modern consumer culture. The novel tells the story of the friendship and rivalry between Nina and Lilian, two attractive young saleswomen in Warenhaus-Zentral, a New York department store. Nina, described by the old store director as "a girl who is both beautiful and proper looking," is chosen to be part of a new window display promoting stockings.[151] The task, which all the saleswomen view as an exciting adventure, involves spending an entire week in a display window with sixteen identically clad mannequins.[152] Nina is intrigued by the possibility of spending her workweek this way and desires the salary bonus that comes with the assignment, ignoring the misgivings of her husband. Dressed like the mannequins, Nina is given the job of demonstrating the durability of the product by lifting her skirt over her knee every few minutes, in regular intervals, and tugging on her stocking, hence suggesting that the stockings do not easily tear.

This assignment thrusts Nina into the liminal space between the department store and the surrounding world, a border between the private retail sphere of the store and the public city streets. As we have seen, the display window was also a controversial site, decried for luring naïve and suggestible passersby into what opponents depicted as the trap of the department store. Window displays that were considered too exciting or stimulating ran afoul of municipal ordinances in many German cities, and in the early twentieth century the Berlin police cracked down on displays that featured moving figures, which were thought to endanger public safety by attracting huge and unruly crowds of onlookers.[153]

Nina soon finds that absorbing the gazes of pedestrians and living among the mannequins does not meet her expectations. The task becomes exhausting and stressful, and, writes Baum, "sometimes it seemed to her that she had become a mannequin, with a stiffly arched back and a wooden smile."[154] After a week with the mannequins, Nina feels less human. The mannequins' close resemblance to people, despite the hard-and-fast boundary separating them, as lifeless objects, from animate beings, is almost uncanny, eerie.

Although Nina is uncomfortable and grows to dislike her position in the window, the display has its intended effect, creating a sensation and drawing crowds into the store. Baum writes that passing pedestrians gather outside the store window and that even the hectic, busy New Yorkers stop and linger, taking in the peculiar sight of a real woman among mannequins. As he is walking by, fifty-two-year-old Steve Thorpe finds himself captivated by the display and especially the woman in it. Thorpe notices that a price tag is affixed to each mannequin, and like the mannequins, the live woman also has a price tag on her knee. Thorpe enters the store and inquires at the information desk. "I'd like to buy the girl who is exhibited in your display window," he says, removing his hat. The woman at the desk is confused, and Thorpe explains, "The girl in the display window. The price is written there, $2.80. I consider that a good deal. Where can I get her?"[155]

Thorpe is joking, and once she realizes it, the woman at the desk has a good laugh. Nevertheless, his comment, along with Nina's feeling that she was starting to become a mannequin, points at Baum's larger themes concerning the eroticization and commodification of saleswomen. Elsewhere in the novel, Baum writes that two men "leaned on the counter and looked over Nina as if she were an object."[156] And later, after Thorpe has come to know Nina, he still can't quite digest the fact that she cannot be bought, joking to Crosby, the store director, that some things aren't for sale even in a department store as comprehensive as the Zentral. In these passages, Baum is clearly thematizing the saleswoman's status between person and thing, as a seller of things and simultaneously as a temptation or thing to be sold. (The writer also evokes Zola's description of headless mannequins in store windows with price tags around their necks and is quite possibly also alluding to the early twentieth-century American practice in which prostitutes sat in display windows with price tags posted.[157]) Indeed, Nina's week among the mannequins exposes the blurry boundary between saleswomen and what they were selling and the eerie encounter between people and mannequins, an encounter that has been treated in fiction and film at least since the 1920s and through today's popular culture. In her classic history of consumer culture, Rosalind Williams writes that department stores and

3.6 KaDeWe "Storage room for mannequins in the cellar. A fantastical group that looks like a throng of seemingly enchanted people." Reprinted from *Das Kaufhaus des Westens: Festschrift zum 25 jährigen Bestehen 1907–1932*, ed. Franz Arnholz and Max Osborn (Berlin, 1932). Bpk, Berlin/Art Resource, NY.

3.7 "Window display humor that caused a general sensation. A raincoat advertisement, portrayed with figures on the upper deck of an autobus." The ad text states: "We are all on top of things no matter the weather. We wear Macintosh raincoats from the KaDeWe." Reprinted from *Das Kaufhaus des Westens: Festschrift zum 25 jährigen Bestehen 1907–1932*, ed. Franz Arnholz and Max Osborn (Berlin, 1932). Bpk, Berlin/Art Resource, NY.

3.8 "This display comically parodies women's frenzied hunt during a remnants sale." Reprinted from *Das Kaufhaus des Westens: Festschrift zum 25 jährigen Bestehen 1907–1932*, ed. Franz Arnholz and Max Osborn (Berlin, 1932). Bpk, Berlin/Art Resource, NY.

the consumer revolution as a whole channeled desires and passions from people to things.[158] The eroticized mannequin and her twin, the objectified saleswoman, compellingly illustrate Williams's point.

A 1932 photograph, published in a book celebrating the KaDeWe's twenty-fifth anniversary, shows a bunch of mannequins in the store's storage area. The accompanying text describes the mannequins as a "fantastical group that looks like a throng of enchanted people," associating the department store and the mannequins in particular with fantasy, magic, and allure.[159] Window displays at the KaDeWe and other department stores placed mannequins in a range of increasingly lifelike situations, as riders on a Berlin bus, for example, in an attention-getting display promoting raincoats, and as eager shoppers zealously competing over items on a sale table. Siegfried Kracauer anthropomorphized the mannequin in his 1931 vignette on the "Temple of Commerce" ("Der Verkaufs-Tempel"), in which a shopgirl, a "bored young lady" and "the keeper of the altar to the temple of consumption" who presides over an empty shop at night, turns out to be a mannequin.[160]

Sigfrid Siwertz's *The Great Department Store* also examines the relationships between men and mannequins and the boundaries between mannequins and saleswomen. This novel features a store decorator, a Mr. Dupré, who treats his mannequins as though they were real people, speaks to them and endows them with names and distinct personalities. Dupré succeeds in convincing Goldmann of the necessity of purchasing new store mannequins, despite his limited budget due to wartime financial hardships. The mannequins, which arrived from Vienna, were, Siwertz notes, marked by "demonstratively contorted gestures," which showed that even they were affected by wartime food scarcities. The narrator further attests to their near humanity, at least in the way they were treated by Dupré: "There was the tall blond Mathilde, the defiant Magdalena, Vera the daydreamer, the impertinent and spirited Odette, and above all, the demonically beautiful Lola, his favorite mannequin with the dangerous smile."[161] Siwertz notes that the decorator always dressed Lola in the finest clothes and would exclaim, "now we are really seductive, Lola!"[162]

Around this time Dupré falls in love with and marries Nina Smith—pointedly described as "a living doll" and as having a "mixture of Slavic, German, and Jewish blood"—and he helps her get a job as a store model in the Goldmann department store. Nina, like the mannequins, came from Vienna, where she had worked as a model. From the moment he met her, Dupré had the uncanny feeling that he had seen her before somewhere, and one day when he is working in a display window he is suddenly struck by the resemblance between Nina and Lola, his favorite mannequin. He realizes that Nina had been the model for Lola. "You can imagine," she says, "that I can be seen in display windows all across Europe."[163] Dupré thus knew Nina first as a mannequin. He had first encountered her in her state as a consumable object, a figure in a display window. Thus, he had formed a kind of erotic attachment and relationship with Lola, Nina's commodity form, before he met the real, living Nina. When Dupré has his epiphany, his first response is laughter, but then his amusement fades as he realizes what he has done.

> "How amusing! So I *had* seen you before. D'you know, when I come to think of it, it's just what I suspected all the time . . . that this woman would be my fate . . . long before I ever met you." And he made a laughing reference to the immobile wax figure.
>
> But deep within him there was something that did not laugh. Suddenly he found the expression on the wax model's face mocking and inimical, and in the innermost recesses of his soul, behind the red mists of passion, there arose a small gray cloud of misgiving lest he had made the greatest mistake of his life.[164]

Note that in this passage, as Dupré begins to realize the consequences of his seduction by the dummy, he refers to Lola as a woman.

Several years before she wrote *The Great Sale*, Vicki Baum dealt with these issues in "Jape im Warenhaus" (Jape in the department store). Published in 1931, while Baum was still in Berlin, "Jape" is a darker and more disturbing work than *The Great Sale* and "Customer Service," both of which date from Baum's Los Angeles period. Her protagonist is Jape Flunt, a young, simple shoemaker's apprentice born into poverty who becomes obsessed with a necktie in a department store display window. Baum pointedly contrasts the dingy grayness of Flunt's life—he was born in a cellar and lived in a rear courtyard—with the bright glamour of a department store, in this case presumably the Wertheim store on Leipziger Strasse. "It was this glimmer, the brightness and the colors that Jape saw for the first time in his life, when his way happened to take him by the department store's display window."[165] Even from the outside, the department store transfixed and transformed Jape. It awakened something new in him: covetousness. Jape had experienced his own consumer revolution.

Captivated by the thought of the necktie, which he associates with his love interest, his young aunt Magda, Jape returns to the display window again and again, gazing at the tie and the cardboard cornucopia that surrounds it. Returning in the evening, he is dazzled by the electric lights and finally notices the other display windows: "On extraordinary furniture made of silk with golden legs sat female figures who looked more beautiful than real women, with more intense smiles and eyes that glowed more, whose hair shined, whose skin shimmered, and who nonetheless were not alive, which seemed eerie to the callow Jape."[166] There were also male mannequins in the window, "fine gentlemen with red cheeks and little silk mustaches. The men also smiled obligingly; the most handsome of them held a bouquet of flowers . . . and on his shirt Jape noticed with a sweet and powerful shock: the necktie."[167] Jape suddenly had a goal and imagined himself transformed into the mannequin—he aimed to save up for the necktie. Standing with Magda, he would strike the male mannequin's pose, pretending that he too held a bouquet. As Baum notes, "he became the young man from the display window, he felt it himself, he could already feel the necktie on his chest."[168]

After managing to scrimp and save one mark, Jape enters the store, only to have his hopes dashed when a saucy saleswoman informs him that the tie actually cost six marks. Showing the shopgirl's characteristic disdain for an uncouth, proletarian customer, she distractedly points Jape toward the cheaper ties. Thus set back, Jape's desire burns all the more intensely. The tie had become the key to winning Magda and other women and to a life of adventure and significance. "It got to the point where Jape had to have the necktie. He would wear it on Sundays and look just like the dazzling man from the display window."[169]

He now hatched a plan, brilliant in its simplicity. Jape would enter the department store in the afternoon, hide behind a pile of clothes, and get himself locked in. Spending the night, he would grab the tie and emerge unnoticed after the morning opening.

The first part of the plan goes smoothly. Jape enters after work, gets lost in the teeming crowds, and hides himself behind a high pile of rolled-up rugs until the store is closed, locked up, and emptied for the night. However, a night in the department store proves to be more than Jape can handle. It seems that the deserted store has everything he could ever need: food to supplement the meager supper he had packed; bedding for a comfortable night's sleep; and even extra clothes—a home away from home and stocked with an unimaginable abundance of goods there for the taking. Yet things quickly go bad. The store's silence is disconcerting, and its dusty smell sickens his lungs. He is soon transported into a semi-fantastical world of consumer abundance, fleeting ecstasy, and mounting terror; Jape has transgressed into the thing world.

When he is certain that the coast is clear, Jape makes his way downstairs to the menswear department and soon finds the necktie display. Grabbing the tie that had so enthralled him, he quickly dons it: "The necktie was lovely, no doubt about it; it was really something, it shined and sparkled, its colors danced. And it clothed him splendidly, his head looked unexpectedly elegant and mature."[170] But suddenly, Jape is overcome with an unfamiliar feeling. Having for the first time participated in an act of frivolous consumption, he now experiences the disappointment of a longing fulfilled, unaware that the pleasure of actually possessing something pales in comparison with the fantasies and desires that goods may arouse. Alas, consumption begets consumption, as the consumer strives to keep his disappointment at bay. Jape thus immediately sets about finding a collar to enhance the look.

In his search, Jape comes upon the staggering abundance of wares that the department store offers, the endless assortment of styles, sizes, and materials.

He loses himself burrowing through and flinging around stacks and stacks of clothes and accoutrements until the goods start to appear as if they have come to life. "The nightly order of the men's fashion department was destroyed and could not be reestablished—this much he could see as he looked away from the mirror and around with a short and harried glance. The items had climbed out of the display cases like sinister, animated beings. They had spread themselves out over tables and cabinets, they had fallen to the floor, crawled into corners, they had unfolded themselves, crumpled themselves up, dirtied themselves, and brought themselves into hopeless disarray."[171] After making a halfhearted attempt to put things back together, Jape flees the scene.

His next encounter is even more unsettling: "Behind a column stood a gentleman with a stern face who waited still and motionless for Jape. They stood facing each other for an eternity and stared at each other with glassy eyes. Jape had the superior courage. He approached the man. The man was made of wax."[172] The mannequin whose pose he had imitated and whom he had aspired to resemble now plays a part in his nightmare. And after a fleeting moment of relief, Jape spies something "white and ghostly." "It threatened, swung fists into the air, had holes instead of eyes. It was Jape's own image, reflected from a distant mirror."[173] The scene evokes the German horror film *The Prague Student* (1926), in which the protagonist is stalked by his mirror image, which he had sold to Satan.[174] Baum, however, gestures at the transformation of Jape's identity through the commodity, in this case the necktie, and his alienation from the thing world of the mannequin as well as from his own selfhood.

Jape has indeed been transformed. As he sits to finish the grubby dinner he has brought, his stomach turning from the liverwurst, he pauses. "Fine gentlemen didn't eat such rubbish. But what did fine gentlemen eat?"[175] Transformed by necktie and collar into a refined man of taste, he begins an imaginary shopping spree, a jaunt through the aisles with his umbrella elegantly placed under his arm, examining, touching, delighting in the store's bounteous offerings and stuffing his pockets full of fineries for his beloved Magda. Entering the food section, Jape is enticed by exotic delicacies like bananas and rare treats like ham rolls, but to prolong the pleasure—he has already started to learn how to manage the pleasures and disappointments of consumption—he takes his time and first grabs something to drink, a mysterious bottle labeled Malaga Gold.

After gorging and guzzling his way through the food section, realizing that he is drunk, Jape crawls up to the third level, the ladies' clothing department, where

> at the end of the stairway, two smiling ladies received him, one in an elegant outfit, the other—"Hey you, do you speak?" [he inquires]—in a silk nightgown. Jape, with his bicycle lantern swinging back and forth between the two, found both of them enchanting. "Good evening, young lady," he said, and then he

tried to flirt with her: Since neither of the two smiling beauties responded, he laughed audibly, grabbed the elegant one on her cold, smooth wax skin, and tried out all of the smooth pickup lines he knew.[176]

Thinking he hears someone coming, Jape descends into a delusional state. He asks himself: "Are you only dreaming of the objects, the treasures, the pleasures that you do not know, the wine that burns, silken women who smile, the shine of the lantern so unspeakably strange between the eerie, unknown world of the objects?"[177]

Coming to his senses a bit, he begins to condemn the excess of the department store and all it represents, pining for the simplicity of his own real life. Stumbling into the art section, he encounters another female likeness, this time a painting of the Venus, standing among other imitations of well-known masterpieces. Fascinated, disturbed, and all but paralyzed by her nakedness, he smashes the painting to pieces and searches for his lantern, finding it on the floor by the two female mannequins. "A hellfire burning inside of him . . . [he] reached behind himself and grasped the smooth skin of the lady who was wearing only a nightgown. The cold, lifeless, not-breathing woman frightened him." Baum now describes the mannequins as "smiling wax ghosts" and notes that everything was quiet and still, "frozen, bewitched."[178]

Baum again draws attention to the troubling boundary between human and object in Jape's confrontation with the store watchman. The watchman, a war invalid—a department store story trope—discovers Jape in the women's fashion department. When the man raises his revolver, Jape, "with the strength of a lunatic," hurls his lantern at the old invalid and kills him. Baum notes wryly that the watchman "was always a quiet person, because of his profession and his disposition, and now had become a bit quieter." Jape ponders the man's humanity, considers that he must have had a mother, a wife, children, and that he was "equipped with the dutifulness and the fear of God, endowed with the inexplicable, awesome, and painful ability of the living—up until now. Now just a bundle of inorganic stuff, material, an object between the piled-up wares of the department store."[179] Disoriented and exhausted, Jape leans his head on the mannequin's leg and begins to doze.

When he comes to, he realizes that he should try to make the watchman's death look like an accident. He decides to burn the store and, as Baum writes, "to let the dead man be killed in the fire."[180] The act of killing a dead man is of course redundant, and thus Baum's language emphasizes the eerie way that the boundaries between organic and inorganic, between alive and dead, have been transcended and blurred during this fateful night in the department store. As the flames begin to spread from the ladies' apparel department throughout the entire floor, the blaze devours the mannequins, and again they appear to "come alive in the heat, they buckle and bend over, they turn their wax limbs like ghosts."[181]

Jape thus experiences a range of uncanny encounters, with lifelike mannequins, with a fresh corpse, and finally with dummies that seem to come to life as they go up in flames. If the mannequin represents one side of women's commodification in the department store, the prostitute signals the other. Both figures draw attention to the objectification of women and the erotic dimensions of department store transactions.

Josef Bernhard Schneider, a sexologist who—using the pen name Lothar Eisen—characterized the department store as an erotic space, explored the libidinal dimensions of shopping and dressing. Schneider observed that store encounters sped up courtship rituals so that what would normally take several months transpired in two or three hours. "They meet each other on the lowest floor, the man reads secret desires in the soul of the girl, or woman as the case may be, in her eyes that longingly look to the right and left. They pass by sparkling jewels and heaps of precious Indian silk on into the refreshment area, and when they have had their coffee, they go further, slowly to the third floor, and up there in some corner they stop speaking and their lips begin to play their silent game."[182] Edmund Edel's account of the "new Berlin," written shortly before the outbreak of World War I, portrayed the KaDeWe as a kind of sex market, referring to its café as a site where neglected wives sought lovers.[183]

The shopgirls themselves were often linked to prostitution, portrayed at times as victims of the stingy practices of the (Jewish) store owners, and in other cases represented as cool and calculating modern women in control of their own sexuality and aware of its market value. For an evocation of the links between consumer culture and the sexual economy, one could turn to Walter Rutmann's 1927 cinematic chronicle of Berlin life, *Berlin: Die Symphonie einer Großstadt*. In one scene a man catches sight of a prostitute through the glass shop windows of a store on a Berlin corner. They glance at each other and then walk off together. The woman is literally framed by the store window as an object for the male spectator to consume.

It seems fitting, then, that in 1920s Berlin prostitutes could often be found outside department stores at night. One observer noted that the streetwalkers in front of the KaDeWe "wore high, bright-red riding-boots as an advertisement for their [sadomasochistic] specialty."[184] Curt Moreck, the author of a guide to Berlin's seamy side, made a similar observation: "In the aura of the display windows of the 'KaDeWe,' which with its range of items satisfies all the needs of modern humanity, stroll those specialists who have cultivated a special erotic demand of the world of modern men." Moreck continues with a description of the tall-booted dominatrices who shout their come-ons like military commands.[185]

Shopgirls became the stuff of erotic fantasy, represented as seductive but morally compromised, indeed suited for trysts but inappropriate marriage material for the proper bourgeois man. In Margarete Stahr's short story "Aus dem Warenhaus," the narrative plays with the notion of going to the department store to obtain a wife, an ironic commentary on the department store's ability to satisfy all needs—in this case erotic and matrimonial—and yet a scandalous act for someone of high social standing.[186] In a humorous plot reversal, it turns out that the lovely *Verkäuferin* in this tale is actually morally upstanding and virtuous (and the respectable lady is a thief) and had only taken the position when her family had fallen on hard times.

Department store selling thus was a highly eroticized act, and the shopgirl participated in what was widely depicted as the store's seduction of customers and passersby. Maria Gleit's *Men's Fashion Department*, a salacious novel that was published just as the Nazis took power (and which quickly ran afoul of Nazi censors), takes place in department store Schack—likely a pun on Schocken—where the menswear section was redesigned to resemble a "brothel" or "bordello." Entering the store was supposed to feel like walking into a nightclub, and the saleswomen, clad in revealing uniforms and trained to flirt, were instructed to make men's purchases "stimulating" and "highly pleasurable." The men streamed in. "It was astounding," Gleit writes, "how great a demand there suddenly was for men's collar buttons. It seemed that all the men of Berlin would be wandering around the world collar buttonless if Schack & Co. hadn't suddenly brought this lamentable situation to an end by opening their fabulous men's department."[187]

The sexologist Schneider, who alleged that most department store girls (*Warenhausfräulein*) practiced prostitution, maintained that the constant exposure to wares aroused a kind of covetousness in female employees, a nearly irrepressible desire to possess the goods they saw and handled all day long. "And since the simplest way to this," he writes, "is secret or open prostitution, most department store girls are clandestine or registered prostitutes as a side profession."[188] Although less theoretically nuanced, Schneider's text echoes the concerns of such contemporaries as Kracauer and Bertolt Brecht, who were similarly convinced of the female spectator's—in their case, film spectators—vulnerability to the seductions of luxury.[189]

The far right wing also seized on the alleged dangers of prolonged exposure to luxury goods and cautioned that women who worked in a department store would aspire to consume and live in a manner beyond their station. An article in the *Hammer-Schriften* declared that prostitution was the inevitable result of this aspiration and cited a (needless to say, rather dubious) study that found that 62 percent of female department store employees suffered from sexually transmitted diseases.[190] Department store critics charged that store conditions forced women into prostitution—that is, it was not their desire for expensive goods, but the fact that they were underpaid by greedy, exploitative bosses that compelled saleswomen to sell their bodies.[191] One anonymous author claimed that a group of female employees appealed to their (Jewish) store director, claiming that their meager salaries were insufficient to meet the requirement that they come to work nicely dressed. The store owner allegedly instructed his employees to become streetwalkers.[192]

The link to prostitution only made explicit what already lurked just under the surface, but the association also resonated with a tradition that associated Jews with prostitution and human trafficking. Paul Dehn, to cite one example, conflated the staffing of department stores with the procurement of women, which, he alleged, was part of the way of life in Galicia.[193] And the anti-Semitic press abounded with rumors of moral corruption and prostitution in Wertheim's tea salon and about sexual encounters in the underground tunnel that linked the Leipziger Strasse store to the Berlin metro.[194]

Du Kommst zu Spät: Eine Szene aus dem Warenhaus (You've come too late: A department store scene), a one-act play from 1914 by Hans Vogt, reflects these perspectives. The play begins with a conversation between Krajevsky, the proprietor of a department store, and Liebhold, his business manager. In the first lines of the play, Liebhold informs Krajevsky that the police had been by the store and apprehended two employees. "Two at once?" asks Krajevsky; "On account of what?" "You have to ask?" his business manager wearily responds, implying that the detention of store employees for prostitution was a regular occurrence. "Always the same thing," responds Krajevsky.[195] Liebhold reports that when asked by the police what led them into this activity, the women responded that they were driven to it by hunger. According to Liebhold, the police commissioner then asked if it was true that the women received a salary of only fifty marks. It was in fact true, and Krajevsky is completely unrepentant about paying his workers such a low wage.

Indeed, Krajevsky embodies the anti-Semitic stereotype of the department store owner. His concern is above all with maximizing his profits, and he disdainfully dismisses Liebhold's concerns with the workers' welfare. "I cannot and do not wish to pay more. . . . Should I throw one hundred marks a month at them, so that they can fully give themselves over to their wild sensual orgies?"[196] Ignoring the apparently legitimate concern that these women were underpaid, Krajevsky simply assumes that any additional wages will encourage further debauchery—in other words, that women are morally corrupt and that the tendency of his female employees to turn to prostitution came not from economic necessity but from moral turpitude. For Krajevsky, women were replaceable parts, although he did have strong feelings for one saleswoman, whom he had secretly transferred from his Frankfurt store. "She does not work as cheaply as the others," Krajevsky confesses to Liebhold, who responds with a cynicism typical of the Weimar period: "He who wishes to love, must pay."[197] While Krajevsky is never explicitly identified as Jewish, his Polish-sounding name is one clue that he is coded as such in the play. That his commercial empire was built on the exploitation of women, their degradation, and ultimately their destruction aligns this set of representations with common notions that Jews were overrepresented in the white slave trade and indeed that their path to the economic domination of the German people lay through women.

3.9 Advertising leaflet featuring Karstadt's "Everything that goes with the woman" jingle, words and music (1929). Stiftung Deutsches Technikmuseum Berlin, Hist. Archiv.

In Weimar culture a fine line separated the prostitute from the new woman. Both were portrayed as calculating and savvy; both were visible in the new commercial centers that sprang up around department stores and other urban attractions; and in the period's visual culture, representations of one easily slid into the other. Unlike the tragic victims in the Vogt play, smart and so-phisticated shopgirls like Evelyne in Kläger's *Incident in the Department Store* understood their commodification and knew how to manipulate it and take advantage of it. As Evelyne tries to seduce the store owner Kreis, she says, "Every-thing marketed is a mass-produced article. Girls are mass-produced wares, consumable articles. You, as a big department store man, know that."[198] Kreis politely rejects her advances, telling her that he does not wish for her to sell herself. "I think," responds Evelyne, "that often one must lead a man in the right direction. But I am a modern girl and my reputation could not get any worse."[199]

The department store, as these examples have demonstrated, was rep-resented and experienced as a site of titillating, transgressive, even eerie possibilities and encounters. Department store tales stoked the fantasy of in-habiting the stores at night, of learning the secrets of these enchanted places where, after hours, the mannequins come to life and the objects dance.[200] Parallel to changes in the kleptomania discourse from the somaticism of the imperial period to the sexual and psychoanalytic conceptions of the Weimar era, the scandalous department store of the *Mittelstand* propaganda, where women were portrayed as exploited by ruthless Jewish businessmen, was gradually replaced by a set of more ambivalent images that depicted women as both victimized and emancipated, as objects to be consumed and simulta-neously as savvy, unsentimental consumers of objects—in short as controlled and controlling inhabitants of their alternative domestic sphere, the new con-sumerist cityscapes of the interwar period.

4 BEYOND THE CONSUMING TEMPLE

*Jewish Dissimilation and Consumer Modernity
in Provincial Germany*

A new rhythm has seized the world, a new movement. Medieval man, from
the horizontal calm of his meditative workday, needed the vertical cathedral
to find his God high above. The man of our times can only find respite from
the excitement of his brisk life in the relaxed horizontal.
                                        —*Erich Mendelsohn (1923)*

I have learnt nothing for my profession from textbooks on commercial
science or national economy, but much from my father, from Hegel, and
from the midrash.
                                        —*Salman Schocken (1957)*

Literary and theatrical treatments of the department store, the fantasies
and nightmares that form much of the subject of this book, were generally set in the metropolis, in most cases a real or imaginary Berlin.
Their plots were typically concerned with the impact of these new forms of
retail on life in Germany's capital city. Many polemical anti–department
store writings, including the anti-Semitic characterizations, were also centered on Berlin, where the eruptions of the new consumer culture were experienced first and felt most strongly. Berlin was furthermore the site of several
of the most architecturally significant German department stores, the iconic
Wertheim "cathedral" on Leipziger Strasse, the sumptuous KaDeWe, and
the imposing Karstadt edifice at Hermannplatz, once described by Siegfried
Kracauer as "a proud, menacing department store."[1] Two of these stores are
still standing and still open for business, albeit in significantly altered form.
Consequently, accounts of the history of department stores and consumer
culture in Germany have focused predominately on the capital, given its
notoriety as a site of leisure, nightlife, and mass consumption during the
Weimar period and as a flashpoint for debates and controversies about the
effects of these new developments.

Jews are also typically associated with Berlin and the urban experience
in this period. Consequently, notions of the "Jewish department store" tend
to focus on the capital city, home of Germany's largest Jewish community
and site of its densest concentration of department stores. However, there
is another dimension to the history of German department stores that this
picture occludes, a story of predominately Jewish-owned businesses opening

up in smaller cities and even large towns and thus transforming architecture, commerce, and streetscapes in provincial German settings.

In Germany, unlike in France, Britain, and the United States, the major department stores had their origin in medium-size towns, as opposed to metropolises like Paris, London, New York, and Chicago. For most of these businesses, the two Tietz firms, Karstadt, Schocken, Barasch, Knopf, and others, even as they began to compete in larger markets and achieve a national reputation, provincial locations remained significant sites of architectural and commercial innovation and the focus of vigorous expansion through the early 1930s. These settings were certainly not immune to the denunciations of anti–department store activists; but in smaller, regional contexts, Jewish business leaders often successfully courted the approval of local elites and found greater popular acceptance than their more metropolitan counterparts.

The Leonhard Tietz and S. Schocken concerns, major firms that had no presence in the capital, touted their regional identity and their role as innovators, bringers of modernity to the provinces. A richly illustrated 1929 volume commemorating the fiftieth anniversary of the Leonhard Tietz company lavishes attention on stores in places such as Hamborn, Kleve and Oberhausen. These buildings featured the most up-to-date architectural and design elements of the time and helped revolutionize life and leisure far away from the capital. In the case of Hamborn, for example, we read that "the newest big city in the Ruhr region has developed over the last twenty-five years with an American tempo. In a new part of town stands the imposing three-facade construction of the Tietz store, one of the most modern department stores in western Germany."[2] The book's descriptions of the various L. Tietz buildings consistently stressed their modernity, in terms of both style and technological innovation, and emphasized features like the escalator, an innovation that Tietz had recently brought to Germany and which remained a novelty into the 1930s. The volume also emphasized that their stores were harbingers of provincial modernity, as in the case of the Kleve emporium, which "brought big-city life into the small town in the lower Rhineland."[3]

The Leonhard Tietz concern was based in Cologne and dominated the department store sector in Germany's western areas, especially around the Rhineland and Westphalia. S. Schocken, a newer and smaller, though rapidly growing business, originated in the Saxon city of Zwickau, where its headquarters remained throughout Salman Schocken's stewardship. Two of its largest and most famous stores did lie beyond the borders of Saxony, in Stuttgart and Nuremberg, and a possible Berlin store was under discussion immediately before the Nazis came to power and put a stop to new department store openings. Nevertheless, Zwickau remained the firm's hub for business operations and for the manufacturing, acquisition, and warehousing of goods.

In November 1928, at the opening ceremonies for a new, modern store in the mountain town of Crimmitschau, Schocken's managing director,

Georg Manasse, acknowledged that the town had fewer than twenty-eight thousand residents, making it Germany's 127th largest city.[4] Addressing an assembly of new employees, Manasse declared that the store would make Crimmitschau a shopping destination in its own right so that its residents would no longer have to travel to larger cities like Zwickau or Dresden to satisfy their needs. At a similar ceremony the following year, he made the exact same point about the town of Waldenburg, where the firm opened an enormous new department store. There he noted that no other city of comparable size—Waldenburg's population was approximately forty-five thousand—could boast of a large and modern retail structure.[5] Schocken's leaders, like L. Tietz's, embraced the role of bringing modernity, that is, consumer culture, big-city fashions, and to some extent American ways, to these small cities and large towns. They promoted their modern, rational approaches to business and modernist principles in architecture, resulting in the formation of centralized, efficient firms and the construction of stores that were free of gratuitous ornamentation or historicism, featuring "clear and straight forms and lines."[6] The intention was to improve life for the residents of these towns through rational architecture and by offering high-quality consumer goods at reasonable prices.

4.1 Kaufhaus Schocken in Waldenburg, opening day, October 21, 1929. Sächsisches Staatsarchiv, Staatsarchiv Chemnitz, 31451 Schocken AG, Zwikau und Nachfolger, No. 270.

Architecture, commerce, and consumption were thus inseparably inter-
woven with Schocken's business and cultural agendas. Schocken's part-
nerships, above all with Erich Mendelsohn, but also with several other,
lesser-known architects, played a crucial role in the realization of these
plans.[7] Schocken and Mendelsohn, who met through Zionist circles after
World War I, were both relatively marginal figures at the time: Schocken,
despite his great business success, remained on the fringes of the world of
German merchants and businesspeople, and Mendelsohn was not accepted
into the ranks of Germany's leading architects, in both cases largely owing
to their Jewish backgrounds. Both men came to be active in the milieu
of German Zionism, and both, especially Mendelsohn, were connected
to communities of avant-garde artists and architects. How, I ask in this
chapter, did these two worlds fit together? Were there connections between
Schocken's commitment to the Zionist goal of revitalizing the Jewish people
and his embrace of modernist aesthetics? How did Salman Schocken's business practices, aesthetic choices, and Jewish engagement set him apart from
the prior generation of department store entrepreneurs?

Although Erich Mendelsohn has received a great deal of attention from
architects and scholars of modernism, and the Schocken stores have been
analyzed in several scholarly works on German business history, historians
have scarcely tried to relate these two sides of Schocken's and Mendelsohn's
activities—Zionism and modernism—at least for Mendelsohn's German period.[8] European modernism, of course, has long been linked to the Jews in
various ways, from early twentieth-century anti-Semitic polemics through a
wave of recent literary-critical and art-historical scholarship, so Schocken's
role as a patron of modernist architecture and design should not come as
a surprise.[9] Furthermore, as the historian Franklin Toker points out, in
1930 Jews lived in four of the five most architecturally radical houses in
the world.[10] Yet, the historical literature has seldom addressed the place of
Zionism in this cultural formation or indeed asked how German Zionism,
modernist aesthetics, and modern retail entrepreneurship came together in
the history of one extraordinarily successful department store chain.

This chapter takes steps in that direction by viewing the Schocken department stores—and also, but to a lesser extent, those of Leonhard Tietz—at the
intersection of German business history, Jewish history, and the history of
modern architecture. I treat Schocken's innovative stores, in part, as a Jewish
response to an earlier generation of department stores and their critics, and as
a kind of corollary to other contemporaneous German Jewish developments
and experiences. Drawing on the work of architectural historian Kathleen
James, especially her comparison of the Wertheim building on Berlin's Leipziger
Strasse with Schocken's Nuremberg store, the chapter is structured around a
series of oppositions, above all between the awe-inspiring, cathedral-like consuming palaces of the Wilhelmine period and the rational, sober (*sachlich*),
and democratizing department stores of the Weimar Republic.

Following James and others, I trace the origins of modernism in department store design to the later 1890s with Alfred Messel's creation of a particularly German department store aesthetic and with the rejection of a style that had been tainted as un-German and "Jewish." The chapter then follows the history of the Schocken firm and explores Schocken's relationship to broader changes in German-Jewish social, cultural, and intellectual history. I discuss the new principles of department store design in the Weimar Republic, focusing on Mendelsohn's Schocken stores and several other modernist department stores in provincial German cities and towns. In its fully realized form in the later 1920s, modernist department store design also helped transcend the obsolescent styles of Wilhelmine architecture and reflected the search for a rational aesthetic, one that appeared to embody the spirit of the new times.[11] Ultimately, however, even Mendelsohn's modernism was condemned as "Jewish architecture." Despite their avowed renunciation of the aristocratic fantasy of Wilhelmine consumer culture, the modernist department stores of the Weimar era, like their prewar predecessors, remained enmeshed in both the dreamworlds of modern consumption and enduring assumptions about Jews and Germany's new consumer culture.

Warenhaus Wertheim, the "Gothic Modern," and Wilhelmine Commercial Architecture

Before turning to Weimar-era architecture, the Schocken stores, and the department store construction boom of the mid- to late 1920s, we need to step back to the turn of the twentieth century, the first golden age of department store building in Germany and the crucible of European architectural modernism. To situate the aesthetic impulses and achievements of Schocken and Mendelsohn, we must first understand what they were responding to in pre–World War I department store design.

The Wertheim department store on Leipziger Strasse, the emblematic German cathedral of consumption, is among the most well-known works of Wilhelmine period architecture. First constructed in 1896–97—additions to the original structure were made in 1899, 1904, and again in the 1920s—it was Germany's largest and most elegant department store at the time of its opening and would soon be its most profitable. The enormous structure had a tremendous impact on Berlin's built environment and on German department store construction for at least the next two decades. Even though it was destroyed during the Second World War, it remains an iconic symbol of the old Berlin.

Originally designed by Alfred Messel, one of the leading architects of the period, the building was notable for its imposing scale, its sweeping facades, and most of all for its starkness and austerity. Paul Göhre's 1907 book *Das Warenhaus* (The department store) focuses above all on this particular store, and was written soon after the completion of its Leipziger Platz extension. Göhre begins his book with vivid descriptions of the building's exterior:

> Silent amid the loud din, proud and self-assured like the enormous trees in front of it, majestic, almost solemn in the way its buttresses reach into the heights. A department store? But no sign, no banners, nothing bright by day, no light effects by night to announce its function. Not the slightest thing about it smacks of advertisement. Not even the slightest sign, at least from afar, of what purpose the house serves. . . . The cumulative impression this house gives is of the most dignified restraint.[12]

He goes on to compare the edifice to a Gothic cathedral, a Greek temple, a chapel at an Oxford college, and even a subtly beautiful woman, who is "nobly but not ostentatiously dressed and only noticed by those whose eyes can appreciate exquisite tastes."[13] The cathedral comparison is based, in part, on the building's verticality, on the way its columns bring the eye skyward, inspiring a sense of awe and majesty, reactions that are a modern-day equivalent to the presumed effect of gazing at the great medieval cathedrals.[14] Göhre also emphasizes the building's dignity and its understated quality—in short, its absence of bombast and its stylistic harmony and integrity. Even the shop windows on the building's other side, he writes, "[are] the most elegant advertisements imaginable: indeed they display the treasures that can be obtained in the house. They are alluring to be sure but they are not obtrusive."[15]

4.2 Wertheim department store, showing Leipziger Strasse and Leipziger Platz extension. From *Wertheim Berlin. Leipziger Strasse und Leipziger Platz.* Courtesy of the University of Southern California, on behalf of the USC Libraries Special Collections.

In her analysis of the Wertheim building, Kathleen James suggests that Messel was responding to the critique of department stores as foreign imports and to the contemporary accusation that they engaged in untoward sales practices, and that they were cluttered and chaotic *Ramschbasare*, destructive of traditional German ways. The historian Kevin Repp strikes a similar chord, noting, for example, that Wertheim benefited from the bad press surrounding Tietz's nearby store, with its much more vaunted edifice and its aggressive advertising campaigns. Restraint was Wertheim's practiced strategy for disarming the anti–department store crusaders and belying the propaganda of the German shopkeeper movement.[16] In contrast to major department stores in France, Belgium, and the United States—often ornate, grandiose metal-and-glass edifices—Messel strove for a new architecture, James writes, "one that was patriotic rather than international in outlook and distinguished as much by its historicism as its forthright expression of skeletal frame construction."[17]

Messel, in short, sought to Germanize the department store. He accomplished this by rooting the building (and thus the department store phenomenon) in German history, through overtures to the style of German towns' late medieval market culture, resulting in what has been called the "new Gothic" or the "Gothic modern"—Gothic in its architectural references and modern in its self-conscious melding of different styles. Urban planner Walter Curt Behrendt characterized the Wertheim building as a "spontaneous expression of national tradition," a continuation of the spirit of Carl Friedrich Schinkel, master builder of Berlin under Frederick William III.[18]

Calling Messel a great artist, Göhre describes the building as an "organic creation full of high harmony and consummate functionalism [*Zweck-dienlichkeit*]." But he adds, crucially, that the architect had not invented a new style for the new function of this building. Rather, "it's much more the case that he made use of old styles."[19] Göhre credits Messel with combining a whole array of period styles, the cathedral-like buttresses, the Greek-classical facade that stretched along Leipziger Strasse, and the Renaissance-era back side, into a harmonious whole, "a triumphal unity" with modern materials like glass and iron in addition to stone.[20] The result, he declares, is the new department store form, a "nearly inescapable model" for all subsequent department stores, which are, Göhre writes, "more or less successful imitations of the Wertheim building."[21]

The building's critical reception was enormously positive, and the store immediately rose to the top of the list of the capital city's tourist attractions.[22] Soon other kinds of commercial buildings followed this style, the so-called "Messel vertical type."[23] Writer Otto Erich von Wussow, in a 1911 text, dubbed this kind of modern commercial construction one of the great achievements of the period's bourgeois architecture, and urban chronicler Max Osborn declared that no new department store designers in Berlin, or anywhere in Germany, could "free themselves from the influence of this model."[24] Kathleen James, similarly noting the influence of Messel's

Wertheim store on contemporary architecture, from office buildings to factories to rural residences, calls Messel's style "rational historicism," seeing it as a bridge between the often elaborate ornamentation popular in imperial Germany and the stark modernism of the post–World War I years.[25]

In contrast to the Messel building, the all-glass facade designed by Bernhard Sehring for the neighboring Tietz store (1899), with its so-called "total display window," might have aroused a great deal of public curiosity, but as one historian points out, architecturally it was a "dead end."[26] A contemporary critic writing under the name "Plutus" excoriated the store, accusing Oscar Tietz of tastelessness, of trying to import American styles into Germany, of oversaturating Berlin with ads—on autobuses, for example—and for trying to reinvent the department store without regard for Berlin's existing aesthetic norms and standards.[27] Göhre conceded that the building was as attention-getting as Wertheim, adding: "It is certainly original that from the street you can see deep into the store, especially at night when it's illuminated, but it is not at all nice."[28] Reflecting back on the Tietz store years later, writer Sammy Gronemann recalled an old Berlin joke: "When Tietz built its palace on Leipziger Strasse with the four imposing female figures floating above the portal, Berliners called it the 'five senses—since taste was missing.'" This in stark contrast to the neighboring Wertheim store, which, for Gronemann, was the "most beautiful creation of modern architecture."[29] Business at the new Tietz store was disappointing too, especially given the building's enormous cost, and rumors circulated that the Hermann Tietz firm was on the verge of bankruptcy. No wonder that the next Tietz structure in Berlin, their 1905 branch at Alexanderplatz, was more conservative, more architecturally "solid," and clearly indebted to the Messel building.[30]

A major wave of department store construction occurred in Germany in the late 1890s and early 1900s. The original department stores of the 1880s and 1890s had occupied relatively small commercial buildings. With their early success, their increasing expansion and diversification of stock, and their ballooning numbers of employees, these businesses soon outgrew their facilities and often took over neighboring properties. Further growth and success by individual firms and by department stores in general helped convince Germany's risk-averse banking establishment—made even more cautious by the 1873 financial crash—that these stores were sound investments, making it easier for department store entrepreneurs to secure loans for ambitious construction projects.[31] Many were thus able to vacate or tear down the hodgepodge of retail spaces they had cobbled together and build larger edifices. This in turn enabled a degree of stylistic cohesion, which, when involving well-known architects, helped publicize the businesses and gave department store firms a particular character, an early form of what we would now call branding. (Those turn-of-the century constructions were, over time, often expanded in several stages and, in some cases, rebuilt and enlarged multiple times.) Simultaneously, the most successful department store owners began to expand their operations into chains, aiming to dominate local and regional and, in several cases, even national markets.

This context helps explain the tremendous influence of Messel's Wertheim store. A major work of enormous size in the heart of Berlin—its surface area, more than twenty-seven thousand square meters, doubled that of the Reichstag, and it dwarfed the adjacent government buildings—executed by one of Germany's most prominent architects, it naturally received a great deal of attention.[32] But the fact that its construction occurred right at the beginning of the first wave of new, purpose-built department store structures made it particularly consequential. Before Messel there was no German department store aesthetic. Early German department stores were, in architectural terms, barely distinguishable from residential constructions; they had large display windows on the ground floor, but the upper floors could have easily been mistaken for apartments.[33] Stylistically, the first wave of major department store constructions tended to be a mishmash, a cacophony of baroque and "oriental" design elements. Hence, Messel's so-called Gothic modern or rational historicism became the dominant style for German department stores and a model for German commercial architecture until the First World War.[34]

Warenhaus Wertheim's interiors were somewhat less revolutionary than the store's arresting exterior, but the selling floors' elegance and sumptuous materials distinguished the store from its predecessors and emphatically distanced Wertheim from the accusation of being a *Ramschbasar*, a cheap or shady discounter. The store's refined dignity was also meant to mollify critics of Germany's new consumer culture, who feared the cultural effects of crass commercialism. Wertheim's tastefulness served to demonstrate the compatibility of art and commerce and of the fine and applied arts.[35] The store's high aesthetic standards could also, Göhre noted, benefit shoppers and browsers alike by teaching them principles of refined organization and display, a notion that was mocked in a vicious, anti-Semitic diatribe against Wertheim that rebuked him as culture-less and un-German.[36]

As in most European department stores of the period, the light court or atrium (*Lichthof*) served as the central point of orientation. In its completed form, the Wertheim store featured three. They served to conduct light through the store's galleries, to orient customers not accustomed to these new retail establishments, and to impart a sense of grandeur, ennobling the middle-class consumer experience with the trappings of aristocracy. The original atrium, with its curved glass, dramatic spaces, and ornate features, achieved a kind of bombast that was somewhat at odds with the sobriety of the building's external form. As described by James: "Rich materials and bold technical effects were almost dwarfed by the spatial drama: barrel-vaulted skylights and two precariously perched bridges eclipsed marble facing and chains of electric lights, still a novelty. Almost lost amid the magnificence of a space which awestruck contemporaries equated with

4.3 Wertheim department store, Leipziger Strasse, Berlin—central atrium. Stiftung Deutsches Technikmuseum Berlin, Hist. Archiv.

princely palaces was the mundane goal of selling."[37] Unlike the atriums in Parisian department stores, whose entryways were dominated by ornate central staircases, the Wertheim court was an enormous open area, bounded by columns, which made it seem like an outdoor space and indeed like a central market square, which, the historian Alarich Rooch writes, appeared from the upper floors like "a theater for the staging of consumer culture."[38] Rooch also notes that the two large standing lights make this part of the central atrium seem like an altar, and that the balcony and the large sun on the wall give it the character of a temple.

As we have seen, Berlin's department stores typically catered to distinct social groups, and although they were also sites of social mixing, it was clear for whom goods in different stores were selected and priced.[39] Wertheim's Leipziger Strasse store was considered "purely a luxury department store" for clientele who had a good deal of disposable income.[40] It represented a departure from existing stores not only in terms of size and architectural form, but also in the display of goods and the manner in which sales were conducted—sales gimmicks or flashy stunts to draw in onlookers were replaced with a more dignified, almost museum-like coolness.[41] In short, Wertheim pioneered the idea of the elegant department store in Germany, making department store shopping an acceptable pastime for German elites. No wonder that Kaiser Wilhelm II chose this store for a ceremonious, albeit ultimately rather ambiguous visit in 1910.[42]

Wertheim's and Messel's response to the critique of department stores as un-German, foreign imports, as chaotic scenes of seduction and chicanery, was thus to turn toward staid dignity, to ground the edifice in German commercial tradition and premodern German history, to reject ostentatious promotion and to embrace luxury, tastefulness, and wealth, resulting in the Gothic modern. The Gothic modern became the dominant architectural style of German retail culture from the beginning of the twentieth century through the First World War, when new department store construction ground to a halt.[43]

The post–World War I world presented a drastically altered cultural and economic landscape for department store organization and construction. In the transition from the partnership of Georg Wertheim and Alfred Messel to that of Salman Schocken and Erich Mendelsohn, we move from the turn-of-the-century synthesis of tradition and modernity to the interwar period's full-on exaltation of the new. Our protagonists change, as well, from two Jewish men who sought acceptance in German-Christian society through conversion (in the case of Messel and many members of the Wertheim family) and intermarriage, to figures who participated in the heady revival of Jewish learning and the strengthening of Jewish solidarity that flourished during the Weimar Republic.

From Margonin to Zwickau: The Schocken Brothers and Consumer Modernity in Saxony

As Salman Schocken presented it in his abundant writings and speeches, modern architecture and modern retail practices, indeed the arts and commerce in general, were parts of an interconnected whole, both serving the demands of the time and both based on rational, scientific thinking that aimed to uplift the consumer's quality of life. Salman Schocken continually stressed the uniqueness of the Schocken stores, which differentiated themselves from most contemporary retail establishments not only in their architecture, but also in their business methods, including their relationships with manufacturers, their administrative centralization, and their treatment of employees and customers.

The story of the Schocken concern's growth from its humble beginnings in Zwickau into a giant commercial empire of nineteen stores (and additional affiliates) has been told in several places, so here only an abbreviated sketch is required.[44] The Schocken family, small storeowners, hailed from the town of Margonin in the province of Posen. Salman, the youngest of ten siblings, had to curtail his studies at an early age and went to work as an apprentice in a small retail shop. Like his older brother Simon—and indeed the majority of the region's ambitious Jewish men—Salman was primed for a career in retail, though the intellectually hungry young man instead longed for a life of scholarship. When he was about thirty and presumed to be too young and inexperienced to operate a department store, the confident Salman invited his doubters to view his private library of "over 900 volumes," which included classic works of political economy and commerce, books he claimed to have worked through systematically and digested thoroughly.[45] He would bring this academic sensibility not only to his Jewish and cultural activities but also to his commercial affairs.[46] His many writings and speeches on economic issues provided historical perspective on retail in Germany and outlined his own commercial and aesthetic principles; these sources are a window onto the history of the firm, illuminating both its actual workings and Salman Schocken's hopes for its reputation.

At the turn of the century, Simon Schocken moved west from Posen to Saxony when he married into the Urys, another family of Posen Jews, and began working for their department store business in Leipzig. He was soon sent to Zwickau, an industrial town in Saxony, to open up a new Ury branch, and Salman joined him in the enterprise several months before the store's grand opening in March 1901. There Simon Schocken oversaw a staff of some forty workers.[47] Advertisements in the Zwickau newspapers announced the store's guiding principles: "steadfast reliability," "the greatest fairness," "extensive assortment," "unlimited exchange of purchased items," "fixed prices," and "cash transactions."[48] The brothers' stated goal was to provide high-quality goods to their customers at the lowest possible prices. Through its promotional campaigns the store rewarded loyal customers and emphasized the quality of its products, strategies that the Schocken brothers continued to employ in the years ahead.

Zwickau, an unremarkable provincial town, was, like much of Saxony, undergoing dramatic changes in this period. Rich in anthracite deposits and the site of growing textile and steel industries, Saxony and neighboring Thuringia began a process of rapid industrialization late in the nineteenth century. Industrial growth was in turn creating an expanding and radicalizing working class that increasingly embraced socialist and social democratic politics—the region would later become a hotbed of revolutionary activity. The local elites, who had managed city affairs unchallenged for centuries, suddenly found themselves threatened by new political developments, nascent social unrest, and unpredictable economic cycles. Saxony's population increased by 23 percent between 1904 and 1914, reaching nearly five million on the eve of World War I.[49] Simultaneously, average income and level of buying power ascended appreciably, creating favorable conditions for new retail ventures.[50]

Despite the opposition of local businesses, the Zwickau store was successful from the beginning, and in the first year of operations business was so good that the Schocken brothers increased their staff from forty to sixty-five.[51] Soon Salman Schocken went off on his own and moved to nearby Oelsnitz, a town of twenty thousand residents, where three years later he opened his own business, a store with a staff of thirty-four employees and a sales area of some eight hundred square meters, making it one of the largest department stores in Saxony at the time. Newspaper ads heralded the store's opening in October 1904, promising customers "the latest thing in *haute couture*" and wares that were "modern," "chic," and "elegant."[52] As had been the case with the Zwickau store, Schocken correctly calculated that the new store's customer base would come not only from the town itself, but from surrounding communities. In an effort to cultivate a loyal following in the region, he even experimented with travel vouchers that reimbursed shoppers from neighboring Saxon towns for their rail fare.[53] He continually stressed customer service—advertising, for example, that when needed, his employees would carry purchased items from the store to a customer's train.[54]

Feeling threatened by the new competition, local business owners launched smear campaigns against the upstart store. The anti–department store movement mobilized, spreading the usual calumny that, for example, Schocken products were of inferior quality and that the brothers engaged in deceptive sales practices. In response, Salman Schocken created a quality-control system, a dedicated site for the scientific testing of goods, which aimed to establish a lasting association between the Schocken name and high-quality merchandise.[55] These efforts reached fruition in the 1920s, a time when rationalization and efficiency became guiding economic principles and even cultural buzzwords across the nation.

In January 1907 when Simon and Salman Schocken rejoined forces and purchased the Zwickau store from the Urys, the firm I. Schocken Sons Zwickau was born. The new enterprise consisted of the Zwickau branch, Salman Schocken's Oelsnitz store, and a purchasing and warehousing center, also in Zwickau. Zwickau was an ideal location for the central offices. As Georg Manasse pointed out years later, it was not by accident that the headquarters stayed there and were not moved to Berlin, even after the firm's substantial growth, since Zwickau lay in a highly industrialized area that facilitated visits to the nearby textile mills and factories with which the Schockens did business.[56] This enabled the Schocken concern to keep a close eye on and influence the production process, which was one of the cornerstones of Salman Schocken's unique approach to the department store business.

The concern grew quickly, and in its first four years the brothers added new locations in the Saxon towns of Lugau, Aue, and Planitz. Lugau had only twelve thousand inhabitants, but like other Schocken locations, it lay in an industrializing area, where increases in textile and iron production accelerated population growth and fueled the expansion of a middle class with money to spend. By studying patterns of economic growth and predicting demographic change, the Schockens were able to capture untapped markets, move in while commercial real estate costs were still reasonable, and create populations of loyal consumers. Indeed, Schocken stores appeared throughout Saxony, forming more or less a circle radiating out from Zwickau in the center.[57] Salman Schocken's biographer Anthony David argues that the strategy of avoiding the major Saxon cities Leipzig and Dresden had the added benefit of not challenging the notables who held sway over their middle-class, urban populations and thus avoiding the wrath of entrenched elites.[58] Instead, Schocken targeted a largely working-class customer base and aimed to improve worker lives by offering goods of exceptional quality and durability at reasonable prices. This also made good business sense: by introducing modern consumer culture to the working classes, the Schocken stores could have this potentially huge regional market all to themselves.

By the eve of World War I, the firm consisted of ten stores and three affiliates—stores not directly owned by the Schockens but which acquired their merchandise through the Zwickau headquarters and made use of the Schockens' purchasing and distribution system. The Schockens now employed some five hundred people. The firm had even made its first forays outside Saxony, with the opening of its Zerbst (Saxony-Anhalt) store in 1913. It was in these years that Salman Schocken worked out his "system," which, as he recounted later, was fully realized just before the outbreak of war.[59]

Schocken's system, based on the modern principles of rationalization and scientific management, can be seen as the antithesis of the consumerist fantasies that earlier department stores had tried to promote, the replacement of temples to aspirational consumerism with venues for the rational and sober presentation of wares. More specifically, the Schocken system rejected the idea of the department store as an unlimited source of variety, as a place for "everything under one roof." Instead of striving for comprehensiveness and promoting his stores as a site of boundless abundance, Schocken limited the selection of goods by establishing certain norms or types. Rather than trying to cater to every possible taste, he developed a rationalized, systematic approach to acquiring merchandise. Carrying fewer items in higher volume gave the concern more power over the manufacturers it dealt with precisely because it was ordering such large quantities. Schocken also ordered farther in advance than its competitors, enabling manufacturers to plan ahead and build in cost-cutting measures.[60] This power over the manufacturers could be wielded to make production serve consumer need, rather than letting consumer choice (and costs) be dictated by the producers.

Explaining this concept in a 1928 speech, Manasse gave the example of curd soap (*Kernseife*), a cleanser that the Schocken stores had originally carried in multiple varieties. The firm then changed course and began stocking only one particular kind. They chose a manufacturer whose factories operated at night when electricity was cheaper, lowering production costs, which translated into cheaper prices. Schocken also dictated the materials that the producer could use. The result, Manasse claimed, was that Schocken's curd soap profits had increased by a factor of twenty and the firm and customers could rest assured that consumers were receiving a fine product.[61] This approach required precise knowledge about buying habits, even consumer psychology, since ordering more than could be sold and carrying excess stock was detrimental to the department store business, which still depended on rapid turnover. The purchasing process was therefore extremely important for the Schockens; they devoted significantly more attention and resources to it than did typical department store firms, which, Salman Schocken noted, paid correspondingly more attention to the art of selling.[62] As a result, the Schockens paid their buyers far more, as much as three or four times the going rate, in part to offset the temptation to accept gifts or meal invitations from supplier representatives, practices that clouded the selection process and at Schocken led to employees' immediate dismissal.[63]

The role of the department store firm, Salman Schocken theorized, lay in the space between production and consumption. As he put it in a 1926 address that was published in the firm's in-house newspaper: "[Retail] is called upon to penetrate the internal logic of consumption and to represent the consumers' interests vis-à-vis production."[64] By ordering fewer items at higher volume, Schocken kept manufacturing costs down, leading to cheaper prices for its customers. In-house production had the same effect, and beginning in 1920, the concern manufactured first its own textiles and soon other products too, enabling it to cut out the middleman entirely in some sectors.[65] Salman Schocken was not exactly a socialist, certainly not in a formal sense: he fleetingly sympathized with the SPD after the November Revolution, before becoming disillusioned, and then briefly belonged to the left-liberal German Democratic Party (DDP). Nevertheless, Schocken was attuned to the injustices and inefficiencies of the capitalist marketplace and was critical of the unchecked power of big agriculture and heavy industry over the economy. Above all, he considered himself a friend to the "little man" and sought to improve the condition of the working class by supplying workers and their families with high-quality, durable goods.[66]

Schocken display windows reinforced the stores' devotion to the practical needs of its modestly earning core customers. Instead of the fantastical displays that stoked the imaginations of metropolitan consumers, Schocken windows often showcased practical goods like miners' uniforms or work boots, and the accompanying text typically pointed out the wares' features in a dispassionate, informative way, often with instructions for practices that could prolong the product's life.[67]

Ever concerned with aesthetic matters, too, Salman Schocken understood the role of large-scale retail as safeguarding not only the quality, but even the tastefulness of consumable goods, and he considered himself responsible for the "cultural level" of his customers.[68] Although the Left generally paid little attention to consumption at this time, and Schocken's desire to uplift the working classes could certainly be seen as paternalistic, his stores were nonetheless lauded by social democratic observers who recognized that they made previously unattainable products available to the working class and thus markedly increased workers' standard of living.[69] The same strategy ingratiated him with those on the higher end of the social spectrum. Indeed, Zwickau elites welcomed the Schockens. Grateful for the business they brought to the city and the role they played in smoothing over social tensions by placating the working class, notables in Zwickau and other Saxon towns secured the goodwill of municipal authorities and helped the brothers swiftly navigate local bureaucracies.[70]

Administrative centralization was crucial for all department store chains, but Schocken implemented an unprecedented degree of centralization and rationalization. The Center (die Zentrale) in Zwickau consisted of three connected buildings: a main warehouse facility, workshops, and a central administration building. In 1930 the Center's staff included over three hundred employees who represented "the common, centralized ideas and energies for the department stores of the Schocken-Concern, which are directed in close harmony."[71]

This office was responsible for all purchasing for the individual Schocken stores, with the exception of fresh produce, which was ordered locally.[72] The Schocken brothers met semiannually with the head buyers from the concern's different departments at the Zwickau offices and examined hundreds of samples, evaluating price and quality before placing their sizable orders.[73] Schocken and his Zwickau staff micromanaged the individual stores, overseeing which departments they were divided into, for example, and even presiding over such details as what to display in the store windows. Gershom Schocken, Salman's son, recalled that his father issued rules and regulations governing every area of department store activity, from washing the floors through the packing of purchased items.[74]

The Zwickau headquarters was also the site for the coordination and printing of the firm's promotional materials. Salman Schocken played an active role in creating the firm's image and iconography; he supervised the choice of fonts and styles for the firm's letterhead, advertisements, and displays. Even proposed product displays from the various stores had to be photographed and sent to the Zwickau offices for approval. The Central also included a construction office for managing new buildings and renovations.

Salman Schocken also created a rigorous bookkeeping method, conducted out of the statistical department in Zwickau, which kept track of all expenses and proceeds for all the stores. Cashiers and bookkeepers at each of the local branches had to gather all sales receipts and ship them at the end of each month to Zwickau for processing, a procedure Manasse likened to the transmission of nerve signals through the body's central nervous system.[75] For every product the stores carried, management kept track of the costs of the raw materials, the labor hours that went into its manufacture, and the associated expenses such as shipping costs and taxes. Drawing on this information, Schocken could estimate products' real costs and judge whether they were being sold at fair prices, or if suppliers were trying to squeeze out excessive profits.[76] Starting in 1922 Salman Schocken kept extensive pricing data, creating the "Schocken Index," which ultimately listed over three hundred different kinds of goods from thirty-six departments. By reading this index alongside official statistics and other economic indicators, he could derive a sense of how his prices compared to the changing cost of living, concluding, for example, that a pair of men's boots cost a German worker sixteen working hours before World War I and fourteen and a half in 1931, or that a pound of margarine required 40 percent less work time in 1931 than it did before the war.[77] The Schocken Index was also used to calculate the supplemental wages given to employees during their paid vacation days.[78]

The quality control efforts first instituted early in the century—to counter the specious accusations of hostile competitors—were further refined when the Schockens hired Dr. Erich Kann in December 1924. Kann, a chemist at the Kaiser Wilhelm Institute in Dresden, established a laboratory for conducting the chemical analysis and physical testing of products in order to ensure high quality and appropriate pricing.[79] Scientists at the Zwickau quality control facility subjected goods to a battery of tests to assay such properties as their resistance to tearing, their durability, or the effectiveness of their waterproofing. Results could show, for example, that a given product was best manufactured out of different materials, in which case Schocken would urge his manufacturers to change production methods to produce a better and more cost-effective item.[80] Between 1926 and 1932 approximately ten thousand tests were conducted at the facility.[81]

A 1927 issue of the Schocken firm's in-house newspaper profiled this quality control system. Featuring a "visit to the laboratory," it described the scene as follows: "In one room stand large bottles with alcohol for the preparation of eau de cologne; smaller bottles with delicate fragrances wait on wooden shelves; clean containers in another room offer up the ingredients for 'Curo' toothpaste; in a neighboring room bottles are being filled with hair tonic and sealed up; mountains of sacks with [instant] pudding powder are piled up on wide tables; thousands of perfume flasks sit on long trays while their formulas are prepared: a cornucopia of good aromas and lovely colors!"[82] The article goes on to describe the operation of the most modern machinery and the highly scientific methods used to produce and test goods useful for daily life. It stresses not only the laboratory's modernity and its exciting gadgetry, but also its strict hygienic standards in the production of items like toothpaste and in the mixing of fragrances. Scientific testing and quality control might well have made the Schocken stores seem more modern, more American, and more advanced and cutting-edge—and also more reliable and responsive to customer need—simultaneously silencing their critics and helping distinguish them from the competition.

Schocken's rationalized, scientific approach also encompassed the promotion and pricing of goods. In 1926 the concern ceased holding special sales events like "white weeks." The stores also discontinued the use of rebates, credit, or other special offers to attract customers—yet another way in which they replaced the techniques of the fantasy-inducing metropolitan department stores with sober and rational practices.[83] In a 1934 report Manasse noted that the Schocken stores could boast of

> an extraordinary number of long-standing customers who know that they can buy at favorable [prices] at any time in the Schocken department stores, even though for many years now [we have had]:
>
> > No special events or teasers [*Lockartikel*],
> > No special prices for particular levels of customers
> > No "free" bonus items
> > No "consumer financing" and
> > No special, overblown customer service,
> > And also the most restrained advertisements in both scale and tone.[84]

Salman Schocken admitted that viewed from afar the department store appeared to be a "confusing complexity," a symbol of the "restlessness of the times." Yet, he continued, those who were familiar with its inner workings would recognize a "fully thought-out organism" and appreciate that behind the "glittery variety of goods and aisles, a law governing orderly function was in effect."[85] He repeatedly stressed his centralized and efficient approach to management, applying the same thoroughness and rationalization that characterized other areas of the business. Schocken staff hierarchies and chains of command led back to the central offices in Zwickau, from where the brothers and their staff devised the distribution of labor, job descriptions for different levels of employment, and guidelines for staff conduct.

Yet even as responsibilities and codes of conduct were prescribed from Zwickau, Schocken and Manasse stressed that employees had to learn to rely on their own judgment and to be responsible for their own spheres of activity. They emphasized that good work would be rewarded with promotion and that the individual should work with an eye toward the smooth functioning of the whole system. And despite the flood of rules and regulations issued by the central offices, Salman Schocken urged employees to help the firm progress by sharing their own observations, thereby countering the "stream of organizational experience that emanates from the Center with an opposing stream leading to simplification, improvement, and additions."[86]

Department store sales personnel, Schocken asserted, had a critical social function. They participated in the fulfillment of the people's needs and served a public with limited buying power who faced difficult decisions about how to allocate scant resources.[87] Schocken, therefore, instructed its salesmen and saleswomen to avoid pressuring shoppers to buy for the sake of pumping up store profits. Rather they were to serve the interests of the customer and to comport themselves in a pleasant and friendly, never overzealous manner.[88] Poorly conceived or ill-advised purchases could have lasting repercussions for the working-class households who shopped at Schocken, whereas sound advice from sales personnel could benefit the consumer and help secure the firm's reputation.[89]

The consideration shown Schocken's customers also applied to the concern's own workforce. Workers enjoyed good job security and relatively favorable wages even in times of economic crisis. During the devastating hyperinflation after World War I, Schocken employees received their salary at the end of every workday. Some 90 percent of apprentice workers were eventually hired for long-term positions, and the firm provided in-house training and education for its new employees.[90] Schocken workers evidently did not share the discontent of other department store employees in the later 1920s. They had collective bargaining rights, and three worker representatives met annually with three representatives of management to review working conditions and address workplace issues.[91] Schocken staff members, in addition, could take advantage of subsidized adult education and fitness classes, and they were given more vacation time than the concern was legally obligated to allow.[92] Vacationing workers were entreated to leave home and received supplemental wages so that they could take advantage of the restorative effect of fresh air and lovely scenery. They were able to stay gratis at the firm's lodge in the Erz Mountains, a thirty-five-guest facility in the woods.[93]

Dynamic Dissimilation: The "New Building" and the Jewish Question in the Weimar Republic

In a 1931 speech Salman Schocken looked back over the preceding five years and the rapid expansion of his firm. In this period, the concern had added seven new department stores, increased its employee rolls to some six thousand workers and reached an annual turnover of nearly 100 million marks. Referring to the new store buildings in Nuremberg, Stuttgart,

4.4 "Partial views of the most recent Schocken concern buildings" (1930). Sächsisches Staatsarchiv, Staatsarchiv Chemnitz, 33309 Georg Manasse Papers, No. 93.

Augsburg, Crimmitschau, Waldenburg, and Chemnitz, he declared that I. Schocken Sons had created a new style in department store architecture, a successor to Messel's Wertheim building and Joseph Olbrich's monumental L. Tietz store in Düsseldorf (1905), which had been the models for earlier generations of German stores. Schocken averred that this style, which, he conceded, perhaps had more influence abroad than in Germany, reflected the spirit of the times, capturing the dynamism and tempo of the modern age.[94] Erich Mendelsohn, too, saw the Nuremberg store, his first Schocken commission—the renovation and expansion of an old factory—as a breakthrough: "Until that point," he observed, "we had only classical structures: the Wertheim building in Berlin and those that followed."[95] His stores for Schocken, Mendelsohn claimed, had created a completely new style in commercial construction, a modern department store aesthetic.

World War I and the revolutionary currents that swept aside Germany's imperial regime rendered both the patriotism and the elegance of Messel's Wertheim store anachronistic and even distasteful in the heady atmosphere of the Weimar Republic's early years. Hyperinflation, wild economic fluctuations, and extreme political polarization stifled commercial life and prolonged the wartime stagnation through the early 1920s. Most retail firms struggled, and few new department stores were created. Yet Salman Schocken proudly testified that he was able to retain his employees and avoid painful layoffs through this period, though the firm's profits were strained as a result of the scarcity of resources, increased production costs, runaway inflation, and his miscalculation that economic order would soon be restored.[96]

Only with the currency stabilization at the end of 1923 and the ensuing economic recovery did the retail sector resume its prewar growth. By 1924–25 a new era of commercial expansion was under way. From that point until the economic crash of 1929, Germany's urban infrastructures developed rapidly. New retail establishments and also schools, hospitals, power plants, and cinemas were built at a steady pace, resulting in the construction of what has been called a "new Germany."[97] These years were the Schocken concern's golden age. The concern resumed the rapid growth of the prewar era, entering larger markets with impressive new buildings and key retail innovations. Profits rose precipitously, reaching around 20 million marks in 1925 and over 26 million the following year.[98]

Architecturally, the new Schocken department stores reflected the altered sensibility of the Weimar period, expressing the democratic and egalitarian principles that underlay the Republic's founding.[99] Indeed, the era's "new building" called for a rejection of the hierarchy, luxury, and ornamentation that characterized such edifices as Wertheim's Leipziger Strasse store, the KaDeWe, and the L. Tietz store in Düsseldorf. Rudolf Stiefler, the architect responsible for the expansion of Schocken's Cottbus store (completed in 1927), enumerated the modern principles in department store construction as "transparency, light, air, clarity, [and] the strictest functionalism allowed by the laws of architectural aesthetics."[100] In some ways the new design principles signaled a return to the populism and mass-marketing impulse, if not the chaos, of the original German department stores.

World War I was also a major watershed in German-Jewish history. The prevailing assimilationist ethos among the German Jewish bourgeoisie came under attack by a new generation who sought a deeper connection to Jewish traditions and hoped to revitalize the Jewish people's intellectual and spiritual livelihood. Exposure to the Jews of Eastern Europe during military service—most famously in the case of Franz Rosenzweig—inspired new feelings of kinship with Polish coreligionists and led many to romanticize the world of Polish Jewry as a more authentic form of life than what their own, deracinated experience in Germany had to offer. Martin Buber typified this search in his research on Hasidism and his valorization of ecstatic worship and spirituality.

Salman Schocken's trajectory reflected this broader pattern among German-Jewish elites. Shortly before the war Schocken began to withdraw somewhat from the trade associations that had taken so much of his time and devoted increasing energy to the Zionist movement, which he had joined in 1910 or 1911.[101] With his growing fortune Schocken had sought acceptance in German bourgeois society—dropping, for example, the Yiddish name Salman for the American-sounding S. Schocken Jr., in official correspondence—but soon reversed course and invested his energies increasingly in Jewish affairs.

A massive migration had carried tens of thousands of Jews westward from the province of Posen in the nineteenth and early twentieth centuries. Some fifty thousand migrants, including the two branches of the Tietz family and many other department store entrepreneurs, came between 1824 and 1871, and another fifty thousand came between 1877 and 1905.[102] Most of these new arrivals had taken the German side in the cultural and linguistic conflicts that roiled Posen. They settled predominately in urban areas like Berlin and Breslau (Wrocław), experienced economic success, and as German speakers acculturated rapidly. In the meantime, however, a newer wave of Jewish immigrants from points farther east had begun to arrive in the 1880s. This group consisted predominately of Yiddish speakers fleeing persecution in the Russian Empire, people who were more likely to bear the outward signs of Jewish religious distinction. In several German cities, including Leipzig, Dresden, and Hamborn, these new arrivals soon outnumbered the members of the established Jewish communities.[103] The combination of a sense of kinship with these so-called Ostjuden, together with the increasingly voluble anti-Semitism that marked German politics and culture during this period, triggered a break with the assimilationist tendencies of earlier generations, and indeed "a turn backward and inward," in the words of the historian Shulamit Volkov, who, in a highly influential essay, labeled this process "dissimilation."[104]

Salman Schocken's life embodied the dynamic of dissimilation that Volkov describes. The Schocken brothers encountered a great many Russian-Jewish immigrants in Saxony, many of whom settled there having fled pogroms after World War I and the Russian Revolution.[105] The Schockens made a point of hiring eastern Jews to work in their stores. They supported Jewish communal philanthropy, demonstrating a sense of solidarity with their newly arrived coreligionists, unlike the established Jewish community, which often turned its back on the newcomers. A generation younger than the Jewish communal leadership—and indeed most of the founding entrepreneurs of the major German department stores—Salman Schocken participated (as thinker, but more significantly as patron) in the heady revival of Jewish learning, the so-called renaissance of Jewish culture that flourished during the Weimar Republic.[106] He also cast his lot with the Zionist movement.

For Schocken, like many other German Jews, the turn to Zionism originally had little to do with the prospect of settling in Palestine. He had reacted with derision at his first reading of Theodor Herzl's writings, and when he did join the Zionist ranks, Schocken was drawn more to the cultural Zionist ideas of Ahad Ha'am (as reworked and promoted by Martin Buber) than to Herzl's political program. Cultural Zionism stressed the need for Jewish cultural rebirth and did not demand immediate relocation to Palestine. Its adherents saw Palestine as a safe haven for persecuted Jews, but for the comfortable Jews of Central Europe, Zion functioned as a cultural and spiritual center, not a necessary destination.[107]

Zionism, for Schocken, represented a rejection of the ideals of the preceding generations of German Jews and a condemnation of the alleged superficiality and emptiness of the German-Jewish bourgeoisie. As his son Gershom put it some years later, Schocken was attracted to Zionism because he found acceptance and community through it, and the movement offered critical, intellectually grounded perspectives on the German-Jewish elites, the "liberal, assimilationist, superficial German Jewry" who had never accepted him, despite his stunning commercial success.[108] Zionism brought him back into active engagement with Judaism, not in the sense of formal religious observance, but rather in terms of an intellectual connection to Jewish texts, a visceral sense of national belonging, and an investment in the project of cultural revitalization. Zionism, in short, was one way of rejecting the assimilationist strategy of the established generation.

Nevertheless, Schocken's journey back to Judaism went through German culture. As Gershom Schocken wrote, it was a "path which led him from Goethe to the Bible, from Novalis to Rabbi Nachman, without him ever giving up Goethe or Novalis."[109] He was so deeply immersed in German literary culture that even when Schocken embraced Zionism and sought to revitalize the Jewish people, he viewed the project through German categories and perspectives and used German national culture as a point of comparison for the Jews. His Zionism, like that of many of his contemporaries, was one steeped in Jewish history and German culture.

The small but dynamic Zionist community that first Simon and later Salman Schocken joined brought the brothers into close contact with intellectuals, writers, and artists, including the architect Erich Mendelsohn. Both Schocken brothers had long been interested in architecture and aesthetic questions. Salman was familiar with the Werkbund, whose coffee kettles and table lamps could be purchased at Schocken stores. In fact, in an address at the 1912 Zionist Congress in Posen, he praised Werkbund artists for breaking free of historicist design and superfluous ornament and creating modern, functionalist style.[110] Why did Schocken mention the Werkbund in a speech before a group of ardent Zionists? His less than enthusiastic audience seems to have been befuddled by this too. The connection, Anthony David suggests, was that Schocken hoped to do for Jewish culture what the Werkbund was doing for German design. He sought to put the Jewish people on a new footing by liberating them from debilitating dependence on the past and excessive reliance on German tradition and influence.[111] In addition to assertions of independence from national traditions, the cultural Zionist project and the Werkbund's modernism shared a utopian strain, a desire to remake life in which material and cultural reform went hand in hand.[112]

In a sense, Messel's Wertheim structure can be seen as a distillation, a highly visible symbol, of what the German Zionists, Schocken included, had come to oppose. The work of a baptized Jewish architect, the building could be read as an attempt to root the department store phenomenon in German history and culture. By the early 1920s, however, these goals seemed anachronistic and were anathema to both modernists and Zionists. Zionists indeed rejected the liberal assimilationist tendencies of their parents' generation, and the Schocken concern—when it reemerged from wartime economic stagnation and began ambitious new expansion and construction plans—embraced the search for a new kind of building rather than trying to adhere to traditional German styles. Its structures represented the architectural equivalent of the rationalized, modern approach that the Schockens developed for the administration of their business.

Erich Mendelsohn gave form to these aspirations. Born in 1887 in the East Prussian town of Allenstein (today Olsztyn), Mendelsohn, like Schocken, came from a shopkeeper family. He concluded his studies in Munich, where he came into contact with expressionist artists around the Blaue Reiter and Die Brücke circles. An early critic of the war, Mendelsohn participated in the radical artists' collectives that emerged during the November Revolution of 1918–19. He set up shop in Berlin after the war, and his wartime sketches were shown at Paul Cassirer's Berlin gallery in 1919, in the exhibition *Architecture in Steel and Reinforced Concrete*, which Salman Schocken attended.

Mendelsohn maintained lifelong connections to leading scientists and musicians, in both cases through his wife, the cellist Luise Maas, and physics and music influenced his work from the beginning. His first major commission was the Einstein Tower at Potsdam's astrophysical observatory, which he intended to be both a monument to Einstein's work on relativity and a laboratory for further study of the physicist's theories.[113] Although controversial at the time, the tower brought Mendelsohn notoriety and was, as James writes, "the most important built symbol of German architecture immediately after the First World War."[114] It marked an early moment in the young architect's lifelong engagement with the study of movement and force and demonstrated his hope to express the spirit of the modern age in concrete.

A committed Jew in a profession historically unwelcoming to Jews, Mendelsohn met most of his employers through Jewish connections. He seldom entered competitions for commissions and received most of his contracts from wealthy Jewish businessmen such as the publishing magnate Rudolf Mosse and retail entrepreneur Hans Petersdorff.[115] German Zionist leader Kurt Blumenfeld, a friend of Mendelsohn's from childhood, recommended the architect to Salman Schocken in 1924, convinced that he would be eager to hire someone who shared his Zionist convictions. Although Mendelsohn was certainly not a major Zionist activist or thinker in these years, as a young man he had been active in the Blau-Weiß (Blue-White), the German Zionist youth movement, and he continued to move in Zionist circles as an adult.

Mendelsohn visited Palestine in 1923 to design a (never built) power station in Haifa and reported that he felt a profound attachment to the land, noting even that he would move there were it not for various practical considerations.[116] More significantly, Mendelsohn shared the sensibility of those members of his generation who rejected the assimilationist goals and the "thin-blooded Judaism" of their parents.[117] Like Salman Schocken, Mendelsohn was inspired by Martin Buber's ideas, specifically his synthesis of religious, aesthetic, and political impulses.[118]

It would be misleading to suggest the existence of direct connections between Mendelsohn's commitment to Zionism and his department store designs, yet similar impulses underlay both spheres of activity. Both architect and patron were on a dissimilationist path. They were searching for new forms and did not feel burdened by German architectural antecedents. Zionism and modernism shared an openness to the new and an antipathy toward artifice and opulence, as well as the key Werkbund assumption that good design would improve quality of life. In his early writings, furthermore, Mendelsohn revealed that he attributed his creative spark to his Judaism, and his emphasis on dynamism betrays the influence of Buber's "Three Lectures on Judaism" (1911), which "orientalized" the Jew and associated him with movement, flow, and constant change, in contrast to the solidity and stasis of the Germanic type, a formulation that Werner Sombart himself would most likely have endorsed, only without the positive connotations.[119] And in an impassioned 1923 text, composed shortly after his first visit to Palestine, Mendelsohn characterized Jews as a bridge between East and West and Jewish settlers as refugees from a decadent civilization, bearing the timeless qualities of Jewish blood, whose return to their land of origin emboldened them to create a new Jewish national culture.[120]

The working relationship between Mendelsohn and Schocken was often tense: Schocken had stronger opinions about architecture than most of Mendelsohn's patrons, and he did not hesitate to express them and to intervene in the creative process. His concerns were unsurprisingly of a more practical nature, and he was willing to compromise aesthetic principles when necessary to cut costs or satisfy municipal authorities, another source of friction with the more idealistic Mendelsohn. Nevertheless, the partnership between the two resulted in several buildings of enormous architectural significance in Germany and Mandate Palestine, including three department stores that were perhaps the fullest expression of new sobriety and Weimar modernism in commercial architecture.

From Vertical to Horizontal: Mendelsohn, Schocken, and the Rhythm of the Machine

One thing the Schocken brothers and Erich Mendelsohn could agree on was that architecture should reflect the spirit of its times. Simon Schocken, a less active public speaker and writer than his more intellectually inclined brother, asserted in a 1928 address that architecture should be the expression of an idea.[121] While the Gothic cathedral was the quintessential architectural expression of medieval religiosity, modernity, he claimed, had yet to come up with its own style, an accomplishment that would require tremendous courage and vision.

Throughout his writings, Mendelsohn contrasted the "verticality" that characterized medieval architecture with modernity's horizontalism: verticality embodied hierarchy, Christian religiosity, and Germanic myths, whereas horizontal lines bespoke the new times, the leveling of hierarchy, and even the release of Jewish creative powers.[122] For Mendelsohn, furthermore, what distinguished modern times above all else was speed, the relentlessly accelerating pace of urban modernity, and the task of modern architecture was to capture this speed and dynamism in concrete form. The historian Janet Ward has pointed out the tension between Mendelsohn's continued emphasis on the rationalization of building and the "nonrational, animalistic energy" of his designs. Their effect, she writes, "mirrors the tempo of the street, and . . . aestheticizes the machinic rhythm of the modern age."[123] Just as trains and rail travel were so important in shaping the history and representation of the department store in the early twentieth century, so Mendelsohn's vision of the modern emporium revolved around new, accelerated forms of transit and circulation. These were the first commercial buildings in Germany designed with the automobile in mind.

The Schocken department store in Nuremberg, the first product of the collaboration between the Schockens and Mendelsohn, marked the beginning of a new era in department store design and construction. Commissioned in 1925, the store was completed a year later. A city of four hundred thousand inhabitants, Nuremberg was the most populous Schocken site up to that point. The second Schocken store in southern Germany, it signaled the firm's bold new expansion plans. The building that was reconstructed to house the store had been a factory, and its stark interiors and austere facades retained a sense of its origins. On a recent trip to the United States,

4.5 Kaufhaus Schocken, Nuremberg, 1926. Foto Marburg / Art Resource, NY.

Mendelsohn had been impressed by the American embrace of an industrial aesthetic. Moreover, Salman Schocken's ascetic preferences dictated that the Nuremberg construction was to be less opulent than Mendelsohn's previous commercial buildings, such as the Petersdorff clothing store in Breslau and the Herpich furrier in Berlin, which sold more luxurious goods to a wealthier customer base.[124]

The Nuremberg store, which consisted of four brightly lit shopping floors, distinguished itself from most major European department stores by not having a central atrium. Indeed, Salman Schocken wanted the building itself to be a space for the clear presentation of wares. Instead of enshrining them in fantasy or distracting bombast, he stressed simplicity and transparency, values he also emphasized in his approach to advertising and packaging. As Schocken put it, the store's spacious interiors were characterized by "well-lit selling floors, sober [sachlich] typography on signs and pricing displays, and a clear organization of the sales stands and product shelves."[125] Consequently, the building reached, as James writes, "an extreme of objective sobriety," thereby embodying the ideal of new sobriety or objectivity, a key Weimar aesthetic principle.[126]

4.6 Kaufhaus Schocken, Nuremberg, opening day, October 11, 1926. Courtesy of Rafael Cazorla, http://www.postalesinventadas.com/. Photographer unknown.

At the opening ceremonies on October 11, 1926, Salman Schocken spoke of the "spirit" and the "principles" that obtained in the new store. To support the building's starkness and lack of ornament, he quoted the German-Jewish painter Max Liebermann, "one of the wisest men of our era," as saying, "In drawing the real art is knowing what to leave out."[127] In architecture, Schocken continued, the goal of eliminating the inessential was an ideal that was seldom met. In a wide-ranging oration that included a quotation from the poet Annette von Droste-Hülshoff and an exhortation from the sacred text *Pirkei Avot* (Ethics of the fathers), Schocken returned to his beloved theme of his firm's unique approach to buying and its modern, efficient, and rational commercial program, stating that rationalization and centralization, now modish catchphrases, had already been the Schocken firm's guiding principles for a quarter century.

Mendelsohn composed a poem of sorts for the occasion, titled "Why this architecture?" He began by contrasting the present with the preceding century:

Think back only a hundred years:
Hoopskirts and wigs
Tallow candle and hand loom

Sedans and horse-drawn carriages
Dry goods stores and artisanal guilds
Then think about us:
Bare knees and short haircuts
Radio and film
Automobile and airplane
Banana shops and department store concerns[128]

The poem exhorted contemporaries to take charge, to free themselves from the styles of the past, styles no longer appropriate in a world of "cities of millions, skyscrapers, eight-hour flights from Moscow to Berlin." It extolled "functionalism, clarity, simplicity" and called for an architecture that reflected the "rhythm of the whizzing autos, the fast traffic" of the times. In his address, Simon Schocken urged the store's employees to take this message to heart: "When you observe the building with its clear forms, you see that straight lines dominate . . . and I advise you to be this direct, clear, and harmonious, not only in your job in the store, but also in your whole approach to life, to take as an example what is embodied architecturally in this building."[129] Nuremberg's lord mayor, Dr. Hermann Luppe, spoke as well. He acknowledged that the building would create controversy, for some critics would object to the existence of such a modern structure in a city famous for its traditional architecture.[130] But he went on to praise the store's modern design, thanking Schocken and Mendelsohn for bringing the trappings of urban modernity to Nuremberg.[131]

Luppe's and Simon Schocken's speeches were captured in a short film that the Schockens produced to record and promote the opening of the Nuremberg store. The film was shown in movie theaters in the winter of 1926–27, and films about the Stuttgart store opening in 1928 and other Schocken events were considered and even commissioned, although it is not clear if they were ever completed. Schocken enlisted the services of László Moholy-Nagy, artistic polymath and key Bauhaus instructor, to direct a promotional film in 1934, but there is no evidence that the project came to fruition.[132] Judging from the promotional material and the extant scripts, the Nuremberg film was done in a modern, avant-garde montage style, not at all uncommon in corporate advertising films of the mid-1920s.[133] The film featured excerpts of the speeches by both Schocken brothers, Erich Mendelsohn, Georg Manasse, and Mayor Luppe before an audience of new store employees and distinguished visitors. It showed the store's portals opening at 3:30 p.m. and the stampede (*Ansturm*) of eager shoppers. The script depicts the excitement of opening day: "The surrounding streets were crowded with tens of thousands of onlookers, who had not yet found entry. Again and again that afternoon the police were forced to temporarily close off the entrance to the store. The number of persons who visited the building between 3:30 and 7 p.m. far exceeded 40,000."[134]

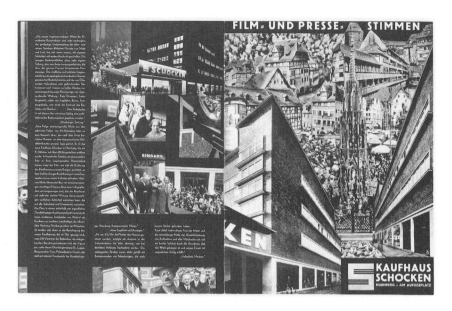

4.7 Press pamphlet, issued on opening of Kaufhaus Schocken, Nuremberg, October 1926. Sächsisches Staatsarchiv, Staatsarchiv Chemnitz, 31451 Schocken AG, Zwickau und Nachfolger, No. 398.

The Schocken stores thus represented a renunciation of the awe-provoking consumer temples like Wertheim's so-called cathedral. Mendelsohn's severe, factory-like horizontal lines countered the religiously uplifting, commodity-fetish inducing verticals of the Messel building with a rational and sober showcase for its goods. Nevertheless, despite the emphasis on these modern principles, the discourse of the store's magnetism, of the crush of excited shoppers, is almost identical to what we saw in our discussion of the "human stream" in chapter 2. The script continues: "All the aisles and stairways, every corner of the great store thickly packed, the masses press each other step by step past the displays of goods whose magnetic pull is unrelenting."[135] Schocken's emphatic commitment to the New Objectivity still left room for the department store's mysterious magnetism and did not fully extinguish the seemingly magical qualities of modern consumer culture.

Reflecting back on the Nuremberg store several years later, Mendelsohn recalled that he and Simon Schocken had embarked on an unprecedented approach to department store architecture, one that made exhibiting the goods its highest imperative.[136] Critics at the time had apparently denounced the building's modern qualities as "unartistic" and its factory-like character as "brutal." A Dresden professor even condemned the style as a "Jewish invention."[137] Others charged that its lack of national referents made it international and therefore un-German. Mendelsohn countered that the style was grounded on reason and objectivity, that it arose seamlessly from the new materials of the age (iron and concrete), and that like all his structures, it was not international but rather rooted in local context.

In light of the Nuremberg store's success, Schocken continued its path of aggressive expansion, and almost exactly two years later it opened a new Mendelsohn-designed store in Stuttgart. The Swabian capital, slightly larger than Nuremberg, lay centrally on rail lines and river ways, making it an ideal location for a major department store. Stuttgart was also a center for banking, insurance, and trade, home to a wealthy population with increasing buying power. The idea for a branch in Stuttgart apparently occurred to Salman Schocken when he passed through the city on his way home from a Zionist meeting in Cologne, although as the historian Konrad Fuchs points out, Schocken had been on the lookout for new locations during this period of rapid expansion, and this, like all his decisions, followed careful planning and deliberation.[138] He discussed the idea with Mendelsohn as early as January 1926, and by that July Mendelsohn reported to his wife, Luise, that much of the design work was finished.[139]

In designing the Stuttgart store, Mendelsohn looked to American commercial architecture, above all the buildings of Louis B. Sullivan, and to factories in Germany for inspiration and produced a design that stressed efficiency, industry, and technology. The architect wrote in a 1928 essay: "Industrial construction is thus leading the way to a new architecture. As industry discovered the new materials or caused their discovery, it inevitably created the necessary means and places of production. . . . Industry . . . is the starting point and bearer of the development that leads from the decay of civilization to a new creative culture. This development is based on the same needs and the same intellectual attitude."[140]

Internally the store stressed practicality and simplicity over pomp. It featured plain wooden furniture and maximized exhibition space, avoiding disruptive columns in the middle of the sales floors. Crucially, like its predecessor in Nuremberg, the store had no central atrium and replaced that space with a loading dock, a move that Mendelsohn saw as an explicit rejection of the Messel model. But unlike the concrete, factory-like Nuremberg store, Kaufhaus Schocken Stuttgart featured enormous windows and was a vision of glass and light. The building's most striking and famous design element was its exposed stairway. Instead of tucking the main stair unobtrusively into a corner, Mendelsohn foregrounded it in a glass cylindrical tower that rose above the store's main entrance. The stunning glass cylinder moved the building's drama to the exterior. This made a profound impression on the public, which naturally helped business, and more importantly left a vast, unobstructed interior space for the selling area.[141]

The building also reflected Mendelsohn's goal of capturing the frenetic tempo of the modern age in concrete. Its horizontal lines, emphasized by black bands atop the stair tower, evoked railway tracks. The horizontal emphasis together with the building's pronounced curvature gave the impression

4.8 Kaufhaus Schocken, Stuttgart, partial view of glass tower, 1928.
Sächsisches Staatsarchiv, Staatsarchiv Chemnitz, 31451 Schocken AG, Zwikau und
Nachfolger, No. 270.

that it was about to take off or launch like an ocean liner.[142] Ward describes
the contrapuntal tension between the Stuttgart store's horizontality and verticality as providing a sense of "machinic control" and making the building
seem like an "animalistic coil ready to spring."[143]

The building's dynamism was all the more striking at night as a result of Mendelsohn's use of lighting. He placed the name "Schocken" in large illuminated letters above the display windows. The stair tower and display windows and the eight bright letters radiated light into the urban night. In the Stuttgart building light was treated as a design material, and Mendelsohn viewed it as means of capturing motion, of reaching and stimulating the mass public.[144] The utilization of light to arouse consumer fantasies seems to run counter to Schocken's emphasis on rationality and his preference for clear, sober announcements over brash, attention-getting advertisements. Indeed, Mendelsohn's use of lighting, as one observer reported, gave the Schocken stores their "secret magic."[145] Another contemporary called the store "an emblem for the city's development" and reported that "during the evening dusk the glass stairwell, magically lit, seems to transport itself out onto the street. . . . The light, as the illuminating potential of the metropolis, becomes a modern form of enchantment. Like a fairytale, its lovely impression beams out something like a spell."[146]

Leading modern architects such as Ludwig Mies van der Rohe, Walter Gropius, and Le Corbusier dutifully visited the Stuttgart store and registered their approval. Although Mendelsohn was not affiliated with the Bauhaus, and his relationship with Gropius was always strained, there was a discernable Bauhaus influence on Schocken's stores. Schocken visited the Bauhaus with his son Gershom in Dessau in 1926, and his stores sold furniture inspired by Bauhaus designs. The firm's typography and advertising incorporated Bauhaus principles, emphasizing above all clarity, readability, and the transmission of information, and its symbol, the famous, squared-off *S*, betrayed the influence of Mondrian.[147] True to the spirit of the New Objectivity, Schocken's ads, as Georg Manasse remarked in 1929, presented the goods themselves and their value, without any gratuitous words of praise.[148] Small newspaper ads, the rectangles of text with small type that the firm favored, had the additional benefit of costing less than the full-page blasts that Tietz and Wertheim tended to use.[149] Schocken hired a Bauhaus designer to direct his construction office in Zwickau, and as we have seen, he enlisted Moholy-Nagy to develop advertisements and direct the concern's promotional films.[150]

After completion of the Stuttgart building, Schocken's expansion became even more rapid. The store in Crimmitschau, another Saxon location, opened its doors less than six weeks later, and in the fall of 1929 the Schockens added additional emporiums in Augsburg and Waldenburg. Waldenburg represented a continuation of their long-standing strategy of serving medium-size towns with substantial department stores, and the choice of Augsburg was, as Salman Schocken saw it, the logical consequence of the success in Nuremberg and Stuttgart, cities with similar profiles.[151]

Neither Simon Schocken's untimely death following a 1929 car accident, nor the economic crisis of the same year, halted the firm's relentless expansion. The Schocken concern, unlike most other department store chains, did not rely on banks to raise capital and was able to finance its construction projects independently, which made it stronger and more secure during difficult economic times.[152] Furthermore, the Augsburg, Nuremberg, and Stuttgart stores were so successful that they contributed as much as half of the firm's overall earnings, sustaining the more modest and vulnerable branches as the economic crisis sank in.[153] Yet it is still striking that the firm opened its largest store yet at a moment when Germany's economic fortunes looked unprecedentedly bleak.

Salman Schocken had long had his eye on Chemnitz. He and Mendelsohn began discussions of a possible project there in late 1927, and Mendelsohn was at work on it in the fall of 1928.[154] The store opened in May 1930. Like its predecessor in Stuttgart, the Chemnitz building had strong horizontal lines, bands of travertine that alternated with windows along the six selling floors (plus three recessed floors above) that ran along the long facade. But compared with the Stuttgart building, the Chemnitz store was marked above all by its simplicity, reflecting a broader tendency in late Weimar commercial architecture and Mendelsohn's escalating rivalry with Mies van der Rohe.[155]

Like the Nuremberg edifice, the Chemnitz building evoked a factory. Again, in explicit contrast to the consuming-temple fantasy of the grandiose Wilhelmine department store, Schocken's Chemnitz store urged consumers to face the factory origins of consumable wares, and it punctured department store commodity fetishism with transparency and sobriety. Simultaneously, its striking curvature and glass facade—all the more enchanting when lit up

4.9 Kaufhaus Schocken, Chemnitz, 1930. Sächsisches Staatsarchiv, Staatsarchiv Chemnitz, 31451 Schocken AG, Zwikau und Nachfolger, No. 270.

against the night sky—reintroduced a sense of dynamism, excitement, and enchantment.

Cutting-edge architecture helped distinguish the Schocken stores, "branding" them as modern and unique. The concern's dynamic and conspicuous constructions captured the attention of city dwellers and served as the stores' best advertisement. As Manasse put it in 1926, it was imperative that the Schocken store be the most interesting building in each town that the firm entered, since "when a woman wants to know where the fashions are, where the fine things can be had, then a visit to one of our stores is a given."[156]

Consumer Modernity in Provincial Germany: Leonhard Tietz in the Rhineland

The Schocken concern went on to open up only one more department store—in Pforzheim in southwestern Germany in September 1931, where it took over and renovated a store that had been part of the Hermann Wronker firm—before the Nazi assumption of power and a 1934 ordinance that banned new department store construction. At that time, the concern was arguably the most important commercial enterprise in the Saxon economy. Its nineteen stores and six thousand employees made it the fifth-largest German department store firm—behind Karstadt, Hermann Tietz, Alsberg Brothers, and Leonhard Tietz—and indeed one of the few that was still on solid financial footing after several years of economic crisis. And as the firm's leaders argued two years later, in the hostile environment of the early Nazi regime, the Schocken company was extremely active in local philanthropic causes, retaining workers even when they were not needed in light of the swelling ranks of the unemployed, and making a positive contribution to local economies and German industry as a whole.[157]

Among Schocken's great achievements in the later 1920s, as we have seen, was to pose an alternative model of department store, bringing modern, *sachlich* structures and the clear and transparent presentation of goods to medium-size cities (Nuremberg, Stuttgart, Chemnitz) and large towns (Crimmitschau, Aue, Waldenburg) and replacing the awe-inspiring verticals of Messel and Olbrich with a "horizontal," more democratic approach to the blessings of German consumer culture. Schocken's regional identity and its role in the life of smaller cities challenge the stereotype of modern European Jewry and Jewish enterprises as belonging purely in the metropolis. Despite early opposition and the continued discontent of members of the shopkeeping middle classes, Jewish-owned department stores (and some non-Jewish-owned businesses) went on to become crucial and valued parts of the economies and cultures of small and medium-size cities throughout Germany.

The evolution of the Leonhard Tietz concern, an older and larger department store firm, helps illustrate the influence of Schocken and Mendelsohn on department store practices and design and provides a second example of a Jewish-owned enterprise that brought modern consumer culture to the German provinces and cultivated an identity that was at once modern and provincial. Leonhard Tietz, based in Cologne starting in 1895, was the leading department store firm in and around the Rhineland. Tietz himself, like the Schocken brothers and so many other department store entrepreneurs, originally hailed from Posen, and he worked in Frankfurt an der Oder and Stralsund before heading west. Ultimately, he successfully acculturated in Cologne, becoming, it seems, a local hero who was referred to in the Rhineland vernacular as "Tietz Leienad."[158]

Although he was neither as prolific a speaker nor as articulate a theorist of the department store business as Salman Schocken, Tietz did introduce several key innovations. For example, the Leonhard Tietz concern was the first publicly held German department store firm. It became a limited joint stock company in 1905, and four years later its shares were being traded on the Berlin stock exchange. In 1901 Tietz opened up an affiliate in Antwerp, becoming the first German-owned transnational department store chain, and several additional branches in Belgium and Switzerland soon followed.[159] In 1925 the L. Tietz firm created Ehape, the *Einheitspreis* (single price) discounter, a Woolworth-like establishment that spread quickly and soon inspired numerous imitators and competitors. Ehape stores consisted of one large selling floor with a simple pricing system and a stock to satisfy the quotidian needs of modestly earning customers.[160] Many of the Tietz buildings, finally, were noted for their architectural and technical innovations, beginning with the 1909 Düsseldorf construction.

L. Tietz's Düsseldorf branch had first opened in 1895 and was renovated and expanded six years later. Soon Tietz was ready for a new, larger, and more conspicuous store building in Düsseldorf and announced a prize competition for the design. The winner was the Darmstadt-based Austrian architect Joseph Olbrich, an erstwhile student of Otto Wagner and an original member of the Viennese Secession. Olbrich died in 1908, before the building was completed, and his students, above all Philipp Schäfer, finished the project in 1909 from Olbrich's notes.[161] Just as Leonhard Tietz was more or less adopted by the Rhinelanders as one of their own, so the Austrian Olbrich, in the words of one contemporary, was "in every respect a modern man and a man who seemed to have been created for the Rhineland and the people of the Rhineland."[162] Here again we see notions of modernity and provincialism coming together around a department store and its architect. In the words of Tietz's own promotional volume: "The monumental Düsseldorf structure, which Olbrich built on the Königsallee . . . would be paradigmatic for the development of large department stores in provincial Germany and would remain one of the most beautiful German commercial buildings."[163]

4.10 Warenhaus Leonhard Tietz, Düsseldorf. Reprinted from *50 Jahre Leonhard Tietz 1879–1929* (Cologne, 1929). Courtesy of the University of Southern California, on behalf of the USC Libraries Special Collections.

Olbrich, like Messel, was part of the first generation of German modernist architects; he was also used to having Jewish patrons, having worked in the milieu of turn-of-the-century Vienna, where Jews were conspicuous and active as sponsors of modernism in the arts.[164] His design, which followed Messel's Wertheim store by about a decade, recapitulated some of Messel's motifs and references. In a 1909 book about the building, the art historian Max Creutz observed that the L. Tietz store dominated the surrounding cityscape just as a Gothic cathedral had towered above neighboring residences in the medieval period.[165] As in the Messel building, the Düsseldorf structure featured pronounced buttresses that directed the viewer's gaze skyward. Its interiors rivaled the Wertheim store in luxury

4.11 Leonhard Tietz, Oberhausen. Reprinted from *50 Jahre Leonhard Tietz 1879–1929* (Cologne, 1929). Courtesy of the University of Southern California, on behalf of the USC Libraries Special Collections.

and splendor, especially in the great central atrium—there were three atriums altogether—which Olbrich tellingly nicknamed the cathedral. Creutz repeatedly compares the Olbrich store to its Berlin counterpart, further confirming that the Messel building stood as the template against which ambitious new German department store constructions were measured in the pre–World War I period.

After little new activity during the war years and in the war's immediate aftermath, the Leonhard Tietz concern embarked on a new wave of renovations, expansions, and new construction. Now under the direction of Alfred Leonhard Tietz—whose father, Leonhard, died in 1914—the firm broke from the Olbrich aesthetic and embraced a new vision of architectural modernism and democratized consumption. As smaller department store firms began to fail in the 1920s, Leonhard Tietz was one of the healthy companies that was able to absorb them, part of a general consolidation in the department store sector starting in the middle of the Weimar period. The L. Tietz firm gobbled up Abraham Brothers department stores in 1927, for example, and renovated their buildings in Mönchen Gladbach and neighboring Rheydt. The Widow Frankfurt department store, Kaufmann Brothers, and Guggenheim & Marks all fell into their hands in the later '20s, bringing Tietz to such locations

4.12 Leonhard Tietz, planned department store in Bonn, reprinted from *50 Jahre Leonhard Tietz 1879–1929* (Cologne, 1929). Courtesy of the University of Southern California, on behalf of the USC Libraries Special Collections.

as Krefeld, Aachen, and Darmstadt. (At its peak, the concern consisted of more than forty department stores in Germany, a Belgian branch of six additional stores, and an affiliate in Paris.) Again and again, Tietz's rhetoric trumpeted the firm's replacement of old department store buildings with modern commercial structures and stressed its role in bringing modernity to the provinces while creating the most beautiful and noteworthy edifices in each location.

The architecture of L. Tietz's building boom of the later 1920s provides another perspective, largely from Germany's west, of the process by which consumer modernity arrived in the German provinces. In 1931 the L. Tietz firm appealed to I. Schocken Sons for samples of its advertising inserts, consciously imitating its styles.[166] Its buildings included the skyscraper-like tower in Oberhausen, a stark brick edifice in Stralsund with its factory references, and the curved glass facades at a planned store in Bonn, a clear nod to the Schocken store in Chemnitz. In each case, the L. Tietz firm, like Schocken and others, having begun to dissimilate from the historical German, embraced the modern in its efforts to balance the local, the regional, and the international, spreading consumer modernity throughout provincial Germany.

5 THE CONSUMING FIRE

Fantasies of Destruction in German Politics and Culture

> The department store is like a fire whose flames, once ignited, devour more
> and more, and that which it once engulfs, it does not easily give up.
>
> —*Erich Köhrer (1909)*

> Lighting a department store on fire is always preferable to operating a
> department store.
>
> —*Fritz Teufel (1967)*

Jape Flunt, the doomed protagonist of Vicki Baum's "Jape in the Department Store," when we left him in chapter 3, had just made the fateful decision to light a fire in the department store to destroy the corpse of the night watchman whom he had inadvertently murdered. After several failed attempts to start a fire with matches, Jape regrouped and began the methodical construction of a "funeral pyre," aided, as Baum points out, by the profusion of flammable material that one finds on hand in a department store. The store's abundance, from which he had adorned himself, drunk, and feasted with such abandon yet again provided for Jape's needs. "The selection . . . is great. You can find things made out of paper, out of cardboard, out of wood."[1] Everything under one roof, Baum might have added. Indeed, Jape even grabbed a bottle of turpentine from the soap department to ignite the pyre. He placed the corpse inside what Baum describes as a mound (*Hügel*) or pyramid, something one can easily imagine highlighting a Tietz display of the exotic East during its famed white weeks.

This time Jape succeeded. As the flames shot up he experienced an enormous sense of relief, a kind of catharsis that reverberated through his body. "Jape leaned on the railing and enjoyed the show," Baum writes. "He shook mightily from pleasure, his whole body trembled, his limbs flapped. Something happened in him, he had to dance, he also had to scream."[2] Yet the fire soon burned beyond his control, and what was meant to be restricted to the lady's apparel department quickly grew into a mighty blaze that ultimately destroyed much of the store and Jape within it. The flames quickly reached beyond the department store, igniting neighboring buildings, turning the heavens red and alarming the city's residents. In the story's concluding paragraph, Jape, now hanging above the store's central atrium, his charred fingers clinging to a railing on the fifth floor, falls into the depths of the inferno just as the flames reach the store's third courtyard and ignite the gas storage tanks. The tanks explode, the department store is instantly leveled, and "the enormous crash of the explosion dashes everything into oblivion."[3]

The deadly fire that closes "Jape in the Department Store" is far from a unique plot element in department store literature. Fire, violence, and destruction were common motifs in the discourse around department stores from the turn of the twentieth century through the post–World War II period. These imagined acts of destruction coincided with actual cases of violence against department stores and the very real threat of fires in stores, theaters, and other large modern structures where crowds gathered. A red thread runs through the German reception of mass consumer society, a history of real and imagined acts of violence to the department store, from the stone-throwing crowds that gathered to protest the opening of Hermann Tietz's Munich store in 1887, through the years of Nazi intimidation and vandalism, to the bombing of two Frankfurt department stores by leftist radicals in 1969. Alongside, indeed embedded within the German fascination with the dreamworld of mass consumption and the consuming temple, lies a fantasy of destruction, of burning down the department store, of attacking the temple and destroying its contents.

On one level, these acts appear straightforward enough, as expressions of hostility to new forms of retail that, so it seemed, threatened the economic livelihood of the German *Mittelstand* and the viability of traditional forms of manufacture and commerce. But that explanation only goes so far. It fails to account for the frequent, almost universal appearance of department store destruction, especially by fire, in literary representations of the department store, and indeed by writers who did not share this economic or cultural sensibility. In fact, nearly all the writers discussed in this chapter—Baum, Siwertz, Georg, Kläger, and most likely Köhrer—were themselves Jewish. Several were active in Jewish communities and causes. This is not to say that Jews cannot give voice to anti-Semitic opinions or ally themselves with anti-Semitic programs, but none of these writers belonged to the anti–department store camp. Baum, in fact, returned again and again to the department store, basing at least three works in such a store, and others in similar retail settings.[4] What then can account for the salience of the image of burning department stores and its staying power in the postwar period, long after the department store had ceased to arouse controversy, and doomsday predictions had given way to more sober assessments of its impact on society and economy?

Whereas economic and anti-Semitic opposition certainly called attention to department store fires and sought to exploit this ever-present threat for their cause, this chapter searches for a broader and more satisfying explanation for the durability and resonance of the fire motif. I maintain that the department store fire operated as a metaphor for the rapid spread of department stores and the explosiveness of the German encounter with new forms of consumer culture, for the power and violence of the stores and the powerful changes in German daily life that stores both reflected and furthered. That is, the theme of fires—along with the department stores' other potential hazards—shoplifting, unethical and unseemly behavior, sexual violence—expressed both the excitements and the dangers associated with these new forms of economic enterprise and leisure activity. Works by Jewish authors may, in addition, have reflected a kind of anxiety about the prominence of these stores in urban settings and the exposure or vulnerability of the Jewish businessmen behind them.

The department store as a space contained, indeed stimulated, highly combustible forces that made it an ideologically laden and psychologically fraught part of daily life. The very act of consumption involves a kind of destruction through the use of a product, commodity, or food. A second, related meaning of consumption, as we have seen, refers to the wasting away of the body through illness.[5] It is not surprising, then, that the mass consumption of the department store is bound up with mass destruction; consumption is inherently a destructive process, the antithesis or end point of production. If the department store embodied mass consumption at an unprecedented scale and tempo, the department store fire appears as its logical consequence, a spectacular, thrilling, and terrifying resolution of the tensions and ambivalences of modern consumer culture. Furthermore, the fantasy of the department store fire, I suggest, drew force from the hidden violence that underlay the conditions of mass production and which, in turn, made possible the store's splendor and sumptuous goods.

The destructive fires at the end of *The Great Department Store* and *Warenhaus Berlin* (Department Store Berlin), as in "Jape in the Department Store," also carried religious connotations. In "Jape" the fire not only destroys the store and kills the protagonist; it "dashes everything into oblivion." It results in the complete destruction of the department store, rendering it into nothingness, an act with theological overtones, which began with Jape's burning of the night watchman's corpse on a funeral pyre. Whereas the religious themes in Baum's story are not Jewish per se, Jewishness is quite explicit in Siwertz's *The Great Department Store* and in Köhrer's *Warenhaus Berlin*. Later in the chapter I read these cases as commentaries on and attempts to work through the coding of the department store as Jewish, the conspicuous presence of Jews in German consumer culture, and the real and symbolic power of the consuming temple over the economy and the urban landscape of modern Germany.

The Fire Safety Debate at the Turn of the Century

In his 1907 treatise, Paul Göhre compared department stores to ocean liners because of their "huge dimensions," their precise compartmentalization, and their modernity. "Both ocean liner and department store," he wrote, "[represent] a triumph of modern, socially organized, human labor."[6] They were both sites of consumption and leisure, products of the new material prosperity and technological revolutions of the modern period, Göhre might have added. "Modern wonders" like ocean liners, airplanes, and zeppelins enthralled early twentieth-century observers, who beheld new achievements in size and speed with a mixture of fear and fascination. Equally fascinating were the accidents and disasters, which contemporary newspapers reported on with grizzly detail and which, in cases like the *Titanic* (1912) and the *Hindenburg* (1937), still exert a powerful hold on the imagination.[7]

The department store provoked a similar ambivalence in early twentieth-century Germany, a combination of excitement and fear: excitement over its novelties, its impressive scale, and its spectacular displays, and fear of its power, its magnetic pull over customers and passersby, and its alleged ability to incite *Kauflust* and turn casual shoppers into a frenzied mob. Akin to airplane crashes and shipwrecks, the department store fire entered the popular imagination at this time. It also became a contentious political issue from the turn of the century through World War I and beyond, the period of the department store's rapid spread and expansion in Germany.

In an era that witnessed several highly destructive urban conflagrations, concern about fires in theaters, cinemas, and other large public buildings remained acute; but to some, department stores represented an even greater danger because of both the goods they carried and the nature of the crowds inside. Clothing, fabrics, and rugs, the core commodities at most of these stores, were composed of highly flammable materials. Furthermore, the infrastructure required to heat, illuminate, and electrify these massive structures was a source of awe and anxiety, as were technical innovations such as elevators and escalators.[8] Display windows with their own lighting systems and often with animatronic figures inspired particular excitement and concern and were frequently linked to deadly blazes.

Above all, it was the crowds, both their size and their behavior, that drew the attention of fire safety campaigners. Department store shoppers, the argument went, stimulated by the stores' many attractions and bargains, acted irrationally, even hysterically. The crush of people, the so-called human stream, could turn even a small fire into a catastrophe since it would spread panic and prevent orderly comportment and evacuation. Some of the same dangers could be found in theaters, too, but as at least one commentator pointed out, theatergoers generally sat in one place for an entire performance and could orient themselves with an eye on an exit sign.[9] Department store customers, on the other hand, were constantly in motion, circulating through the store's numerous departments, sections, and floors, leading to disorientation and preventing quick escape.

Although there was indeed a series of fires in German department stores at the end of the nineteenth century and the beginning of the twentieth, most of them were limited in scale, with, at worst, a handful of casualties.

More serious fires occurred outside Germany, including one in Budapest that had a lasting impact on German observers; but there was no conflagration at a German department store to match the literary imaginings of Baum, Köhrer, and Siwertz, and no disaster whose death toll or drama remotely approached that of the sinking of the *Titanic* or the *Hindenburg* crash. The equivalent of these modern wonders, immense and spectacular structures like the Wertheim store on Leipziger Strasse (1897), the KaDeWe (1907), the Karstadt at Hermannplatz (1929), or the Schocken building in Chemnitz (1931), were never the site of destructive fires—at least not until Allied bombing in World War II—and the catastrophic department store fire proved to be more powerful as a metaphor than as an actual phenomenon. In fact, the largest and most modern department stores, those that inspired the most awe and fear, turned out to be the safest.

Nevertheless, German department store fires did command popular and media attention. Ferdinand Bucholtz, for example, included a picture of a burning Hamburg department store, with employees huddled on a balcony waiting for rescue, in his 1931 compendium of dangers and thrills, experiences that distinguished the modern "risk society" from bourgeois complacency, as Ernst Jünger explained in the book's introduction.[10]

The trope of the burning department store resonated most strongly in anti-Semitic newspapers, which returned again and again to these fires long after other papers had ceased to cover them. Starting with a deadly blaze in the Braunschweig Karstadt in 1899 or perhaps with the fire in a Landauer department store in Karlsruhe the next year, department store fires triggered debate in municipal and state assemblies about the stores' potential dangers and how they should be regulated. The Braunschweig fire, determined to be the likely result of a short circuit in the electrical system, caused the deaths of at least six employees. Thick smoke prevented one worker from getting to the emergency exit—he jumped out a window to his death—and five seamstresses apparently suffocated inside. Investigators identified the presence of flammable materials in the corridors and stairways as the cause of the fire's rapid spread. One account of the horrifying ordeal described the building's interior as a "fire-spewing smokestack."[11]

Concern about the Braunschweig fire and a blaze at department store Aron in Berlin-Rixdorf the following January led Prussian officials to devise a range of new fire safety ordinances for any business that stored great quantities of flammable goods or worked with highly combustible materials.[12] These ordinances, first drafted by a working group of architects, city officials, businessmen, and fire safety experts in 1900 and 1901, and given final approval by Berlin's police president in 1907, ruled that police must perform fire safety checks in new department stores and other large business buildings before they could open, and that goods could not be exhibited in stairways or customers allowed in store basements and attics.[13] Bavaria adopted similar measures in 1903, and two years later the state

5.1 "Burning Department Store in Hamburg." Reprinted from Ferdinand Bucholtz, *Der gefährliche Augenblick* (Berlin, 1931). Bpk/Staatsbibliothek zu Berlin.

of Hesse followed suit.[14] Department store owners and other businessmen protested these measures at a demonstration in Berlin in December 1900, claiming that they would have severe financial consequences and threaten retailers' economic livelihood.[15]

Yet these measures did nothing to quell unease about department stores and the threat of fire. Even as store owners protested the regulations' severity, activists on the other side continued to push for more stringent guidelines. The *völkisch Staatsbürger-Zeitung*, for example, a newspaper that relentlessly attacked department stores in the last years of the nineteenth century and the beginning of the twentieth, criticized the "mildness" of the regulations, accusing state officials of being in the department store owners' pockets, a state of affairs that allegedly imperiled "thousands of human lives, daily and hourly."[16]

The *Staatsbürger-Zeitung* stepped up its attacks in August 1903 in the immediate aftermath of a catastrophic fire at the Goldbergers' "Paris" department store in Budapest. As many as thirty people were killed by the fire, and many more injured.[17] Reports in the sensationalist newspaper listed significantly higher figures, but those numbers do not stand up to scrutiny. Beyond dispute, however, is that about a dozen people plummeted from the store's fifth-floor windows in a desperate attempt to escape.[18] Later reports blamed their deaths on fire department disorganization and incompetence. Apparently it took thirty minutes for the firefighters to set up their safety nets, which they then held onto incorrectly while a number of victims fatally plunged out the windows.[19]

The fire broke out around 7 p.m. when a technician switched on the electrical lighting in a display window.[20] Fire engines arrived quickly but lacked sufficient means to keep order on the streets or combat the rapidly spreading conflagration. The military and Budapest police force soon secured the scene, and Emperor Franz Joseph, who happened to be in Budapest at the time, visited the injured survivors in the hospital the next evening. The first victims to be buried, the six Jewish casualties, were laid to rest in Budapest's Israelite Cemetery two days later, and more than ten thousand residents attended the funeral, giving an indication of the enormity of the catastrophe and the deep and widespread grief it caused in the Hungarian capital.[21]

In its coverage of the event, the *Staatsbürger-Zeitung* emphasized several themes: that the mainstream Berlin press had given scant attention to the fire, that the fire should serve as a warning for what could happen in one of the major Berlin department stores, and that the fire directly resulted from the Goldbergers' business practices. All three themes revolved around the Jewishness of the department store.

The lack of coverage in the mainstream Berlin newspapers, the *Staatsbürger-Zeitung* writers implied, resulted from a kind of conspiracy between the Jewish-dominated liberal media, the so-called "Department store press," and the Jewish economic elite. In its reportage, the *Staatsbürger-Zeitung* continually referred to the Paris department store as a *Ramsch basar*, signaling the Jewishness of the store and its association with cheap, peddled goods. The store, alleged the *Staatsbürger-Zeitung*, was a mess, with piles of goods strewn about in ways that presented a clear fire hazard. (The less polemical *Wiener Bilder* described the building somewhat similarly as "a tangle of nooks and crannies," not suitable for large concentrations of people.)[22] The Goldbergers' greed, it was further alleged, had led them to try to cut costs by not following through on fire safety regulations and not marking and designating sufficient emergency evacuation routes for employees and customers. Indeed, articles in the right-wing, anti-Semitic press seldom failed to note that the Goldbergers were insured, implying that the fire benefited them financially, all the more reason for their alleged indifference to fire safety and prevention. Human life, so went the argument, was a matter of indifference to the greedy and ruthless Jewish department store owner whose businesses, after all, had destroyed thousands of German middle-class livelihoods.

This view dovetailed with the widely shared notion that department stores were dangerous for their workers and customers and for the general public. These fears were bound up with a kind of collective anxiety about the stores' size and power and the destabilizing effects of the consumer revolution. A right-wing deputy warned in a Prussian Landtag debate on department stores and fires in 1908:

> Gentlemen, I would like to speak to the great danger to body and life to which visitors to the powerful [*gewaltig*] department stores are subjected the moment they enter these huge spaces. . . . Our department stores are growing more and more into mighty, I can only say, enormous structures [*Reisenhausbauten*], and I think it's not an unreasonable assumption when I maintain that the larger a department store is, the more people it can contain, all the more dangerous it is for the residents and especially the shopping public.[23]

Even more alarming to the speaker was that the great majority of department store customers were women, and women's clothing, he claimed, was more highly flammable than men's; its excessive fabric, its frills and lace, could easily catch fire and spread flames.[24] In short, the speaker shares the assumption, common in the discourse on department stores, that women were at once more vulnerable than men and more dangerous.[25]

As we have seen, the danger associated with the stores had to do with their size, their conspicuous presence in busy and crowded commercial centers, the concentration of people within them, and their assumed impact on the German economy and society. The threat of fire, although very real and potentially consequential, became more or less an excuse to rail against the stores and to inhibit their growth and spread through new regulations. (In one case, in an absurd demonstration of circular reasoning, department store opponents expressed regret that more customers had not been caught in a fearsome blaze in Magdeburg's Barasch emporium, for the experience would have surely taught them to stay out of department stores.[26]) Indeed, the fire issue was taken up by the German Anti-Semitic League (Deutscher Antisemiten-Bund), which held an event on August 28, 1903, on "the department store fire in Pest and what it can teach us about Berlin."[27] Two members of the Reichstag, Otto Böckler of Berlin and Wilhelm Bruhn from Frankfurt an der Oder, addressed the crowd.

The Reichstag deputies, both of whom were heavily involved in the *Staatsbürger-Zeitung*, had made a tour of Berlin department stores to assess conditions and safety practices. They found, according to Böckler, frequent violations, such as the continued presence of goods in the stairways. More disturbing, Böckler maintained, was the department store's labyrinthine environment, which could make it difficult for customers to find their bearings and reach emergency exits. Conditions around Christmastime would be particularly dangerous, Böckler warned: "You have to imagine Golden Sunday when the public fills the rooms standing shoulder to shoulder, with the result that women become lightheaded in the crowds, when a large portion of the workers are temporary help, who themselves barely know their way around the department store. What if a fire suddenly broke out!"[28] Böckler's observations about the dangerous pre-Christmas crowds, while not entirely without validity, were likely intended to stir up discomfort with the notion of Jewish storeowners profiting from the Christian holiday, a theme that reverberated throughout department store critiques.[29]

Bruhn followed Böckler's speech with a more general condemnation of the department store's impact on German economic life. He characterized the stores as a threat to the German middle classes and attacked the hypocrisy of those who acted as if they supported German shopkeepers yet still shopped in the big stores, urging his listeners to take their business to traditional German specialty shops. While these comments, like Böckler's, may have reflected a legitimate concern with safety, it is clear, as defenders of the department store owners and the League for Combating Anti-Semitism pointed out, that the crusade against department store fires was for the most part disingenuous, an attempt to halt the growth and development of these businesses. Surely it was not a coincidence, argued one department store backer, that the leaders of the fire safety campaign were the same people who had sought to impose punitive taxes and other impediments to the stores' spread and growth.[30]

Opponents, for example, had consistently invoked the danger of fire as an argument for restricting the construction of new stores in Berlin and elsewhere. Yet, as the stores' defenders pointed out, older, smaller shops were more likely to pose fire hazards than were the new department stores, with their steel frames, large glass windows, and central atriums.[31] As Oscar Tietz, chairman of the German Department Store Association, argued in January 1906, fires had seldom broken out in the new department store structures, either in Germany or abroad. Instead the great majority of such incidents occurred in older buildings, in stores that shared space with residences and had originated as factories, as was the case in all of the twelve major department store fires in Germany between 1897 and 1906. The Goldbergers' Paris department store, he explained, occupied only the bottom two floors of a mixed residential and commercial building. In fact, a letter from the Berlin Police Department to the Prussian Ministry of the Interior asserts that the Goldbergers' building would not have passed Prussian safety regulations and would not have been approved for use as a department store.[32] (After the fire, Goldberger had a new building constructed, a six-story emporium that more closely resembled modern Western European department stores.)[33] Most of the victims were actually the apartment dwellers on the upper floors, not store workers or customers. In short, modern structures built specifically to house department stores were not the problem and should not have been the focus of the fire safety movement. With their large central atriums and wide stairways, they were, in fact, safer. The Royal Prussian fire chief Reichel actually confirmed this by building two models, one of the Tietz store on Leipziger Strasse and another of a store without a central atrium. He ignited the two models and found that the fire spread more quickly in the old-style store.[34]

Many of those concerned with fire safety proposed limiting customers to the two lower floors and reserving the upper levels for storage.[35] Friedrich Hammer, a deputy to the Prussian Diet, argued in the spring of 1906 that the police ordinances would not suffice, or could not be followed when a department store was crowded with several thousand people, in which case orderly evacuation would be impossible. Making matters worse, he asserted, was the fact that the workforce was composed mostly of women, the shopgirls who, in moments of danger, "certainly aren't as mentally present as men."[36] A liberal opponent mockingly responded that perhaps department stores should be forbidden from hiring women. He then noted that there are also a lot of cowardly men.

Hammer's colleague Eckart from the Free Conservative Party made an impassioned plea:

> If you ever enter one of these huge bazaars around a holiday, especially Christmas, and if you see the thousands upon thousands of shoppers and the hundreds of employees who go from stairway to stairway in one of these four-, five-, even six-story houses and who wander and push and shove each other between highly flammable objects, and if you just imagine a fire breaking out or even if someone just shouts out "fire," or if panic spreads for any other reason, gentlemen, not even a tenth of the people are going to get out alive, the others will be fatally trampled.[37]

Several German cities did enact temporary measures that restricted customers to the lower floors.[38] But as Oscar Tietz and liberal members of the Prussian Diet pointed out, this would actually increase the risk and severity of fires, since it would make those areas more crowded and dangerous and would mean that the upper floors were filled with a dense concentration of textiles and other flammable materials. Even Reichel noted in a 1906 statement that "the larger a department store, the more means there are to use against the danger of fire."[39] He noted approvingly that large department stores had ample corridors and wide stairways for quick evacuation and display areas that provided abundant space for customers. Reichel also pointed out that the new department stores featured sufficient numbers of sprinklers and fire extinguishers, and that management instructed their staff members in proper evacuation procedures. He rejected Hammer's suggestions as counterproductive, but did propose a series of measures, such as more clearly marked exits, wider stairways, and a system whereby the most frequently purchased goods be stored on the lower floors to keep crowd sizes down on the upper stories. He also recommended that directors consider charging an entry fee at the busiest times of year, such as Christmas, to reduce the crowds by discouraging casual browsers. Not surprisingly, this measure, which would most likely have cut significantly into store profits, was never seriously entertained. Nevertheless, in the weeks leading up to Christmas, guards were posted at Tietz stores in Munich to keep crowds below a certain threshold, a policy that became standard practice during busy seasons.[40]

As Reichel stated, new department store buildings were generally equipped with fire prevention and alarm systems that met or exceeded governmental requirements. Indeed, in their promotional materials, these stores tended to boast of the massive water flow from city lines, their house fire watchmen, and their sprinklers and alarms, features that helped emphasize their enormous size, their modernity, and their safety. The KaDeWe, for example, was equipped

with approximately 80 manually operated fire alarms that their watchmen could ring, some 850 automatic alarms throughout the store, a house fire crew with direct lines to the Charlottenburg fire department, and automatic alarms in the cellar and attics that sounded when temperatures rose above a safe threshold.[41]

The fire safety issue, as a political topic, began to fade in the years leading up to World War I. State and city officials must have begun to lose interest and ceased to pay heed to the anti-fire crusaders, and incidences of department store fire began to decline as modern

5.2 Warenhaus Tietz, Berlin, January 1929. Bundesarchiv, Bild 102-07256 / Photo: Georg Pahl.

and more secure constructions replaced older mixed-use buildings and as safer electric lighting began to replace gas. There were several notable department store fires in the later 1920s and early 1930s, including a blaze at Kaufhaus Schocken in Cottbus in 1930, evidently started by an iron that had been left on, and two at Tietz stores in Berlin in 1928 and 1929, but these incidents did not trigger a new wave of anti–department store agitation.[42] Yet, even as the fire safety campaigns waned and the issue began to lose its political traction, the department store fire entered the early twentieth-century literary imagination.

The Department Store Fire as Literary Motif

The catastrophic fires and the references to the threat of fire in department store fiction bear little resemblance to the actual fires mentioned above. In contrast to the fires in Budapest and Braunschweig, the imagined conflagrations in *Warenhaus Berlin*, *The Great Department Store*, and "Jape in the Department Store" did not result from accidents or equipment failure. They were intentionally set, with destructive intent. These fires all came in the aftermath of a crime, a moral transgression, thwarted romantic longings, or some combination of the three. In the moral universe of these stories, the fires result from the hubris of department store owners and the sexual and gender dynamics at work in mass consumption. They function as a kind of catharsis, a purging of the affront of the great department store and a resolution of the tensions it provoked.

Take, for example, Wilhelm Stücklen's play *Purpus*. As we saw in chapter 3, department store owner T. T. Purpus revels in the store's power to attract women. Early in the play he delights in the fact that the store had had fifteen thousand female customers on the prior day. When Purpus's plan to win over his beloved Hulle and cause her to break off her engagement fails, he abruptly decides to hold a sale of unprecedented proportion to bring in as many women as possible as compensation for losing her. He dictates the text of the promotional flyer to the house inspector, Herr Kalender, a nervous little man with sweaty palms: " 'To all Women! Department Store T. T. Purpus is clearing out its entire inventory tomorrow. . . . All prices are cut by a third—no, are cut in half!' "[43]

Purpus, the reader learns, had never shown much interest in the business side of the department store he had inherited from his father. It became important to him only as a means of attracting women. As he says on the day of the sale: "I love you all so deeply, you women! You lovely women! How I love the dreadful ones among you and the ugly ones and the superficial [ones]! . . . Be happy! . . . Be joyful! . . . And be good to me! . . . for one of you has Hulle's voice and one has her hair and her moods and her smile."[44] The store owner's power over collective womanhood works to compensate for his powerlessness toward one woman.

Meanwhile the store's order has been completely turned on its head. Kalender, who had incessantly expressed his concern about shoplifting for the first two acts, turns out to be a shoplifter himself. When caught by Pursch, the store's general manager, Kalender replies: "You really should try it sometime, Pursch! It's crazily exciting! And not at all easy!"[45] Orge, Hulle's fiancé, upon learning that his embezzlement has been discovered, grabs a revolver and nearly kills himself out of shame, until Purpus allows him and Hulle to leave the store without legal consequences. On the morning of the sale, Purpus has been locked in his office since the evening before, as desperate crowds of would-be shoppers bang on the store's front doors, demanding to be let in. The play can almost be read as an inversion of Zola's *Ladies' Paradise*. Whereas in Zola's work, Denise's love tames Mouret and saves the day by resolving the social tensions that the department store caused, in *Purpus*, Hulle's rejection exposes the morally distorted world of crime, immorality, and suppressed violence behind the store's facade, a world that explodes in the play's final scene.

Once the desperate women are allowed to enter the store and take advantage of the sale, Purpus basks in their love. As he showers gifts upon them, they storm through the aisles and shout "Hail Purpus!" In the play's closing moments, Hulle returns to the store to tell Purpus that she and Orge will soon marry. Flying into a rage, he demands that she leave immediately and threatens to burn the store down. Herr Pursch, the only major character who is not at all morally compromised, then enters to talk to Purpus about reestablishing order in the store. He sees Purpus break down, and then, the reader may infer from the stage notes, seeing that Purpus has indeed started a fire, shouts out the play's final line: "Evacuate the store!"[46]

T. T. Purpus had built a commercial empire by understanding, flattering, and exploiting women's desires. Not unlike Zola's Mouret, Purpus considered himself an expert on and a great lover of women. In both stories a major sale attracts countless adoring and semi-hysterical customers, and the event is described as a war, the store a battlefield. For example, Purpus remarks on the day of the sale: "Is this the battlefield of a defeated one? For whom is this sea of delight burning?"[47] The fire at the end of *Purpus*, while only hinted at, seems to represent the eruption of the collective *Kauflust* in the store, the explosion of the intense consuming desires, both material and erotic, that fill the store on its last day. Its consequence, we may presume, is the making right of the corrupted moral order that underlay the store's success.

The connection between *Kauflust* and fire is abundantly apparent in the language and symbolism of department store fiction. It appears in the very first sentence of Baum's "Jape in the Department Store": "The object on which the dull manner and consciousness of seventeen-year-old Jape Flunt ignited itself [*sich entzündete*] was a colorful, silk necktie that lay in the display window of a department store."[48] The story then follows a trajectory from the moment that desire for an object sparks Jape's awakening through to the department store's fiery destruction. Baum uses loaded language like this throughout the work, language that foreshadows and anticipates the conflagration. Thus, when Jape recalls the mannequin wearing the necktie in the window display, the image "burned in him," and when he wakes from his post-revelry sleep and catches sight of the reflection of two female mannequins, their image "ignites hellfire within him."[49]

The display window, of course, had functioned as the contact point, the spot where desires were kindled, and whose lights attract the attention of passersby and spark their interest. Desires burn. They spark, ignite, are inflamed. In the language of department store novels, too much desire, or morally compromised desire, can erupt into a destructive blaze. Fire, both physically and in the literary imagination, is connected to light, and the lights of the display windows and store facades help ignite consuming desires. Indeed, as Wolfgang Schivelbusch notes, artificial light began with fire. Gas and electric lights "burn."[50]

Light plays a pronounced role in the history of the department store. Zola, for one, vividly contrasts the dank interiors of Baudu's old shop with the shining, "furnace-like glare" and bright interiors of Mouret's store.[51] Throughout *The Ladies' Paradise*, he describes women as white and luminescent and the department store as a white chapel. Schivelbusch and other scholars have shown how changes in artificial lighting influenced the development of the display window, the department store, and modern urban culture, and how managing and directing light posed a major challenge to department store architects and planners, dictating important and lasting design choices.

The gaslights that illuminated late nineteenth-century display windows and city streets burned with open flames, giving them an aura of excitement and magic, yet also a sense of danger. New structures in the early twentieth century began to feature large atriums with skylights, the *Lichthof*, which channeled sunlight through the store's galleries. As Janet Ward points out, these atriums originally appeared in Paris in response to the dangers of gas lighting in a store's interior, and not long afterward they became an indispensable component of Wilhelmine department store design.[52]

Enormous display windows also became increasingly common in the later nineteenth century as glass became more affordable and thus began a new era of glass-and-steel department store structures. Hermann Tietz's building on Leipziger Strasse, designed by the architect Bernhard Sehring, was mockingly nicknamed "the Aquarium" for its massive glass facade. At its grand opening in 1900, the gigantic store was lit brightly from within to show off the power and spectacle of its illumination against the night sky—a controversial exhibition that must have been extremely striking, given that it occurred a quarter century before internally lit display windows became common.[53] The effect, the historian Siegfried Gerlach notes, was a style of architecture that featured enormous "glass curtains" and made the display window the central motif.[54] Tietz's Alexanderplatz store (1904) and the Wertheim store on Leipziger Strasse (1897) used even more glass, but showed a great deal more architectural restraint by framing the glass windows and evoking traditional architectural motifs. The glass roofs above their light courts were some 650 square meters, more than double the size of the average light-court roof in Berlin and second only to the Galeries Lafayette in Paris, which boasted the largest light court in Europe.[55]

In addition to conducting sunlight through the store's departments, light courts had the added benefit of giving consumers a way of orienting themselves in these vast and often confusing structures, functioning like the central square of a big city.[56] The light court also could have a soothing effect. It provided "a peaceful respite from congested urban conditions," writes Ward, who notes that spending time in these tranquil yet awe-inspiring spaces could be a moving, transcendent experience, conjuring the same emotions as a visit to an urban cathedral.[57]

The advent of electric lighting in the late nineteenth century and its rapid spread in the mid-1920s had a revolutionary impact on urban culture and consumption. Although electricity lacked the more mysterious and magical qualities of gas lighting, critics soon reconciled themselves to its advantages. Electric advertising and neon signs, both of which took off in the 1920s, transformed the nighttime city into a spectacle of advertising, entertainment, and consumerism. The spread of electric lighting and the "mastery of the night" became signs of increasing modernity.[58] In department stores and at other retailers goods were henceforth on display long after the stores closed. Stores were built with glass not only to conduct light inside during the day but to illuminate the nights with their bright displays. Their intense brightness burned in the evening sky, making the store itself seem aglow like a fire.

5.3 "KaDeWe in Light and Beauty." *Berliner Tageblatt*, October 14, 1928.

5.4 Hermann Tietz advertisement: Berlin in Lights Week.
Berliner Tageblatt, October 13, 1928.

The German obsession with the spectacle of light may have reached its peak in October 1928 when the capital city celebrated "Berlin in Lights" with parades, songs, illumination of commercial buildings, and lighting competitions in a series of events organized by the chamber of commerce. Berlin in Lights coincided with the white weeks sales at major Berlin department stores and was accompanied by new advertising campaigns that stressed the stores' luminosity. An ad for the KaDeWe, "KaDeWe in Light and Beauty," shows the store surrounded by a nimbus, a fiery glow emanating outward. A Tietz advertisement from the same week shows bright rays emanating from the Tietz "T" and announces a special sale that coincided with the festivities. In one case the celebrations narrowly averted disaster. On the same day as the *Graf Zeppelin* airship crossed the Azores, reaching the halfway point on its journey to New York, a short circuit in a display window being decorated for the festivities caused a fire at the Tietz "Aquarium."[59] Store employees and the fire department quickly contained the blaze, and the store reopened the next day.

Burning the Jewish Temple of Commerce

Sigfrid Siwertz's *The Great Department Store* contains many of the elements commonly found in department store novels going back to *The Ladies' Paradise*. Characters and plotlines typical to the genre are introduced, including the display window decorator, the venerable store detective who holds forth on shoplifting and kleptomania, and an assistant manager who falls in love with and marries a shopgirl. The store owner, Goldmann, is a Polish Jew who arrived in Sweden with only a crate full of clothing, soaps, and accessories, which he sold to girls and women in the Swedish countryside, gradually building up his capital. An avuncular, beneficent, and excessively modest figure, Goldmann bears little resemblance to the Jewish economic elite of Western Europe. In contrast to the refined manners and imposing bearing of the German department store kings, Goldmann is represented as a stereotypical shtetl Jew, a stooped-over man of advanced years who speaks with a strong accent, drops Yiddish into his expression, and wears wrinkled clothes, in part to look so modest that his employees will be discouraged from demanding raises.

Goldmann's Jewishness is not at all incidental; it plays a prominent role throughout the novel, from the anti-Semitic caricatures of himself that he collects, to his business practices (the restless energy, ceaseless expansion, and risk taking as discussed in chapter 2), to his final testament, which states that a Jew must be put on the board of directors after his death: "One of the Ashkenazis, a real Eastern Jew like me."[60] Nor is Jewishness incidental to the department store. In one of the caricatures Goldmann keeps in his desk, a giant nose with the frenetic gestures of the stereotypically twitchy Jewish merchant adorns the department store's main portal. The nose presides over an "oriental bazaar" full of fabrics, remnants, and slippers. Goldmann is unperturbed. Referring to himself in the third person, he muses: "The Swedes are so envious; although they laugh at Goldmann and feel superior to him, they still come with their money."[61]

Portrayed as a source of both life and death, Siwertz's "great" or "large" department store has formidable powers. In the book's opening pages, a child is conceived in the bedding department by a couple who, venturing into the department store after hours, find themselves locked in for the night. And crime, suicide, and a deadly fire propel the plot forward. As in *Purpus*, "Jape in the Department Store" and *Warenhaus Berlin*, this fire is intentionally set and related to an ethical breach. A wave of shoplifting is revealed to be an inside job, the work of a crime ring of employees directed by Philipp Sporre, the son of the house detective, referred to as "a kind of department head in Goldmann's thievery department."[62] After the younger Sporre is imprisoned, his father hangs himself in the department store out of shame, leaving an apologetic suicide note for Goldmann.

When released, Philipp Sporre is determined to take revenge on the department store, which he blames for his father's death. His deprivation resulting from prison and poverty makes the store, with its glittery abundance and luxury, appear all the more galling. Hungry and miserable in the bitter Stockholm winter, Philipp, like Jape, finds himself drawn to a display window, where he lingers for hours, enamored with two mannequins in a fur display. It is New Year's Eve in Stockholm, and the streets outside Goldmann's are full of activity, with throngs of celebrants pushing up against the store's portals. "Above [Philipp] hummed the great department store, which had everything that he had to do without: food, warmth, luxury, love. On floor after floor were piled up all the magnificence of the world."[63]

He loses himself in the crowds and slips, unnoticed, into a packing crate half filled with wood shavings. Unobserved, he closes the lid and, like Jape, finds his way into the department store after hours. Unlike Jape, however, he ends up not on the shopping floors, but in a storage room above. Still not decided on how to wreak his revenge—he originally planned simple acts of vandalism—Philipp finds some red silk, which he tears up. Reaching for the matches in his pocket, he decides to start a fire, but again like Jape, he has some difficulty igniting the "funeral pyre" (*Scheiterhaufen*) he has arranged. At last the flames take. Siwertz describes the scene: "He stood there with the pale face of a madman and stared into the flames, which quickly consumed his small funeral pyre. Then he began to throw silks atop it. . . . It must become a huge funeral pyre, everything must burn, the cheap trinkets, the luxury goods, the perfumes, the undergarments, the mannequins."[64]

Fantasizing about how famous he will become and how he will be known through the city as the one who burned down Goldmann's, he is "licked" by a "flame tongue" and is soon devoured by the fire. Goldmann, who is in the store at the time, notices the smell of smoke and alerts the fire department but is not able to escape without serious injury.

The crowds of New Year's Eve celebrants gather around to watch the show, "but it was not only fun and games in the crowd. Some, shaken up by the spectacle, saw the fire as divine judgment, a great misfortune, a secret crime."[65] Some spectators worry about the fate of Goldmann's employees; others have personal grievances with Goldmann and feel vindicated that the store is burning, seeing it as fair retribution. One onlooker speaks of his brother-in-law whom Goldmann had fired and who was now unemployed. Siwertz adds, "The brother-in-law in this case thus corresponded to the ten righteous ones for whom Sodom and Gomorrah could have been saved."[66] Here the author is referring to the biblical passage in which God destroyed Sodom and Gomorrah when ten righteous people could not be found. The firing of the brother-in-law, to this member of the crowd, meant the removal of the last worthy person from the department store. Everything and everyone that remained was morally compromised.

The reference to Sodom and Gomorrah at once equates Goldmann's store with the infamous biblical sites of debauchery and the store's burning with their destruction. Sodom and Gomorrah did not merely burn; they were destroyed, annihilated by divine act. Significantly, Siwertz places the metaphor in a hostile character's mouth, suggesting not that the writer saw the department store in these terms—indeed, the authorial voice is quite sympathetic to Goldmann and his store throughout the book—but that it was a contemporary perspective, that subjects in the interwar period may well have viewed the department store as a site of debauchery, as a sin worthy of divine condemnation. An additional layer of religious significance is added by the fact that the store burned on New Year's Eve, which, in German-speaking countries, is called "Sylvester Evening" and commemorates the death of Saint Sylvester, the pope who presided over the emperor Constantine's conversion to Christianity. What could be more fitting than the destruction of the Jewish temple of commerce before rapturous crowds on a day of Christian rejoicing!

Other onlookers on the crowded Stockholm streets regard the fire less theologically, reflecting a more mundane anti-Semitic point of view. One viewer who suspects insurance fraud asserts: "I'd bet anything the haggling Jew set it himself."[67] A kindhearted and honest businessman, who treats employees well, Goldmann is continually misunderstood and unjustly condemned by the public, who seem both to revel in the splendor of his fine department store and to take great pleasure in its destruction.

Fire crews contain the blaze by morning and are able to save much of Goldmann's store. Only the remnant fabrics, toys, and bedding departments are destroyed—the remnants, one can infer, because fabrics are so flammable, and the beds, on a more symbolic level, because that department was the site of the act at the book's beginning, the sexual liaison by the young couple who were locked in after hours. Goldmann, who is placed in the hospital's section for indigents because of his shabby attire—he does not have his papers with him—is severely injured in the fire and dies soon afterward. The store soon reopens but under new, mostly non-Jewish ownership. Although Goldmann had stipulated that a Jew be placed on the board of directors, his death means that the store will no longer be controlled by a Jew. Thus, the New Year's Eve fire serves to resolve the tension and controversy—which the character Goldmann was well aware of—that stemmed from the presence of a Jew behind the consuming temple.

Erich Köhrer's *Warenhaus Berlin* (1909) was written when massive department stores were still a new phenomenon in German cities and towns and when Germans were first dealing with the changes brought by new forms of retail and leisure. The destructive fire at the end of this novel also operates as an allegory with heavy religious overtones and also results from disturbances in the moral order.[68] The book's protagonist, Friedrich Nielandt, like Goldmann, hails from an Eastern European shtetl and has worked his way up to become a wealthy and important businessman. Whereas in the Siwertz novel, Goldmann's relentless drive to expand his store and increase his fortune is attributed to Jewish restlessness and insecurity, Nielandt's ambitions can be traced, above all, to his wife's demand for luxury. With a background similar to her husband's, Frau Nielandt was working as a shopgirl in his store when they married, but her vanity has grown even faster than Nielandt's wealth. She sheds the prosaic Anne Maria and becomes Jane, a name that evokes American sophistication and Hollywood glamour. Although not exactly beautiful—Köhrer describes her sharp nose and wildly curly, untamable hair, traits that mark her appearance as Jewish—the "little Jewess" possesses a fiery, almost magical personality.[69]

Jane's material demands pressure Nielandt to expand his modest store again and again, propelling him to launch a new business venture and create the immense department store of the title, a transparently fictionalized version of the KaDeWe, which had opened two years before Köhrer's book was published. Nielandt recognizes that "the department stores that already existed in Berlin lay in the north and center of the city. In recent times, the city's development has pushed westward from Potsdamer Tor, and whole cities have arisen where there were once only remote deserts. The residents of these western districts, if they don't want to take care of their shopping needs in the small stores, must make a big trip to reach the department stores in the city center."[70] Hence Nielandt decides to construct his new store "out there in the west, around the zoological garden," where "a department store could certainly do magnificent business."[71] Jane's material desires, then, and Nielandt's drive to satisfy them, will power a fundamental transformation in Berlin's commercial topography.

Nielandt requires capital for his ambitious plans and finds an eager investor in the dissolute Günther Duessen, an elegant, bored noble, described by Köhrer as a blond and "Germanic" type. Duessen is not interested in the business per se—he can muster, at best, a few moments' passing attention for Nielandt's grandiose plans—but rather in Jane. He involves himself in the venture as an excuse to be near her and, he hopes, to seduce her. In short the giant department store and indeed the commercialization of western Berlin will result from both a Jewish woman's greed and a decadent German nobleman's lecherous desire to possess her.

The proposed store's location, proximate to the actual KaDeWe on Berlin's Wittenbergplatz, lies centrally on Berlin's transit grid, near the Zoo train station and a number of streetcar lines. However, this location, close by the Kaiser Wilhelm Gedächtniskirche (memorial church), gives city officials pause. Building regulators fear that the department store might block the church and that "the church's sanctity would be desecrated if the doors to a department store opened right across from its main entrance."[72]

The church then provides a backdrop for subsequent events. On the day of Department Store Berlin's grand opening, Köhrer writes, "as the chimes of the Kaiser Wilhelm Gedächtniskirche's bell tower trailed off into the clear winter air, the sea of lights of the new house flamed up."[73] The juxtaposition of the Christian church and the Jewish temple of commerce frames the novel's climactic events, which, like those in Siewertz's *The Great Department Store*, unfold in a highly allegorical manner. The church itself, which was commissioned by the German emperor Wilhelm II to commemorate his grandfather Wilhelm I, harks back to an imagined traditional Germany starkly at odds with the consumer-oriented modernity of the department store. The appearance of the department store next to the cathedral can be read as reflecting a larger tension in a society that was responding to rapid changes by looking backward, attempting to revive discarded traditions just as they were on the verge of obsolescence.

In describing Department Store Berlin's grand opening, Köhrer emphasizes its brightness, its shimmering advertisements and lustrous glow, suggesting that the department store's very existence represents a kind of burning. "At five o'clock sharp," he narrates, "a surging sea of light began to pour out over Joachimstaler-, Hardenberg-, and Kantstrasse." Nielandt and Griebner, his business manager, fully understand the significance of light in advertising. "The entire ground floor and the first upper story were completely surrounded by a thick ring of arc lights behind which were mounted spotlights, which spun out the light waves in a huge circle into the surrounding area. The display windows . . . themselves lustrously appointed, were also bathed in a flood of light."[74] This rich imagery gives the store an ethereal and spiritual quality, suggesting that it is surrounded by an aura or even a kind of halo or nimbus, similar to the KaDeWe's appearance in the 1928 Berlin in Lights advertisement.

Judging by the crowds on opening day—nearly fifty thousand customers show up—the store is bound to be a great success. Griebner compares the crowds to rushing water as he triumphantly reports on the day to his boss: "Hurray Mr. Nielandt, a success; it will be an enormous success. Our house is besieged by an impenetrable throng. Like a levee that stops the rushing of flooding seawaters, a black wall is being drawn around the gleaming lights of Department Store Berlin."[75] Indeed, the store's remarkable success during its first several months brings Nielandt tremendous wealth and power. At this point in the novel, he is already preparing to expand the store by purchasing an adjacent hotel, thus encroaching even more closely on the Kaiser Wilhelm Church.

Yet Nielandt feels pangs of remorse for having buried himself so deeply in his work and thereby neglecting his wife. Jane, by this point, is deep in her affair with Günther Duessen. Rumors of the affair do not come as a surprise to Griebner, who admits that he finds it implausible that the "youthful, elegant" Jane could have remained true to the "aged, somewhat pudgy and ungainly body of Nielandt."[76] Like Goldmann in *The Great Department Store*, Nielandt is portrayed as an asexual figure. A stereotype of Jewish masculinity, he is physically unattractive and more interested in business than love or sex. In fact, early in the novel, as Duessen is trying to seduce Jane, he assures Jane that her husband would not mind if she took a lover: a parvenu like Nielandt, an unrefined man who had risen socially through his own labor, could not appreciate her beauty, and his business was more important to him than his wife's loyalty. When Nielandt finally learns about Jane's infidelity, Jane tries this approach with him: "You have your business, which keeps you very busy and which preoccupies you completely. Let me have my lover!"[77] And, as she confesses her lover's identity, Jane doubly emasculates her husband: "he's the same man who through his millions has made the fulfillment of your wishes possible even as he satisfies my desires."[78]

At least from Jane's and Duessen's perspectives, then, Nielandt, the prototypical Jewish man, is incapable of devoted romantic love and obsessed solely with commercial ventures. Nevertheless, Nielandt is devastated by news of the affair. He now sees Jane and the department store as rivals for his love and devotion, ultimately blaming the store, the "ravenous Moloch"—which he had established to satisfy his wife's desires—for tearing him away from her. Throughout the novel, Nielandt had waxed enthusiastic about the store's power over women shoppers. Now, caught in an untenable position by his dependence on Duessen's capital, he realizes the store's power over him and concludes that he must put it back in its place. "Yes, this house was responsible for all the suffering that had been brought down on him. Like an alluring phantom in all of its splendor and power it had stood day and night foremost in his thoughts and dreams and had not let him go until he was completely ensnared in its web and had forgotten about everything beautiful and precious beyond it. And now it was wresting from him the most exquisite thing that still remained his."[79]

Nielandt resolves to win Jane back and reassert himself, to restore order and reestablish his control over the department store. Smashing a pitcher against a porcelain display, he works himself into a rage: "Yes, he was the master. He could destroy what he had built up. He could smash his own child that aimed to become his tyrannical ruler."[80] Fire seems the solution. The only way to reassert his control, to tame the "Moloch," is to raze it. Like Jape and Philipp Sporre, Nielandt does not escape the blaze that he ignites, an inferno that not only levels Department Store Berlin but convulses the entire city, "which, struck in the heart, writhed in weary paroxysms."[81]

Köhrer describes the fire in frankly biblical terms. "It was," he recounts, "as though the earth reared up in a mighty rage. A huge fist [of flame], glowing red, raised itself up, stretched the tower up into the heavens and then tore it down deep into the ground with an abrupt lurch. . . . The store's entire interior collapsed in on itself with dull claps of thunder."[82] Whereas the fire at the end The Great Department Store was likened to the destruction of Sodom and Gomorrah, here the allegory more closely resembles the Tower of Babel. Nielandt's hubris, the majesty and grandeur of his colossal department store, which, as in the biblical tale, resembles a city, calls upon itself destructive divine wrath.

Yet again the church provides a backdrop, a screen for observing the department store's destruction. "The church stood there like a black silhouette against the burning horizon. In its windows the eerie beauty of the furious blaze was reflected magically."[83] But with the store's destruction, the provocation of the Moloch, the secular temple of greed, is resolved, dictating the novel's peaceful, poetic ending, on a lovely Sunday morning, no less: "A thick, yellow shower of sparks rained down like a fluttering veil of majestic beauty out into the dark night," writes Köhrer.[84]

For the historian Detlef Briesen this climactic scene staged the defeat of the upstart and threatening consumer culture at the hands of traditional German mores. This "auto-da-fé of mass culture," he argues, accounted for the great popularity of Köhrer's work.[85] Briesen may have formulated this a bit too one-dimensionally. Most of Köhrer's readers—like Köhrer himself, who contributed essays to Kaufhaus Israel's albums—were probably not opponents of Germany's nascent consumer culture.[86] It is more likely that readers felt uneasy about new forms of mass consumption, that the consumer revolution, still only in its infancy, was bringing new pleasures while also causing a sense of disorientation and fear. The department store's destruction may have provided a pleasurable, temporary resolution of those anxieties and a restoration of the moral order that the store's growth had shattered. Rather than simply opposing the department store and modern consumption, it seems much more likely that Köhrer was portraying its tremendous power and dynamism, describing the formidable force of the store and the unsettling desires it unleashed.

If modernity's vast energies led to the production of what the historian Bernhard Rieger calls modern wonders—ever-larger ocean liners, faster, more powerful airplanes, and (one could add) more comprehensive and stunning department stores—they simultaneously fed a fascination with destruction, with crashes, shipwrecks, and department store blazes.[87] The destructive fires at the end of these fictional works bespeak this fascination, this sense of the powerful destructive force that modernity carries within it. Inasmuch as humanity longs for greater, more impressive, and more powerful creations, Siwertz and Köhrer suggest that early twentieth-century subjects feared the power of these creations and fantasized about their annihilation. If the department store and the new regime of mass consumption spread like wildfire, as a commonly used metaphor had it, their rise must culminate in their self-destruction through fire, the only way to resolve modernity's relentless energies and the tensions they spark.

Department Store Violence

Fire can also be seen as part of the larger topic of violence within and against the stores, their employees, and customers. Department stores provoked a whole spectrum of violent acts, both real and fantasized, from their emergence through the Nazi assumption of power in the 1930s and even into the postwar period. Literature and theater often used the department store as a setting for violent acts, including rape and murder—even warfare in the case of Manfred Georg's 1928 novel *Aufruhr im Warenhaus* (Insurrection in the department store). The stores' political opponents attacked them in a number of actions during this period, with greater frequency shortly before and immediately after the Nazis came into power. Whereas attacks on department stores were generally overt political acts, literary representation of violence typically operated with a related but distinct set of assumptions. Like the fictional fires discussed above, these imagined acts of violence reflected the belief that the department store contained unstable, combustible tensions, sometimes manifested in the violent subordination of women.

The fact that so many department store dramas and novels feature violent endings demands closer scrutiny. It betrays an impulse to bring to the surface the violence that, it could be argued, lay behind the scenes and made possible the department store's luxury and splendor. Georg Heym's "Der Irre" (The mad man), from 1913, an expressionist short story told from the perspective of a violent, hallucinating mental patient, uses the department store as background for its protagonist's deranged acts.[88] The story begins with the unnamed patient's release from an asylum, from which he slowly makes his way into central Berlin, coming in and out of lucidity and murdering two children on the way. It reaches its climax when he arrives at a department store. By juxtaposing insane asylums and department stores, the narrative arc suggests that the latter can also be seen as a site of violent and disturbed behavior. The character's hallucinatory impressions of the lavish store resonate with many of the themes we have already encountered, including the brightness of the department store, its frenetic activity and motion, and its cathedral-like qualities. "Damn, this is a fine church," he thinks to himself, impressed by its splendor, light, and vast open spaces.[89] Entering the store, the protagonist sees "countless tables, full of fabrics, clothes. Everything swam in a lovely light, which radiated through the twilight of the huge palace's high windows. From the ceiling hung an enormous chandelier with countless, glittering brilliant diamonds."[90] The store's brightness and opulence are striking to be sure, but it's the quality of the store's light that Heym emphasizes, describing the ground floor, for example, as an "ocean filled with tremendous light."[91]

The character makes his way upstairs in the elevator, feeling like a "bird swooping up to the sky," and from that point on the department store's activities begin to lull him into a haze.[92] "He leaned on a railing, under which he saw the people streaming in like countless black flies with their heads, legs, and arms in constant motion, so that they seemed to emit a ceaseless hum. . . . He was a great white bird above a large, isolated sea, soothed by the eternal brightness, high up in the blue. His head climbed up the white clouds, he was nearing the sun, which filled the skies beyond his head, a large golden bowl that began to buzz mightily."[93] Delighting in the illusion that he can fly, he climbs onto the balustrade, contemplates swooping down into the "sea," and then zeroes in on a disturbing dark shape below. At this point he has attracted the attention of customers and employees. Ladies are staring, store workers are rushing about, looking for their managers. He then springs down, landing atop—and smashing, we can assume—Japanese glasswork, Chinese lacquer paintings, and Tiffany crystal. The dark shape, it turns out, is a shopgirl, and the protagonist grabs her throat and begins slowly squeezing. The store is now complete chaos: "And the crowd flees through the aisles, people trample each other on their way down the stairs. Clamorous screaming fills the house. Someone yells 'fire, fire.' In an instant the whole floor is empty. There only remain a pair of little children before the stairway door, kicked to death or crushed."[94] The maniac, meanwhile, strangles the shopgirl until she dies, and then he is shot to death by a police officer who has been called to the scene.

The climax of "Der Irre" embodies the deepest fears conjured up by anti–department store agitators. A stampeding crowd incited by the threat of fire, with deadly, nightmarish consequences, evokes the warnings of the crusaders discussed earlier in this chapter. Furthermore, the story's violent, murderous altercation, the mad scene triggered by a madman, reflects the assumption that department stores were mysterious, dangerous places. The store's lights, whose brightness created such a sense of spectacle, fuel the character's descent into murderous insanity. That the story ends with the murder of a store worker reinforces the notion that department stores were a site of violence and that shopgirls were at particular risk.

Hans Vogt's *Du Kommst zu Spät* (You're too late), a 1914 play set in a department store, likewise dramatizes (and exaggerates) the abject condition of women in department stores, ending with a rape and a shooting. This highly melodramatic one act concerns Krajewsky, a department store owner; Klärle, a beautiful shopgirl whom he has transferred from the Frankfurt store so he can be near her at Berlin headquarters; and Schmidt the bookkeeper, who falls in love with her. Klärle and Schmidt become engaged before Krajewsky has had a chance to try to win her over. Karajewsky calls her up to his office, and when she rejects his advances, he forces himself on her. After finding out, Schmidt shoots Krajewsky and kills himself, apparently out of shame that Krajewsky had violated and disgraced his fiancé.[95] Vogt presents a particularly histrionic version of what department store critics saw as the oppressive relationship between male department store owners and their female employees.

In Georg's 1928 novel *Aufruhr im Warenhaus* (Insurrection in the department store), New York's Spring Department Store, a massive, sixty-story skyscraper, becomes the headquarters of a group of Bessarabian revolutionaries who have fled Europe after their unsuccessful attempt to assassinate a Romanian minister of state.[96] The group's leader, Viktor, bears an uncanny resemblance to Winfried T. Booker, owner of the Spring Department Store, whom he had encountered on the boat to America, a man who exudes power and ambition. Viktor kills his doppelgänger and assumes his place as the store's director. He uses his new power and wealth subversively to support revolutionary causes, funding, for example, a group of rebels in Latin America and offering free merchandise to New York's poor. In the novel's climactic scenes, Viktor closes the store, hoists a red flag atop its tower, and demands fair treatment for the workers whose labor makes the department store possible. With an army of African Americans and other disenfranchised groups, he attacks the Woolworth building, New York's next largest structure in the world of the novel. Department Store Spring becomes a site of chaos and insanity, and American bombers ultimately destroy the store.

Georg, a journalist and later the editor of the New York–based *Aufbau*, the leading newspaper for German-speaking Jews in the United States, sets his novel in the United States presumably because America signified the heart of consumer capitalism. (Nevertheless, it is worth noting that Georg was willing to move the setting to a different country and remove the story's political dimensions for the anticipated filming.)[97] Viktor and his band of radicals try to subvert American consumer culture from within, acts that earn them the suspicion and hostility of the united department store owners of New York and ultimately the U.S. government. The novel's ending, in which the department store is turned into a scene of battle, seems less outlandish when we consider the common use of military metaphors to describe the stores and the frenzy of buying and selling that takes place in their galleries, especially after major sales and promotions.

The store's violent destruction, finally, can be seen as a way of calling attention to the often violent and oppressive conditions that make mass production possible, an uncovering of the hidden violence and exploitative labor upon which the store was built. In this sense, Georg is staging the de-fetishizing of the commodity, an explosive act that strikes at the heart of modern consumer culture. Unlike Köhrer's 1909 novel, in which the department store is framed as a threat to traditional German ways, Georg's story, written in the heady political context of the Weimar Republic, presents a left-wing critique of the department store as part of the American capitalist machine, a machine that sees to the store's destruction once it has gone over to the opposing political camp. The novel was published even as right-wing violence toward department stores began to flare up in cities and towns across Germany.

It is not clear whether Georg's novel rivaled the popular success of Köhrer's, or, for that matter, whether his treatment of consumer capitalism resonated with a broad readership. Georg himself noted that interest in filming the novel stemmed from the appeal of the characters and exciting plot and not the political message.[98] We do know, however, that the novel was critically acclaimed. Writers such as Kurt Hiller, Kurt Pinthus, and Joseph Roth, reviewing the book in some of the major newspapers of the period, praised Georg effusively for his literary style and his insights into human nature.[99]

Emil Kläger's 1933 play *Incident in the Department Store* also draws connections between modern mass consumption, exploitation, and violence at a time when violence against department stores had become increasingly common and visible. It features a business manager explicitly identified as Jewish and a sprinkling of Yiddish words in the text. Kläger's work brings to mind the parallels between department stores and theaters. One character has left his job at the Kreis department store to pursue a career in the theater, and the dialogue is filled with references to the store's theatrical qualities—in fact the characters even talk about how the play should end—and the final scene is played out by four mannequins. Indeed, department stores provided an ideal setting for literary and theatrical work, offering an abundant supply of potential props and ready-made story lines. In fact, as Mila Ganeva has pointed out, theater and clothing retail began to intersect in the late nineteenth century, a moment when fashion marketing became increasingly theatrical, and theater authors became interested in the dramatic dimensions of dressing and changing clothes.[100]

The play concludes in a fantastical, surrealistic atmosphere, played, as the stage directions inform, "in the light streaming from the street, especially from the rotating advertisements."[101] Amid the refracted lights of consumer culture, Kreis, the store owner, having fallen to the brink of financial ruin, pulls a revolver out of his desk. Just at that moment, his friend Fehring rushes in frantically. Fehring has smelled fire and suspects the source is in Kreis's office. Although there was no fire, the play closes with a violent suicide in the director's office.

From the beginning, violence and the threat of fire haunted the department store. They were exploited by the stores' opponents in their appeals to state officials to limit new competitors' ability to expand and grow. In department store literature and drama, fires and violent endings resolve the tensions of nascent consumer culture, right the distorted moral order, and bring out the violence that lurks below its glittery surfaces. Yet some of these works portrayed consumer culture as growing and spreading like an unstoppable force, a raging fire. All the more fitting, then, that fires felled so many of the fictional department stores, not only in the times and places analyzed here, but well beyond. In Michael Pearson's pulpy novel *The Store* (1986), based on Harrods in London, Kingstons department store is attacked and set afire by butchers angry that the store has moved into the meat trade. And the zany 2004 Spanish film *El Crimen Ferpecto* (The ferpect crime), which takes place in Madrid's Yeyo's department store, features the murder of a salesman, the incineration of his corpse, and a blaze that burns down the store and allows the protagonist to fake his death.[102] That fire occurs at Christmastime, and pandemonium ensues as the huge crowds try to evacuate the burning store while others loot its contents. In a rapturous scene strangely reminiscent of the novels by Siwertz and Köhrer, flames consume the store and its holiday displays to the strains of "Jingle Bells." Even though the golden age of the department store waned decades ago and the stores have lost much of their ability to excite, provoke, and frighten, the theme of the consuming fire continues to exert a hold on our imagination.

The Politics of Shattered Glass

Actual acts of violence against German department stores, like anti–department store agitation, came in two waves: the first began in the 1890s, the period of the stores' rapid expansion and growth, and waned in the years preceding World War I; the second, more pronounced phase gained strength in the late 1920s, the years of rising economic uncertainty and political polarization during which the Nazis gained national prominence and reaped major electoral successes.

The violence of the first wave was limited in scope. It coincided with the movement to levy special taxes on department stores, the publication of a spate of anti–department store treatises, and the fire safety campaigns. For example, the success of the Hermann Tietz store in Munich, one of Germany's first fully fledged department stores, had been met in the late 1880s with a great deal of opposition, which on at least one occasion turned into violence.

A group of protesters, chiefly rival businessmen, met in a beer hall to voice their grievances. After working themselves up into an alcohol-induced furor, they marched on the store, blocked its doors, and passed out defamatory leaflets. Soon student activists from the university's *Burschenschaften* (student corps) joined the fray and began hurling rocks and harassing employees and shoppers who tried to enter the store. The police refused to take action against the students on the grounds that these were sons of notable families, even as the young activists began smashing windows, beating employees, and destroying merchandise. Finally, the military was called in to restore order and scatter the crowds. University and city officials refused to bring charges against the demonstrators or take action of any kind against them until Hermann Tietz, who had American citizenship, appealed to the U.S. consulate. Soon thereafter a student corps member was sent to make official apologies on behalf of his corps and the university.[103]

Violence in this early period was generally the expression of economic resentment and a fear that often overlapped and intersected with anti-Semitism. There were cases in which department store owners—Jacques Raphaeli in Berlin, for example—were threatened and intimidated, and anti–department store agitation did, at times, grow violent amid the intense struggles for economic survival and "street territory" among merchants in Berlin and other major cities.[104] Yet things calmed down with the gradual acceptance of the department store before World War I, and there is little evidence of anti–department store violence in the early and middle years of the Weimar Republic.

Starting in 1928, attacks picked up in frequency and intensity. The new wave of attacks, both verbal and physical, were most often led by Nazi militants, who resurrected the anti–department store slogans and symbols of the preceding generation but articulated them in a sharper key in a political culture marked by increasing violence.[105] In the 1928 celebrations of the entry of Nazi deputies into the Reichstag, rioters hurled rocks at department store display windows in Berlin.[106] A 1931 anti-Nazi propaganda film, made by the Social Democrats, captured these events, depicting Nazi celebrants smashing store windows on Berlin's Leipziger Strasse.[107] Nazi organs published lists of "acceptable" stores and urged party members to avoid those not on the lists, including Jewish-owned stores and consumer cooperatives. SA thugs were arrested for attacks on several department stores in the cities of Darmstadt and Mainz in December 1932, in actions that apparently protested Jewish-owned stores' marketing of Christmas goods and themes, an old anti-Semitic issue that the Nazis took up with new fervor.[108] A 1932 report on these incidents in the Berlin-based *Vossische Zeitung* warned readers to expect more of these attacks in the Christmas season.[109]

The summer of 1932 was the high-water mark for anti–department store violence in the Weimar Republic. Heinrich Uhlig, the author of a 1956 study on department stores under the Nazi dictatorship, counts ten acts of terror against department stores and discount retailers like Woolworth and Ehape in the three-week period between July 28 and August 12, 1932.[110] In two separate incidents in July and August 1932, SA members sprayed tear gas and set off small explosives in L. Tietz and Woolworth stores in the northwestern German cities of Krefeld, Wuppertal, and Düsseldorf, apparently laboring under the misconception that the Woolworth chain was owned by Jews.[111] Several of the stores had to be evacuated completely while authorities cleared the gas and protected merchandise from theft. That same summer also saw numerous cases of intimidation, shop-window smashing, pistol shots, tear gas and bomb throwing, and the firebombing of an East Prussian department store at night.

To be sure, department stores were far from the only target of these uniformed thugs. Around the same time, similar disruptions occurred during screenings of the antiwar film *All Quiet on the Western Front* and at meetings of other political groups and organizations.[112] In the late 1920s and early 1930s Nazis also attacked KPD activists as they staged their own demonstrations outside store window displays at Christmastime. The communists for their part objected to the commercialization of the holiday and the way its appropriation by German consumer capitalism distracted attention from such serious political and social issues as growing poverty and income disparity.[113] Still, the department store, as a highly visible symbol of Jewish power—power over the German economy and power over women—was a particularly tempting target for Nazi protesters.[114]

Weimar's urban modernity, its bustling commercial and leisure spheres, and its nightscapes of brightly lit, ever-larger show windows and signs represented, in the Nazi mind, the decadence and depravity of the Republic, a reminder of all that had gone wrong in Germany. The Nazis, in contrast, brought their own culture of darkness and light. Through their mastery of fire, in the torchlight parade, and their evening campaigns of brutality and intimidation, the Nazis turned the night into a primal scene of awe and terror. Nights under Nazi rule brought, at first, an escalation of protests and violence against department stores and other institutions and businesses associated with Jews. In the weeks following Hitler's appointment as chancellor, display windows of (Jewish and non-Jewish) department stores and other Jewish-owned businesses were smashed, and a fire was set at an Ehape shop in the town of Pirmasens in the Rhineland Palatinate.[115] In Braunschweig that March, Karstadt stores were vandalized, shots were fired at an Epa store (a discount department store) in Magdeburg, and a Woolworth store in the town of Gotha was nearly completely destroyed.[116] Demonstrators regularly encamped outside department stores and discounters in Berlin and other cities, demanding that German women shop elsewhere and shaming those who entered.

The Nazi Party, however, did not officially condone such actions—certainly not out of sympathy for Jewish store owners, but rather to avoid creating the appearance of disorder or inflicting a shock on the economy. As employers of some ninety thousand (mostly non-Jewish) workers, department stores were crucial to Germany's economic livelihood at a time of crippling unemployment. Thus, despite all their propaganda against one of their oldest targets, the Nazi regime made only halfhearted attempts to restrict department stores' growth and expansion and actually rescued one major store, floating the bankrupt Hermann Tietz concern with favorable loans in June 1933.[117] Tietz employed some fourteen thousand workers at the time, the great majority of whom were not Jewish. While preventing the opening of new department stores and enacting special taxes on them, the party endorsed a wait-and-see approach in the period between 1933 and 1936–37, claiming that the "department store question" would be dealt with in due course—as soon as the unemployment problem was solved and the economy placed on a proper footing.[118] As Hitler's adjutant Rudolf Hess declared in a July 1933 statement, party members were forbidden from taking matters into their own hands and acting independently against department stores. This did not mean, he hastened to point out, that Nazis could support or promote the stores; and as Martin Bormann, Hess's deputy, added in his own statement, the stores were forbidden from flying Nazi flags, displaying pictures of the führer, or carrying SS-men figurines or other Nazi symbols until further notice.[119]

The tension between Nazi economic populism and the party's sympathy with big business, which mirrored the conflict between SA zealots and the more restrained, bureaucratic approach of the party once in power, endured through the 1930s. While the latter approach generally prevailed, there were nonetheless occasional boycotts and outbursts of violence against stores in these years. The most notorious was the so-called Night of the Broken Glass or Kristallnacht, November 9–10, 1938, a night of anti-Jewish violence, round-ups of Jewish men, and officially sponsored actions against Jewish shops and synagogues that proved to be a major turning point in the Nazi persecution of the Jews. Some twenty-nine department stores were set on fire or destroyed. Among the ninety-one Jews killed that night was the manager of a Chemnitz department store, who was beaten to death in the store's cellar.[120]

Soon thereafter the last remaining Jewish-owned department stores were Aryanized, auctioned to non-Jewish competitors for a fraction of their worth, completing a process that had begun in 1933 with the forced removal of many Jewish employees. Names were changed: Leonhard Tietz became Kaufhof already in 1933; Wertheim became AWAG (Allgemeine Warenhandelsgesellschaft AG, or General Retail Company Inc.) several years later. Amid Hermann Göring's final push to remove Jews from the German economy, N. Israel, Berlin's oldest department store and one of the last holdouts, finally surrendered control in February 1939.[121] Once sold off to non-Jewish investors, the stores were allowed, in slightly modified form, to conduct business as usual until wartime scarcities severely limited their supplies.

Burn, Department Store, Burn!

The next significant attacks on German department stores occurred thirty years later, in a completely different context. These acts were inspired not by Nazi condemnations but rather by a new source of opposition, the student movement, with its left-wing critique of consumer culture and its message of anticapitalism, anti-Americanism, and anti-Zionism.

On May 5, 1967, L'Innovation, a popular Brussels department store, opened an exhibition on American fashion, displaying blue jeans and other trappings of contemporary American life. The heavily promoted exhibition became an instant source of controversy as activists began to protest this celebration of Americana in light of the United States' actions in Vietnam. Three weeks later, when fire broke out on May 22, many blamed the protesters or assumed the involvement of anti-American groups. The fire, which was actually caused by an electrical failure, spread quickly through the crowded store and soon devoured the 1897 structure, which evidently had no sprinkler system. Some employees, having listened to protester fireworks for three weeks, assumed this was simply more of the same and did not evacuate in time. In all 322 people perished.

The Brussels fire generated a great deal of sympathy, especially in Germany. One of its consequences was to inspire a series of pamphlets by members of Kommune 1, the radical Berlin commune, which decried the apparent hypocrisy of mourning the victims of the blaze while ignoring the situation in Southeast Asia. A flyer headlined "When will the Berlin department stores burn!" appeared two days after the fire, seeking to stir readers' consciousness: "A burning department store with burning people conveys that crackling Vietnam feeling for the first time in a major European city, being there, burning with it, that is something we've had to do without in Berlin so far."[122] It went on to place the consumer at the heart of the American imperium, equating advertising slogans and the hyper-marketing of American commodities on the one hand with American military interventions in the guise of spreading freedom and democracy on the other.[123] It ended with the militant cry: "Burn warehouse, burn!" Notwithstanding the poor English translation of *Warenhaus*, readers would have understood the reference to African American protest movements in the United States and their call to burn the "decencies and dignities" of American consumer culture, the material benefits of capitalist abundance enjoyed disproportionately by white America.[124]

Some nine months after the leaflet appeared in Berlin, Andreas Baader, Gudrun Ensslin, Thorwald Proll, and Horst Söhnlein took seriously what the authors had evidently meant as merely a provocation. Shortly before closing time they planted homemade explosives in the Kaufhof and Schneider department stores on the Zeil, Frankfurt's busy commercial strip. The bombs exploded around midnight, causing no casualties but leading to significant property damage. The ensuing trial, a media frenzy in West Germany, notable for the attention-getting theatrics of the defendants, brought convictions and prison sentences to the four. In May 1970, Ensslin, journalist Ulrike Meinhof, and others helped Baader escape prison and flee underground, the founding moment in the history of the Red Army Faction, leading to years of violent, left-wing activism in West Germany.[125] In Proll's notebooks the police later found the line, "When will the Berlin department stores burn!"—a direct quote from the 1967 Kommune 1 flyer.[126]

For the militant activists of the late 1960s and early 1970s, living amid the bounty of West Germany's economic miracle, the department store symbolized consumerist excess. They condemned it for numbing consumers into complacency and passive acquiescence with the crimes of both the Nazi past and the capitalist present. For them the department store bombing was not just an attack on two stores; it was a wake-up call against the United States, simultaneously the belly of the consumer-culture beast and perpetrator of an imperialist war in Southeast Asia. Having been taken out of Jewish hands by the Nazis, department stores were now linked with fascism, rounding out the equation of America, consumerism, imperialism, and fascism, the moving targets against which the New Left mobilized. Although explicit references to the Jewish origins of the German department stores do not appear in the Red Army Faction literature, the group's militant support for the PLO, its aggressive stance against Zionism, and Meinhof's recycling of the stereotypical "money-Jews" in her explanation of anti-Semitism suggest that the memory of the "Jewish department store" lingered still.[127]

Less than a century after their emergence in German cities and towns, scrubbed of their Jewish management, the department stores were fully accepted by the political Right, which had gradually made its peace with commercial capitalism. Just when their economic significance was falling from its 1950s peak, and soon before a series of bankruptcies threatened to eradicate them altogether, German department stores experienced one final moment in the political and cultural spotlight, standing, many believed, at the center of a nexus of nefarious international forces. For one last time, attacking and burning the temple of consumption would be the means of striking a blow against the power of consumer culture and commercial capitalism.

CONCLUSION

Nazi Aryanization measures, followed by years of war, terror, and devastation, weakened the association between Jews and department stores in Germany and Europe. The German department store became the Jewish department store once again in the 1990s, however, after the collapse of the German Democratic Republic, but this time purely as a historical and legal issue. The end of the GDR brought a wave of new restitution cases for formerly Jewish-owned properties, assets, and businesses that fell on the east side of the German-German border. The Wertheim building on Berlin's Leipziger Strasse, once the iconic German department store, having been destroyed during World War II, became iconic again, this time as a symbol of unresolved justice and the limits of the German state's goodwill toward the victims of Nazi-era crimes.

The Wertheim case was brought on behalf of Wertheim's chicken-farming, New Jersey descendants by the New York–based Conference on Material Claims against the Federal Republic of Germany. Benefiting from the canny detective work of a Berlin graduate student, the case ultimately hinged on an act of fraud perpetrated by Arthur Lindgens, a Wertheim family friend and adviser who had married Georg Wertheim's (non-Jewish) widow in 1939 and guided the company through the treacherous years of the Third Reich.[1] In 1951 Lindgens defrauded the two surviving Wertheim heirs. He claimed that the business lay in shambles and had no value. Perpetrating this deception, he flew to New York—preventing the brothers from seeing the actual state of things in Berlin—and bought what remained of the business from them for a fraction of its worth. Lindgens had actually already concluded a deal to sell the business to Karstadt-Quelle, the Karstadt department stores' parent company, for a much higher sum.[2] After years of legal battles, the case was settled in 2007, with Karstadt-Quelle agreeing to pay 88 million euros to the Claims Conference, although Wertheim descendants continued to fight for a more favorable settlement for the valuable properties the Wertheims had owned around Leipziger Platz and for the family's once-flourishing department store firm.

The streetscapes of today's Berlin and other German cities are filled with conspicuous and wrenching memorials to the Nazi past. Prime real estate in the capital city, a stone's throw from where the Leipziger Strasse store once stood, is devoted to a field of concrete slabs or stelae commemorating the victims of Nazi genocide. Throughout the city, shiny pavement stones bearing the names of deported and murdered Jews force pedestrians literally to stumble out of their complacency and face up to history. Nevertheless, in this culture of memory, the department store's Jewish origins seem largely forgotten. Berlin's Jewish Museum and occasional magazine articles remind visitors and readers of the tremendous economic and cultural role that Germany's Jewish department store kings once played, but the stores themselves, now consolidated into two nationwide conglomerates, show no trace of their origins and no sign of the fierce political, economic, and cultural controversies they once inspired.

In this book I have argued that those controversies revolved around Jews and "the Jew" for some sixty years. In each chapter I analyzed the German department store from a distinct perspective and then linked that perspective to a particular set of images of the Jew or a specific theme in Jewish history. Debates about the rising power and prominence of the department store often invoked the anti-Semitic notion of the Jew as a parasite, as an "economic vampire," indeed a hostile, external force feeding off the German body politic. Jewish entrepreneurs were portrayed both as ur-capitalists, circulating economic actors constitutionally suited for risky capitalist endeavors, and as worldly agents, exemplars and purveyors of a kind of cosmopolitanism that either enriched or threatened German life. The department store's eroticization, its sex-gender order, and the notion that it represented an alternative domestic space for women focused attention on the Jewish store owners' power over female shoppers and prompted the Nazis and others to defame the Jew as exploiter and rapist. The associations between Jews and modernism also played an important role, revealing themselves above all in the architecture of the modernist department stores of the 1920s and the commercial and aesthetic causes pursued by the entrepreneur, literary patron, and Zionist Salman Schocken. Many of these themes came together in the image of the department store fire expressed both in the literary imagination and in actual acts of violence and intimidation from the 1880s through the 1930s and beyond. Several works of fiction represented the unease of Jews themselves with the conspicuous presence of Jewish-owned consuming palaces, yielding an image of the self-conscious Jew who imagines the purging of the Jewish-owned department store from Germany's urban landscape. These stories, with their explicit biblical imagery, illustrate the anxiety that came with Jewish success and the longed-for resolution of the tension provoked by the Jewish temple of consumption and its threat to German and Christian traditions.

Jews as bloodsuckers, as archetypal capitalists, as exploiters of women, as modernists, and as anti-Christians—these disparate but often overlapping images waxed and waned over the course of German and European Jewish history. By emphasizing them I do not mean to downplay the positive sides of German Jewish history, the tremendous achievements of German Jews, the dynamic movements that shaped Jewish religious and cultural life in these years, or the strong sense of belonging and affiliation that so many Jews felt in Germany and with German society and culture. It would be misleading to overlook the extent to which many German Jews were integrated into German society or of course to suggest that German Jews were inevitably doomed. Rather, I am arguing that these images of Jews lurked in the culture, that they were visible and legible to Jews and non-Jews alike—including anti-Semites, Zionists, and everyone in between—and that they were available for deployment by foes (and sometimes friends) of the department store and critics of modern German life.

In excavating the deep entanglement of department stores and Jews in the German past, I have also tried to shed light on another German peculiarity, namely the astonishing persistence of supernatural themes in treatments of the department store across a wide variety of media and sources. These varied from the department store monsters and economic vampires that filled the propaganda sheets of anti–department store activists, to representations of eerie encounters in the stores, especially after hours, when mannequins seemed to come to life and the boundaries between the living world and the "thing world" appeared terrifyingly permeable. On one level, the persistence of these themes suggests widespread unease with the new stores and their apparent powers, their ability to awaken *Kauflust* and turn passersby into eager consumers, a bundle of forces that seemed to defy rational explanation. On another level, they betray that the Jewish department store had a metaphysical resonance in pre-Nazi Germany, that the debate about consumer culture had strong ontological, even theological overtones.

In Wilhelmine Germany, religious traditions and consumer culture seemed to be two opposing forces, and traditional, religious values appeared to provide insulation from the contagious sway of commodity worship and greed allegedly embodied by the power of the market and the new forms of consumerism. In Erich Köhrer's *Warenhaus Berlin*, this opposition was embodied in the allegorical face-off between two adjacent structures: "Department Store Berlin"—a fictionalized KaDeWe—and the Kaiser Wilhelm Memorial Church, symbol of throne, altar, and traditional Prussian values. The stakes could not have been higher; this was a struggle between different movements, groups, and ideologies not only over economy and urban space, but also over Germans' imagination, desires, and fantasies.

In other cultures—the United States, for example—consumerism and religion overcame their initial antipathy and eventually reconciled; one scholar has shown, in fact, that American department stores and holidays worked in tandem, representing alternately the "spatial" and "temporal" embodiment of the culture of American consumption.[3] In Germany, this reconciliation took much longer. For decades after the consumer revolution, consumerism continued to represent the negation of religious devotion, a threat to established Christian values. The consuming temple, that is, the Jewish temple of commerce, was the site of a false god, a department store Moloch, and remained antithetical to the welfare of the German polity.

Only in the postwar years, as West Germany rose from the rubble to experience an unprecedented period of peace and economic growth, did the opposition to consumer culture weaken and eventually fade away, save for a few academic departments and tenacious outposts of radicalism. And even these once-strident youths gradually turned the page on their anti-consumerism and came to embrace the blessings of commodity culture.[4] Germans as a whole became consummate consumers, developing, as one scholar puts it, "a new liberation theology of individual happiness and consumer comfort."[5] In today's Berlin, a glitzy and elegant, if rather unimaginative, shopping arcade called the Mall of Berlin has arisen at the site of Wertheim's Leipziger Strasse emporium, beckoning tourists and investors by marketing nostalgia for the glamour of a lost Berlin in the idiom of globalized American consumer culture. The KaDeWe is still open for business, having been rebuilt, restored, and recently expanded. After the war, it quickly climbed its way back to the top of the list of Berlin tourist attractions. The Kaiser Wilhelm Memorial Church, on the other hand, stands as a perpetual ruin, once a symbolic bulwark against the encroachment of modern commercial culture, today a monument to the murderous barbarism of the Nazi past.

NOTES

Introduction

1 Thomas Theodor Heine, "Der Teufel im Warenhaus," in *Die Märchen* (Berlin, 1978), 7.

2 Ibid., 9. All translations from German are by the author unless stated otherwise.

3 Max Weber, "Science as a Vocation," in *From Max Weber: Essays in Sociology*, ed. H. H. Gerth and C. Wright Mills (Oxford, 1958), 139. For similar perspectives on the impact of capitalist modernity on culture, society, and psyche see Georg Simmel, "The Metropolis and Mental Life," in *Simmel on Culture: Selected Writings*, ed. David Frisby and Mike Featherstone (London, 1998), esp. 176; Werner Sombart, "Das Warenhaus. Ein Gebilde des hochkapitalischer Zeitalters," in *Probleme des Warenhauses: Beiträge zur Geschichte und Erkenntnis der Entwicklung des Warenhauses in Deutschland* (Berlin, 1928), 77–87.

4 Susan Buck-Morss, *The Dialectics of Seeing: Walter Benjamin and the Arcades Project* (Cambridge, MA, 1989), 254.

5 Sigfrid Siwertz, *Das große Warenhaus*, trans. from Swedish by Alfons Fedor Cohn (Berlin, 1928), 11.

6 Lothar Eisen, "Psychologie des Warenhauses," *Geschlecht und Gesellschaft* 8 (1913): 391.

7 Emil Kläger, *Zwischenfall im Warenhaus. Komödie in drei Akten* (Vienna, 1933).

8 Alfred Döblin, *Berlin Alexanderplatz* (Munich, 1965), 56.

9 See, for example, "Der Warenhausmoloch in München," *Volkischer Beobachter* 40 (April 6, 1927); Karl Gerstenberg, "Memorien von Karl Gerstenberg: geb. 1891 Berlin, gest. 1965 New York," unpublished manuscript in possession of Bess Rothenberg, New York City.

10 On Jews and the fashion industry see Roberta S. Kremer, ed., *Broken Threads: The Destruction of the Jewish Fashion Industry in Germany and Austria* (Oxford, 2007), and Uwe Westphal, *Berliner Konfektion und Mode: Die Zerstörung einer Tradition* (Berlin, 1986).

11 Sombart, "Das Warenhaus"; Sombart, *Die Juden und das Wirtschaftsleben* (Leipzig, 1911).

12 See, for example, Plutus, "Tietz," *Die Zukunft* 35 (1901), 127.

13 Michael Brenner, *The Renaissance of Jewish Culture in Weimar Germany* (New Haven, CT, 1998), 92; Kerry Wallach, "Kosher Seductions," in *Das Berliner Warenhaus: Geschichte und Diskurse / The Berlin Department Store: History and Discourse*, ed. Godela Weiss-Sussex and Ulrike Zitzlsperger (Frankfurt, 2013), 125–26.

14 H. G. Reissner, "The Histories of 'Kaufhaus N. Israel' and of Wilfried Israel," *Leo Baeck Institute Year Book* 3 (1958): 227–56; Nils Busch-Petersen, *Oscar Tietz: Von Birnbaum / Provinz Posen zum Warenhauskönig von Berlin* (Berlin, 2004), 44–50; Werner E. Mosse, "Terms of Successful Integration: The Tietz Family, 1858–1923," *Leo Baeck Institute Year Book* 34 (1989): 131–61.

15 In her treatment of early Lubitsch films, Sabine Hake argues that the setting—usually a clothing or shoe store—reinforces the characters' Jewishness. See Sabine Hake, *Passions and Deceptions: The Early Films of Ernst Lubitsch* (Princeton, NJ, 1992), 30–33.

16 Werner Türk, *Konfektion* (Berlin, 1932), 66.

17 Siwertz, *Das große Warenhaus*, 37.

18 Quoted in Michael B. Miller, *The Bon Marché: Bourgeois Culture and the Department Store, 1869–1920* (Princeton, NJ, 1981), 177.

19 Émile Zola, *The Ladies' Paradise*, trans. Brian Nelson (Oxford, 1995), 427.

20 Karl Marx, *Capital: A Critique of Political Economy*, vol. 1, trans. Ben Fowkes (New York, 1976), 163–77.

21 See, for example, Peter Stürzebecher, *Das Berliner Warenhaus* (Berlin, 1979), 25.

22 For the critical reception of this often-repeated comment from the *Berliner Börsen-Courrier* see Paul Dehn, *Die Großbazare und Massenzweiggeschäfte* (Berlin, 1899), 34.

23 Walter Benjamin, *The Arcades Project*, trans. Howard Eiland and Kevin McLaughlin (Cambridge, MA, 1999), 61.

24 Jean Baudrillard, *Consumer Society: Myths and Structures* (London, 1998), 195–96.

25 See Rosalind Williams, *Dream Worlds: Mass Consumption in Late Nineteenth-Century France* (Berkeley, CA, 1982), 4–6.

26 Leo Deutsch, "Zur Frage der Kleptomanie," *Zeitschrift für die gesamte Neurologie und Psychiatrie* 152 (1935): 213. Deutsch thought a more apt comparison would be to Anky's drama *Day and Night*, in which a respected rabbi "falls prey to perversions" at night but acts perfectly normally during the day.

27 Hans Buchner, *Dämonen der Wirtschaft: Gestalten und dunkle Gewalten aus dem Leben unserer Tage* (Munich, 1928).

28 Erich Köhrer, *Warenhaus Berlin: Ein Roman aus der Weltstadt* (Berlin, 1909).

29 For overviews of consumer culture in twentieth-century Germany see Alon Confino and Rudy Koshar, "Régimes of Consumer Culture: New Narratives in Twentieth-Century German History," *German History* 19 (April 2001): 135–61, the special issue of *Le Mouvement Social*, edited by Gerhard Haupt, "Au bonheur des allemands. La consommation en Allemagne au xxe siècle," *Le Mouvement Social*, no. 206 (January–March 2004), and Paul Lerner, "An All-Consuming History? Recent Works on Consumer Culture in Twentieth-Century Germany," *Central European History* 42 (2009): 509–43.

30 Konrad H. Jarausch and Michael Geyer, *Shattered Past: Reconstructing German Histories* (Princeton, NJ, 2003), 273.

31 See, for example, Neil McKendrick, "The Consumer Revolution of Eighteenth-Century England," in *The Birth of a Consumer Society: The Commercialization of Eighteenth-Century England*, ed. McKendrick, J. Brewer, and J. H. Plumb (London, 1982), 9–11; James Axtell, "The First Consumer Revolution," in *Consumer Society in American History: A Reader*, ed. Lawrence B. Glickman (Ithaca, NY, 1999), 85–99.

32 Leora Auslander, *Taste and Power: Furnishing Modern France* (Berkeley, CA, 1996); Williams, *Dream Worlds*.

33 Quoted in Ellen Furlough, *Consumer Cooperation in France: The Politics of Consumption* (Ithaca, NY, 1991), 3. See also Ulrich Wyrwa, "Consumption and Consumer Society: Contribution to the History of Ideas," in *Getting and Spending: European and American Consumer Societies in the Twentieth Century*, ed. Susan Strasser, Charles McGovern, and Matthias Judt (Cambridge, 1998), 431–47; and Frank Trentmann, "Beyond Consumerism: New Historical Perspectives on Consumption," *Journal of Contemporary History* 39 (2005): 373–401.

34 Baudrillard, *Consumer Society*, 75.

35 Furlough, *Consumer Cooperation*, 3.

36 Jarausch and Geyer, *Shattered Past*, 271.

37 Miller, *Bon Marché*, 185.

38 Susan Porter Benson, *Counter Cultures: Saleswomen, Managers, and Customers in American Department Stores, 1890–1940* (Urbana, IL, 1986), 75.

39 Rudi Laermans, "Learning to Consume: Early Department Stores and the Shaping of Modern Consumer Culture (1860–1914)," *Theory, Culture, Society* 10 (1993): 94. See also Gudrun König, *Konsumkultur: Inszenierte Warenwelt um 1900* (Vienna, 2010).

40 On the comparative history of consumer culture and the department store see Jeffrey Crossick and Serge Jaumain, eds., *Cathedrals of Consumption: The European Department Store, 1850–1939* (Aldershot, UK, 1999). Important works on the modern history of consumerism include Peter N. Stearns, *Consumerism in World History: The Global Transformation*

of Desire (New York, 2006); Heinz-Gerhard Haupt, *Konsum und Handel: Europa im 19. und 20. Jahrhundert* (Göttingen, 2003); Martin Daunton and Matthew Hilton, eds., *The Politics of Consumption: Material Culture and Citizenship in Europe and America* (Oxford, 2001); Strasser, McGovern, and Judt, *Getting and Spending*; Frank Trentmann and John Brewer, *Consuming Cultures, Global Perspectives: Historical Trajectories, Transnational Exchanges* (Oxford, 2006); and Victoria de Grazia, ed., with Ellen Furlough, *The Sex of Things: Gender and Consumption in Historical Perspective* (Berkeley, CA, 1996).

41 See Uwe Spiekermann, *Basis der Konsumgesellschaft* (Munich, 1999).

42 Dirk Reinhardt, *Von der Reklame zum Marketing: Geschichte der Wirtschaftswerbung in Deutschland* (Berlin, 1993); Christiane Lamberty, *Reklame in Deutschland: Wahrnehmung, Professionalisierung und Kritik der Wirtschaftswerbung* (Berlin, 2000); Pamela Swett, S. Jonathan Wiesen, and Jonathan Zatlin, eds., *Selling Modernity: Advertising in Twentieth-Century Germany* (Durham, NC, 2007).

43 Erika Rappaport, *Shopping for Pleasure: Women in the Making of London's West End* (Princeton, NJ, 2000), esp. chap. 4.

44 On luxury, consumption, and class see above all Warren Breckman, "Disciplining Consumption: The Debate about Luxury in Wilhelmine Germany, 1890–1914," *Journal of Social History* 24 (Spring 1991): 485–505.

45 In addition to works cited above see Peter Fritzsche, *Reading Berlin 1900* (Cambridge, MA, 1998); Peter Jelavich, *Berlin Cabaret* (Cambridge, MA, 1996); Jelavich, *Berlin Alexanderplatz: Radio, Film, and the Death of Weimar Culture* (Berkeley, CA, 2006).

46 On consumer culture in the Nazi period see, among others, Shelley Baranowski, *Strength through Joy: Consumerism and Mass Tourism in the Third Reich* (New York, 2004); Wolfgang König, *Volkswagen, Volksempfänger, Volksgemeinschaft. "Volksprodukte" im Dritten Reich. Vom Scheitern einer nationalsozialistischen Konsumgesellschaft* (Paderborn, 2004); S. Jonathan Wiesen, *Creating the Nazi Marketplace: Commerce and Consumption in the Third Reich* (New York, 2011); Hartmut Berghoff, "Enticement and Deprivation: The Regulation of Consumption in Pre-War Nazi Germany," in Daunton and Hilton, *Politics of Consumption*, 165–84.

47 On wartime clothing and fashions see Irene Guenther, *Nazi Chic? Fashioning Women in the Third Reich* (Oxford, 2004), 265–77.

48 Detlef Briesen, *Warenhaus, Massenkonsum und Sozialmoral: Zur Geschichte der Konsumkritik im 20. Jahrhundert* (Frankfurt, 2001).

49 Erica Carter, *How German Is She? Postwar West German Reconstruction and the Consuming Woman* (Ann Arbor, MI, 1997). See also Michael Wildt, *Am Beginn der "Konsumgesellschaft": Mangelerfahrung, Lebenshaltung, Wohlstandshoffnung in Westdeutschland in den fünfziger Jahren* (Hamburg, 1994).

50 Mark Landsman, *Dictatorship and Demand: The Politics of Consumerism in East Germany* (Cambridge, MA, 2005); Judd Stitziel, *Fashioning Socialism: Clothing, Politics and Consumer Culture in East Germany* (Oxford, 2005).

51 David Crew, ed., *Consuming Germany in the Cold War* (Oxford, 2003), introduction.

52 Briesen, *Warenhaus*, 26.

53 On the history of department stores in Germany see Weiss-Sussex and Zitzlsperger, *Das Berliner Warenhaus*; Thomas Lenz, *Konsum und Modernisierung. Die Debatte um das Warenhaus als Diskurs um die Moderne* (Bielefeld, 2011); Jürgen Schwarz, *Architektur und Kommerz. Studien zur deutschen Kauf-und Warenhausarchitektur vor dem Ersten Weltkrieg am Beispiel der Frankfurter Zeil* (Frankfurt, 1995); König, *Konsumkultur*, esp. chap. 4; Helmut Frei, *Tempel der Kauflust: Eine Geschichte der Warenhauskulture* (Leipzig, 1997); and Siegfried Gerlach, *Das Warenhaus in Deutschland: Seine Entwicklung bis zum Ersten Weltkrieg in historisch-geographischer Sicht* (Stuttgart, 1988); Robert Gellately, "An der Schwelle der Moderne. Warenhäuser und Ihre Feinde in Deutschland," in *Im Banne der Metropole. Berlin und London in den zwanziger Jahren*, ed. Peter Alter, (Göttingen 1993), 131–56; and Hans-Peter Ullmann, "'Der Kaiser bei Wertheim'—Warenhäuser im wilhelminischen Deutschland," in *Europäische Sozialgeschichte. Festschrift*

für Wolfgang Schieder, ed. Christof Dipper, Lutz Klinkhammer, and Alexander Nützenadel (Berlin, 2000), 223–36. On Aryanization see, above all, Simone Ladwig-Winters, *Wertheim: Ein Warenhausunternehmer und seine Eigentümer: Ein Beispiel der Entwicklung der Berliner Warenhäuser bis zur "Arisierung"* (Münster, 1997); Hannah Ahlheim, *"Deutsche, Kauft Nicht Bei Juden!": Antisemitismus und Politischer Boykott in Deutschland 1924 bis 1935* (Göttingen, 2011); Christoph Kreutzmüller, *Ausverkauf: Die Vernichtung der jüdischen Gewerbetätigkeit in Berlin 1930–1945* (Berlin, 2012).

54 See Fritz Backhaus, Raphael Gross, and Liliane Weissberg, *Juden. Geld. Eine Vorstellung* (Frankfurt, 2013); Jonathan Karp, *The Politics of Jewish Commerce: Economic Thought and Emancipation in Europe, 1638–1848* (New York, 2008); Gideon Reuveni and Sarah Wobick-Segev, *The Economy in Jewish History: New Perspectives on the Relationship between Ethnicity and Economic Life* (New York, 2010); Rebecca Kobrin, ed., *Chosen Capital: The Jewish Encounter with American Capitalism* (New Brunswick, NJ, 2012); Derek J. Penslar, *Shylock's Children: Economics and Jewish Identity in Modern Europe* (Berkeley, CA, 2001); and Sarah A. Stein, *Plumes: Ostrich Feathers, Jews, and a Lost World of Global Commerce* (New Haven, CT, 2008). On Jews and consumer culture see Gideon Reuveni and Nils Roemer, eds., *Longing, Belonging, and the Making of Jewish Consumer Culture* (Leiden, 2010).

55 See, for example, the essays by Leora Auslander, Darcy Buerkle, Lisa Silverman, and Na'ama Rokem, in "Jewish Studies Meets Cultural Studies," *Journal of Modern Jewish History* 8 (2009): 41–120; Lisa Silverman, "Beyond Antisemitism: A Critical Approach to German-Jewish Cultural History," *Nexus: The Duke Journal of German Jewish Studies* 1 (2011): 27–45; Klaus Hödl, "The Elusiveness of Jewishness: Jews in Viennese Popular Culture around 1900," *Journal of Modern Jewish History* 12 (2013): 379–97; Paul Reiter, *The Anti-Journalist: Karl Krauss and Jewish Self-Fashioning in Fin-de-Siècle Europe* (Chicago, 2008).

56 Above all, Silverman, "Beyond Antisemitism."

57 Till van Rahden, "Jews and the Ambivalences of Civil Society in Germany, 1800 to 1933—Assessment and Reassessment," *Journal of Modern History* 77 (2005): 1024–47; Robert Gellately and Nathan Stolzfus, eds., *Social Outsiders in Nazi Germany* (Princeton, NJ, 2001); Neil Gregor, Mark Roseman, and Nils Roemer, eds., *German History from the Margins* (Bloomington, IN, 2006); Till van Rahden, *Juden und andere Breslauer: Die Beziehungen zwischen Juden, Protestanten und Katholiken in einer deutschen Großstadt von 1860 bis 1925* (Göttingen, 2000).

58 George L. Mosse, "The Image of the Jew in German Popular Culture: Felix Dahn and Gustav Freytag," *Leo Baeck Institute Year Book* 2 (1957): 218–27.

59 "Bericht für Herrn Schocken, 23.3.1932," Schocken Institute Jerusalem 185/228/1 Propaganda und Information.

60 For this analysis I have used the 1928 German translation, which like the subsequent American edition was slightly altered to make sense in a different national and cultural context.

61 For a thought-provoking discussion of Jews in the German imagination see Alon Confino, "Fantasies about the Jews: Cultural Reflections on the Holocaust," *History and Memory* 17 (2005): 296–322.

1. Jerusalem's Terrain

1 Leo Colze, *Berliner Warenhäuser* (1908; repr., Berlin, 1989), 8.

2 Käthe Lux, *Studien über die Entwicklung der Warenhäuser in Deutschland* (Jena, 1910), 1.

3 David Ciarlo has examined the simultaneous emergence and reciprocal influence of German mass (visual) culture and imperialism. See David Ciarlo, *Advertising Empire: Race and Visual Culture in Imperial Germany* (Cambridge, MA, 2011).

4 Colze, *Berliner Warenhäuser*, 11.

5 Lamberty, *Reklame in Deutschland*, 36; Lenz, *Konsum und Modernisierung*; Uwe Spiekermann, *Warenhaussteuer in Deutschland:Mittelstandsbewegung, Kapitalismus und Rechtsstaat im späten Kaiserreich* (Frankfurt, 1994), 13.

6 Lux, *Studien*, 1

7 Protocols of the Haus der Abgeordneten, 76. Sitzung am 16. Juni 1899 in GehStA PK I HA Rep. 93 B, Nr. 1435. Waren u. Geschäftshäuser, Bd. 1, 1899–1902.

8 Ibid.

9 Colze, *Berliner Warenhäuser*, 11.

10 Margarete Böhme, *W.A.G.M.U.S.* (Berlin, 1911), 49.

11 Esra Bennathan, "Die demographische und wirtschafliche Struktur der Juden," in *Entscheidungsjahr 1932. Zur Judenfrage in der Endphase der Weimarer Republik*, ed. Werner E. Mosse (Tübingen, 1965), 114.

12 I take this definition from J. Wernicke, "Der Kampf um das Warenhaus," in *Probleme des Warenhauses*, 14.

13 Marie Netter, "Das Moderne Warenhaus," in *Frankfurter Zeitung*, September 28, 1903, clipping in GehStA PK I HA Rep. 93 B, Nr. 1436.

14 Sombart, "Das Warenhaus," 83.

15 *Es Liegt in der Luft (Ein Spiel im Warenhaus)*, Revue in 24 Bildern, text by Marcellus Schiffer, music by Mischa Spoliansky, courtesy of Felix Bloch Erben, Bühnenvertrieb, 9–10.

16 Böhme, *W.A.G.M.U.S.*, 122.

17 Alfred Wiener, *Das Warenhaus: Kauf-, Geschäfts-, Büro-Haus* (Berlin, 1912), 22.

18 "Das Waarenhaus," *Berliner Börsen-Courier*, November 8, 1898, clipping in GehStA I HA Rep. 120 CV Nr. 68a, Bd. 1.

19 Wiener, *Das Warenhaus*, 22–23.

20 Arthur Wilke, "Die Psychologie des Warenhauses," *Der Deutsche* 5 (February 2, 1907): 550–54.

21 Ibid., 214.

22 On department stores as tourist attractions see Fritzsche, *Reading Berlin*, 163–65.

23 Williams, *Dream Worlds*, 67.

24 Wiener, *Das Warenhaus*, 22.

25 Gustav Stresemann, "Die Warenhäuser: Ihre Entstehung, Entwicklung, und volkswirtschaftliche Bedeutung," *Zeitschrift für die gesamte Staatswissenschaft* 56 (1900): 714.

26 Sombart, "Das Warenhaus," 79.

27 Williams, *Dream Worlds*, 67.

28 Wolfgang Schivelbusch, *The Railway Journey: The Industrialization of Time and Space* (Berkeley, CA, 1986), 190.

29 See Elaine S. Abelson, *When Ladies Go A-Thieving: Middle-Class Shoplifters in the Victrian Department Store* (New York, 1989), chap. 3.

30 Philip G. Nord, *The Politics of Resentment: Shopkeeper Protest in Nineteenth-Century Paris* (New Brunswick, NJ, 2005), 73. Salman Schocken once remarked that department store goods were gazed upon by thousands of customers each day. Salman Schocken, *Die Entwicklung der Warenhäuser in Deutschland und die kaufmännischen Voraussetzungen der Warenhausbauten* (Leipzig, 1911), 22.

31 Sombart, "Das Warenhaus," 78.

32 Köhrer, *Warenhaus Berlin*, 30–31.

33 Böhme, *W.A.G.M.U.S.*, 27.

34 R. Hartmann, "Großer Umsatz, Kleiner Nutzen," in *Hermann Tietz, der grösste Warenhaus-Konzern Europas im Eigenbesitz. Ein Buch sichtbarer Erfolge* (Berlin, 1932), 57.

35 See Gerlach, *Das Warenhaus in Deutschland*, 41.

36 Sombart, "Das Warenhaus," 78.

37 Lamberty, *Reklame in Deutschland*, 132.

38 The Paris store Au Coin de la Rue was built five years before the Bon Marché, but it only lasted to 1880. A three-story structure, it pioneered the typical department store

architectural form (central atrium with departments built around it), but it lacked the splendor of the Bon Marché. See Rudi Laermans, "Learning to Consume," 84.

39 See above all Miller, *Bon Marché*.

40 Geoffrey Crossick and Serge Jaumain, "The World of the Department Store: Distribution, Culture, and Social Change," in Crossick and Jaumain, *Cathedrals of Consumption*, 16.

41 For example, the Bazar de l'Hôtel de Ville was founded in 1854, Le Louvre in 1855, Au Printemps a decade later, La Samaritaine in 1869, and Les Galeries Lafayette in 1895.

42 Nord, *Politics of Resentment*, 80–81.

43 Miller, *Bon Marché*, 25–27.

44 Heidrun Homburg, "Warenhausunternehmen und ihre Gründer in Frankreich und Deutschland," *Jahrbuch für Wirtschaftsgeschichte* (1992): 184; Miller, *Bon Marché*, 25.

45 Miller, *Bon Marché*, 192–206.

46 Miller, *Bon Marché*; Lisa Tiersten, *Marianne in the Market: Envisioning Consumer Society in Fin-de-Siècle France* (Berkeley, CA, 2001).

47 Nord, *Politics of Resentment*, 7.

48 Yet, as Nord concedes, department store development was tied to the broader transformation that undermined neighborhood allegiances—which older stores depended on—and led to the formation of dedicated commercial areas within Paris and other cities. *Politics of Resentment*, 82–99.

49 Gellately, "An der Schwelle der Moderne," 137–38; Nord, *Politics of Resentment*, 83–84.

50 Nord, *Politics of Resentment*, 84.

51 Benson, *Counter Cultures*, 12.

52 William Leach, *Land of Desire: Merchants, Power, and the Rise of a New American Culture* (New York, 1992), 22.

53 Ibid., 23.

54 Ibid., 27.

55 Gellately, "An der Schwelle der Moderne," 138–39.

56 See Rappaport, *Shopping for Pleasure*, esp. chap. 5.

57 Quoted in Crossick and Jaumain, "World of the Department Store," 29–30.

58 On developments in Austria see above all Andreas Lehne, *Wiener Warenhäuser, 1865–1914* (Vienna, 1990).

59 See, for example, Shulamit Volkov, "The Dynamics of Dissimilation: *Ostjuden* and German Jews," in *The Jewish Response to German Culture: From the Enlightenment to the Second World War*, ed. Jehuda Reinharz and Walter Schatzberg (Hanover, NH, 1985), 204; Jack Wertheimer, *Unwelcome Strangers: East European Jews in Imperial Germany* (Oxford, 1987).

60 On Jewish department store entrepreneurs in the United States see Leon Harris, *Merchant Princes: An Intimate History of Jewish Families Who Built Great Department Stores* (New York, 1979). See also Avi Y. Decter, "Memory and Meaning in Baltimore's Jewish-Owned Department Stores," in *Enterprising Entrepreneurs: The Jewish Department Stores of Downtown Baltimore* (Baltimore, 2001), 3–11.

61 Werner E. Mosse, *Jews in the German Economy: The German-Jewish Economic Élite, 1820–1935* (New York, 1987), 25.

62 Kremer, *Broken Threads*; Mila Gineva, *Women in Weimar Fashion: Discourses and Displays in German Culture, 1918–1933* (Rochester, NY, 2008); Westphal, *Berliner Konfektion und Mode*; Guenther, *Nazi Chic?*

63 Günther Rohdenburg, *"Das War Das Neue Leben": Leben und Wirkung des Jüdischen Kaufhausbesitzers Julius Bamberger und seiner Familie* (Bremen, 2000), 12.

64 Frei, *Tempel der Kauflust*, 75.

65 Ibid., 69.

66 Schocken, *Die Entwicklung der Warenhäuser*, 18.

67 "Drei Tage in Berlin," Reisebrief von H. Blankenburg in N. Israel Album "Deutschland zur See" (1903), Landesarchiv Berlin.

68 See Erica Fischer and Simone Ladwig-Winters, *Die Wertheims. Geschichte einer Familie* (Berlin, 2011), 48–49.

69 See, for example, Stresemann, "Die Warenhäuser," 707.

70 Busch-Petersen, *Oscar Tietz*, 14.

71 See Harry Jandorf, "Erinnerungen an meinen Vater Adolf Jandorf," LBI NY ME 335.

72 Rudolf Karstadt Incorporated, *The Largest Chain Store Enterprise in Germany* (New York; privately printed for Dillon, Read & Co., 1928), 15.

73 Frei, *Tempel der Kauflust*, 75.

74 See Gerlach, *Das Warenhaus in Deutschland*; John F. Mueller, "'Eine Zierde jeder Stadt': Placing Provincial Department Stores in German Historiography and on the High Street," in Weiss-Sussex and Zitzlsperger, *Das Berliner Warenhaus*, 241–55.

75 Paul Göhre, *Das Warenhaus* (Frankfurt, 1907), 90.

76 Johannes Wernicke, *Das Waren-und Kaufhaus* (Leipzig, 1913), 28, cited in Tim Coles, "Department Stores as Retail Innovations in Germany," in Crossick and Jaumain, *Cathedrals of Consumption*, 73.

77 Lux, *Studien*, 8.

78 Ibid., 9.

79 Otto Erich von Wussow, *Geschichte und Entwicklung der Warenhäuser* (Berlin, 1906), 32.

80 Netter, "Das Moderne Warenhaus."

81 Ibid.

82 Mosse, *Jews in the German Economy*, 189.

83 Julius Hirsch, *Das Warenhaus in Westdeutschland. Organization und Wirkung* (Leipzig, 1910), 79–80.

84 Spiekermann, *Warenhaussteuer*, 8–9; Briesen, *Warenhaus*, 78–79. See also Shulamit Volkov, *The Rise of Popular Anti-modernism in Germany: The Master Artisans, 1873–1896* (Princeton, NJ, 1978).

85 Briesen, *Warenhaus*, 78.

86 Spiekermann, *Warenhaussteuer*, 24–25.

87 Wilhelm Liebknecht, "Zukunftstaatliches," in *Cosmopolis: Revue Internationale* 9 (January 1898): 227.

88 Ibid., 227. Emphasis in text.

89 On communist critiques of department store exploitation see, for example, "'Weise Woche' bei Wertheim," *Rote Fahne*, February 6, 1927.

90 See Robert Gellately, *The Politics of Economic Despair* (London, 1974), 50–57; Hans-Gerhard Haupt, ed., *Die radikale Mitte: Lebensweise und Politik von Handwerkern und Kleinhändlern in Deutschland seit 1848* (Munich, 1985), esp. 235–91.

91 Spiekermann, *Warenhaussteur*, 32–33.

92 Kurt Stefan Baer, *Der Kampf gegen Großbetriebe des Einzelhandels und die Volkswirtschaft* (Jena, 1932), 7.

93 Wernicke, "Der Kampf," 13.

94 See Lamberty, *Reklame in Deutschland*, 158–61.

95 Ibid., 477–90.

96 Wernicke, "Der Kampf," 16.

97 See Spiekermann, *Warenhaussteuer*, 112; F. W. R. Zimmermann, "Warenhaus und Warenhaussteuer," *Zeitschrift für die Gesamte Staatswissenschaft* 68 (1912): 701–6; Rudolf Lenz, *Karstadt: Ein Deutscher Warenhauskonzern* (Stuttgart, 1995), 22–23.

98 Spiekermann, *Warenhaussteuer*, 144.

99 Heinrich Uhlig, *Die Warenhäuser im Dritten Reich* (Köln, 1956), 52.

100 Wussow, *Geschichte und Entwicklung*, 44.

101 On images of Jews as economic actors see Penslar, *Shylock's Children*; Karp, *Politics of Jewish Commerce*; Nicolas Berg, ed., *Kapitalismusdebatten um 1900: Über antisemitisierende Semantiken des Jüdischen* (Leipzig, 2011); Mosse, "Image of the Jew."

102 Quoted in Spiekermann, *Warenhaussteuer*, 161.

103 Apparently several Berlin department store owners brought lawsuits for defamation against newspapers that used these terms. See Dehn, *Die Großbasare*, esp. 18.

104 Ibid., 57.

105 "Aus der Praxis der Ramschbazare und Warenhäuser," *Hammer* 9 (1910), 129.

106 See Wussow, *Geschichte und Entwicklung*, 43.

107 "Ramschbasare," *Staatsbürger-Zeitung* 34 (November 15, 1898), 1.

108 "Der unlauterer Wettbewerb der Ramschbasare," *Staatsbürger-Zeitung* 35 (February 8, 1899), 1.

109 Clipping, "Aus der Kaufmännischen Reform," 23.3.1894 in GehStA PK I HA, Rep. 120 CIX 1 Nr. 53, vol. 1, "betr. den unlauteren Wettbewerb im Handel und Verkehr." The same point can be found in Hausschildt, *Der Kampf gegen die Waarenhäuser. Praktische Vorschläge zur Beseitigung derselben* (Friedeberg z. Queis. 1898), in GehStA PK Rep 120 C VIII 1 Nr. 134, vol. 1, 5–6.

110 Hausschildt, *Der Kampf gegen die Waarenhäuser*, 5–6.

111 H.M., "Das Warenhaus, eine Gefahr? Was jeder Deutsche über das Warenhaus und seine Auswirkungen wissen muß," *Totgeschwiegene Wahrheiten* 5 (June 20, 1930), 3–4.

112 F. Roderich-Stoltheim, "Die Tricks der Warenhäuser," *Hammer: Blätter für deutschen Sinn* 12 JG (May 1, 1913), 225–30.

113 See the clippings in GehStA PK I HA, Rep. 120 CIX 1 Nr. 53, vol. 1, "betr. den unlauteren Wettbewerb im Handel und Verkehr."

114 On the Wertheim family see Fischer and Ladwig-Winters, *Die Wertheims*.

115 "Intimes aus dem Kaufhaus Franz Sonntag," *Die Wahrheit* 3 (November 16, 1907), 2.

116 Hauschildt, *Der Kampf gegen die Waarenhäuser*, 6, 10.

117 Anonymous, "Die Moral im Warenhause," *Hammer* 11 (May 15, 1912), 295.

118 Dehn, *Die Großbazare*, 20–21; "Intimes von Wertheim," *Die Wahrheit: Freies Deutsches Volksblatt* 3 (August 31, 1907), 3.

119 For one example see the report in *Mitteilungen aus dem Verband zur Abwehr des Antisemitismus* 8 (October 1, 1898), 318.

120 For example, F. Roderich-Stoltheim, "Warenhäuser und öffentliche Sittlichkeit," *Hammer: Blätter für deutschen Sinn* 12 (May 15, 1915), 264.

121 Ibid., 263.

122 "Liebes-Fallstricke im Warenhaus Wertheim," *Die Wahrheit* 4 (February 29, 1908), 1–2.

123 See, for example, G. Gerber, *Warenhauspest* (Plauen, 1932); Hauschildt, *Der Kampf gegen die Waarenhäuser*; Anonymous, "Der Warenhaus-Unfug," *Hammer* 11 (January 15, 1912), 43–45; and Anonymous, "Wertheim Triumphator!" *Staatsbürger-Zeitung* (27.11.1906), clipping in LAB A Pr. Br. Rep. 30, Tit 94, Nr. 14311 (Wertheim); Anonymous, "Der Warenhausmoloch in München," *Volkischer Beobachter*, April 6, 1927.

124 Spiekermann, *Warenhaussteuer*, 85–87.

125 Anonymous, "Die Moral im Warenhause," 295.

126 Stoltheim, "Warenhäuser und öffentliche Sittlichkeit," 267.

127 "Behördliche Reklame für Warenhäuser," in *Staatsbürger-Zeitung* 39 (November 24, 1903), clipping in GehStA Rep. 93 B, 1436.

128 Böhme, *W.A.G.M.U.S.*, 36.

129 See David Biale, *Blood and Belief: The Circulation of a Symbol between Jews and Christians* (Berkeley, CA, 2007), 144.

130 *Die Wahrheit* 4 (March 21, 1908), clipping in LAB A Pr. Br. Rep. 30, Tit 94, Nr. 14311.

131 Ibid. See also Gerber, *Warenhauspest*.

132 Dehn, *Die Großbasare*, 37.

133 Anonymous, "Warenhäuser und Umsatzsteuer," *Hammer* 11 (December 1, 1912), 621.

134 Clipping from *Staatsbürger-Zeitung*, 15.12.12 in LAB A Pr. Br. Rep. 30, Tit 94, Nr. 14311 (Wertheim).

135 Dehn, *Die Großbasare*, 64.

136 See Hauschildt, *Der Kampf gegen die Waarenhäuser*, 3.

137 H.M., "Das Warenhaus, eine Gefahr," 4.

138 Interestingly, the anti-Semitic, anti–department store newspaper *Die Wahrheit* featured numerous ads for the KaDeWe around its opening in 1907.

139 H.M., "Das Warenhaus, eine Gefahr," 10.
140 Beno, "Sie machen in Weihnachten," *Illustrierter Beobachter* 4 (December 7, 1929), 655.
141 Wernicke, "Der Kampf," 17.
142 Quoted in Joe Perry, *Christmas in Germany: A Cultural History* (Chapel Hill, NC, 2010), 170.
143 Ibid., 170.
144 Paul Dehn, *Hinter den Kulissen des modernen Geschäfts* (Berlin, 1897), 80.
145 See, for example, Felix Goldmann, "Das Warenhaus. Was Wird aus dem jüdischen Mittelstand?" *CV Zeitung* 1929, Heft 1 (April 1, 1929).
146 Walter E. Schulz, "Warenhäuser," in *Hermann Tietz, der grösste Warenhaus-Konzern Europas im Eigenbesitz*, 5–6.

2. Dreamworlds in Motion

1 On Jews and cosmopolitanism see M. S. Miller and Scott Ury, "Cosmopolitanism: The End of Jewishness?," *European Review of History—Revue européene d'histoire* 17 (June 2010): 337–59, and Natan Sznaider, *Jewish Memory and the Cosmopolitan Order* (London, 2011).
2 See Sebastian Conrad, *Globalisation and the Nation in Imperial Germany*, trans. Sorcha O'Hagan (Cambridge, 2010).
3 Mary Douglas and Baron Isherwood, *The World of Goods: Towards an Anthropology of Consumption* (1979; repr., London, 1996); Williams, *Dream Worlds*. See also Crossick and Jaumain, "World of the Department Store," 1–45. See also Arjun Appadurai, ed., *The Social Life of Things: Commodities in Cultural Perspective* (Cambridge, 1988).
4 Jean Baudrillard, "For a Critique of the Political Economy of the Sign," in *Jean Baudrillard, Selected Writings*, ed. Mark Poster (Stanford, CA, 2002), 60–100.
5 Marx, *Capital*, 1:163–77.
6 "Welt der schönen Dinge." I take this quote from the Kaufhof store in Leipzig, which like most Kaufhof stores designates each floor and each category of product as a kind of world: e.g., "Kinderwelt," "Herrenwelt."
7 Karl Marx, *Grundrisse: Foundations of the Critique of Political Economy*, trans. Martin Nicolaus (London, 1973), 533–34.
8 See the analysis in Schivelbusch, *Railway Journey*, 41. The sociologist Georg Simmel, a keen observer of this phenomenon, noted that the increasing distance between producer and purchaser under modern capitalism led to a "rationally calculated economic egoism" and a "relentless matter of factness" on the part of urban consumers. Simmel, "Metropolis and Mental Life," 176.
9 On department stores as exhibition spaces see Alarich Rooch, *Zwischen Museum und Warenhaus: Ästhetisierungsprozesse und sozial-kommunikative Raumaneignungen des Bürgertums (1823–1920)* (Oberhausen, 2001).
10 Max Osborn, "Moderne Verkaufsräume," in *Hermann Tietz, der grösste Warenhaus-Konzern*, 86–87.
11 Doris Wittner, "Seine Gründer und die Junge Generation," in *Hermann Tietz, der grösste Warenhaus-Konzern*, 16.
12 Lion Feuchtwanger, "Warenhaus-Revue," unpublished ms., no date, Archive of the Feuchtwanger Memorial Library, USC, "Plays, Poetry and Short Stories," box D2, 2–3. The manuscript presumably dates from around 1931 when Feuchtwanger moved to Berlin.
13 Vicki Baum, *Der große Ausverkauf* (1937; repr., Cologne, 1983), 18.
14 Lamberty, *Reklame in Deutschland*, 50.
15 Feuchtwanger, "Warenhaus-Revue," 2.
16 Williams, *Dream Worlds*, 69–70.
17 Leo Colze ends his 1908 book on the KaDeWe with an extensive list of the wares available at that store, from *Alfenidewaren* (Goods made from Alfenide, an alloy of nickel and silver) to *Zimmereinrichtungen* (room furnishings). See Colze, *Berliner Warenhäuser*, 79–81.

18 Thorwald Andersen et al., *Die Frau und ihre Welt* (Berlin, 1910); Gustav Meinecke, *"Die Deutschen Kolonien." Ein Beitrag zur Geschichte und Völkerkunde der Deutschen überseeischen Besitzungen. Nach amtlichen Quellen bearbeitet. Nebst einem Anhang Ereignisse des Jahres 1900 in China* (Berlin, 1901); Siegfried Hartmann, Rudolf Kreuschner, and Karl Bröckelmann, *Unter und über der Erde* (Berlin, 1908); and Eugen Zabel: *Eine Weltreise. Kriegsschauplatz—Weltausstellung* (Berlin, 1905). A complete set of these albums can be found in the Landesarchiv Berlin.

19 Ciarlo, *Advertising Empire*, 28–30.

20 Feuchtwanger, "Warenhaus-Revue," 4. "Es war nicht einfach, Kaufer, es derart zu fügen, daß die Dinge so handlich zu deiner Verfügung liegen. Bei Hitze und Frost mußten sie viele abplagen, dir deine Waren zusammenzutragen. . . . Im kanadischen Forst schweigsame Männer Bäume fällen, Flößen sie zu Tal über stilles Wasser und Stromschnellen. In einem anderen Erdteil machen sie Maschinen, beim Zersägen der Bäume zu dienen . . . Gelbe, schwarze, weiße Hände wirken vereint, daß, Käufer, Tisch und Stuhl dir passend scheint."

21 Berliners joked that "Wertheim bears the weight of the world." See Fischer and Ladwig-Winters, *Die Wertheims*, 103. On Israel see "Das Theater," in N. Israel Album (1906), Landesarchiv Berlin.

22 Wertheim's Leipziger Strasse store was considered a "Weltstadtwarenhaus für die Welt" in contrast to the Tietz store at Alexanderplatz, which was thought of as a "Volkswarenhaus" [a (common) people's department store] for Berliners. See Gernot Jochheim, *Der Berliner Alexanderplatz* (Berlin, 2006), 107. The origin of this quote is unclear. On the Wertheim lawsuit see Ladwig-Winters, *Wertheim*, 31.

23 See *Hermann Tietz, der grösste Warenhaus-Konzern*, 27, 44, 49.

24 Pictures of these stores can be found in Helga Behn, "Die Architektur des Deutschen Warenhausees von Ihren Anfängen bis 1933" (PhD dissertation, University of Cologne, 1984).

25 Ciarlo, *Advertising Empire*.

26 Meinecke, *Die Deutschen Kolonien*.

27 This is not to say that Israel and other German department stores did not carry goods bearing racial iconography on their labels, only that they did not regularly integrate such imagery into their store advertisements and representations.

28 http://germanhistorydocs.ghi-dc.org/sub_image.cfm?image_id=2179&language=german.

29 Petia Sierschynski argues that the Wertheim store on Leipziger Strasse was architecturally and stylistically bound up with the aesthetic dimensions of German colonialism, which turned on the opposition between culture (*Kultur*) and civilization (*Civilization*) and that Wertheim's status as an exemplar of "culture" stood in implicit opposition to the colonial world. An interesting, if a bit forced, approach to reading department stores in the context of empire. See Petia Sierschynski, "The *Warenhaus* in the Competition of the Nations: Alfred Messel's Wertheim and Wilhelmine Imperial Ambitions (1898–1905), in *The Berlin Department Store*, 199–222.

30 Feuchtwanger, "Warenhaus-Revue," 3.

31 Quoted in Anthony David, *The Patron: A Life of Salman Schocken, 1877–1959* (New York, 2003), 44–45.

32 Siwertz, *Das große Warenhaus*. As Goldmann's associate says to him: "Isn't the department store your love and your life? And now you're having a child with it! Yes, Goldmann, you're having a child with your department store. That is fantastic! Fantastic!" (p. 102).

33 On the female flâneur or flâneuse and spectatorship in the department store see Anne Friedberg, *Window Shopping: Cinema and the Postmodern* (Berkeley, CA, 1993), and Katharina von Ankum, *Women in the Metropolis: Gender and Modernity in Weimar Culture* (Berkeley, CA, 1997).

34 Gerhard Tietz, "Der Verkäufer und die Verkäuferin im Warenhaus (Unter besonderer Berücksichtigung der Verhältnisse im Leonhard Tietz-Konzern)," 25 Jahre Verband deutscher Waren-u. Kaufhäuser in *Zeitschrift für Waren-und Kaufhäuser* (Berlin, May 9, 1928), 15.

35 Köhrer, *Warenhaus Berlin*, 23.
36 See "Berlin und das Welthaus N. Israel," in *Unser Kaiserhaus* (Berlin, 1902).
37 *Chauffeur ins Metropol! Die neue Revue*, 3. Genehmigt für das Metropol-Theater am 19.9.1912. LAB A Pr. Br. Rep. 030–05–05–02, 5439.
38 Lothar Eisen (pseud. for Josef Bernhard Schneider), "Psychologie des Warenhauses," *Geschlecht und Gesellschaft* 8 (1913): 391.
39 Köhrer, *Warenhaus Berlin*, 85.
40 Göhre, *Das Warenhaus*, 136.
41 Stresemann, "Die Warenhäuser," 714.
42 Colze, *Berliner Warenhäuser*, 9–10.
43 Georg Tietz, *Hermann Tietz. Geschichte einer Familie* (Stuttgart, 1965), 30–31.
44 Siwertz, *Das große Warenhaus*, 7.
45 Göhre, *Das Warenhaus*, 21.
46 Zola, *Ladies' Paradise*, 28, 49, 56, etc.
47 Theodor Herzl, *Old New Land*, trans. Lotta Levensohn (Princeton, NJ, 1997), 98.
48 The best treatment of the railway's impact on European life remains Schivelbusch, *Raiway Journey*. See esp. chap. 13, "Circulation," for a discussion of mobility, travel, and consumer culture.
49 Todd Presner, *Mobile Modernity: Germans, Jews, Trains* (New York, 2007), 2–3.
50 Schivelbusch, *Railway Journey*, 190.
51 Schocken, *Die Entwicklung der Warenhäuser*, 19.
52 Rudy Koshar, "Seeing, Traveling, and Consuming: An Introduction," in *Histories of Leisure*, ed. Koshar (Oxford, 2002), 1–24, and Shelley Baranowski and Ellen Furlough, *Being Elsewhere: Tourism, Consumer Culture, and Identity in Modern Europe and North America* (Ann Arbor, MI, 2001).
53 Schivelbusch, *Railway Journey*, 197.
54 Ladwig-Winters, *Wertheim*, 66.
55 Colze, *Berliner Warenhäuser*, 20–21.
56 Köhrer, *Warenhaus Berlin*, 21.
57 Israel Family Collection, Leo Baeck Institute AR 187. This store, it should be noted, was unrelated to the department store chain "Warenhaus Centrum" of East Germany.
58 Baum, *Der große Ausverkauf*. Vicki Baum, *Central Store*, trans. Paul Selver (London, 1940).
59 Israel Family Collection, Leo Baeck Institute AR 25140, Series III, Kaufhaus N. Israel.
60 David, *Patron*, esp. 45, 145. See also Untitled Document, dated April 19, 1944, Archive of the Leo Baeck Institute AR 6379, George Manasse Collection, doc. 11 (draft by George Manasse recalling business practices of Schocken concern.) And doc. 13, speech by Manasse to employees on the opening of new department store in Pforzheim, September 24, 1931, p. 2. On centralized display window design see Janet Ward, *Weimar Surfaces: Urban Visual Culture in 1920s Germany* (Berkeley, CA, 2001), 216.
61 George Manasse Collection, Leo Baeck Institute, doc. 15, address to new workers (April 19, 1933), p. 2.
62 Michael Bienert, "Neuyork in Neukölln: Hybris und Untergang des Karstadt-Warenhauses am Berliner Hermannplatz," in Weiss-Sussex and Zitzlsperger, *Das Berliner Warenhaus*, 224–25.
63 "Direkt im besonderem Tunnel vom Bahnsteig ins Warenhaus," undated, unreferenced newspaper clipping in Schocken Institute Archive (concern), box 115/111: Zeitungsausschnitte zum Thema "Kampf gegen die Warenhäuser" 7.3.33–2.2.35.
64 For example, "Stützen Sie sich voll Vertrauen auf uns bei Ihren Einkäufen. . . . Das deutsche Großkaufhaus Karstadt, U-Bahnhof Hermannplatz—der Karstadt Bahnhof," Deutsches Technikmuseum, Berlin, Historisches Archiv, Sig III.2, 15751.
65 Ladwig-Winters, *Wertheim*, 49.
66 Stürzebecher, *Das Berliner Warenhaus*, 41. See also Bienert, "Neuyork in Neukölln," 225.
67 "Über den Dächern von Berlin . . . ," Deutsches Technikmuseum, Historisches Archiv, Sig III.2, 02399.

68 "Das Warenhaus Wertheim, der Polizeipräsident und der unterirdische Sauglauch," *Die Wahrheit* 2 (November 24, 1906), 2–3; "Die Glücksschwemme des Warenhauses Wertheim," *Die Wahrheit* 3 (November 2, 1907), 1–2; "Wertheim und die Untergrundbahn," *Staatsbürger-Zeitung* (May 5, 1903), 1. Wertheim's attempts to create direct access from the *U-Bahn* into their store were unsuccessful at Leipziger Platz, and then again at their Moritzplatz store. The 1929 Karstadt store was the first to have an entrance from the *U-Bahn* directly into the store.

69 See, for example, "Die Geheimnisse des Teesalons im Warenhaus Wertheim," *Die Wahrheit* 3 (January 19, 1907).

70 Stürzebecher, *Das Berliner Warenhaus*, 32.

71 I have not been able to determine whether the display window pictured here coincided with the tracks exhibition.

72 Antonia Meiners, *100 Jahre KaDeWe* (Berlin, 2007), 35.

73 Göhre, *Das Warenhaus*, 36.

74 Ibid., 116–17.

75 Renate Palmer, *Der Stuttgarter Schocken-Bau von Erich Mendelsohn. Die Geschichte eines Kaufhauses und seiner Architektur* (Tübingen, 1995), 47–48.

76 "Luftfahrt-Werbewoche," Deutsches Technikmuseum, Historisches Archiv, Sig VI.1.040, Nr. 1895. On the aviation craze in Weimar Germany see Peter Fritzsche, *A Nation of Fliers: German Aviation and the Popular Imagination* (Cambridge, MA, 1992).

77 Max Osborn, ed., *Das Kaufhaus des Westens, 1907–1932. Festschrift anläßlich des 25-jährigen Bestehens* (Berlin, 1932), 118.

78 Ladwig-Winters, *Wertheim*, 66.

79 See "Imperial Panorama," in Walter Benjamin, *Berlin Childhood around 1900*, trans. Howard Eiland (Cambridge, MA, 2006). See also Friedberg, *Window Shopping*, and Vanessa Schwartz, *Spectacular Realities: Early Mass Culture in Fin-de-Siècle Paris* (Berkeley, CA, 1998).

80 Quoted in Helmut Lethen, *Cool Conduct: The Culture of Distance in Weimar Germany*, trans. Don Reneau (Berkeley, CA, 2001), 26.

81 Schivelbusch, *Railway Journey*, 195.

82 Lethen, *Cool Conduct*, chap. 2.

83 Simmel, "Metropolis and Mental Life," and Simmel, *The Philosophy of Money*, trans, David Frisby (New York, 2011).

84 Stürzebecher, *Berliner Warenhaus*, 39.

85 See Sabine Hake, *Topographies of Class: Modern Architecture and Mass Society in Weimar Berlin* (Ann Arbor, MI, 2008), 32.

86 Gerhard Tietz, "Der Verkäufer und die Verkäuferin," 15.

87 See Anthony McElligott, *The German Urban Experience, 1900–1945: Modernity and Crisis* (London, 2001), 132.

88 Colze, *Berliner Warenhäuser*, 11–12.

89 Köhrer, *Warenhaus Berlin*, 107.

90 Feuchtwanger, "Warenhaus-Revue," 1, 2.

91 Walter E. Schulz, "Warenhäuser," in *Hermann Tietz, der grösste Warenhaus-Konzern*, 6.

92 Siegfried Kracauer, "Der Dichter im Warenhaus," in *Siegfried Kracauer Aufsätze, 1927–1931*, ed. Inka Mülder-Bach (Frankfurt, 1990), 229.

93 Oscar Schweriner, *Arbeit: Ein Warenhausroman* (Berlin, 1912), 7.

94 Quoted in Ladwig-Winters, *Wertheim*, 41. On the idea of the irrational consuming crowd see Lamberty, *Reklame in Deutschland*, 80.

95 Uwe Spiekermann, "Thieves and Theft in German Department Stores, 1895–1930: A Discourse on Morality, Crime and Gender," in Crossick and Jaumain, *Cathedrals of Consumption*, 141; Briesen, *Warenhaus*, 26.

96 Böhme, *W.A.G.M.U.S.*, 80.

97 Perry, *Christmas in Germany*, 166.

98 From *Die Welt am Sonntag*, December 9, 1901, clipping in LAB A. Pr. Br. Repositorium 30 (Polizeipräsidium), Titel 133, Nr. 18627.

99 For police interventions in shop window design see LAB A. Pr. Br. Rep. 30 (Polizeipräsidium), Titel 133, Nr. 18627.

100 Ward, *Weimar Surfaces*, 221.

101 Kurt Pinthus, "Warenhaus-Propaganda. Ein Dialog von Dr. Kurt Pinthus," in *Hermann Tietz, der grösste Warenhaus-Konzern*, 124.

102 Göhre, *Das Warenhaus*, 35.

103 Manfred Georg, *Aufruhr im Warenhaus* (Berlin-Friedenau, 1928).

104 Reprinted in Michael Bienert, ed., *Joseph Roth in Berlin: Ein Lesebuch für Spaziergänger* (Cologne, 1996), 159.

105 See reports on the first escalator in Zwickau in SSSA Akte 294, G.B. Nr 1129 B, 20.10.32.

106 Schocken Archive, Jerusalem, in 185/228/1 Propaganda und Information. Verschiedene Einzelfragen.

107 In Bienert, *Joseph Roth in Berlin*, 160–61.

108 Ibid., 160.

109 H. Wagner, *Über die Organisation der Warenhäuser, Kaufhäuser und der großen Spezialgeschäfte* (Leipzig, 1911).

110 For the same idea see Wiener, *Das Warenhaus*, 22.

111 Colze, *Berliner Warenhäuser*, 31. The Wertheim store on Leipziger Strasse had seventy stations and encompassed over three miles. See Matheo Quinz, "Wertheim," *Der Querschnitt* 8 (1928), 9. On the need for constant repair and eventual replacement see Harry Jandorf, "Erinnerungen an meinen Vater Adolf Jandorf," 2, LBI NY ME 335.

112 See Walter E. Schulz, "Warenhäuser," in *Hermann Tietz, der größte Warenhauskonzern*, 190.

113 "Das Theater," N. Israel Album, 1906.

114 Gellately, *Politics of Economic Despair*, 44.

115 Herzl, *Old New Land*, esp. 98.

116 Ibid., 84

117 See Presner, *Mobile Modernity*, esp. 147–79.

118 Presner writes that "Herzl imagines the transformation of Palestine from a barren wasteland into a fantastic, colonial wonderland modeled on the cosmopolitanism of the German universal." *Mobile Modernity*, 197.

119 Sznaider, *Jewish Memory*, 6.

120 See Lerner, "Consuming Powers: The 'Jewish Department Store' in German Politics and Culture," in Reuveni and Wobick-Segev, *Economy in Jewish History*, 135–56.

121 Paul Dehn, *Hinter den Kulissen*, 6.

122 Ibid., 85.

123 Stoltheim, *Das Rätsel des jüdischen Erfolges* (Leipzig, 1928), 109.

124 For example, "Der Harem im Warenhaus am Andreasplatz," *Die Wahrheit* 4 (May 30, 1908), 1–2, and "Die Geheimnisse des Teesalons im Warenhaus Wertheim," *Die Wahrheit* 3 (January 19, 1907), 1. For a discussion of this theme see my essay "Consuming Pathologies: Kleptomania, Magazinitis, and the Problem of Female Consumption in Wilhelmine and Weimar Germany," in *WerkstattGeschichte* 42 (Summer 2006): 46–56.

125 Hans Buchner, *Warenhauspolitik und Nationalsozialismus* (Munich, 1929); Buchner, *Dämonen der Wirtschaft: Gestalten und dunkle Gewalten aus dem Leben unserer Tage* (Munich, 1928). On Nazi approaches to mass consumption see above all Wiesen, *Creating the Nazi Marketplace*; Baranowski, *Strength through Joy*; König, *Volkswagen, Volksempfänger, Volksgemeinschaft*; Berghoff, "Enticement and Deprivation"; Lerner, "All-Consuming History?"

126 Buchner, *Warenhauspolitik*, 4. The same passage appears verbatim in *Dämonen der Wirtschaft*.

127 Benjamin, *Arcades*, 48.

128 Buchner, *Warenhauspolitik*, 4.

129 Walter Boehlich, ed., *Der Berliner Antisemitismusstreit* (Frankfurt, 1965).

130 Gustav Freytag, *Soll und Haben* (Leipzig, 1855; repr., Berlin, 2014).

131 Werner Sombart, "Die Reklame," in *Morgen: Wochenschrift für deutsche Kultur* 2 (March 6, 1908), 283.

132 Conrad, *Globalisation*, 359.

133 Sombart, "Die Reklame," 283.

134 A. Waldmann, "Soziale Einrichtungen und Angestellten-Fürsorge," in *Hermann Tietz, der grösste Warenhaus-Konzern*, 182.

135 Pinthus, "Warenhaus-Propaganda," 122.

136 Sombart, "Das Warenhaus," 77–87.

137 Simmel, "Metropolis and Mental Life," 178.

138 Böhme, *W.A.G.M.U.S.*, 17–18.

139 Moritz Loeb, *Berliner Konfektion* (Berlin, 1906), 50–51.

140 See Conrad, *Globalisation*, 373.

141 Zola, *Ladies' Paradise*, 35.

142 Siwertz, *Das große Warenhaus*, 49.

143 See Paul Mendes-Flohr, "The Berlin Jew as Cosmpolitan," in *Berlin Metropolis: Jews and the New Culture*, ed. Emily Bilski (Berkeley, CA, 2000), 17–18.

144 On Jews and economic thought see Penslar, *Shylock's Children*; Karp, *The Politics of Jewish Commerce*; Moishe Postone, "The Holocaust and the Trajectory of the Twentieth Century," in *Catastrophe and Meaning: The Holocaust and the Twentieth Century*, ed. Postone and Eric Santner (Chicago, 2003), 81–116.

145 Karl Marx, *Zur Judenfrage* (1844; repr., Berlin, 1920); Sombart, *Die Juden und das Wirtschaftsleben*; Yuri Slezkine, *The Jewish Century* (Princeton, NJ, 2004). For an excellent historical and historiographic treatment see Berg, *Kapitalismusdebatten um 1900*.

146 See, for example, Mitchell B. Hart, "Jews, Race, and Capitalism in the German-Jewish Context," *Jewish History* 19 (2005): 49–63.

147 Quoted in Konrad Fuchs, "Jüdische Unternehmer im deutschen Gross-und Einzelhandel Dargestellt an ausgewählten Beispeilen," in *Jüdische Unternehmer in Deutschland im 19. und 20. Jahrhundert*, ed. Werner E. Mosse and Hans Pohl (Stuttgart, 1992), 178.

148 Rudolf Karstadt A.G., *The Largest Chain Store Enterprise in Germany* (New York, 1928), 15.

3. Uncanny Encounters

1 One doctor estimated that women comprised 97–98 percent of department store thieves. Cajus Nordmann, "Die Warenhausdiebinnen," in *Die Welt der Frau* 26 (1907), 85.

2 Kläger, *Zwischenfall im Warenhaus*, 62.

3 Leopold Laquer, *Der Warenhaus-Diebstahl* (Halle, 1907), 7.

4 Stücklen, *Purpus*, 26.

5 Susan Porter Benson, *Counter Cultures* (Urbana, IL, 1988), 76.

6 Sigmund Freud, *Das Unheimliche* (Frankfurt, 1968). Originally published as Sigmund Freud, "Das Unheimliche," *Imago. Zeitschrift für Anwendung der Psychoanalyse auf die Geisteswissenschaften* 5 (1919): 297–324.

7 See Brian Nelson, "Zola and the Counter Revolution: Au Bonheur des Dames," *Australian Journal of French Studies* 30 (1993): esp. 236.

8 Zola, *Ladies' Paradise*, 77.

9 "Das Waarenhaus in *Berliner Börsen-Courier* (November 8, 1898), clipping in GehStA I HA Rep. 120 CV Nr. 68a, Bd. 1.

10 Eduard-Rudolf Müllener, "Die Entstehung des Kleptomaniebegriffes," *Suddhoffs Archiv für Geschichte der Medizin und der Naturwissenschaften* 48 (1964): 233

11 Laquer, *Der Warenhaus-Diebstahl*, 8; Gerhard Schmidt, "Der Stehltrieb oder die Kleptomanie," *Zentralblatt für die gesamte Neurologie und Psychiatrie* 92 (1939): 3.

12 Siwertz, *Das große Warenhaus*, 246, 247.

13 The quote, no doubt a reference to *The Ladies' Paradise*, is from Colze, *Berliner Warenhäuser*, 73. On department store shoplifting in the United States see Abelson, *When Ladies*

Go A-Thieving. On the earlier history of shoplifting see Rachel Shteir, *The Steal: A Cultural History of Shoplifting* (New York, 2011), chap. 1.

14 Stücklen, *Purpus*, 13.

15 Lamberty, *Reklame in Deutschland*, 67.

16 Ibid., 95; Colze, *Berliner Warenhäuser*, 74–75.

17 Colze, *Berliner Warenhäuser*, 73.

18 "Entlarvte Ladendiebinnen," *Die Praktische Berlinerin* 34 (1910), 11.

19 See, for example, Laquer, *Der Warenhaus-Diebstahl*, 9.

20 Colze, *Berliner Warenhäuser*, 75.

21 Briesen, *Warenhaus*, 83–149; Gudrun M. König, "Zum Warenhausdiebstahl um 1900: Über juristische Definitionen, medizinische Interpretamente und die Geschlechterforschung," in *Geschlecht und Materielle Kultur: Frauen-Sachen, Männer-Sachen, Sach-Kulturen*, ed. Gabriele Mentges, Ruth-E. Mohrmann, and Cornelia Foerster (Münster, 2000), 49–66.

22 See Hans Bernd Thiekötter, *Die psychologischen Wurzel und strafrechtliche Bewertung von Warenhausdiebstählen* (Bochum, 1933), 1.

23 This most likely refers to Christmas 1910. Colze, *Berliner Warenhäuser*, 73. Concerning Tietz, see Hirsch, *Das Warenhaus in Westdeutschland*, 116. The other report comes from Göhre, *Das Warenhaus*, 132.

24 Schweriner, *Arbeit*, 223.

25 Uwe Spiekermann, "Theft and Thieves in German Department Stores, 1895–1930: A Discourse on Morality, Crime and Gender," in Crossick and Jaumain, *Cathedrals of Consumption*, 137.

26 See Abelson, *When Ladies Go A-Thieving.*

27 For background on the film see Charles Musser, *Before the Nickelodeon: Edwin S. Porter and the Edison Manufacturing Company* (Berkeley, CA, 1991), 292–302.

28 Zola, *Ladies' Paradise*, 255.

29 Max Hartung, *Kleptomanie: Schwank in einem Aufzug* (Leipzig, 1900).

30 *Lustige Blätter* 31 (1906), 1–22.

31 See Eugen Wilhelm, "Ein Fall von sogenannter Kleptomanie," *Archiv für Kriminal-Anthropologie und Kriminalistik* 16 (1904): 160–61.

32 Gerhard Schmidt, "Der Stehltrieb oder die Kleptomanie," *Zentralblatt für die gesamte Neurologie und Psychiatrie* 92 (1939): 12.

33 Ibid., 12.

34 Quoted in Thiekötter, *Die psychologischen Wurzel*, 20.

35 Paul Lerner, "Hysterical Cures: Hypnosis, Gender and Performance in World War I and Weimar Germany," *History Workshop Journal* 45 (March 1998): 79–101; Ruth Harris, *Murders and Madness: Medicine, Law, and Society in the Fin de Siècle* (Oxford, 1989).

36 Ann Friedberg, *Window Shopping: Cinema and the Postmodern* (Berkeley, CA, 1994), chap. 3.

37 Wilhelm Stekel, *Impulshandlungen: Wandertrieb, Dipsomanie, Kleptomanie, Pyromanie und verwandte Zustände* (Berlin, 1922), 214.

38 Ibid., 213; Schmidt, "Der Stehltrieb," 12; Laquer, *Der Warenhaus-Diebstahl*, 9.

39 Paul Dubuisson, *Les Voleuses de Grands Magasin* (Paris, 1902). The German translation of Dubuisson's work appeared in 1904.

40 Laquer, *Der Warenhaus-Diebstahl*, 11.

41 Nordmann, "Die Warenhausdiebinnen," 85.

42 Dubuisson, quoted in Laquer, *Der Warenhaus-Diebstahl*, 11.

43 Thiekötter, *Die psychologischen Wurzel*, 17.

44 Stücklen, *Purpus*, 10.

45 Siwertz, *Das große Warenhaus*, 169.

46 Stücklen, *Purpus*, 17.

47 Quoted in Spiekermann, "Theft and Thieves," 141.

48 Stresemann, "Die Warenhäuser," 714.

49 Prentice Mulford, *Unfug des Lebens und des Sterbens* (1913; repr., Frankfurt, 1977), 109.
50 Dehn, *Die Großbazare*, 33. See also F. Roderich Stoltheim, "Warenhäuser und öffentliche Sittlichkeit," 263.
51 Laquer, *Der Warenhaus-Diebstahl*, 12.
52 Leo Deutsch, "Zur Frage der Kleptomanie," 213; Nordmann, "Die Warenhausdiebinnen," 88.
53 Quoted in Shteir, *Steal*, 43.
54 Georg Buschan, *Geschlecht und Verbrechen* (Berlin, 1908), 11.
55 Ibid., 13.
56 Laquer, *Der Warenhaus-Diebstahl*, 41–42. See also Stekel, *Impulshandlungen*, 209, for an overview of the psychiatric literature on these connections.
57 Thiekötter, *Die psychologischen Wurzel*, 23.
58 See Buschan, *Geschlecht und Verbrechen*, 13–14. On the construction of the sexualized, gendered consumer-citizen see Christoph Conrad, "Observer les consommateurs. Études de marché et histoire de la consommation en Allemagne, des années 1930 aux années 1960," *Le Mouvement Social* no. 206 (January–March 2004): esp. 16.
59 A. Lepmann, "Über Diebstähle in den grossen Kaufhäusern," *Ärztliche Sachverständigen-Zeitung* 7 (January 1, 1901), 32.
60 See Rappaport, *Shopping for Pleasure*, 53, and Dorothy Rowe, *Representing Berlin: Sexuality and the City in Imperial and Weimar Germany* (Aldershot, UK, 2003).
61 See, for example, Göhre, *Das Warenhaus*, 133.
62 Zola, *Ladies' Paradise*, 243.
63 Siwertz, *Das große Warenhaus*, 158.
64 Spiekermann, "Theft and Thieves."
65 Rachel Bowlby, *Shopping with Freud* (London, 1993), 5.
66 Stekel, *Impulshandlungen*.
67 Olga Wohlbrück, *Der große Rachen* (Berlin, 1915).
68 Ibid., 13.
69 Siwertz, *Das große Warenhaus*, 247.
70 Stekel, *Impulshandlungen*, 207.
71 Schiffer and Spoliansky, *Es Liegt in der Luft*, 22–23.
72 Wilhelm Carlé, "Die Rolltreppe. Der Roman eines jungen Mädchens," 3, manuscript fragment in Schocken Institute Archive: 185/228/1 Propaganda und Information. Verschiedene Einzelfragen.
73 Vicki Baum, "Dienst am Kunden," 7. MS in University of Southern California Feuchtwanger Memorial Library, Felix Guggenheim Papers, box 171, folder 16. Unpublished manuscript, no date.
74 See Shteir, *Steal*, 44.
75 See also Deutsch, "Zur Frage der Kleptomanie," 214.
76 Göhre, *Das Warenhaus*, 65.
77 Ibid. See also Hirsch, *Das Warenhaus in Westdeutschland*, 54.
78 Hirsch, *Das Warenhaus in Westdeutschland*, 52–54. See also Lux, *Studien*, 23.
79 Werner Sombart, "Das Warenhaus," 87.
80 Mitteilungen des Verbands der Werbetätigen Frauen Deutschlands e.V., 3 (1931). Schocken Institute Archive: 185/228/1, Propaganda und Information. Verschiedene Einzelfragen.
81 A. Waldmann, "Soziale Einrichtungen und Angestellten-Fürsorge," in *Hermann Tietz, der grösste Warenhaus-Konzern Europas im Eigenbesitz. Ein Buch sichtbarer Erfolge*, ed. Walter E. Schulz (Berlin, 1932), 182.
82 Lux, *Studien*, 24.
83 "Fünfzehn Leitsätze für das Verkaufspersonal des Kaufhauses Manasse," George Manasse Collection, Leo Baeck Institute Archive AR/6379, (probably) 1927, 84. The same document, for Kaufhaus Schocken, can be found in *Das Kaufhaus Schocken im Jahre 1926*.

Vorträge, Ansprachen und Leitsätze aus früheren Schocken-Hauszeitungen (Nuremberg, 1952), 18–21.

84 Salman Schocken, May 6, 1926, box 149/224: Sammlung sämtlicher Referate, den Schocken Konzern betreffend, Schocken Institute, Jerusalem.

85 Dorothy Rowe, *Representing Berlin: Sexuality and the City in Imperial and Weimar Germany* (London, 2003), 163–64.

86 Böhme, *W.A.G.M.U.S.*, 347. Ellipsis points in text.

87 Ibid., 347.

88 Ibid., 348.

89 Ibid.

90 Ibid., 271.

91 Hans Fallada, *Kleiner Mann—Was Nun?* (1932; repr., Berlin, 2012), 331.

92 Colze, *Berliner Warenhäuser*, 9.

93 Böhme, *W.A.G.M.U.S.*, 513.

94 Köhrer, *Warenhaus Berlin*, 76.

95 Böhme, *W.A.G.M.U.S.*, 107.

96 Ibid., 397.

97 Ibid., 164.

98 Ibid., 128.

99 Josef Wiener-Braunsberg, *Warenhausmädchen: Roman aus Berlin der Gegenwart* (Berlin, 1922), 117.

100 Mulford, *Unfug des Lebens*, 111.

101 L. Herzberg, "Der Angestellte des Warenhauses," 25 Jahre Verband deutscher Waren-u. Kaufhäuser," *Zeitschrift für Waren-und Kaufhäuser* (May 9, 1928), 12.

102 Hirsch, *Das Warenhaus in Westdeutschland*, 64.

103 Colze, *Berliner Warenhäuser*, 33.

104 Köhrer, *Warenhaus Berlin*, 58–59.

105 Colze, *Berliner Warenhäuser*, 34.

106 Sombart, "Das Warenhaus," 84.

107 Colze, *Berliner Warenhäuser*, 33; Lux, *Studien*, 23.

108 Sammy Gronemann, *Erinnerungen an Meine Jahre in Berlin* (Berlin, 2004), 16.

109 Schweriner, *Arbeit*, 23. See Atina Grossmann, "*Girlkultur* or the Thoroughly Rationalized Female," in *Women in Culture and Politics*, ed. J. Friedlander (Bloomington, IN, 1986), 62–80.

110 Maria Gleit (pseud. for Hertha Gleitsmann), *Abetilung Herrenmode. Roman eines Warenhausmädels* (Vienna, 1933), 72.

111 Göhre, *Das Warenhaus*, 86–87.

112 On the military metaphor in French department stores see Nord, *Politics of Resentment*, 63.

113 Waldmann, "Soziale Einrichtungen," 182.

114 Göhre, *Das Warenhaus*, 79–80.

115 Lux, *Studien*, 33.

116 Hirsch, *Das Warenhaus in Westdeutschland*, 63–64.

117 Ladwig-Winters, *Wertheim*, 61; Anonymous, *Aus den Warenhäusern beider Welten. Die Organisation der größten Berliner, Pariser, und Amerikanischen Warenhäusern* (Berlin, 1908), 70.

118 Waldmann, "Soziale Einrichtungen," 184; "Bekanntmachung from Abt. Personal-Wohlfahrt, Zwickau, May 25, 1926," SSSC 31451 Schocken-Konzern & Nachfolger, Akte 307.

119 Leonhard Tietz Aktiengesellschaft, *50 Jahre Leonhard Tietz 1879–1929* (Cologne, 1929), 101–2.

120 Hirsch, *Das Warenhaus in Westdeutschland*, 70. Apparently Wertheim paid higher wages than Hermann Tietz. Heinrich Hartmann, "Wohltätigkeit zwischen humanistischen Werten und sozialem Kapital. Oscar Tietz (1858–1932)," in *Jüdische Wohlfahrt im Spiegel von Biographien* 2 (2007): 422.

121 Lux, *Studien*, 39; Waldmann, "Soziale Einrichtungen," 183–84.

122 "Regelung der Urlaubs-Zeit, -Dauer,-Beihilfe der Schocken Kommandit-Gesellschaft. . . ." April 1932, George Manasse Collection, Archive of the Leo Baeck Institute, AR 6379.

123 "An die Mitarbeiter," May 1, 1933 (date is probable), G. Manasse, in George Manasse Collection, Archive of the Leo Baeck Institute, AR 6379.

124 Ladwig-Winters, *Wertheim*, 61; Hirsch, *Das Warenhaus in Westdeutschland*, 68.

125 Colze, *Berliner Warenhäuser*, 35.

126 For a list of Oscar Tietz's charitable activities see the documents pertaining to his (unsuccessful) application for recognition as a councilor (*Kommerzienrat*). In LAB A Pr. Br. Rep. 30 Tit. 94, Nr. 13810. See also Hartmann, "Wohltätigkeit," 416–26; Mosse, *German-Jewish Economic Elite*, 71–75.

127 For a detailed account of wages and other incentives at the L. Tietz firm and a comparison of L. Tietz and Wertheim see Hirsch, *Das Warenhaus in Westdeutschland*, 57–63. See also Lux, *Studien*, for a breakdown of wages, 27–33.

128 Hirsch, *Das Warenhaus in Westdeutschland*, 55–56.

129 Zola, *Ladies' Paradise*, 311.

130 Waldmann, "Soziale Einrichtungen," 187.

131 Herzberg, "Der Angestellte des Warenhauses," 13.

132 See P. G. Nasher, "Tietz," in *Der Querschnitt* 8 (January 1, 1928), 8; Lux, *Studien*, 39; Karrtte, "Die Personal-Erziehung in den Warenhäusern Hermann Tietz," in *Hermann Tietz, der grösste Warenhaus-Konzern Europas*, 162–81.

133 "Education und Service: Verkäuferausbildung bei der Leonhard Tietz A.-G.," *Zeitschrift für Waren-und-Kaufhäuser* 27 (June 2, 1929), 1.

134 See, for example, Wilhelm Rubiner, *Die Warenhausgräfin* (Leipzig, 1923). Rubiner was the nom de plume of Walter Gerhard.

135 Ibid., 12.

136 "Terrorismus in der Konfektion," *Die Wahrheit* 3 (March 9, 1907), 3.

137 Letter from the Minister für Handel und Gewerbe to the Polizeipräsident Berlin, March 28, 1908. Landesarchiv Berlin, A Pr. Br. Rep. 30, Tit 94, Nr. 10937 (Jandorf).

138 Lothar Eisen (pseud. for Josef Bernhard Schneider), "Psychologie des Warenhauses," *Geschlecht und Gesellschaft* 8 (1913), 394.

139 See, for example, "Die Kellnerinnen im Warenhaus Wertheim," *Die Wahrheit* 3 (May 18, 1907), and "Liebes-Fallstricke im Warenhaus Wertheim," *Die Wahrheit* 4 (February 29, 1908), 1–2.

140 Miller, *Bon Marché*, 194.

141 *Simplicissimus* 31 (May 3, 1926), 70.

142 Irmgard Keun, *The Artificial Silk Girl*, trans. Katharina von Ankum (1932; repr., New York, 2002). See also the introduction to this edition by Maria Tatar.

143 "Im Zuchthaus des Warenhausjuden," *Illustrierter Beobachter* 4 (December 21, 1929), 678–79, 690.

144 Ibid., 690.

145 Anonymous, *Aus den Warenhäusern beider Welten*, 70.

146 Ladwig-Winters, *Wertheim*, 61.

147 "Im Zuchthaus," 690.

148 Ward, *Weimar Surfaces*, 230–31; Mila Ganeva, "The Beautiful Body of the Mannequin: Display Practices in Weimar Germany," in *Leibhaftige Moderne: Körper in Kunst und Massenmedien, 1918–1933*, ed. Michael Cowan and Kai Marcel Sicks (Bielefeld, 2005), 152–69.

149 Freud, "Das Unheimliche."

150 Zola, *Ladies' Paradise*, 6.

151 Baum, *Der große Ausverkauf*, 83.

152 The practice of mixing a live model with a group of mannequins in a store window, as in the Baum novel, was in fact a common occurrence in Europe and the United States, and the live models were typically made up to look just like the wax dummies.

153 See the files in Landesarchiv Berlin, A. Pr. Br. Repositorium 30 (Polizeipräsidium), Titel 133, Nr. 18627.

154 Baum, *Der große Ausverkauf*, 88.

155 Ibid., 96.

156 Ibid., 107.

157 See Leach, *Land of Desire*, 58.

158 Williams, *Dream Worlds*, 67.

159 In *Das Kaufhaus des Westens: Festschrift zum 25 jährigen Bestehen 1907–1932*, ed. Franz Arnholz and Max Osborn (Berlin, 1932), 177.

160 Siegfried Kracauer, "Der Verkaufs-Tempel," in *Siegfried Kracauer Aufsätze, 1927–1931*, ed. Inka Mülder-Bach (Frankfurt, 1990), 350.

161 Siwertz, *Das große Warenhaus*, 106–7.

162 Ibid., 107.

163 Ibid., 130.

164 Sigfried Siwertz, *Goldman's*, trans. E. Gee Nash (New York, 1930), 117–18. In this case I have used the published English translation.

165 Vicki Baum, "Jape im Warenhaus," in *Die anderen Tage. Novellen von Vicki Baum* (Berlin, 1931), 217.

166 Ibid., 219.

167 Ibid.

168 Ibid.

169 Ibid., 221.

170 Ibid., 225.

171 Ibid., 227.

172 Ibid.

173 Ibid.

174 See Baudrillard, *Consumer Society*, 187–90.

175 Baum, "Jape im Warenhaus," 228.

176 Ibid., 231.

177 Ibid.

178 Ibid., 233–34.

179 Ibid., 236.

180 Ibid., 237.

181 Ibid., 239.

182 Eisen, "Psychologie des Warenhauses," 394.

183 Edmund Edel, *Neu-Berlin*, 2nd ed. (Berlin, 1914).

184 See, for example, Egon Larsen, *Weimar Eyewitness* (London, 1976), 95.

185 Curt Moreck, *Führer durch das "lasterhafte" Berlin* (Leipzig, 1931), 29–30.

186 Margarete Stahr, "Aus dem Warenhaus," in *Illustrirte Zeitung* 121 (1903), 39–40, 77–78.

187 Gleit, *Abetilung Herrenmode*, 75.

188 Eisen, "Psychologie des Warenhauses," 395.

189 See Jill Suzanne Smith, "Just How Naughty Was Berlin? The Geography of Prostitution and Female Sexuality in Curt Moreck's Erotic Travel Guide," in *Spatial Turns: Space, Place and Mobility in German Literary and Visual Culture*, ed. Jaimey Fisher and Barbara Mennel (Amsterdam, 2010), 60–61; Deborah Smail, *White-Collar Workers, Mass Culture and Neue Sachlichkeit in Weimar Berlin* (Bern, 1999), 49.

190 F. Roderich Stoltheim, "Warenhäuser und öffentliche Sittlichkeit," 264.

191 For example, Hausschildt, *Der Kampf gegen die Waarenhäuser*, 2.

192 H.M., "Das Warenhaus, eine Gefahr?," 7.

193 Dehn, *Die Großbazare*, 45.

194 For example, see anonymous, "Der Fünf-Uhr-Tee im Warenhaus Wertheim," *Die Wahrheit* 2 (June 30, 1906), 1–2; anonymous, Die Geheimnisse des Teesalons im Warenhaus Wertheim," *Die Wahrheit* 3 (January 19, 1907), 1–2.

195 Hans Vogt, *Du Kommst zu Spät: Eine Szene aus dem Warenhaus* (Leipzig, 1914), 5.

196 Ibid., 6.

197 Ibid., 7.

198 Kläger, *Zwischenfall im Warenhaus*, 74–75.

199 Ibid., 78.

200 A 1960 *Twilight Zone* episode called "The After Hours" dramatizes this issue. In the show, which takes place in a department store, the viewer gradually realizes that the main character is actually a mannequin. In this store, it turns out, mannequins take turns passing as people for a month. In the story, the mannequin-turned-woman tries to remain human because she enjoyed the experience so much, but she gives in to her reality and gradually transforms back into the mute stillness of an object.

4. Beyond the Consuming Temple

1 Siegfried Kracauer, "Der Dichter im Warenhaus," in *Siegfried Kracauer Aufsätze, 1927–1931* (Frankfurt, 1990), 228.

2 *50 Jahre Leonhard Tietz 1879–1929* (Cologne, 1929), 67.

3 Ibid., 65. I am borrowing the term "provincial modernity" from Jennifer Jenkins, *Provincial Modernity: Local Culture and Liberal Politics in Fin-de-Siècle Hamburg* (Ithaca, NY, 2003). For a regional perspective on the German department store see Mueller, "'Eine Zierde jeder Stadt.'"

4 "Ansprache des Herrn Manasse an das neu engagierte Crimmitschauer Personal am 1.11.1928, im Kaufhaus Schocken, Crimmitschau," SSSC 33309, Akte 39. On Manasse see Jürgen Nitsche, *Georg Manasse: Schockens Generaldirektor—Sozialdemokrat—Pazifist* (Berlin, 2013).

5 "Ansprache des Herrn Direktor Manasse anlässlich der Pressebesprechung am Montag, den 21. Oktober 1929 nachmittags 3 Uhr 30 im Gesellschaftssaal des Hotel 'Waldenburger Hof,'" SSSC 33309, Akte 39.

6 "Ansprache des Herrn Manasse an das neu engagierte Crimmitschauer Personal," 2.

7 Lars Scharnholz, *Kaufhaus Schocken Cottbus* (Leipzig, 2000), 9–10.

8 On Mendelsohn's architecture in Palestine/Israel and its connections to German Zionism see Alona Nitzan-Shaftan, "Erich Mendelsohn: From Berlin to Jerusalem" (master's thesis, architecture studies, Massachusetts Institute of Technology, 1993). Nitzan-Shaftan fleshes out links between the philosophical underpinnings of German Zionism and Mendelsohn's architectural work, a useful intervention to be sure, but one that has little or nothing to say about Schocken's business practices or about Mendelsohn's department store designs. Siegfried Moses connects Schocken's Zionism and his commercial activities in terms of his character. He finds that Schocken approached both spheres with a unique singularity of purpose, self-discipline, and deliberateness, but he makes no substantive connections between the world of Zionism and the department store business, with the exception of pointing out other individuals who inhabited both milieu. Moses, "Salman Schocken: His Economic and Zionist Activities," *Leo Baeck Institute Year Book* 5 (1960), 73–104. One exception that does explore Mendelsohn's Jewishness and Zionism in relation to his architectural practice, but most of all to his Dutch connections, is Herbert and Liliane Richter, *Through a Clouded Glass: Mendelsohn, Wijdeveld, and the Jewish Connection* (Tübingen, 2008).

9 See, for example, Elana Shapira, "Jewish Identity, Mass Consumption, and Modern Design," in Reuveni and Roemer, *Longing, Belonging, and the Making of Jewish Consumer Culture*, 61–90; Abigail Gillman, *Viennese Jewish Modernism: Freud, Hofmannsthal, Beer-Hofmann, and Schnitzler* (University Park, PA, 2009); Leora Auslander, "The Boundaries of Jewishness: Or When Is a Cultural Practice Jewish?" *Journal of Modern Jewish History* 8 (2009): 47–64; Emily Bilski, ed., *Berlin Metropolis: Jews and the New Culture, 1890–1918* (Berkeley, CA, 2000); Reiter, *Anti-Journalist*. See also the thought-provoking insights in Scott Spector, "Modernism without the Jews," *Modernism/Modernity* 13 (2006): 615–33.

10 Franklin Toker, *Fallingwater Rising: Frank Lloyd Wright, E. J. Kaufmann, and America's Most Extraordinary House* (New York, 2003), 69.

11 See Kathleen James, *Erich Mendelsohn and the Architecture of German Modernism* (Cambridge, 1997), and "From Messel to Mendelsohn: German Department Store Architecture in Defense of Urban and Economic Change," in Crossick and Jaumain, *Cathedrals of Consumption*, 252–78.

12 Göhre, *Das Warenhaus*, 7–8.

13 Ibid., 8–9.

14 See Alarich Rooch, "Wertheim, Tietz und das KaDeWe in Berlin. Zur Architektursprache eies Kulturraumes," in Weiss-Sussex and Zitzlsperger, *Das Berliner Warenhaus*, 180.

15 Göhre, *Das Warenhaus*, 10. See also Albert Hoffmann, "Das Warenhaus A. Wertheim in der Leipziger Strasse," *Deutsche Bauzeitung* 32 (April 30, 1898), 217–19; (May 7, 1898), 229–32.

16 Kevin Repp, "Marketing, Modernity and the 'German People's Soul': Advertising and Its Enemies in Late Imperial Germany," in *Selling Modernity: Advertising in Twentieth-Century Germany*, ed. Pamela E. Swett, S. Jonathan Wiesen, and Jonathan B. Zatlin (Durham, NC, 2010), 30–32.

17 James, "From Messel to Mendelsohn," 261.

18 Quoted in Repp, "Marketing," 37.

19 Göhre, *Das Warenhaus*, 13.

20 Ibid., 14.

21 Ibid.

22 Fritzsche, *Reading Berlin 1900*, 164.

23 Rooch, "Wertheim, Tietz und das KaDeWe," 178.

24 Wussow, *Geschichte und Entwicklung*, 56; Max Osborn, *Berlins Aufstieg zur Weltstadt* (Berlin, 1929), 182.

25 James, "From Messel to Mendelsohn," 263.

26 Ullmann, " 'Der Kaiser bei Wertheim,' " 228.

27 Plutus, "Tietz," *Die Zukunft* 35 (April 1901): 126–27.

28 Göhre, *Das Warenhaus*, 92.

29 Sammy Gronemann, *Erinnerungen* (Berlin, 2002), 16.

30 Rooch, "Wertheim, Tietz und das KaDeWe," 194.

31 See Tim Coles, "Department Stores as Retail Innovations in Germany: A Historical-Geographical Perspective on the Period 1870–1914," in Crossick and Jaumain, *Cathedrals of Consumption*, 82–83.

32 Matheo Quinz, "Wertheim," *Der Querschnitt* 8 (1928): 11; *Wertheim Berlin. Leipziger Strasse und Leipziger Platz* (Berlin, ca. 1928–30).

33 Rooch, "Wertheim, Tietz und das KaDeWe," 177.

34 Kevin Repp writes of the "monotonous repetition of Messel's masterpiece all across the land": Repp, "Marketing," 38. See also Helga Behn, "Die Architektur des deutschen Warenhauses von ihren Anfängen bis 1933" (PhD dissertation, University of Cologne, 1984), 92, and Christian Schramm, "Architecture of the German Department Store," in Kremer, *Broken Threads*, 32–33.

35 For the idea that Wertheim's elegant interiors can be see as a rejection of the stylistic disunity of earlier department stores, which was associated with "Jewish capitalism" and crass commercial culture, see Shapira, "Jewish Identity," 64.

36 See Breckman, "Disciplining Consumption," 499; Karl Graebel, "Wertheim als Erzieher," *Hammer, Blätter für deutschen Sinn* 6 (December 1, 1907), 708.

37 James, "From Messel to Mendelsohn," 262–63.

38 Rooch, "Wertheim, Tietz und das KaDeWe," 183.

39 Gerhard Tietz pointed out that different departments in the same store often catered to different social groups. See Gerhard Tietz, "Der Verkäufer und die Verkäuferin im Warenhaus (Unter besonderer Berücksichtigung der Verhältnisse im Leonhard Tietz-Konzern)," in 25 Jahre Verband deutscher Waren-u. Kaufhäuser, in *Zeitschrift für Waren-u. Kaufhäuser* (Berlin, May 9, 1928), 14.

40 See Colze, *Berliner Warenhäuser*, 12.

41 Stresemann, "Die Warenhäuser," 706.

42 Ullmann, "'Der Kaiser bei Wertheim,'" 223–36. Ullmann writes that the visit, which occurred on a Sunday when the store was closed, was an ambiguous political statement that could easily be read as either a statement of support of or opposition to the department store phenomenon.

43 James, "From Messel to Mendelsohn," 263.

44 See, above all, Konrad Fuchs, *Ein Konzern aus Sachsen. Das Kaufhaus Schocken 1901–1953* (Stuttgart, 1990). Also see David, *Patron*; G. Schocken, "Salman Schocken: Ich Werde Seinesgleichen Nicht Mehr Sehen," *Der Monat* 20 (1968): 13–30.

45 Fuchs, *Ein Konzern aus Sachsen*, 32.

46 G. Schocken, "Salman Schocken," 13. Indeed, Schocken is known today, at least in the Jewish world, far more for his collection of Judaica, his publishing ventures, and his patronage of Jewish writers and intellectuals than for his business achievements.

47 Ibid., 21.

48 Ibid.

49 Ibid., 26.

50 Ibid.

51 Ibid., 21.

52 Quoted in David, *Patron*, 49.

53 Fuchs, *Ein Konzern aus Sachsen*, 27.

54 Ibid., 30.

55 Ibid.

56 "Ansprache des Herrn Direktor Manasse . . . 21. Oktober 1929 . . ." SSSC 33309, Akte 39.

57 "Ansprache des Herrn Direktor Manasse an das neu engagierte Crimmitschauer Personal am1/11/1928, im Kaufhaus Schocken, Crimmitschau," SSSC 33309, Akte 39.

58 David, *Patron*, 45.

59 Salman Schocken, "Zur Eröffnung des Kaufhauses Schocken in Nürnberg, Ansprache an die Gäste, 11. Okt. 1926," in *Das Kaufhaus Schocken im Jahre 1926. Vorträge, Ansprachen und Leitsätze aus früheren Schocken-Hauszeitungen* (Nuremberg, 1952), 9.

60 Renata Manasse Schwebel, Stories, LBI MS 766, 24.

61 "Ansprache des Herrn Direktor Manasse . . . 1/11/1928," SSSC 33309, Akte 39.

62 "Unser Einkauf," in SSSC 33309, Akte 39.

63 Schwebel, Stories, 28.

64 Schocken, "Zur Eröffnung des Kaufhauses Schocken" (1926), in "Aus frühreren Schocken Hauszeitungen," SSSC 31451, Akte 398.

65 Fuchs, *Ein Konzern aus Sachsen*, 177.

66 G. Schocken, "Salman Schocken," 15.

67 See SSSC 31451, Akten 403/2 and 403/3 for pictures of Schocken window displays.

68 Salman Schocken, "Zwischen Produktion und Konsum," in *Vier Vorträge über den gegenwärtigen Stand und die Aufgaben des Großeinzelhandels*, 36. In GehStA PK I HA Rep 120 CVIII 2a Nr. 31, Bd. 7.

69 See G. Schocken, "Salman Schocken," 19.

70 David, *Patron*, 53.

71 "Die Zentrale," in Die Zentrale: Mitteilungen der Schocken Kommandit-Gesellschaft A. Aktien 8 (1931) SSSC 31451, Akte 398.

72 Moses, "Salman Schocken," 52.

73 G. Schocken, "Salman Schocken," 17.

74 Ibid., 18.

75 "Dienstanweisung," January 20, 1926, in SSSC 31451, Akte 81 (film).

76 G. Schocken, "Salman Schocken," 18.

77 Schocken, "Zwischen Produktion und Konsum," 40–44.

78 "Regelung der Ulaubs-Zeit, -Dauer, -Beihilfe der Schocken KG, Zwickau, April 1931, in Manasse Papers, LBI AR 6379, doc. 7.

79 Kann held the position until he left Germany in 1933 for Britain, where he came to work in a similar capacity for fellow Zionist Simon Marks, cofounder of Marks & Spencer. As a young man Marks had been sent to learn the department store business from Schocken and Manasse. G. Schocken, "Salman Schocken," 18. See also Judi Bevan, *The Rise and Fall of Marks & Spencer . . . and How It Rose Again* (London, 2010), 36, and Schwebel, Stories, 27.

80 Salman Schocken, "Zwischen Produktion und Konsum," Ein Vortrag, gehalten am 12.11.1931 in der Hauptversammlung des Verbandes Deutscher Waren und Kaufhäuser, in *Das Kaufhaus Schocken im Jahre 1926. Vorträge, Ansprachen und Leitsätze aus früheren Schocken-Hauszeitungen* (Nuremberg, 1952), 37.

81 "Gepflogenheit der Kaufhäuser Schocken" (September 18, 1933), SSSC 33309, Akte 72.

82 "Ein Besuch im Laboratorium," Schocken-Hauszeitung (January/March 1927), 6 in SSSC 31451, Akte 398.

83 "Von der Gepflogenheit der Kaufhäuser Schocken," 2 SSSC 31451, Akte 417, p. 54; also "Referat des Herrn Direktor Georg Manasse vor dem Reichswirtschaftsamt (February 3, 1932), Manasse Papers, LBI New York, 7–8.

84 "Besonderheiten des Schockenkonzerns gegenüber anderen Konzernen, in SSSC 33309, Akte 72.

85 Schocken, "Zwischen Produktion und Konsum," 37.

86 Schocken, "Personalerziehung," in *Das Kaufhaus Schocken im Jahre 1926*, 19.

87 Fünfzehn Leitsätze für das Verkaufspersonal der Käufhäuser Schocken, in "Aus frühreren Schocken Hauszeitungen," SSSC 31451, Akte 398.

88 Ibid.

89 See "Ansprache des Herrn Direktor Manasse . . . am 1/11.1928," SSSC 33309, Akte 39, p. 4.

90 "Gepflogenheit der Kaufhäuser Schocken."

91 Schwebel, Stories, 25–26.

92 "Regelung der Urlaubszeit," Manasse Papers, LBI New York, AR6379.

93 "Ansprache von Herrn Direktor Manasse an die Lehrlinge am 5. April 1932," 5, SSSC 33309 Manasse Papers, Akte 39.

94 Salman Schocken, Pforzheim, 24.9.1931, Schocken Institute Jerusalem, box 149/225.

95 "Ansprache des Herrn Architekt Erich Mendelsohn anlässlich der Vorbesichtigung des Kaufhauses Schocken am 15.Mai.1930 vormittags," SSSC 33309, p. 40.

96 Schwebel, Stories, 26; Fuchs, *Ein Konzern aus Sachsen*, 74–76.

97 Fuchs, *Ein Konzern aus Sachsen*, 131.

98 Ibid., 133.

99 See, among others, Hake, *Topographies of Class*, 112–13.

100 Salman Schocken, "Eröffnung des Erweiterungsbaues im Kaufhaus Schocken, Cottbus" (January–March 1927), in "Aus frühreren Schocken Hauszeitungen," SSSC 31451, Akte 398.

101 Moses, "Salman Schocken," 83.

102 Shulamit Volkov, "The Dynamics of Dissimilation: Ostjuden and German Jews," in *The Jewish Response to German Culture: From the Enlightenment to the Second World War*, ed. J. Reinharz and W. Schatzberg (Hanover, NH, 1985), 204.

103 Brenner, *Renaissance*, 33.

104 Volkov credits historian Saul Friedländer for bringing the term to her attention. See Volkov, "Dynamics of Dissimilation," 196 fn.

105 See Jon Gunnar Molstre Simonsen, "Perfect Targets: Anti-Semitism and Eastern Jews in Leipzig, 1919–1923," *Leo Baeck Institute Year Book* 51 (2006): 79–101.

106 I take the term from Brenner, *Renaissance*.

107 See Stephen M. Poppel, *Zionism in Germany, 1897–1933: The Shaping of a Jewish Identity* (Philadelphia, 1977), esp. chap. 6.

108 G. Schocken, "Salman Schocken," 25.

109 Ibid., 25.

110 David, *Patron*, 83–84.

111 Ibid., 84.

112 Poppel, *Zionism in Germany*, 129.

113 James, *Erich Mendelsohn and the Architecture of German Modernism*, 11–13.

114 Ibid., 12.

115 Author interview with Rudy Petersdorf and Rikki Horne, August 23, 2009, Ojai, CA.

116 Arnold Whittick, *Erich Mendelsohn* (London, 1956), 67; Gilbert Herbert and Liliane Richter, *Through a Clouded Glass: Mendelsohn, Wijdeveld, and the Jewish Connection* (Tübingen, 2008), 94–95.

117 The term is from Alona Nitzan-Shiftan, "Contested Zionism—Alternative Modernism: Erich Mendelsohn and the Tel Aviv Chug in Mandate Palestine," in *Constructing a Sense of Place: Architecture and the Zionist Discourse*, ed. Haim Yacobi (Aldershot, UK, 2004), 32.

118 See Herbert and Richter, *Through a Clouded Glass*, 30–31. Ultimately, such ideas, Mendelsohn's aestheticized notion of Jewish peoplehood, his imagined Arab-Jewish cultural synthesis, and the explicit "oriental" references in his designs for buildings in Mandate Palestine and Israel—reflections of ideas that were common among young German Zionists—ran him afoul of the Zionist leadership and the leading modernist architects in Tel Aviv. See Nitzan-Shiftan, "Contested Zionism," for a full explication of Mendelsohn's relationship to the political and architectural establishment in the *Yishuv*.

119 See Nitzan-Shiftan, "Erich Mendelsohn: From Berlin to Jerusalem," 32–33.

120 Erich Mendelsohn, "Palästina als künstlerisches Erlbenis," in Mendelsohn Papers, Kunstbibliothek Berlin IV 5 a (1).

121 "Ansprachen in Crimmitschau am 15.11.1928," SSSC 33309, Akte 40.

122 See Renate Palmer, *Der Stuttgarter Schocken-Bau von Erich Mendelsohn. Die Geschichte eines Kaufhauses und seiner Architektur* (Tübingen, 1995), 28–30. Also see Mendelsohn's letter to Luise Maas (September 29, 1914), in *Erich Mendelsohn. Briefe eines Architekten*, ed. Oskar Beyer (Munich, 1961), 33–34. Many American department stores reinforced this notion of verticality standing for hierarchy in that the lower selling floors, often the cellars, were reserved for cheaper goods and poorer or more "ethnic" customers while the upper floors catered to a more elite clientele.

123 Ward, *Weimar Surfaces*, 118.

124 James, *Erich Mendelsohn and the Architecture of German Modernism*, 174–75.

125 Quoted in Thilo Richter, *Erich Mendelsohns Kaufhaus Schocken. Jüdische Kulturgeschichte in Chemnitz* (Leipzig, 1998), 100.

126 Ibid., 177.

127 "Zur Eröffnung des Kaufhauses Schocken in Nürnberg. . . ." in Aus früheren Schocken Hauszeitungen, SSSC 31451, Akte 398.

128 "Warum diese Architektur?," in *Die neuen Bauten: Mitteilungen der Schocken Kommandit-Gesellschaft A. Aktien 7* in SSSC 31451, Akte 398.

129 In "Textänderungen für den Eröffnungsfilm," SSSC 31451, Akte 604. Ellipsis points in original.

130 In fact Luppe was bitterly attacked by the anti-Semitic press for bringing the Jewish-owned company into Nuremberg. Alexander Schmidt, "Das Schockenkaufhaus in Nürnberg—Beginn der Moderne vor Ort und Zielscheibe des Antisemitismus," unpublished paper, Chemnitz, October 8, 2013.

131 SSSC 31451, Akte 604. In the context of increasing attacks on the Schocken store in Nuremberg, Luppe later distanced himself from the Schockens.

132 Letter from Moholy-Nagy to Schocken AG, May 28, 1934, in SSSC 31451, Akte 604.

133 Reinhardt, *Von der Reklame zum Marketing*, 343–50.

134 "Die Eröffnung des Kaufhauses Schocken–Nürnberg im Lichtspiel," in SSSC 31451, Akte 604. P. 4.

135 Ibid., 4–5.

136 Although most of the secondary literature on Mendelsohn's work for the Schocken concern stresses his relationship with Salman Schocken, the brother who was more involved in aesthetic questions, Mendelsohn frequently mentioned his relationship with Simon Schocken in his public speeches and writings.

137 Ansprache des Herrn Architekt Erich Mendelsohn. . . ." SSSC 33309, Akte 40.

138 Fuchs, *Ein Konzern aus Sachsen*, 141–42.

139 James, *Erich Mendelsohn and the Architecture of German Modernism*, 178.

140 Quoted ibid., 187–88.

141 Ibid., 189.

142 Ward, *Weimar Surfaces*, 119; see also Palmer, *Der Stuttgarter Schocken-Bau*, 47–48.

143 Ward, *Weimar Surfaces*, 211.

144 See Erich Mendelsohn, "Gedanken zur neuen Architektur (im Felde), 1914–17," in Mendelsohn, *Bauten und Skizzen* (Berlin, 1924), 3.

145 "Allerlei Reklame," in *Zwickauer Tageblatt und Anzeiger* (21.1.27), clipping in SSSC 31451, Akte 399.

146 Quoted in David, *Patron*, 170.

147 Palmer, *Der Stuttgarter Schocken-Bau*, 117. The Schocken S was designed by Josef Neustadt, an associate of Mendelsohn's.

148 "Ansprache des Herrn Direktor Manasse am 21 October 1929," SSSC 33309, Akte 39, p. 4.

149 "Referat des Herrn Director Manasse zu der Sonntags-Tagung der Schocken Kommanditgesellschaft auf Aktien Zwickau, am 6 June 1926," 8, SSSC 33309, Akte 39.

150 David, *Patron*, 165; letter from Moholy-Nagy to Schocken firm, Berlin, May 28, 1934, SSSC 31451, Akte 604.

151 Fuchs, *Ein Konzern aus Sachsen*, 148–49.

152 Moses, "Salman Schocken," 79.

153 Fuchs, *Ein Konzern aus Sachsen*, 154.

154 James, *Erich Mendelsohn and the Architecture of German Modernism*, 194.

155 Ibid., 193–200.

156 "Referat des Herrn Director Manasse zu der Sonntags-Tagung der Schocken Kommanditgesellschaft auf Aktien Zwickau, am 6 June 1926," 5, SSSC 33309, Akte 39.

157 See, for example, the section "Was zählen wir zu unseren sozialen Pflichten?," in Gepflogenheiten der Kaufhäuser Schocken," 3–4 in SSSC 33309, Akte 72.

158 Das Gedenken an Tietze Leienad" von Redakteur Josef Thur "Er verzehrte sich im Dienst am Fortschritt im Handel," *Kölner Zeitung* no. 265 (November 13, 1964), LBI AR 2434 C, Leonhard Tietz Clippings Collection.

159 Hirsch, *Das Warenhaus in Westdeutschland*, 23.

160 Heinrich Uhlig, *Die Warenhäuser im Dritten Reich* (Cologne, 1956), 27.

161 Max Creutz, *Joseph M. Olbrich. Das Warenhaus Tietz in Düsseldorf* (Berlin, 1909), 12.

162 Ibid., 11–12.

163 *50 Jahre Leonhard Tietz*, 14.

164 Shapira, "Jewish Identity."

165 Creutz, *Joseph M. Olbrich*, 6.

166 Letter from L. Tietz AG Reklame Zentral to I. Schocken Sons, April 14, 1931, SSSC 31451, Akte 313.

5. The Consuming Fire

1 Baum, "Jape im Warenhaus," 238.

2 Ibid., 239.

3 Ibid., 240.

4 On Baum see Nicole Nottelmann, *Die Karrieren der Vicki Baum: Eine Biographie* (Cologne, 2007).

5 Williams, *Dream Worlds*, 4–6.

6 Göhre, *Das Warenhaus*, 35.

7 See Bernhard Rieger, *Technology and the Culture of Modernity in Britain and Germany, 1890–1945* (Cambridge, 2005).

8 For a description see, for example, Colze, *Berliner Warenhäuser*, 64–72.

9 See protocols of the Haus der Abgeordneten, 27. Sitzung am 8. Februar 1908. Abg. Felisch in GehStA I HA Rep. 93 B, Nr. 1439 Waren und Geschäftshäuser, Bd. 5, 1907–13.

10 Ferdinand Bucholtz, *Der gefährliche Augenblick: Eine Sammlung von Bildern und Berichten* (Berlin, 1931).

11 Clipping from *Hannoverscher Courier*, May 31, 1899. See also clipping from *Magdeburgische Zeitung*, June 4, 1899, in GehStA I HA Rep. 93 B, Nr. 1435.

12 "Sozialpolitische Bauordnung," in *Deutsche Rundschau*, April 4, 1906, clipping in GehStaA I HA Rep. 93B, Nr. 1437.

13 Stürzebecher, *Das Berliner Warenhaus*, 23. See "Sonderanforderungen an Warenhäuser und an Solche Anderen Geschäftshäuser, in welchen größere mengen brennbarer Stoffe feilgehalten werden vom 2. November 1907," LAB A. Pr. Br. Rep 30 (Polizeipräsidium), Titel 133, Nr. 18627

14 "Sozialpolitische Bauordnung."

15 "Protest der Hausbesitzer gegen die geplanten baupolizeilichen Beschränkungen," *Berliner Tageblatt*, May 12, 1900, in GehStA I HA Rep. 93 B, Nr. 1435.

16 In *Staatsbürger-Zeitung*, May 29, 1901, GehStA I HA Rep. 93 B, Nr. 1435.

17 "Die Brandkatastrophe in Budapest," *Wiener Bilder: Illustrirtes Familienblatt* 8, no. 36 (September 2, 1903), 4–6. For more on the Goldberger department store see Gábor Gyáni, "Department Stores and Middle-Class Consumerism in Budapest, 1896–1939," in Crossick and Jaumain, *Cathedrals of Consumption*, 208–24. Gyáni notes that the fire caused fourteen deaths, including that of the owner's wife (p. 212).

18 See "Bazarbrand in Budapest," *Österreichische Verbands-Feuerwehr-Zeitung* 27, no. 17 (September 5, 1903), 201–2.

19 "Die Brandkatastrophe in Budapest."

20 "Der Budapester Warenhausbrand," *Österreichische Verbands-Feuerwehr-Zeitung* 27 (October 20, 1903), 238–39.

21 "Die Brandkatastrophe in Budapest."

22 Ibid.

23 In GehStA PK I HA Rep. 93 B, Nr. 1439 Waren und Geschäftshäuser, Bd. 5, 1907–13.

24 Ibid.

25 See also "Die Warenhäuser als Mausefallen des Todes," *Deutsche-Jugend-Zeitung*, January 6, 1904, in GehStA I HA Rep. 93B, 1436.

26 See *Im deutschen Reich* 10 (1904, Nr. 7), 427.

27 *Staatsbürger-Zeitung*, August 28, 1903.

28 "Der Warenhausbrand in Peßt und die Berliner Warenhäuser," *Staatsbürger-Zeitung*, August 29, 1903.

29 Perry, *Christmas in Germany*, 169–71. See also "Der goldene Sonntag," in *Staatsbürger-Zeitung*, December 12, 1903, and "Sie machen im Weihnachten," *Illustrierter Beobachter* 49 (December 7, 1929), 655.

30 See, for example, Itzberner, "Feuergefährliche Geschäftshäuser," *Zeitschrift für Waren-und Kaufhäuser*, April 12, 1906, and "Sozialpolitische Bauordnung."

31 GehStA I HA Rep. 93B, no. 1437. See also Wussow, *Geschichte und Entwicklung*, 48–49.

32 GehStA I HA Rep. 93B, 1436 letter from Polizeipräsident to Ministerium des Innern, 1904.

33 Gyáni, "Department Stores," 212.

34 GehStA I HA Rep. 93B, no. 1439.

35 See remarks by Hammer before Abg. Haus, in GehStA I HA Rep. 93 B, no. 1437.

36 Ibid.

37 Ibid.

38 "Bauordnungen für Waren-und Geschäftshäuser," *Zeitschrift f. Waren-u. Kaufhäuser*, May 18, 1904, clipping in GehStA I HA Rep. 93B, no. 1436.

39 Ibid., Berlin, February 4, 1906 (gez. Reichel, Königliche Branddirektor).

40 Schocken, *Die Entwicklung der Warenhäuser*, 15–17.

41 See Colze, *Berliner Warenhäuser*, 63–64, 70–71.

42 *Berlin Morgen-Zeitung*, January 31, 1929.

43 Stücklen, *Purpus*, 85.

44 Ibid., 95.

45 Ibid., 99.

46 Ibid., 111.

47 Ibid., 95.

48 Baum, "Jape im Warenhaus," 215.

49 Ibid., 220, 233.

50 Wolfgang Schivelbusch, *Disenchanted Night: The Industrialization of Light in the Nineteenth Century*, trans. Angela Davies (Berkeley, CA, 1995), 4.

51 Zola, *Ladies' Paradise*, 28.

52 Ward, *Weimar Surfaces*, 200.

53 Repp, "Marketing," 30; Reinhardt, *Von der Reklame zum Marketing*, 280.

54 Gerlach, *Das Warenhaus*, 102.

55 Stürzebecher, *Das Berliner Warenhaus*, 25.

56 Ibid., 25.

57 Ibid., 200.

58 Joachim Schlör, *Nights in the Big City* (London, 1998), 66.

59 *Berliner Morgen-Zeitung*, October 13, 1928; "Warenhausbrand in der City," *Vossische Zeitung*, October 12, 1928.

60 Siwertz, *Das große Warenhaus*, 324.

61 Ibid., 37.

62 Ibid., 158.

63 Ibid., 304.

64 Ibid., 308.

65 Ibid., 320.

66 Ibid.

67 Ibid.

68 See Franziska Schößler, *Börsenfieber und Kaufrusch: Ökonomie, Judentum und Weiblichkeit bei Theodor Fontane, Heinrich Mann, Thomas Mann, Arthur Schnitzler und Émile Zola* (Bielefeld, 2009), 301.

69 Köhrer, *Warenhaus Berlin*, 20.

70 Ibid., 16–17.

71 Ibid., 17.

72 Ibid., 39.

73 Ibid., 138.

74 Ibid., 39.

75 Ibid., 47.

76 Ibid., 93.

77 Ibid., 122.

78 Ibid.,

79 Ibid., 129.

80 Ibid., 131.

81 Ibid., 135.

82 Ibid., 138.

83 Ibid., 144.

84 Ibid.

85 Briesen, *Warenhaus*, 14. See also Schößler, *Börsenfieber*, which, unlike Briesen, brings Jewishness into the analysis.

86 See, for example, Erich Köhrer, "Die Kunst als Arbeit und Genuss," in Kaufhaus Israel Album 1914: *Arbeit und Erholung*.

87 Rieger, *Technology and the Culture of Modernity*, 2.

88 Georg Heym, "Der Irre," in *Der Dieb. Ein Novellbuch* (Leipzig, 1913), 27–50.

89 Ibid., 46.

90 Ibid.

91 Ibid., 49.

92 Ibid., 47.

93 Ibid.

94 Ibid., 49.

95 Hans Vogt, *Du Kommst zu Spät: Eine Szene aus dem Warenhaus* (Leipzig, 1914).

96 Manfred Georg, *Aufruhr im Warenhaus* (Berlin-Friedenau, 1928).

97 Manfred Georg, "Aufruhr im Warenhaus: Inhaltsangabe und Handlungsumriß," Deutsches Literaturarchiv A: George 75.5887.

98 Ibid.

99 "Kritiken über Manfred Georg," in Manfred Georg, "Aufruhr im Warenhaus: Inhaltsangabe und Handlungsumriß," Deutsches Literaturarchiv A: George 75.5887.

100 Mila Ganeva, "Elegance and Spectacle in Berlin: The Gerson Fashion Store and the Rise of the Modern Fashion Show," in *The Places and Spaces of Fashion, 1800–2007*, ed. John Potvin (New York, 2009), 126–27, and Ganeva, "Weimar Film as Fashion Show: *Konfektionskomödien* or Fashion Farces from Lubitsch to the End of the Silent Era," *German Studies Review* 30 (2007): 288–310. See also Rappaport, *Shopping for Pleasure*, chap. 6, and Hake, *Passions and Deceptions*, 26–28. Lubitsch's family was in the clothing business, and he was school friends with Georg Manasse, managing director of Kaufhaus Schocken.

101 Kläger, *Zwischenfall im Warenhaus*, 109.

102 Michael Pearson, *The Store* (New York, 1986).

103 The incident is recounted in Werner Mosse, "Terms of Successful Integration: The Tietz Family, 1858–1923," *Leo Baeck Institute Year Book* 34 (1989): 137.

104 See LAB A Pr.Br.Rep 030, Nr. 12005; Molly Loberg, "The Streetscape of Economic Crisis: Politics, Commerce, and Urban Space in Interwar Berlin," *Journal of Modern History* 85 (June 2013): 364–402; Loberg, "The Fortress Shop: Consumer Culture, Violence, and Security in Weimar Berlin," *Journal of Contemporary History* 49, no. 4 (October 2014): 675–701.

105 See Heinrich Uhlig, *Die Warenhäuser im Dritten Reich* (Cologne, 1956), 34.

106 Simone Ladwig-Winters, "The Attack on Berlin Department Stores (Warenhäuser) after 1933," in *Probing the Depths of German Anti-Semitism: German Society and the Persecution of the Jews*, ed. David Bankier (New York, 2000), 246–70.

107 Bundesarchiv Berlin R 1501/125683 (Filmangelegenheiten), Berlin, February 1931, Bl. 277.

108 Uhlig, *Die Warenhäuser*; Perry, *Christmas in Germany*, 183–85.

109 "Anschläge auf Warenhäuser," in *Vossische Zeitung*, December 20, 1932.

110 Uhlig, *Die Warenhäuser*, 68.

111 Letter to Oberpresident der Reinprovinz in Koblenz, Koblenz, September 16, 1932, GehStA I HA Rep. 120 CVIII 1 Nr. 54, Bd. 39.

112 Letter from Preußischer Minister des Innern, Berlin, den 1. November 1932, to Minister für Handel und Gewerbe, GehStA I HA Rep. 120 CVIII 1 Nr. 54, Bd. 39.

113 Perry, *Christmas in Germany*, 182–83.

114 Loberg, "Fortress Shop."

115 "Gegen Gewalttätigkeiten," in *Vossische Zeitung*, March 2, 1933, clipping in Schocken Institute Archive, box 115/111: Zeitungsausschnitte zum Thema "Kampf gegen die Warenhäuser" 7.3.33–2.2.35.

116 Uhlig, *Die Warenhäuser*, 78.

117 Avraham Barkai, *From Boycott to Annihilation: The Economic Struggle of German Jews, 1933–1943* (Boston, 1990); Gellately, "An der Schwelle der Moderne," 153–54; Uhlig, *Die Warenhäuser*, 115–16.

118 "Ein Erlass zur Warenhausfrage," clipping from *Frankfurter Zeitung*, July 9, 1933, in Schocken Institute Archive, box 115/111: Zeitungsausschnitte zum Thema "Kampf gegen die Warenhäuser" 7.3.33–2.2.35.

119 Schocken Institute Archive, box 115/111: Zeitungsausschnitte zum Thema "Kampf gegen die Warenhäuser" 7.3.33–2.2.35. In 1928 *Simplicissimus* ran a cartoon, drawn by Thomas Theodor Heine, showing a Nazi official caught while purchasing cloth for German flags at a Wertheim store. *Simplicissimus* 33 (August 27, 1928), 280.

120 Uhlig, *Die Warenhäuser*, 179.

121 See H. G. Reissner, "The Histories of 'Kaufhaus N. Israel' and of Wilfrid Israel," *Leo Baeck Institute Year Book* 3 (1958): 227.

122 "Wann Brennen die Kaufhäuser?" (April 25, 1967), Kommune 1 pamphlet 8, http://www.infopartisan.net/archive/1967/2667118.html.

123 See Victoria de Grazia, *Irresistible Empire: American's Advance through Twentieth-Century Europe* (Cambridge, MA, 2005), introduction.

124 See Wilfried Mausbach, "'Burn, warehouse, burn!': Modernity, Counterculture, and the Vietnam War in West Germany," in *Between Marx and Coca-Cola: Youth Cultures in Changing European Societies*, ed. Alex Schildt and Detlef Siegfried (New York, 2006), 175.

125 See Gerd Koenen, *Vesper, Ensslin, Baader. Urszenen des deutschen Terrorismus* (Frankfurt, 2005).

126 Sara Hakemi, *Anschlag und Spektakel: Flugblätter der Kommune 1, Erklärungen von Ensslin/Baader und der frühen RAF* (Berlin, 2010), 10.

127 J. Smith and André Moncourt, eds., *The Red Army Faction: A Documentary History* (Montreal, 2009).

Conclusion

1 Fischer and Ladwig-Winters, *Die Wertheims*, 347–58.

2 Ronald Smothers, "A Holocaust Reparations Settlement Makes Its Way to South Jersey," *New York Times*, January 24, 2006.

3 See Leigh Schmidt, "The Commercialization of the Calendar: American Holidays and the Culture of Consumption, 1870–1930," *Journal of American History* 78 (December 1991): 887–916, esp. 899.

4 Jarausch and Geyer, *Shattered Past*, 313.
5 Paul Betts, "The *Nierentisch* Nemesis: Organic Design as West German Pop Culture," *German History* 19 (2001): 209.

SELECTED BIBLIOGRAPHY

Interviews

Arlen, Walter, and Howard Myers. August 3, 2011, Santa Monica, CA.
Petersdorf, Rudy, and Rikki Horne. August 23, 2009, Ojai, CA.

Unpublished Memoirs

Bamberger, Lotte. "A Family History for My Children and Grandchildren," 1992.
Gerstenberg, Karl. "Memorien von Karl Gerstenberg: geb. 1891 Berlin, gest. 1965 New York." No date.
Jandorf, Adolf. "Erinnerungen an Meinen Vater," Leo Baeck Institute, ME 335, 1967.
Schwabe, Carl. "Mein Leben in Deutschland," Leo Baeck Institute, ME 586, 1941.
Winterfeldt, Hans. "Deutschland: Ein Zeitbild, 1926–1945. Leidensweg eines deutschen Juden in den ersten 19 Jahren seines Lebens," MM 81, 1969.

Archival Collections

Bundesarchiv Berlin-Lichterfelde (BARCH)
    NS26 Hautparchiv der NSDAP
    R5 Reichsverkehrsministerium
    R/8051 Vereinigung für freie Wirtschaft, e.V.
Deutsches Technikmuseum, Historical Archive, Berlin
Geheimes Staatsarchiv Preußischer Kulturbesitz (GehStA), Berlin
    Repositorium 93B Ministerium für öffentliche Arbeiten
    Repositorium 120 Ministerium für Handel und Gewerbe
Getty Research Institute, Los Angeles
    Erich and Luise Mendelsohn Papers
Kunstbibliothek Berlin
    Erich Mendelsohn Papers
Landesarchiv Berlin (LAB)
    -A Pr. Br. Rep 030. Polizeipräsidium
    -A Rep 342–02. Amtsgericht Charlottenburg. Handelsregister. Library
Leo Baeck Institute (LBI), New York
    Israel Family Collection (AR 187; AR 783; AR 4790)
    Carl Jaburg Collection (AR 10067)
    Adolf Jandorf Collection (AR 3144)
    George Manasse Collection (AR 6379)
    Hermann Tietz Collection (AR 1943)
    Leonhard Tietz Collection (AR 2434)
    Wertheim Department Store Berlin Collection (AR 2630)

Sächsisches Staatsarchiv, Chemnitz (SSSC)
   33309 Georg Manasse Papers
   31451 Schocken-Konzern & Nachfolger
Schocken Institute, Concern Archive, Jerusalem
University of Southern California Library, Special Collections, Feuchtwanger Memorial Library

Fiction and Stage

Baum, Vicki. *Der große Ausverkauf.* Cologne: Kiepenheuer & Witsch, 1983. Originally published in 1937.
——. "Jape im Warenhaus." In *Die anderen Tage. Novellen von Vicki Baum.* Berlin: Ullstein Verlag, 1931, 215–41.
Böhme, Margarete. *W.A.G.M.U.S.* Berlin: Fontane, 1911.
Carlé, Wilhelm. "Die Rolltreppe. Der Roman eines jungen Mädchens." Novel fragment in Schocken Institute Archive. Box 185/228/1.
Ely, Leopold. *Das Warenhausmädchen, Volksstück mit Gesang in 1 Akt.* LAB A Pr.Br. Rep. 030–05–02—Polizeipräsidium, Theaterzensur (neu), Nr. 5743. No date.
Feuchtwanger, Lion. "Warenhaus-Revue." USC Special Collections. Feuchtwanger Papers. Box D2.
Freund, Julius. *Chauffeur ins Metropol! Die neue Revue.* LAB A Pr. Br. Rep. 030–05–02, Nr. 5439 (1912).
Freund, Max. *Der Warenhauskönig.* Barmen: Eos-Verlag, 1912.
Georg, Manfred. *Aufruhr im Warenhaus.* Berlin-Friedenau: Weltbücher-Verlag, 1928.
Georgy, Ernst. *Der Konfektionsbaron. Ein Zeitbild aus der Konfektion.* Stuttgart: Union Deutsche Verlagsgesellschaft, 1923.
Gerhard, Walter (pseud. for Wilhelm Rubiner). *Die Warenhausgräfin.* Leipzig: Rekord Verlag Krömer & Co., 1923.
Gernsheim, Walter. *Der Warenhaus-König.* Dresden: Mignon-Verlag, 1921.
Gleit, Maria (pseud. for Hertha Gleitsmann). *Abetilung Herrenmode. Roman eines Warenhausmädels.* Vienna: Umonesta-Verlag, 1933.
Hartung, Max. *Kleptomanie. Schwank in einem Aufzug.* Leipzig: Reclam Verlag, 1900.
Heine, Thomas Theodor. "Der Teufel im Warenhaus." In *Die Märchen,* 7–14. (East) Berlin: Aufbau Verlag, 1978. Originally published in 1935.
Heym, Georg. "Der Irre." In *Der Dieb. Ein Novellbuch.* Leipzig: Rowohlt, 1913.
Kläger, Emil. *Zwischenfall im Warenhaus. Komödie in drei Akten.* Vienna: Georg Marton, 1933.
Köhrer, Erich. *Warenhaus Berlin: Ein Roman aus der Weltstadt.* Berlin: Wedekind, 1909.
Popper, Otto Reinhardt. *Das Warenhausfräulein, Volksstück in 5 Akten von dem Messingputzer.* 1908. LAB A Pr.Br.Rep. 030–05–02—Polizeipräsidium, Theaterzensur (neu), Nr. 4337.
Schiffer, Marcellus (text), and Mischa Spoliansky (music). *Es Liegt in der Luft (Ein Speil im Warenhaus).* Munich: Dreiklang-Dreimasken, 1928. Provided by Felix Bloch Erben Theater Company.
Schweriner, Oscar. *Arbeit: Ein Warenhausroman.* Berlin: Duncker, 1912.
Siwertz, Sigfrid. *Das große Warenhaus.* Translated from the Swedish by Alfons Fedor Cohn. Berlin: Brandusche Verlag, Jüdischer Buchverlag, 1928.
Stahr, Margarete. "Aus dem Warenhaus." *Illustrirte Zeitung* 121 (1903), 39–40, 77–78.
Sternberg, Alexander. *Ein Warenhaus-Mädchen: Schicksale einer Gefallenen.* Berlin: Verlag moderner Lektüre, 1909.

Stücklen, Wilhelm. *Purpus: Ein Schauspiel in drei Akten*. Berlin: Drei Masken Verlag, 1918.
Trott, Magda. *Der Schöne Abteilungschef*. Leipzig: Rekord Verlag Krömer & Co., 1923.
Türk, Werner. *Konfektion*. Berlin: Agis-Verlag, 1932.
Vogt, Hans. *Du Kommst zu Spät: Eine Szene aus dem Warenhaus*. Leipzig: Bruno Volger Verlag, 1914.
Wiener-Braunsberg, Josef. *Warenhausmädchen: Roman aus Berlin der Gegenwart*. Berlin: Ehrlich, 1922.
Wohlbrück, Olga. *Der große Rachen*. Berlin: Scherl, 1915.
Zola, Émile. *The Ladies' Paradise*. Translated by Brian Nelson. Oxford: Oxford University Press, 1995.

Newspapers

Beriner Tageblatt
Berliner Morgen-Zeitung
Cosmopolis: Revue Internationale
Deutsche-Jugend-Zeitung
Deutsche Rundschau
Fliegende Blätter
Hammer: Blätter für deutschen Sinn
Hannoverscher Courier
Illustrierter Beobachter
Jüdisches Gemeindeblatt Berlin
Lustige Blätter
Magdeburgische Zeitung
Mitteilungen aus dem Verein zur Abwehr des Antisemitismus
Morgen: Wochenschrift für Deutsche Kultur
Österreichische Verbands-Feuerwehr-Zeitung
Praktische Berlinerin
Querschnitt
Rote Fahne
Simplicissimus
Staatsbürger-Zeitung
Völkischer Beobachter
Vossische Zeitung
Wahrheit
Wiener Bilder: Illustrirtes Familienblatt
Zeitschrift für Waren-und Kaufhäuser

Selected Published Works

Primary Sources

Anonymous. *Aus den Warenhäusern beider Welten. Die Organisation der größten Berliner, Pariser, und Amerikanischen Warenhäusern*. Berlin: L. Schottlaender, 1908.
Anonymous. *Das Warenhaus, eine Gefahr? Was jeder Deutsche über das Warenhaus und seine Auswirkungen wissen Muß*. Munich: Deutscher Volksverlag, 1930.
Baer, Kurt Stefan. *Der Kampf gegen Großbetriebe des Einzelhandels und die Volkswirtschaft*. Jena: Fischer, 1932

Benjamin, Walter. *The Arcades Project*. Translated by Howard Eiland and Kevin McLaughlin. Cambridge, MA: Harvard University Press, 1999.

Buchner, Hans. *Dämonen der Wirtschaft: Gestalten und dunkle Gewalten aus dem Leben unserer Tage*. Munich: F. Eher, 1928.

———. *Warenhauspolitik und Nationalsozialismus*. Munich: F. Eher Nachfolger, 1929.

Buschan, Georg. *Geschlecht und Verbrechen*. Berlin: Hermann Seemann Nachfolger, 1908.

Colze, Leo (Leo Cohn). *Berliner Warenhäuser*. Berlin Hermann Seemann Nachfolger, 1908.

Creutz, Max. *Joseph M. Olbrich. Das Warenhaus Tietz in Düsseldorf*. Berlin: E. Wasmuth, 1909.

Das Kaufhaus Schocken im Jahre 1926. Vorträge, Ansprachen und Leitsätze aus früheren Schocken-Hauszeitungen. Nuremberg: Merkur AG, 1952.

Dehn, Paul, *Die Großbazare und Massenzweiggeschäfte*. Berlin: Trowitzsch & Sohn, 1899.

———. *Hinter den Kulissen des modernen Geschäfts*. Berlin: Trowitzsch & Sohn, 1897.

Deutsch, Leo. "Zur Frage der Kleptomanie." *Zeitschrift für die gesamte Neurologie und Psychiatrie* 152 (1935): 208–34.

Eisen, Lothar (pseud. for Joseph Bernhard Schneider). "Psychologie des Warenhauses," *Geschlecht und Gesellschaft* 8 (1913): 388–97.

50 Jahre Leonhard Tietz 1879–1929. Cologne: L. Tietz AG, 1929.

Gerber, G. *Warenhauspest*. Plauen: Kampfgemeinschaft gegen Warenhaus und Konsum der NSDAP, 1932.

Göhre, Paul. *Das Warenhaus*. Frankfurt: Rütten & Loening, 1907.

Gronemann, Sammy. *Erinnerungen*. Berlin: Philo Fine Arts, 2002.

Hermann Tietz, der grösste Warenhaus-Konzern Europas im Eigenbesitz. Ein Buch sichtbarer Erfolge. Berlin: M. Schröder, 1932.

Hirsch, Julius. *Das Warenhaus in Westdeutschland; seine Organisation und Wirkungen*. Leipzig: Deichert, 1910.

Kracauer, Siegfried. "Der Dichter im Warenhaus." In *Siegfried Kracauer. Aufsätze, 1927–1931*, edited by Inka Mülder-Bach, 228–31. Frankfurt: Suhrkamp, 1990.

———. "Der Verkaufs-Tempel." In *Siegfried Kracauer. Aufsätze, 1927–1931*, edited by Inka Mülder-Bach, 349–51. Frankfurt: Suhrkamp, 1990.

Laquer, Leopold. *Der Warenhaus-Diebstahl*. Halle: Marhold, 1907.

Leppmann, A. "Über Ladendiebinnen." *Archiv für Psychiatrie* 35 (1902): 264.

Lux, Käthe. *Studien über die Entwicklung der Warenhäuser in Deutschland*. Jena: Fischer, 1910.

Mendelsohn, Erich. *Bauten und Skizzen*. Berlin (1924).

Nordmann, Cajus. "Die Warenhausdiebinnen." *Die Welt der Frau* 26 (1907), 85–86.

Osborn, Max. *KaDeWe. Kaufhaus des Westens. 1907–1932. Festschrift anläßlich des 25-jährigen Bestehens*. Berlin, 1932.

Plaut, Felix. "Ueber krankhafte Kaufsucht." *Monatsschrift für Kriminalpsychologie und Strafrechtsreform* 3 (1906): 409–16.

Probleme des Warenhauses. Beiträge zur Geschichte und Erkenntnis der Entwicklung des Warenhauses in Deutschland. Berlin: Verband Deutscher Waren-und Kaufhäuser, 1928.

Roth, Joseph. "Das ganz große Warenhaus." In *Joseph Roth in Berlin: Ein Lesebuch für Spaziergänger*, edited by Michael Bienert, 159–61. Cologne: Kiepenheuer & Witsch, 1996.

Schocken, Salman. *Die Entwicklung der Warenhäuser in Deutschland und die Kaufmännischen Voraussetzungen der Warenhausbauten*. Leipzig: Poeschel, 1911.

Sombart, Werner. *Die Juden und das Wirtschaftsleben*. Leipzig: Duncker & Humblot, 1911.

——. "Die Reklame." *Morgen: Wochenschrift für deutsche Kultur* 2 (March 6, 1908): 281–86.

——. "Das Warenhaus. Ein Gebilde des hochkapitalischer Zeitalters." In *Probleme des Warenhauses: Beiträge zur Geschichte und Erkenntnis der Entwicklung des Warenhauses in Deutschland*, 77–87. Berlin, 1928.

Stekel, Wilhelm. *Impulshandlungen: Wandertrieb, Dipsomanie, Kleptomanie, Pyromanie und verwandte Zustände*. Berlin: Urban & Schwarzenberg, 1922.

Vier Vorträge über den gegenwärtigen Stand und die Aufgaben des Großeinzelhandels. Berlin: Verband Deutscher Waren-und Kaufhäuser, 1931.

Wagner, H. *Über die Organisation der Warenhäuser, Kaufhäuser und der großen Spezialgeschäfte*. Leipzig: Carl Ernst Poeschel, 1911.

Wiener, Alfred. *Das Warenhaus: Kauf-, Geschäfts-, Büro-Haus*. Berlin: Wasmuth, 1912.

Wilhelm, Eugen. "Ein Fall von sogenannter Kleptomanie." *Archiv für Kriminal-Anthropologie und Kriminalistik* 16 (1904): 156–66.

Wilke, Arthur. "Die Psychologie des Warenhauses." *Der Deutsche* 5 (February 2, 1907): 550–54.

Wussow, Otto Erich von. *Geschichte und Entwicklung der Warenhäuser*. Berlin: S. Simon, 1906.

Secondary Sources

Abelson, Elaine S. *When Ladies Go A-Thieving: Middle-Class Shoplifters in the Victorian Department Store*. New York: Oxford University Press, 1989.

Auslander, Leora. *Taste and Power: Furnishing Modern France*. Berkeley: University of California Press, 1996.

Baranowski, Shelley, *Strength through Joy*. Cambridge: Cambridge University Press, 2004.

Baranowski, Shelley, and Ellen Furlough. *Being Elsewhere: Tourism, Consumer Culture, and Identity in Modern Europe and North America*. Ann Arbor: University of Michigan Press, 2001.

Barkai, Avraham. *From Boycott to Annihilation: The Economic Struggle of German Jews, 1933–1943*. Boston: Brandeis University Press, 1990.

Baudrillard, Jean. *Consumer Society: Myths and Structures*. London: Sage Publications, 1998.

——. "For a Critique of the Political Economy of the Sign." In *Jean Baudrillard, Selected Writings*, edited by Mark Poster, 60–100. Stanford, CA: Stanford University Press, 2002.

Behn, Helga, "Die Architektur des deutschen Warenhauses von ihren Anfängen bis 1933." PhD dissertation, University of Cologne, 1984.

Bennathan, Esra. "Die demographische und wirtschafliche Struktur der Juden." In *Entscheidungsjahr 1932. Zur Judenfrage in der Endphase der Weimarer Republik*, edited by Werner E. Mosse, 87–131. Tübingen: Paul Siebeck, 1965.

Benson, Susan Porter. *Counter Cultures: Saleswomen, Managers and Customers in American Department Stores, 1890–1940*. Urbana: University of Illinois Press, 1986.

Bowlby, Rachel. *Shopping with Freud*. London: Taylor & Francis, 1993.

Breckman, Warren. "Disciplining Consumption: The Debate about Luxury in Wilhelmine Germany, 1890–1914." *Journal of Social History* 24 (September 1991): 485–505.

Brenner, Michael. *The Renaissance of Jewish Culture in Weimar Germany.* New Haven, CT: Yale University Press, 1998.

Briesen, Detlef. *Warenhaus, Massenkonsum und Sozialmoral: Zur Geschichte der Konsumkritik im 20. Jahrhundert.* Frankfurt: Campus, 2001.

Buck-Morss, Susan. *The Dialectics of Seeing: Walter Benjamin and the Arcades Project.* Cambridge, MA: MIT Press, 1989.

Busch-Petersen, Nils. *Oscar Tietz: Von Birnbaum / Provinz Posen zum Warenhauskönig von Berlin.* Berlin: Hentrich & Hentrich, 2004.

Ciarlo, David. *Advertising Empire: Race and Visual Culture in Imperial Germany.* Cambridge, MA: Harvard University Press, 2011.

Conrad, Sebastian. *Globalisation and the Nation in Imperial Germany.* Translated by Sorcha O'Hagan. Cambridge: Cambridge University Press, 2010.

Crew, David, ed. *Consuming Germany in the Cold War.* Oxford: Bloomsbury, 2003.

Crossick, Geoffrey, and Serge Jaumain, eds. *Cathedrals of Consumption: The European Department Store, 1850–1939.* Aldershot, UK: Ashgate, 1999.

David, Anthony. *The Patron: A Life of Salman Schocken, 1877–1959.* New York: Metropolitan Books, 2003.

de Grazia, Victoria. *Irresistible Empire: America's Advance through 20th-Century Europe.* Cambridge, MA: Harvard University Press, 2005.

de Grazia, Victoria, with Ellen Furlough, eds. *The Sex of Things: Gender and Consumption in Historical Perspective.* Berkeley: University of California Press, 1996.

Dessa (Deborah Petroz-Abeles). *A Tribute to Kaufhaus N. Israel, 1815–1939: Collages and Paintings Based on the N. Israel Album 1912 "Hygiene im Wandel der Zeiten."* Pully, Switzerland: self-published, 2003.

Fischer, Erica, and Simone Ladwig-Winters. *Die Wertheims. Geschichte einer Familie.* Berlin: Rowolt, 2004.

Frei, Helmut. *Tempel der Kauflust: Eine Geschichte der Warenhauskultur.* Leipzig: Edition Leipzig, 1997.

Friedberg, Ann. *Window Shopping: Cinema and the Postmodern.* Berkeley: University of California Press, 1994.

Fritzsche, Peter. *Reading Berlin 1900.* Cambridge, MA: Harvard University Press, 1998.

Fuchs, Konrad. *Ein Konzern aus Sachsen. Das Kaufhaus Schocken 1901–1953.* Stuttgart: Deutsche Verlagsanstalt, 1990.

Furlough, Ellen. *Consumer Cooperation in France: The Politics of Consumption.* Ithaca, NY: Cornell University Press, 1991.

Ganeva, Mila. "The Beautiful Body of the Mannequin: Display Practices in Weimar Germany." In *Leibhaftige Moderne: Körper in Kunst und Massenmedien, 1918–1933,* edited by Michael Cowan and Kai Marcel Sicks, 152–69. Bielefeld: Transcript, 2005.

——. "Elegance and Spectacle in Berlin: The Gerson Fashion Store and the Rise of the Modern Fashion Show." In *The Places and Spaces of Fashion, 1800–2007,* edited by John Potvin, 121–38. New York: Routledge, 2009.

——. "Weimar Film as Fashion Show: *Konfektionskomödien* or Fashion Farces from Lubitsch to the End of the Silent Era." *German Studies Review* 30 (2007): 288–310.

——. *Women in Weimar Fashion: Discourses and Displays in German Culture, 1918–1933.* Rochester, NY: Camden House, 2008.

Gellately, Robert. "An der Schwelle der Moderne. Warenhäuser und Ihre Feinde in Deutschland." In *Im Banne der Metropole. Berlin und London in den zwanziger Jahren,* edited by Peter Alter, 131–56. Göttingen: Vandenhoeck & Ruprecht, 1993.

——. *The Politics of Economic Despair: Shopkeepers and German Politics, 1890–1914.* London: Sage Publications, 1974.

Gellately, Robert, and Nathan Stolzfus, eds. *Social Outsiders in Nazi Germany.* Princeton, NJ: Princeton University Press, 2001.

Gerlach, Siegfried. *Das Warenhaus in Deutschland.* Wiesbaden: F. Steiner Verlag, 1988.

Guenther, Irene. *Nazi Chic? Fashioning Women in the Third Reich.* Oxford: Bloomsbury Academic, 2004.

Hamlin, David D. *Work and Play. The Production and Consumption of Toys in Germany, 1870–1914.* Ann Arbor: University of Michigan Press, 2007.

Hart, Mitchell B. "Jews, Race, and Capitalism in the German-Jewish Context." *Jewish History* 19, no. 1 (2005): 49–63.

Herbert, Gilbert, and Liliane Richter. *Through a Clouded Glass: Mendelsohn, Wijdeveld, and the Jewish Connection.* Tübingen: Ernst Wasmuth Verlag, 2008.

Homburg, Heidrun. "Warenhausunternehmen und ihre Gründer in Frankreich und Deutschland." *Jahrbuch für Wirtschaftsgeschichte* (1992/1), 183–219.

James, Kathleen. *Erich Mendelsohn and the Architecture of German Modernism.* Cambridge: Cambridge University Press, 1997.

Jarausch, Konrad H., and Michael Geyer. *Shattered Past: Reconstructing German Histories.* Princeton, NJ: Princeton University Press, 2002.

Jelavich, Peter. *Berlin Cabaret.* Cambridge, MA: Harvard University Press, 1996.

König, Gudrun M. *Konsumkultur. Inszenierte Warenwelt um 1900.* Vienna: Böhlau Verlag, 2009.

——. "Zum Warenhausdiebstahl um 1900: Über juristische Definitionen, medizinische Interpretamente und die Geschlechterforschung." In *Geschlecht und Materielle Kultur: Frauen-Sachen, Männer-Sachen, Sach-Kulturen,* edited by Gabriele Mentges, Ruth-E. Mohrmann, and Cornelia Foerster, 49–66. Münster: Waxmann, 2000.

Kremer, Roberta S., ed. *Broken Threads: The Destruction of the Jewish Fashion Industry in Germany and Austria.* Oxford: Berg Publishers, 2007.

Kreutzmüller, Christoph. *Ausverkauf: Die Vernichtung der jüdischen Gewerbetätigkeit in Berlin 1930–1945.* Berlin: Metropol, 2012.

Ladwig-Winters, Simone. "The Attack on Berlin Department Stores (Warenhäuser) after 1933." In *Probing the Depths of German Anti-Semitism: German Society and the Persecution of the Jews,* edited by David Bankier, 246–70. New York: Berghahn Books, 2000.

——. *Wertheim: Geschichte eines Warenhauses.* Berlin: Be.Bra Verlag, 1997.

Laermans, Rudi. "Learning to Consume: Early Department Stores and the Shaping of Modern Consumer Culture (1860–1914)." *Theory, Culture, Society* 10, no. 4 (1993): 79–102.

Lamberty, Christiane. *Reklame in Deutschland: Wahrnehmung, Professionalisierung und Kritik der Wirtschaftswerbung.* Berlin: Duncker & Humblot, 2000.

Leach, William. *Land of Desire: Merchants, Power, and the Rise of a New American Culture.* New York: Vintage, 1992.

Lenz, Thomas. *Konsum und Modernisierung. Die Debatte um das Warenhaus als Diskurs um die Moderne.* Bielefeld: Transcript Verlag, 2011.

Lethen, Helmut. *Cool Conduct: The Culture of Distance in Weimar Germany.* Translated by Don Reneau. Berkeley: University of California Press, 2001.

Loberg, Molly. "The Fortress Shop: Consumer Culture, Violence, and Security in Weimar Berlin." *Journal of Contemporary History* 49, no. 4 (October 2014): 675–701.

Makela, Maria. "The Rise and Fall of the Flapper Dress: Nationalism and Anti-Semitism in Early-Twentieth-Century Discourses on German Fashion." *Journal of Popular Culture* 34, no. 3 (Winter 2000): 183–208.

Marx, Karl. *Capital: A Critique of Political Economy.* Vol. 1. Translated by Ben Fowkes. New York: Penguin Books, 1976.

——. *Grundrisse: Foundations of the Critique of Political Economy.* Translated by Martin Nicolaus. London: Penguin Classics, 1973.

Meiners, Antonia. *100 Jahre KaDeWe.* Berlin: Nicolaische Verlagsbuchhandlung, 2007.

Miller, Michael B. *The Bon Marché: Bourgeois Culture and the Department Store, 1869–1920.* Princeton, NJ: Princeton University Press, 1981.

Moses, Siegfried. "Salman Schocken: His Economic and Zionist Activities." *Leo Baeck Institute Year Book* 5 (1960): 73–104.

Mosse, George L. "The Image of the Jew in German Popular Culture: Felix Dahn and Gustav Freytag." *Leo Baeck Institute Year Book* 2 (1957): 218–27.

Mosse, Werner E. *Jews in the German Economy: The German-Jewish Economic Élite, 1820–1935.* New York: Clarendon Press, 1987.

——. "Terms of Successful Integration: The Tietz Family, 1858–1923." *Leo Baeck Institute Year Book* 34 (1989): 131–61.

Müllener, Eduard-Rudolf. "Die Entstehung des Kleptomaniebegriffes." *Suddhoffs Archiv für Geschichte der Medizin und der Naturwissenschaften* 48 (1964): 216–32.

Nitzan-Shiftan, Alona. "Erich Mendelsohn: From Berlin to Jerusalem." Master's thesis, Massachusetts Institute of Technology, 1993.

Nord, Philip G. *The Politics of Resentment: Shopkeeper Protest in Nineteenth-Century Paris.* New Brunswick, NJ: Transaction Publishers, 2005.

Palmer, Renate. *Der Stuttgarter Schocken-Bau von Erich Mendelsohn. Die Geschichte eines Kaufhauses und seiner Architektur.* Tübingen: Silberburg-Verlag, 1995.

Perry, Joe. *Christmas in Germany: A Cultural History.* Chapel Hill: University of North Carolina Press, 2010.

Poppel, Stephen M. *Zionism in Germany, 1897–1933: The Shaping of a Jewish Identity.* Philadelphia: Jewish Publication Society, 1977.

Presner, Todd. *Mobile Modernity: Germans, Jews, Trains.* New York: Columbia University Press, 2007.

Rappaport, Erika. *Shopping for Pleasure: Women in the Making of London's West End.* Princeton, NJ: Princeton University Press, 2000.

Reinhardt, Dirk. *Von der Reklame zum Marketing: Geschichte der Wirtschaftswerbung in Deutschland.* Berlin: Wiley-VCH Verlag, 1993.

Reissner, H. G. "The Histories of 'Kaufhaus N. Israel' and of Wilfrid Israel." *Leo Baeck Institute Year Book* 3 (1958): 227–56.

Reuveni, Gideon, and Nils H. Roemer, eds. *Longing, Belonging, and the Making of Jewish Consumer Culture.* Leiden: Brill, 2010.

Reuveni, Gideon, and Sarah Wobick-Segev, eds. *The Economy in Jewish History: New Perspectives on the Relationship between Ethnicity and Economic Life.* New York, Berghahn Books, 2010.

Richter, Thilo. *Erich Mendelsohns Kaufhaus Schocken. Jüdische kulturgeschichte in Chemnitz.* Leipzig: Passage, 1998.

Rohdenburg, Günther. *Das War Das Neue Leben: Leben und Wirkung des Jüdischen Kaufhausbesitzers Julius Bamberger und seiner Familie.* Bremen: Edition Temmen, 2000.

Rooch, Alarich. *Zwischen Museum und Warenhaus: Ästhetisierungsprozesse und sozial-kommunikative Raumaneignungen des Bürgertums (1823–1920)*. Oberhausen: Athena, 2001.

Rowe, Dorothy. *Representing Berlin: Sexuality and the City in Imperial and Weimar Germany*. London: Ashgate, 2003.

Rürup, Reinhard, ed. *Jüdische Geschichte in Berlin: Bilder und Dokumente*. Berlin: Edition Hentrich, 1995.

Scharnholz, Lars. *Kaufhaus Schocken Cottbus*. Leipzig: Diekmann, 2000.

Schivelbusch, Wolfgang. *Disenchanted Night: The Industrialization of Light in the Nineteenth Century*. Translated by Angela Davies. Berkeley: University of California Press, 1995.

——. *The Railway Journey: The Industrialization of Time and Space*. Berkeley: University of California Press, 1986.

Schlör, Joachim. *Nights in the Big City*. Translated by Pierre Gottfried Imhof and Dafydd Rees Roberts. London: Reaktion Books, 1998.

Schocken, G. "Salman Schocken: Ich Werde Seinesgleichen Nicht Mehr Sehen." *Der Monat* 20 (1968), 13–30.

Schößler, Franziska, *Börsenfieber und Kaufrusch: Ökonomie, Judentum und Weiblichkeit bei Theodor Fontane, Heinrich Mann, Thomas Mann, Arthur Schnitzler und Émile Zola*. Bielefeld: Antithesis Verlag, 2009.

Schwarz, Jürgen. "Architektur und Kommerz. Studien zur deutschen Kauf-und Warenhausarchitektur vor dem Ersten Weltkrieg am Beispiel der Frankfurter Zeil." PhD dissertation, Johann-Wolfgang-Goethe-Universität, Frankfurt, 1995.

Shteir, Rachel. *The Steal: A Cultural History of Shoplifting*. New York: Penguin Books, 2012.

Smail, Deborah. " 'Sadly Materialistic . . .': Perceptions of Shops and Shopping Streets in Weimar Germany." *Journal of Popular Culture* 34, no. 3 (Winter 2000): 141–61.

Spiekermann, Uwe. *Basis der Konsumgesellschaft. Entstehung und Entwicklung des modernen Kleinhandels in Deutschland 1850–1914*. Munich: Beck, 1999.

——. *Warenhaussteuer in Deutschland: Mittelstandsbewegung, Kapitalismus und Rechtsstaat im späten Kaiserreich*. Frankfurt: Lang Publishing, 1994.

Strasser, Susan, Charles McGovern, and Matthias Judt, eds. *Getting and Spending: European and American Consumer Societies in the Twentieth Century*. New York: Cambridge University Press, 1998.

Stürzebecher, Peter. *Das Berliner Warenhaus: Bautypus, Element der Stadtorganisation, Raumsphäre der Warenwelt*. Berlin: Archibook-Verlag, 1979.

Swett, Pamela, S. Jonathan Wiesen, and Jonathan Zatlin, eds. *Selling Modernity: Advertising in Twentieth-Century Germany*. Durham, NC: Duke University Press, 2007.

Sznaider, Natan. *Jewish Memory and the Cosmopolitan Order*. Cambridge: Polity Press, 2011.

Tiersten, Lisa. *Marianne in the Market: Envisioning Consumer Society in Fin-de-Siècle France*. Berkeley: University of California Press, 2001.

Tietz, Georg. *Hermann Tietz: Geschichte einer Familie und ihrer Warenhäuser*. Stuttgart: Deutsche Verlags Anstalt, 1965.

Uhlig, Heinrich. *Die Warenhäuser im dritten Reich*. Cologne: Westdeutscher Verlag, 1956.

Ullmann, Hans-Peter. "Der Kaiser bei Wertheim–Warenhäuser im wilhelminischen Deutschland." In *Europäische Sozialgeschichte. Festschrift fur Wolfgang Schieder*, edited by Christof Dipper, Lutz Klinkhammer, and Alexander Nützenadel, 223–36. Berlin: Duncker & Humblot, 2000.

Van Rahden, Till. "Jews and the Ambivalences of Civil Society in Germany, 1800 to 1933—Assessment and Reassessment." *Journal of Modern History* 77, no. 4 (2005): 1024–47.

——. *Juden und andere Breslauer: Die Beziehungen zwischen Juden, Protestanten und Katholiken in einer deutschen Großstadt von 1860 bis 1925.* Göttingen: Vandenhoeck & Ruprecht, 2000.

Volkov, Shulamit. "The Dynamics of Dissimilation: Ostjuden and German Jews." In *The Jewish Response to German Culture: From the Enlightenment to the Second World War,* edited by J. Reinharz and W. Schatzberg, 192–211. Hanover, NH: University Press of New England, 1985.

Ward, Janet. *Weimar Surfaces: Urban Visual Culture in 1920s Germany.* Berkeley: University of California Press, 2001.

Weiss-Sussex, Godela, and Ulrike Zitzlsperger, eds. *Das Berliner Warenhaus: Geschichte und Diskurse / The Berlin Department Store: History and Discourse.* Frankfurt: Peter Lang, 2013.

Westphal, Uwe. *Berliner Konfektion und Mode: Die Zerstörung einer Tradition.* Berlin: Edition Hentrich, 1986.

Whittick, Arnold. *Erich Mendelsohn.* London: F. W. Dodge Corp., 1956.

Williams, Rosalind. *Dream Worlds: Mass Consumption in Late Nineteenth-Century France.* Berkeley: University of California Press, 1982.

INDEX

Page numbers followed by *f* indicate illustrations.

Abelson, Elaine, 101
Abteilung Herrenmode (Gleit), 117, 135
Advertising, 128*f*, 137*f*, 144–45, 150–51,
    154–56, 165, 167, 171, 178
  advertising profession, 61–62, 84
  consumer revolution and, 10, 12–13
  criticisms of, 32, 47, 53, 103
  film and, 167, 171
  light and, 193, 194*f*, 195, 199–200
  racial imagery and, 6–7, 6*f*, 62–63,
    63*f*, 226n27
  rapid growth of, 32–33
  themes of, 58–61, 70–74, 72*f*, 78–79,
    150
  ZDK and, 43–44
Agnew, Jean-Christophe, 11
Air travel, store advertising and,
  77, 77*f*
Alsberg family, 5, 40
Althoff, Theodor, 40
Althoff firm, 38, 56
Altneuland (Herzl), 69, 85
Ansky, S. (*The Dybbuk*), 9
Anti–department store movement
  anti-Semitism and, 7, 23, 24–25, 43,
    45, 46–55, 49*f*, 50*f*, 51*f*
  centered on Berlin stores, 139
  department store responses to, 45
  kleptomania and, 105
  lack of impact on department stores,
    54–55
  Mittelstand and economic anxiety,
    42–45, 52–54
  Schocken stores and, 151
Anti-Semitism
  anti–department store movement, 7, 23,
    24–25, 43, 45, 46–55, 49*f*, 50*f*, 51*f*

  department store safety and, 183
  stereotypes of Jewish store owners,
    122–25, 135–36
Arbeit: Ein Warenhausroman
  (Schweriner), 81, 101
Arcades Project (Benjamin), 4
Arendt, Hannah, 86
Aryanization, of department stores in
  1930s, 9–10, 15, 71, 91–92, 209,
  212
Association of German Department Stores
  (Verband Deutscher Waren-und
  Kaufhäuser), 45, 53
Association to Combat Anti-Semitism, 45
Atriums, in stores, 31, 68, 77, 147–48,
  148*f*, 176–77, 187–88, 192
Aufruhr im Warenhaus (Georg), 17, 202,
  204–5
"Aus dem Warenhaus" (Stahr),
  134–35

Baader, Andreas, 210–11
Bamberger, Julius, 37
Barasch Brothers store, 61
Barasch family, 5, 40
Baudrillard, Jean, 8, 11, 57
Bauhaus, 171
Baum, Vicki
  Der große Ausverkauf, 17, 18, 58–59,
    71, 125–27
  Dienst am Kunden, 18, 108–9
  "Jape im Warenhaus," 17, 130–34,
    179–80, 181, 190, 191–92
Behind the Scenes in the Modern Store
  (Dehn), 54, 86
Behrendt, Walter Curt, 145
Benjamin, Walter, 4, 8, 9, 14, 57, 88

Benson, Susan Porter, 12, 35
Berlin
  advertisements and displays in, 126,
    146
  anti–department store activism and,
    42, 45, 52–54, 139, 207
  crowds in, 81–82
  department store as symbol and center
    of, 65–66, 70–71, 72f, 73–75, 73f,
    74f, 75f
  department store employees in, 117,
    118
  department stores in, generally, 13–14,
    21–23, 38–41
  fires and, 185–90, 189f, 210–11
  Jews in, 5–6, 88, 91, 114, 160
  theft in stores, 99–101
  in twenty-first century, 212–13, 215
  See also specific stores and literary
    works
Berlin Alexanderplatz (Döblin), 5
Berlin: Die Symphonie einer Großstadt
  (Rutmann), 134
Berliner Warenhäuser (Colze), 17, 39,
  70, 80, 114
Berlin in Lights promotion, 195
Bismarck, Otto von, 61
Blumenfeld, Kurt, 163
Böckler, Otto, 187
Böhme, Margarete (W.A.G.M.U.S.), 17,
  24–25, 28, 32, 52, 55, 81, 90–91,
  113–15
Bon Marché stores, 12, 33
Bormann, Martin, 209
Boucicaut, Aristide, 33, 34
Bowlby, Rachel, 107
Brecht, Bertolt, 135
Briesen, Detlef, 15, 201
Bruhn, Wilhelm, 187
Buber, Martin, 160, 161, 163
Buchner, Hans, 87–88, 92
Bucholtz, Ferdinand, 183
Buck-Morss, Susan, 4
Buschan, Georg, 105–6

Capital (Marx), 8, 57
Carlé, Wilhelm ("Die Rolltreppe"), 17,
  83, 108
Carson, Pirie, Scott store, 35

Central Association of German
  Shopkeepers and Artisans. See
  Zentralverband Deutscher Kaufleute
  und Gewerbetreibender (ZDK)
Chauffeur ins Metropol! (musical revue),
  22, 65–66
Chemnitz, Schocken store in, 172–73,
  172f
Christmas
  anti–department store activism and
    Jewish profits from, 53–54
  stores open Sundays before, 81–82
Ciarlo, David, 61–62
Circulation
  of capital, 42, 46, 57, 80, 88, 92
  of goods, 57, 79–84, 92
  of Jews, 58, 88–90
  of people in stores, 79–83
Cohn, Leo. See Colze, Leo
Colze, Leo (Leo Cohn), 21, 22–23, 25,
  54, 116, 120
  Berliner Warenhäuser, 17, 39, 70, 80,
    114
  on shoplifting, 99–100
Commodity fetish concept, of Marx, 8,
  57
Conference on Material Claims against
  the Federal Republic of Germany,
  212
Conrad, Sebastian, 90
Consumer cooperatives, 13, 26
Consumer revolution, history of, 10–15
Consumption, connotations of word,
  9, 181. See also Cosmopolitan
  consumption
Cosmopolitan consumption, 56–58
  as code for threat of Jewish economic
    power, 74, 85–93, 89f
  department store as metropolis and,
    64–68
  department store world and,
    56–64
  movement of goods to and within
    stores, 57, 79–84, 92
  travel and centrality of stores, 68–77,
    72f, 73f, 74f, 75f, 76f, 77, 77f, 78f,
    79
Creutz, Max, 176
Crimen Ferpecto, El (film), 206

Crimmitschau, Schocken store in, 140–41

David, Anthony, 152, 162
Dehn, Paul
  Behind the Scenes in the Modern Store, 54, 86
  criticisms of department stores, 46–47, 52–53, 86, 88
  on Jews and prostitution, 136
  on shoplifting, 105
Department stores in Germany, generally
  contrasted with specialty shops, 25–33, 90
  dream-like magic of, 4–5
  growth in late nineteenth and early twentieth centuries, 21–25, 146–47
  Jews and growth of, 36–42
  origins in medium-size towns, 13, 140
  regulation of, 24, 43
  as secular temple, 7–10, 29, 214–15
  and shopping seen as leisure activity, 28–30
Der große Ausverkauf (Baum), 17, 18, 58–59, 71, 125–27
Deutsch, Leo, 105
"Devil in the Department Store, The" (Heine), 1, *2f*, 3–4, *3f*, 6, 18
Dienst am Kunden (Baum), 18, 108–9
Dissimilation, of Jews, 159–64
Döblin, Alfred (*Berlin Alexanderplatz*), 5
Droste-Hülshoff, Annette von, 166
Du Kommst zu Spät: Eine Szene aus dem Warenhaus (Vogt), 136, 204
Düsseldorf, Tietz store in, 158, 159, 174–77, *175f*, *189f*
Dybbuk, The (Ansky), 9

East Germany (German Democratic Republic), 14–15, 212
Economic rationalization. *See* Rationalization (economic)
Edel, Edmund, 134
Ehape (*Einheitspreis*), 174, 208
Eiffel, Gustave, 33
Einstein, Albert, 162
Einstein Tower, 162

Eisen, Lothar (pseudonym). *See* Schneider, Josef Bernhard
Electric lighting, 193
Elevators, introduction of, 83
Ensslin, Gudrun, 210–11
Escalators, introduction of, 83
Es Liegt in der Luft (revue), 26–27, 107–8
Esquirol, Jean-Étienne Dominique, 98
"Everything under one roof" (*alles unter einem Dach*) motto, 26–28, *27f*, 35, 60
  Schocken's rejection of, 152

Fallada, Hans (*Kleiner Mann—Was Nun?*), 114
Famous-Barr store, 35
Feuchtwanger, Lion, 64
  "Warenhaus-Revue," 58, 59, 60–61, 80–81, 93
Filene, Edward, 96
Filene's, 35, 37
Fire, 179–81
  catharsis and Jewish temple of commerce, 190–202
  department store fires, 183, *184f*, 185
  department stores and safety issues, 181–90, *184f*
  kauflust connected to, 182, 191–92
  and violence against Jews, 206–9
  and violence in 1960s and 1970s, 210–11
  and violence within and against stores, 202–6, 209
France
  consumer revolution in, 11, 12–13
  development of and opposition to department stores in, 33–35
  international goods and, 64
Frankfurt department stores, 1968 bombing of, 15, 210–11
Frankfurt School, 15, 102–3
Frankfurt Zeil, 14, 210–11
Freud, Sigmund
  repetition compulsion and, 109
  "uncanny" and, 96–97, 125
Freytag, Gustav (*Soll und Haben*), 17, 88
Fritsch, Theodor, 48, 49, 51–52, 86, 88
Fuchs, Konrad, 169
Furlough, Ellen, 11–12

Galeries Lafayette, 34, 193
Ganeva, Mila, 205
Georg, Manfred (*Aufruhr im
     Warenhaus*), 17, 202, 204–5
Gera, 13, 39, 110
Gerhard, Walter (pseudonym). *See*
     Rubiner, Wilhelm
Gerlach, Siegfried, 192
German Anti-Semitic League (Deutscher
     Antisemiten-Bund), 187
German Democratic Party (DDP), 153
German Democratic Republic (GDR),
     14–15, 212
German Department Store Association,
     17
German National Party, 53
Gerson, Hermann, 37
Geyer, Michael, 10–11
Giffard, Pierre, 34
Gleit, Maria (pseudonym for
     Hertha Gleitsmann; *Abteilung
     Herrenmode*), 117, 135
Globe, used as symbol by stores, 61
Göhre, Paul, 17, 82, 110, 117, 146
     comparison of department stores to
          ocean liners, 46, 77, 181–82
     Das Warenhaus, 40, 66, 68, 69,
          143–44, 145, 147
Goldberger "Paris" department store, in
     Budapest, 185–86, 188
Goods, movement within stores and
     delivery of, 83–84, 92
Göring, Hermann, 209
Gothic modern architecture style, 145,
     147, 149
Grands magasins, 12, 33–35
Grands Magasins du Louvre, Les, 34
Great Britain
     consumer revolution in, 13
     development of and opposition to
          department stores in, 36
     international goods and, 64
Gronemann, Sammy, 146
Gross, Otto, 109
Große Rachen, Das (Wohlbrück), 107
Große Warenhaus, Das (Siwertz), 7, 18,
     64, 67, 91, 104, 106, 107, 116,
     129–30
     fire and, 181, 190, 195–98, 201, 202

Grünbaum, Adolf, 88
Grundrisse (Marx), 57

Hamburg department store fire, 183,
     184f
Hammer, Friedrich, 188–89
"Hammer-Schriften" (anti-Semitic
     booklets), 16, 48, 51, 52, 135
Hartung, Max (*Kleptomanie: Schwank in
     einem Aufzug*), 101
Hausschildt, J. W., 47, 48
Heine, Thomas Theodor, 9
     "The Devil in the Department Store,"
          1, 2f, 3–4, 3f, 6, 18
Hermann Tietz firm, 17, 39–41, 56, 58,
     70, 84, 79, 188
     architecture of, 61, 62f, 146, 192
     financial condition of, 146, 209
     Jewishness and, 5, 6
     light and, 192–95
     success of, 32, 54–55
     violence against, 180, 206–7
     women employees of, 110, 118,
          120
Hermann Wronker firm, 173
Hertzog, Rudolf, 64
Herzl, Theodor, 161, 229n118
     Altneuland and Herzl on department
          stores, 69, 85
Hess, Rudolf, 209
Heym, Georg ("Der Irre"), 202–4
Hirsch, Julius, 41, 110
H. J. Emden Sons, 39
H.M. (author), 47–48, 53
Hoffman, E. T. A. ("Sandman"), 125
Horkheimer, Max, 14
Hubbuch, Karl (*Der Traum des
     Tietzmädchens*), 111–12, 112f
Hypnotic state, kleptomania and, 102–3,
     105

Illustrierter Beobachter, 124
Imperialism and colonialism, German,
     61–64, 63f, 226n29
Innovation, L', 210
"Irre, Der" (Heym), 202–4
I. Schocken Sons. *See* Schocken firm
Israel, Berthold, 6, 41
Israel, Nathan, 25

James, Kathleen, 142, 145–46, 147–48, 162–63, 165
Jandorf, Adolf (Abraham), 25, 39, 48, 87, 122
Jandorf family, 5, 37, 39
Jandorf firm, 66–67. *See also* KaDeWe
"Jape im Warenhaus" (Baum), 17, 130–34
    fire and, 179–80, 181, 190, 191–92
Jarausch, Konrad, 10–11, 12
Jews
    cosmopolitan consumption and, 74, 85–93, 89*f*
    cosmopolitanism and, 56–58
    department store development and, 5–7, 34, 36–42
    migration from Posen, 9, 37, 150, 160, 174
    See also Anti-Semitism
John Wanamaker stores, 35
Julius Bormaß Department Store, 61
Jünger, Ernst, 183
Junk dealing, association of Jews with, 38, 46–47

KaDeWe (Kaufhaus des Westens; Department Store of the West), 6, 23, 39, 67, 139, 183
    cash handling in, 84
    fire safety and, 189
    light and, 193*f*, 195
    mannequin storage in, 127*f*, 129
    prostitution and, 134
    railroads and centrality of, 70, 75, 75*f*, 76*f*, 77
    rooftop terrace of, 63*f*
    shopgirls and, 118
    travel and, 79
    in twenty-first century, 215
KPD (Communist Party of Germany), 208
Kampfgemeinschaft gegen Warenhaus und Konsumverein (Combat League against Department Stores and Consumer Cooperatives), 51, 51*f*
Kann, Erich, 155, 239n79
Karstadt, Rudolf, 40
Karstadt firm, 37, 38, 54, 56, 61, 82, 137*f*, 183
    centrality of stores, 71, 72*f*, 73–75, 73*f*, 74*f*, 82, 139

Jews and, 5, 25
    mobility and, 77
    violence against, 208
Karstadt-Quelle, 212
Kaufhäuser, defined, 40, 44
Kaufhaus Israel, 38, 44, 84
    centrality slogan of, 70–71
    Jewishness and, 6, 6*f*
    promotional albums of, 60, 63–64, 63*f*, 65
Kaufhaus Manasse, 118
Kauflust (desire to consume), 28, 47
    connected to fire, 182, 191–92
    women and, 5, 29, 81
Kaufmann family, 37
Keun, Irmgard (*Das Kunstseidene Mädchen*), 123–24
Kläger, Emil (*Zwischenfall im Warenhaus*), 5, 94–95, 96, 109, 138, 205–6
Klein, César, 79
Kleiner Mann—Was Nun? (Fallada), 114
Kleptomania, women and, 9, 34, 49, 98–102, 100*f*
    male crime contrasted, 98–99
    as psychiatric and sexual diagnosis and, 5, 94–97, 101–10
Kleptomaniac, The (Porter), 101
Kleptomanie: Schwank in einem Aufzug (Hartung), 101
Knopf family, 5, 40
Köhrer, Erich (*Warenhaus Berlin*), 10, 17, 31, 39, 65, 66, 70, 80, 92, 114–15, 181, 190, 198–202, 214
Konfektion (Türk), 6–7
Konsum-Tempel (consuming temple), 8–9
Kracauer, Siegfried, 14, 81, 135, 139
    "Temple of Commerce," 129
Kraepelin, Emil, 101–2
Kundenfang (attempt to capture customers from others), 32
Kunstseidene Mädchen, Das (Keun), 123–24

Ladies' Paradise, The (*Au Bonheur des Dames*; Zola), 7–8, 17–18, 33, 49, 60, 68, 90–91, 97, 101, 106, 113, 120, 125, 127, 191, 192

Laermanns, Rudi, 12
Lamberty, Christiane, 59
Laquer, Leopold, 95, 103, 105,
    106
Leach, William, 36
LeBon, Gustave, 81
Leonhard Tietz firm, 17, 40, 56, 158,
    159
    architecture of, 140, 173–78, 175*f*,
        176*f*, 177*f*
    building boom in 1920s, 177–78
    name change in 1933, 209
    success of, 41, 54
    violence against, 208
    women employees of, 110, 111, 118,
        121
Leppmann, Arthur, 106
Lethen, Helmut, 79
Liebermann, Max, 166
Liebknecht, Wilhelm, 42–43
Light, in department stores, 192–95,
    193*f*, 194*f*. *See also* Atriums, in
    stores
Ligue syndicale du travail, de l'industrie
    et du commerce (Syndical League
    of Labor, Industry, and Commerce),
    34
Lindgrens, Arthur, 212
Lockartikel (teasers), anti–department
    store activism and, 47–48
Loeb, Moritz, 91
Lombroso, Cesare, 105
Luppe, Hermann, 167
Lustige Blätter magazine, 101
Lux, Käthe, 21, 24, 40

Maas, Luise, 162, 169
Macy's, 35
"Magasinitis," 5, 103
Magasins de nouveautés, 34
Manasse, Georg, 71, 141, 151, 153, 155,
    156–57, 167, 171, 173
Mannequins
    boundaries between people and,
        129–34, 236n200
    commodification of women and,
        125–27, 127*f*, 128*f*, 129
Marc, C.-C., 98
Marks, Simon, 239n79

Marshall Field's, 35
Marx, Karl
    Capital, 8, 57
    commodity fetish concept of, 8, 57
    Grundrisse, 57
Marxism, anti–department store activism
    and, 42–43, 53
Matthey, André, 97–98
Meinhof, Ulrike, 211
Mendelsohn, Erich, 149, 162
    architectural philosophy of, 77, 80, 164
    poetry of, 166–67
    Einstein Tower, 162
    Schocken's Chemnitz store and,
        172–73, 172*f*
    Schocken's Nuremberg store and, 159,
        164–69, 165*f*, 166*f*, 168*f*
    Schocken's Stuttgart store and,
        169–71, 170*f*
    Zionism and, 142, 161–64, 236n8,
        240n118
Messel, Alfred, 8, 39, 143–47, 149,
    158–59, 173
Miller, Michael B., 12, 123
Mittelstand (shopkeeping and artisanal
    middle classes)
    anti–department store activism and,
        42–45, 52–54
    defense of, 24
    threat of Jewish economic power and,
        86, 87–88
Mobility. *See* Cosmopolitan consumption
Modernism and modernity
    capitalism and, 4–10, 84–86
    department store design and, 157–60,
        175–77
    Jews and, 19, 142, 175, 213
    Leonhard Tietz firm and, 173–78
    Schocken firm and, 141, 149–57
    Zionism and, 142, 162–64
    See also Messel, Alfred;
        Mendelsohn, Erich; Schocken
        firm
Moholy-Nagy, László, 167, 171
Moreck, Curt, 134
Moses, Siegfried, 236n8
Mosse, George, 17
Mosse, Rudolf, 163
Mulford, Prentice, 104, 115–16

National Socialist party
  anti–department store activism and,
    14, 50–51, 50f
  banning of department store
    construction, 173
  platform of 1920 and department store
    ownership, 6
  threat of Jewish economic power and,
    87
  violence against stores and,
    206–9
  women employees and, 124–25
Netter, Marie, 26, 41
New Objectivity, 80, 168, 171
Night of the Broken Glass (Kristallnacht),
    209
Nitzan-Shaftan, Alona, 236n8
Nord, Philip, 34–35
Nordmann, Caius, 103, 105
Nuremberg, Schocken store in, 159,
    164–69, 165f, 166f, 168f

Olbrich, Joseph, 158, 159, 173, 174–75,
    177
Osborn, Max, 58, 145
Oscar and Betty Tietz Foundation,
    120

Palestine. See Zionism
Pearson, Michael (The Store), 206
Peddling, association of Jews with, 38,
    46–47, 88
Perry, Joe, 53–54
Petersdorff, Hans, 163
Petersdorff clothing store, 165
Pinthus, Kurt, 82, 90, 93
Plessner, Helmut, 79
Porter, Edwin S. (The Kleptomaniac),
    101
Posen (Poznań), Jewish migration from, 9,
    37, 150, 160, 174
Presner, Todd, 85–86, 229n118
Printemps, 34
Proll, Thorwald, 210–11
Prostitution, 34, 106, 135
  shopgirls linked to, 134–35, 137–38,
    137f
Purpus (Stücklen), 95–96, 98, 104,
    190–91

Railroad stations, and mobility and
  centrality of stores, 68–75, 72f, 73f,
    74f, 75f, 76f
Railway Journey, The (Schivelbusch), 69
Raimann, Emil, 102
Ramschbasare (rummage bazaars), 46,
    145, 147, 186
Raphaeli, Jacques, 207
Rappaport, Erika, 14
Rationalization (economic), 4, 54, 71,
    80, 151–57, 164
Reichel, Maximilian, 188, 189
Repp, Kevin, 145
Rhineland, L. Tietz stores in, 39–40,
    140, 173–78
Rieger, Bernhard, 202
Roeren, Hermann, 24
"Rolltreppe, Die" (Carlé), 17, 83, 108
Roman Emperor Department
  Store, 61
Rooch, Alarich, 148
Rosenzweig, Franz, 160
Roth, Joseph, 82
Rowe, Dorothy, 111–12
Rubiner, Wilhelm (Warenhausgräfin),
    122, 234n134
Rudolph Hertzog store, 38
Ruppin, Arthur, 92
Rutmann, Walter (Berlin: Die Symphonie
    einer Großstadt), 134

"Sandman" (Hoffman), 125
Saxony, 19, 37, 40, 44, 71, 140, 150–52,
    160
Schäfer, Philipp, 174
Schiffer, Marcellus, 107–8
Schinkel, Carl Friedrich, 145
Schivelbusch, Wolfgang, 30–31, 79, 192
  The Railway Journey, 69
Schmidt, Gerhard, 102
Schneider, Josef Bernhard, 66, 122, 134, 135
Schocken, Gershom, 154, 161, 171
Schocken, Salman, 38, 69, 88, 111, 120
  business plan for stores, 71
  Jewish learning and, 150, 160
  Mendelshon and, 162, 163–64
  Zionism and, 142, 161–62, 213,
    236n8
  See also Schocken firm

Schocken, Simon, 150–51, 161, 164, 167–68, 171–72
Schocken family, 37, 40
Schocken firm, 17, 54, 56
  modern architecture of, 157–60, 158*f*, 164–73, 165*f*, 166*f*, 168*f*, 170*f*, 172*f*
  modern business practices of, 149, 151, 152–57
  regional identity and, 140–41
  women employees of, 111, 118, 120
Schulz, Walter E., 55, 81
Schweriner, Oscar (*Arbeit: Ein Warenhausroman*), 81, 101
Sehring, Bernhard, 146, 192
Selfridge, Henry, 36
Shopgirls, 110–12
  anti-Semitic press and depiction of Jewish business practices, 122–25
  linked to prostitution and seduction of customers, 134–35, 137–38, 137*f*
  worklife and treatment of, 112–18, 119*f*, 120–25, 121*f*
Shopkeeper movement, 43–45, 145
Shoplifting. *See* Kleptomania, women and
Siegel-Cooper stores, 35
Sierschynski, Petia, 226n29
Simmel, Georg, 80, 90, 225n8
Simplicissimus cartoons
  department store all inclusiveness, 27–28, 27*f*
  employees and Jewish owners, 123, 123*f*
Siwertz, Siegfried (*Das Große Warenhaus*), 7, 18, 64, 67, 91, 104, 106, 107, 116, 129–30, 181, 190, 195–98, 201, 202
Slezkine, Yuri, 91
Social Democratic Party of Germany (SDP)
  anti–department store activism and, 42–45, 53
  Schocken and, 153
Social leveling, in department stores, 66–67
Söhnlein, Horst, 210–11
Soll und Haben (Freytag), 17, 88
Sombart, Werner, 110, 117

characterization of Jews, 88, 90, 91–92, 163
on department stores, 26, 80
Jews and capitalism and, 5–6
on specialty shops, 30, 31
Specialty shops (*Spezialgeschäfte*)
  department stores contrasted, in France, 34–35
  department stores contrasted, in Germany, 25–33, 90
Spiekermann, Uwe, 42, 44, 101
Spoliansky, Mischa, 107–8
Staatsbürger-Zeitung, 52, 52–53, 185–87
Stahr, Margarete ("Aus dem Warenhaus"), 134–35
Stekel, Wilhelm, 103, 107, 109
Stewart, A. T., 35
Stiefler, Rudolf, 159
Stoltheim, F. Roderich (pseudonym). *See* Fritsch, Theodor
Store, The (Pearson), 206
Stralsund, 13, 38, 39, 174, 178
Strauss family, 37
Stresemann, Gustav, 30, 66, 104
Stücklen, Wilhelm (*Purpus*), 95–96, 98, 104, 190–91
Stuttgart, Schocken store in, 169–71, 170*f*
Süße Geschäftsmädels series, 113, 122

Taxes, imposed on department stores, 36, 44–45
Taylorism. *See* Rationalization (economic)
"Temple of Commerce" (Kracauer), 129
Theft. *See* Kleptomania, women and
Thiekötter, Hans-Bernd, 103, 106, 107, 109
Tietz, Alfred Leonhard, 177
Tietz, Gerhard, 65, 80
Tietz, Hermann, 37, 207. *See also* Hermann Tietz firm
Tietz, Leonhard, 25, 39–40, 174, 177. *See also* Leonhard Tietz firm
Tietz, Oscar, 6, 25, 45, 67, 146, 187–88, 189
Toker, Franklin, 142
Traum des Tietzmädchens, Der (Hubbuch), 111–12, 112*f*

Travel agencies, in department stores, 78–79
Treitschke, Heinrich von, 88
Türk, Werner (*Konfektion*), 6–7
Twilight Zone (television program), 236n200

Uhlig, Heinrich, 207–8
"Uncanny," of Freud, 96–97, 125
United States
consumerism and religion in, 214–15
consumer revolution in, 13
development of and opposition to department stores in, 35–36
shopping and travel in twentieth century, 69–70
Ury family, 5, 37, 40, 150, 151

Vietnam, student protests and, 210–11
Violence, within and against department stores, 202–6, 209
Vogt, Hans (*Du Kommst zu Spät: Eine Szene aus dem Warenhaus*), 136, 204
Volkov, Shulamit, 160
Vossische Zeitung, 207

W.A.G.M.U.S. (Böhme), 17, 24–25, 28, 32, 52, 55, 81, 90–91
shopgirls and, 113–15
Wagner, H., 83
Wahrheit, Die (newspaper), 122
Waldenburg, Schocken store in, 141, 141f
Waldmann, A., 90, 117
Wanamaker, John, 36
Ward, Janet, 82, 164, 170, 192
Warenhaus, Das (Göhre), 40, 66, 68, 69, 143–44, 145, 147
Warenhaus Berlin (Köhrer), 10, 17, 31, 39, 65, 66, 70, 80, 92, 114–15, 116, 214
fire and, 181, 190, 196, 198–202
Warenhäuser, defined, 40, 44
Warenhausgräfin (Rubiner), 122, 234n134
Warenhausmädchen: Roman aus Berlin der Gegenwart (Wiener-Braunsberg), 115

"Warenhaus-Revue" (Feuchtwanger), 58, 59, 60–61, 80–81, 93
Warenhaus Wertheim, 5, 26, 38, 41, 91–92, 104, 117–18, 139, 183
architecture of, 8, 39, 143–47, 144f, 158–59, 226n29
centrality and, 77
destroyed during World War II, 212
as "gravedigger" of middle class, 52–53
interior of, 78f, 79, 147–49, 148f
light and, 192–95
name change in 1933, 209
social leveling and, 66–67
thefts from, 100–101
in twenty-first century, 215
women employees of, 110
Weber, Max, 4, 91
Weisse Wochen (White weeks), 79
Werkbund, 162, 163
Wernicke, Johannes, 45, 53
Wertheim, Abraham, 25, 39
Wertheim, Georg, 38–39, 61, 75, 87, 122, 149
Wertheim, Hugo, 38–39
Wertheim family, 37, 41, 212
West Germany, 14–15, 215
Whiteley's Universal Provider, 36
Wiener, Alfred, 29
Wiener Bilder, 186
Wiener-Braunsberg, Josef (*Warenhausmädchen: Roman aus Berlin der Gegenwart*), 115
Wilhelm II, Kaiser, 149, 199
Wilke, Arthur, 29
Williams, Rosalind, 30, 60, 127, 129
Window displays
abundance and, 58–60, 59f
lure of department stores and, 22, 26, 30, 32, 41, 47–50
mannequins and, 125–27, 128f, 129
Schocken stores and, 153–54
stores and light, 192–95
Wittner, Doris, 58
Wohlbrück, Olga (*Das Große Rachen*), 107
Women, 7, 49, 81
crime while menstruating, 105–6
department store as both safe and dangerous place for, 65, 96–97, 109–10

Women *(continued)*
  growth of department stores and,
    21–22
  imagery of entrapment of, 50–51, 50*f*,
    103–4
  kauflust and, 5, 28–29, 81
  social leveling in stores and, 66
  see also Kleptomania, women and;
    Mannequins; Shopgirls
Woolworth stores, 204, 208
Wronker family, 5, 37, 40, 56
Wussow, Otto Erich von, 40, 145

Zentralverband Deutscher Kaufleute
    und Gewerbetreibender (ZDK),
    43–45

Zionism
  Herzl and cosmopolitanism, 85,
    229n118
  Mendelsohn and, 142, 161–64,
    236n8, 240n118
  modernism and, 163–64
  Salman Schocken and, 142, 161–62,
    213, 236n8
Zola, Émile (*The Ladies' Paradise*), 7–8,
    17–18, 33, 49, 60, 68, 90–91, 97, 101,
    106, 113, 120, 125, 127, 191, 192
Zwickau, Schocken concern in, 71, 83,
    140–41, 150–57
*Zwischenfall im Warenhaus Incident in
    the Department Store* (Kläger), 5,
    94–95, 96, 109, 138, 205–6